Fred Halliday, who died in April 2010 aged 64, was Professor Emeritus of International Relations at the London School of Economics and a Research Professor at the Barcelona Institute for International Studies. He was familiar with 10 languages, including Arabic and Persian, and published over 20 books, including *Islam and the Myth of Confrontation* (I.B. Tauris).

Shocked and Awed

A Dictionary of the War on Terror

Fred Halliday

Former ICREA Research Professor, IBEI
(Barcelona Institute for International Studies)

University of California Press

Berkeley   Los Angeles

The University of California Press, one of the most distinguished university presses in the United States, enriches lives around the world by advancing scholarship in the humanities, social sciences, and natural sciences. Its activities are supported by the UC Press Foundation and by philanthropic contributions from individuals and institutions. For more information, visit www.ucpress.edu.

University of California Press
Berkeley and Los Angeles, California

Originally published in 2010 in the United Kingdom by
I.B.Tauris & Co. Ltd., London
www.ibtauris.com

Library of Congress Control Number: 2010925508
ISBN: 978-0-520-26870-8 (paper : alk. paper)

17 16 15 14 13 12 11 10
10 9 8 7 6 5 4 3 2 1

Typeset in Minion by MPS Limited, a Macmillan Company
Printed and bound in Great Britain by TJ International Ltd, Padstow, Cornwall

Mixed Sources
Product group from well-managed
forests and other controlled sources
www.fsc.org Cert no. SGS-COC-2482
© 1996 Forest Stewardship Council
FSC

Contents

Publisher's Note

On 26 April 2010, Fred Halliday died in Barcelona following a long illness, and will be sadly missed by those lucky enough to have known and worked with him. He had already submitted the final version of *Shocked and Awed* before his condition became too severe for him to work. Nevertheless he was unable to respond to all of the queries generated by the copyediting process of his text. In his absence, I.B.Tauris drew on years of experience of working with Halliday to respond to these queries in his place. After academic advisors deemed their inclusion necessary, we have also added entries on 'Yellowcake', 'Salafism', 'Project for the New American Century', 'Adam Gadahn' and 'Ayaan Hirsi Ali'. We have endeavoured to ensure that the final product reflects the author's style, purpose and thinking as closely as possible. Any errors which may have crept into the text due to this unusual editing arrangement are entirely the publisher's responsibility, though we have done our best to ensure it maintains the level of rigour the author always demanded of himself.

INTRODUCTION

Language and Politics in the Post-9/11 Era

> Wheresoever manners and fashions are corrupted, language is.
> It imitates the public riot.
>
> —Ben Johnson, early 17c[1]
>
> What use are poets in a time of crisis?
>
> —Hölderlin[2]

This is a book about the vitality, and the uses and misuses, of language, but also about something more dangerous and perhaps more immediate: the turmoil and uncertainty of the contemporary world, specifically in the years following the 2001 Al-Qa'ida attack on New York and the ensuing 'War on Terror' pursued in riposte by the USA. Rather than aspiring to being comprehensive in any sense, *Shocked and Awed* is an attempt to illustrate the richness and malleability of words; the ever-changing character of language; how words and phrases are thrown up by such events; how bits of the past, often historical and religious symbols, are recycled for contemporary uses. It also demonstrates the intersection of words with power; how, as the very title of the book suggests, states seek to use language to control events, how insurgents use their own vocabulary to justify their actions and discredit opponents. In a phrase, it is a study of the order *and* the disorder of words.

That those who seek to control events, people and their minds also seek to control language is a truism of modern politics, as it is of the major religions.[3] The title of the book itself, *Shocked and Awed,* stands as an example of one case of the political and military use of words, and of the illusions they embody, in this case, words chosen by a powerful state, the USA, to symbolise the attempt to dominate another country (Iraq), only to find its mission very much unaccomplished, facing years of war and turmoil and, in the end, a disorderly retreat. However, the aspiration to control through language, and the resultant failure to do so, are also evident in the language of those opposed to such states. With some hindsight, we can see that the verbal excesses of Osama bin Laden have done little better than those of George W. Bush: the all-encompassing 'Global *jihad*' so dramatically announced to the youth of the Islamic world by Al-Qa'ida before and after 9/11 is, in large measure, a catchword for ongoing conflict within a dozen or so countries while the *International Islamic Front Against Jews and Crusaders*, first proclaimed by Al-Qa'ida and its associates in 1998, although responsible for the 2001 and many other attacks and massacres, has failed to win over most Muslims or to defeat its foes. In all likelihood, in some form, and in some countries, such contestation will continue for years to come: it will not fundamentally change the world, or destroy the power of the USA, or convert Europe to Islam.

Shocked and Awed's first goal is, for sure, to serve as a work of reference, however unorthodox or incomplete, to words and phrases used about 9/11, and the events that have followed them, as well as about the ongoing issues of cultural conflict, terrorism and Middle Eastern politics linked to those events. In so doing it also aims to make a broader contribution to understanding the politics *and* thinking of the contemporary Middle East, linking up with the ongoing discussion of how far culture, religion and 'Islam' explain the politics and society of the region today. Against the tendency of many in the East and West to explain these events in terms of something fixed by the past by tradition, sacred texts or, most confusingly, as a product of 'culture', this book argues that the meaning of words, and the selection political actors today make about the use of symbols from the past, are largely a matter of contemporary selection and choice. The oft-heard excuses, 'They were always like that', 'It was always so', do not resist serious examination. While many of those involved in politics today certainly do invoke the past, history and tradition to give meaning to what they do, the actual use of these reflects contemporary needs, meanings and ideologies. In particular, this emphasis on the contemporary, on what makes sense in the world now, is the key to understanding the thinking of Islamist militants: we cannot understand the thinking, methods or goals of Osama bin Laden by going back to the Middle Ages, or holy texts, any more than we can comprehend the thinking and policies of the 43rd president of the USA by watching Hollywood films that portray an idyllic American past of cowboys and Indians.[4] Osama bin Laden *did* read the Quran. George W. Bush *did* watch *Westerns*; each cites such influences in their public statements. However, the use to which they put such influences, and the impact such uses had, are a matter of contemporary history and meaning.

There is, however, one more general goal, or intellectual aspiration, underlying this book: to illustrate *the linguistic consequences of major international crises*. The events of 9/11 and all that followed in Afghanistan and Iraq, and more generally in relations between the Muslim and non-Muslim worlds, had a significant impact on language, creating new words and phrases and reviving, and often redefining, already existing ones. This was always so: each of the great cataclysms of modern times has left its impact on language, be it World War I, World War II, the Spanish Civil War, the Cold War or Vietnam.[5] Yet if this linguistic harvest of war was always the case, in some ways it may be even more the case in the contemporary world than before: the spread of communications, the importance of the 'information war', the chaotic enticements of cyberspace, all make this, in addition to being a war for security and control of states, a 'global vocabulary war'.

Anyone embarking on a dictionary has to make, or at least attempt to make, claims about the principles of inclusion and exclusion. In my case, taking the events of 9/11 as a starting point, and following the fate of language through the associated wars of Afghanistan, Iraq and the Arab–Israeli dispute, through the reaction of Western governments and societies, particularly that of the USA, to these events and the associated public controversies over culture, violence and security so occasioned, I have sought as much as anything to illustrate how words are shaped and redefined, how new situations throw up fresh vocabulary, how old words are taken up and redefined, sometimes wilfully, often by natural linguistic change. All works of reference and dictionaries involve a set of contradictory qualities – rigour and eccentricity, reliability and serendipity, consistency and *bricolage*,[6] an awareness of the precise, correct meaning of words and of the constant changes of meaning and phrase that all languages exhibit. *Shocked and Awed* is no exception.

Shocked and Awed makes no claim to being comprehensive, but aspires to cover a wide ground, from the uses of religious tradition and symbol in Islam and Judaism to the myriad innovations, some official, many informal and colloquial, that maintain the vitality of American English. This broad remit, limited to a large extent by the events following 9/11 but incorporating terms already in currency but used in this period, explains the division of the book into its 12 chapters. Chapter 1 focusses on 9/11 itself and on the American intelligence response to it. Chapter 2 looks at the language of Osama bin Laden and of Islamist movements more generally. Chapter 3 is devoted to the vocabulary associated with the US detention and treatment of suspects. Chapter 4 covers the wars in Afghanistan and Iraq, the most direct outcomes of 9/11. Chapter 5 examines terminology commonly used in and about the Middle East, more so words taken from Arabic. Chapter 6 looks at the ways in which Muslims are portrayed and stereotyped in contemporary discourses. Chapter 7 looks at the Arab–Israeli dispute, both because of its close association in the minds of everyone – Israelis, Arabs and Americans – with the 'Global *jihad'*/'War against Terror' and also to provide a comparative example of how a particular conflict generates its own recycling of language and its own justificatory terms. Chapter 8 looks in some more detail at the euphemisms and some of the technical terms used in war, above all at the way in which they serve to obscure the death and suffering involved. Chapter 9 looks at the way in which, side by side with the often deadening official terms and acronyms generated by the US government, American colloquial has responded to this crisis. Chapter 10 illustrates the ways in which new place names, some actual, some imaginary prompted by the crisis, have come to prominence. Chapter 11 examines the role of euphemism and evasion in general in the face of 9/11 and its aftermath. Chapter 12 brings the story back to the realm of international politics, and to some of the terms and concepts that these events have brought into public debate. While much has for sure been left out, perhaps enough has been included.[7]

If this book has a clear starting point – the events of September 2001 – it also has, of necessity and by dint of some historical logic, a concluding point, the departure of President George W. Bush from the White House, and the inauguration of President Barack Obama in January 2009. In themselves, these changes will not conclude the conflicts covered in this volume, or consign the issues raised – political, cultural and historical – to oblivion: but they do provide a suitable point at which to draw a line under at least one chapter of the wars and conflicts reflected here. On his part, President Obama and his advisers have made clear that, while committed to maintaining the security of the USA, they no longer see the conflict with Islamist armed movements as their priority, or the basis of a global strategy or 'war', and are, at the same time, committed to changing some of the counterterrorism policies pursued by the preceding administration. For their part, the Islamist forces – Al-Qa'ida and many others – opposing the USA and its allies, have, while maintaining their commitment to pursuing their goals, and, we can only surmise, being capable of doing so for many years to come, moved from what appeared in 2001–3 to be a *worldwide* challenge to the West, to a more focussed, country-specific, if potentially more deadly, assault on particular countries, among them Afghanistan, Pakistan, Yemen and Somalia.

For myself, I can claim no special skills as a lexicographer, other than curiosity and a critical sense about the uses and definitions of words, and some training in relevant language skills: Latin and Greek, French and German at school; Arabic and Persian in later life. Other forms of inspiration have also had their impact. Working for 25 years at LSE, a stone's throw from the house into which he moved in 1746 and where he lived while compiling his dictionary, at 17 Gough Square, and with his statue a minute from my office in the Strand, I could not but be aware of the spirit of Dr. Samuel Johnson, to me, as a critical student of language, the greatest of all English social scientists and a model of that mixture of dedication and eccentricity that lexicography requires. That a similar distance in the opposite direction from LSE was Bush House, the home of the BBC international services, broadcasting in over 60 tongues, was also an inspiration. To work and live, as I now do in Catalonia, as a Research Professor with ICREA, the *Institció Catalana de Recerca i Estudis Avançats,* and in a research and teaching environment in which on any one day I have to operate in three languages at least – Spanish, Catalan, English – is also a great stimulus to precision and curiosity in matters of language.

In conceiving of, and working on, this book I have, however, drawn special inspiration and encouragement from others who have attempted work of this kind before: the spirit, dedication and intermittent distempers of Dr. Johnson;[8] the great compilation of an earlier linguistic interface between the Muslim and Western vocabularies; the 'Anglo-Indian' *Hobson-Jobson*; Raymond Williams's 1976 *Keywords;* and Lynne Truss's *Eats, Shoots and Leaves,* the reading of which in 2004 did much to validate my initial, but wavering, enthusiasm in this project. Equally important were those classic writings on language, power and politics that were influential on my generation of the 1960s.[9] Their studies of language were not simply lexicographical. For them the critique of language was part of the critique of power, of lies that served to kill, torture, oppress and seal off chances for life enhancement and freedom.

The material used here was collected over a seven-year period, from late 2001 to the end of 2008, as part of other work I was writing on the Middle East, but also as an alternative, perhaps less clamorous, more meticulous, in some ways more intellectually gratifying, way of responding to, and commenting on, events that were fast-moving, complex, many-centred and, in many ways, disturbing when not frightening. Such work is, moreover, part of the broader challenge of our times, that of enabling people to comprehend, and hence in some degree better control, the events and world that surround them. In the end, precision in language, the challenging of essentialist meanings, the explication of obscure terms and phrases, are not a purely scholarly pursuit, although eminently justifiable in those terms alone: they are an essential part of maintaining a democratic and peaceful world. Words can exalt and can explain, but, as is shown by *shock and awe*, jihad and many other entries in this book can also kill, and promote fear, hatred and misunderstanding. For that reason, too, they need to be studied, challenged and controlled.

Notes

1. Quoted in Frank Kermode, 'Lives of Dr. Johnson', *New York Review of Books*, 22 June 2006, p. 28.
2. 'und wozu Dichter in dürftiger Zeit', 'Brot und Wein', in Friedrich Hölderlin, *Gedichte*, Jochen Schmidt ed. Frankfurt am Main: Insel Verlag, 1984, pp. 114–119, line 122. I am most grateful to Ekkehart Krippendoff, himself a fine writer on language and politics, for locating the original of this quotation.
3. As many writers in the twentieth century have shown – among them George Orwell in *1984*; Victor Klemperer in his analysis of the language of the Third Reich, *MTI* and Noam Chomsky in his 1966 essay 'The Responsibility of Intellectuals'; the British sociologists of language and meaning; Richard Hoggart in his *The Uses of Literacy* and Raymond Williams in his *Keywords;* but above all Antonio Gramsci, supreme analyst of the role of discourse in reinforcing 'hegemony' – language is itself a constituent of social and political power.
4. On the general 'modernity' of Al-Qa'ida's vocabulary and imagery, see Denis McAuley, '"Fundamentalism or Populism?": The Ideology of Osama bin Laden. Nation, Tribe and World Economy', *Journal of Politcal Ideologies,* Vol. 10, no. 3, October 2005; on a similar argument with regard to the language of the Iranian Revolution of 1978–1979, Ervand Abrahamian, *Khomeinism. Essays on the Islamic Republic,* London: I.B.Tauris, 1993, Chapter 1; and Sami Zubaida *Islam, the People and the State,* London: Routledge, 1993.
5. On World War I, John Brophy and Eric Partridge, *The Daily Telegraph Dictionary of Tommies' Songs and Slang, 1914–18* Barnsley, Yorkshire: Frontline Books, 2008. On World War II, Gordon L. Rottman, *FUBAR: Soldier Slang of World War II,* Botley, Oxford: Osprey, 2007 (the acronym in the title, 'FUBAR', stands for 'Fucked up Beyond All Recognition'). On the Spanish Civil War, the Cold War and Vietnam, I am not aware of any systematic study or listing, but examples are many: for example, from the first *fifth column, supremo,*

weapons of mass destruction; from the second, *arms control, commissar, defector, fellow traveller, KGB, mole, revisionist, running dog, Sputnik;* from the last, *DMZ, frag, pacification, swiftboard, Tet, VC.* From the Napoleonic Wars in Spain we get *guerrilla,* from the Boer War *concentration camp,* etc.

6. In his classic *Tristes Tropiques,* Claude Levi-Strauss argues for *bricolage,* literally collecting odd items – here a general curiosity about, and unfettered interest in, human affairs – and, in his view, the primary task of a social scientist. This would, for sure, be news to the straight-jacketed and 'professional' editors of the referred journals that now constitute the zenith of academic excellence.

7. As defence for what I have included and missed out, I can only invoke the words of Dr. Johnson: 'Every other author may aspire to praise; the lexicographer can only hope to escape reproach, and even this negative recompense has been yet granted to very few.' (Samuel Johnson, from the Preface to his *Dictionary of the English Language* 1755, reprinted as *Samuel Johnson's Dictionary, Selections from the 1755 Work That Defined the English Language,* ed. Jack Lynch, London: Atlantic Books, 2004, p. 25.)

8. 'When I took the first survey of my undertaking, I found our speech copious without order, and energetic without rules: wherever I turned my view, there was perplexity to be disentangled, and confusion to be regulated.' Preface, p. 25.

9. See note 3 above.

CHAPTER 1

9/11, US Intelligence and Counterterrorism

> 9/11 did not change the world, it changed the way Americans look at the world.
>
> —President George W. Bush
>
> God has struck America at its Achilles heel and destroyed its greatest buildings, praise and blessings to him. America has been filled with terror from north to south and from east to west, praise and blessings to God. What America is tasting today is but a fraction of what we have tasted for decades.
>
> —Osama bin Laden's statement of 7 October 2001, 'In the Winds of Faith', in *Messages to the World*, p. 104

1 per cent doctrine   Term used by writer Ron Suskind of Vice-President Dick Cheney's principle that the merest whiff of a threat put the USA in enormous danger and hence had to be annihilated (H. D. S. Greenway, 'Bush's Losing Team', *IHT*, 27 December 2006). See **pre-emption**.

9/11   American system of dating (which runs month, day, year as opposed to the European system of day, month, year) for 11 September 2001, the date of the **Al-Qa'ida** attacks on New York and Washington. Shorthand for start of widespread, but not 'global', conflict between the USA and radical Islamist groups, linked to, or in some way associated with, **Al-Qa'ida**. No convincing explanation has ever been offered, other than logistical and operative readiness, for the choice of this date, which Osama bin Laden subsequently termed *Yaum Niu York* – 'the Day of New York'. It is, however, one that was already freighted with significance in different countries: in Chile, as the anniversary of the September 1973 coup by General Agusto Pinochet that ousted President Salvador Allende and his Popular Unity government; in the

Catalonia province of Spain, where it is the national day, commemorating the defeat of Catalan forces by the Bourbons in 1713. Some have associated the date with the day in 1683 when the Austrian forces broke the Muslim siege of Vienna. By coincidence, 911 is a number familiar to all Americans as the telephone for the emergency services.

9/11 Commission   See *National Commission on Terrorist Attacks upon the United States.*

A

active millimetre wave   A new security scanning system first tested in Schiphol Airport in Amsterdam as well as in others around the world, said to be fast and efficient and as 'safe to use as a cell phone'. The American Civil Liberties Union (ACLU) expressed concern about the not-mentioned aspects of the technology: it produces precise images of passengers' bodies, revealing private body parts and intimate medical details such as colostomy bags. This raised doubts as to the 'voluntary nature' of the scan, since people are not aware of what they are revealing of themselves. The US Transport Security Administration insisted that faces are obscured, but the software is very easy to reverse, according to ACLU, which also expressed concern about the 'irresistible pull that images created by this system will create on some employees (e.g. when a celebrity like George Clooney or someone with an unusual or 'freakish' body goes through the system)' ('Schiphol Body-scanning Prompts No Complaint Yet', *IHT*, 17 May 2007; also 'New Airport Body Scanners Troubling to ACLU Privacy Expert', ACLU Press Release, 11 October 2007; www.mindfully.org/Technology/2007/Active-Millimeter-Wave11oct07.htm).

Advanced Research Development Activity (ARDA)   US intelligence analysis programme. According to a report entitled *Data Mining and Homeland Security*, issued by the Congressional Research Service in January 2006, **ARDA**'s role was to spend National Security Agency (NSA) money in order to 'solve some of the most critical problems facing the US intelligence community [see **fifteen squabbling baronies**]', notable among which was 'making sense' of the massive amounts of data the NSA collected, frequently from online social networks. **ARDA** research aimed at discovering whether the semantic web could easily be used to connect people, e.g. in tracking financial dealings by linking 'who knows who' through purchasing or bank records, in order to uncover groups of terrorists, money launderers or blacklisted groups. **ARDA**'s name was changed in 2006 to **Disruptive Technology Office**. Its concern with online social network analysis and **automated intelligence profiling** echoed the Pentagon's **Total Information Awareness** project (Paul Marks, 'Pentagon Sets Its Sights on Social Networking Websites', *New Scientist*, 9 June 2006).

anthrax A piece of coal (hence *anthracite*), boil or carbuncle, from Greek *anthrax*. Since 1876, also a fever caused by minute, rapidly multiplying, organisms in the blood. After 9/11 **anthrax** soon joined the list of 'terror weapons', since letters containing anthrax spores were mailed in September 2001 to several news media offices and two Democratic US senators, killing 5 people and infecting 17 others. At the time many believed the **anthrax** attacks were a follow-up to 9/11. The FBI file name for the case was *Amerithrax*. Treatment with the antibiotic Ciprofloxacin is regarded by many doctors as an expensive, and more risky, response than others, such as the generic drug Doxycycline. In 2008 it appeared that the FBI might have finally identified the perpetrator as Bruce Ivins, a 61-year-old scientist: Evins had worked for 18 years at the Fort Detrick BioDefense Laboratory in Maryland and apparently committed suicide in August 2008. According to some reports, Evins had worked on anthrax antidotes for the US government and was thought to have despatched the samples in 2001, taking advantage of the public alarm after 9/11, as a means of testing his anti-anthrax vaccine. His family and friends continued to deny these charges.

anti-terrorism In US and British parlance, policies *responding to* terrorist acts. Contrast with **counterterrorism** which is preventive.

Anti-terrorism, Crime and Security Act 2001 UK law, passed in the aftermath of 9/11, and building on the law passed in 2000. Involved substantial curtailment of civil liberties, but did not go as far as the 2001 USA **Patriot Act.**

automated intelligence profiling See **Advanced Research Development Activity** and **Total Information Awareness.**

B

Bali to Beslan to Baghdad Grandiloquent and alliterative phrase used in the second of a series of speeches in 2006 on the global war on terror and coinciding with the release of an updated version of the White House anti-terrorism strategy by President George W. Bush to denote the strike capacity of terrorists. Noting that Al-Qa'ida was 'evil but not insane', he mentioned Osama bin Laden 18 times in his 40-minute speech. Bush warned that bin Laden was still pursuing his vision of 'a unified totalitarian Islamic state that can confront and eventually destroy the free world' (Sheryl Stolberg and Brian Knowlton, 'Bush, in Political Mode, Warns of Qaeda Threat', *IHT*, 6 September 2006). **Bali** in Indonesia had been the site of a terrorist attack on tourists in 2002; **Beslan**, a town in the North Caucasus republic of Ingushetia, was the scene of an attack by Chechen rebels in which they held school pupils hostage.

Binladengate   Term coined by French intelligence expert Richard Labeviere to denote US intelligence failures, and past association with bin Laden, in relation to 9/11.

biometrics   Application of supposedly scientific methods to suspect identification, using data from their iris, fingerprints and face. Basis of US government campaign after 2001 to get other states to issue passports with biometric data. Biometrics uses a binary image to register such data. After 2001, major problems arose with this technology: eyes that were blue, or watery, or had contact lenses were registered inaccurately, as were those with Asian eyelashes. Biometric data also presuppose accurate databases which, in regard to the iris, do not exist.

bioterrorism   1990s term used to denote the use by terrorists of biological weapons, e.g. **anthrax**, botulism, plague, smallpox.

Black Dawn   NATO simulation exercise, conducted in Brussels in June 2005, in which a *jihadist* terrorist network acquires nuclear material, makes a crude nuclear device and detonates it outside NATO headquarters. More than 300 representatives from NATO countries witnessed this fictionalised account of 'catastrophic terrorism'. See **Global Threat Reduction Initiative** (Sam Nunn and Pierre Lellouche, 'Now in Rehearsal, the Unthinkable', *IHT*, 31 May 2005).

breach of security   Recognition by FBI director Robert Mueller III soon after the 9/11 attacks that the US administration's Arabic language skills were abysmal, which led to jokes among intelligence officials about his admission breaching security.

C

censoring impulses Term used for what cinema director Brian de Palma calls 'a mission to misinform', on the failure of films on the war on terror to address underlying issues or include themes unwelcome to mainstream American audiences (Nigel Andrews, 'Hollywood's Explosive Talent', *FT*, 8–9 March 2008). An example of this was the removal from the original film script of *Charlie Wilson's War*, as written by Aaron Sorkin, of a scene in which the hero, an anti-communist Congressman and supporter of the Afghan *mujahidin* in the 1980s, hears of the 9/11 attacks. Cf. **redact**.

Citizen Patrols US freelance vigilantes who, after 9/11 in particular, converged in southeast Arizona to patrol the frontier with Mexico and, as some supporters argued, defend it 'from terrorist attack'. Participants came from as far afield as Buffalo, New York, and Orange County, California, and numbered over a thousand former soldiers and policemen, public servants and retired citizens. This group and a rival organisation called the Minuteman Civil Defense Corps (described by President Bush as 'vigilantes') patrolled the Arizona border with Mexico, and particularly the Naco Corridor, to prevent illegal immigrants from slipping into the country. While the official border patrol detained almost a million would-be immigrants each year, another half a million were managing to cross into the harsh Arizona Desert (Carlos Ramos, 'Patrulla ciudadana en Arizona', *El País*, 5 April 2005; and www.lewrockwell.com/gaddy/gaddy16.html)

Citizen Soldiers US citizens who serve in the National Guard. In the past their service typically extended to a few days a month, but in recent years has become much more integrated into the regular armed forces and they are now on longer periods of duty after 9/11 to guard public buildings and generally reassure the public. Also known as 'Weekend Warriors' and, in Washington, DC, 'Capitol Guardians'. The National Guard is, in fact, the oldest component of the US forces, going back over 360 years to the Massachusetts Bay Colony. They can perform both federal and state roles.

Code Orange US Homeland Security term signifying 'high' risk of attack. One stage higher than 'Yellow' designating an 'elevated' risk. Used on several occasions after 9/11 (the *Guardian*, 3 August 2004).

complex phenomenon In reference to US government agencies, a mess. See **assumption train, Babel of war assessments, connect the dots,**

groupthink, rearrange wiring diagrams (Joel Brinkley, 'Colombia Drug Fight Sees Mixed Results', *IHT*, 28 April 2005).

compound   An enclosed area surrounding a house. Also a closed area where dangerous or otherwise legally suspect entities, e.g. dogs or impounded cars, are placed. As distinct from the homonym meaning 'to combine', which is of Latin origin, this is a colonial term, used by the Dutch and British in Asia, and is believed to be derived, despite its Latinate sound, from the Malayan *kampung*. For extensive discussion of this usage, see *Hobson-Jobson. A Glossary of Colloquial Anglo-Indian Words and Phrases, and of Kindred Terms, Etymological, Historical Geographical and Discursive* (1886), pp. 240–4. Now generically used to denote a fenced-off, private zone inhabited by expatriates in, say, Afghanistan or Saudi Arabia, similar to a 'gated community' in Western countries. One of the signs of serious escalation in the Al-Qa'ida campaign against expatriates in Saudi Arabia in 2003–4 was its ability to enter and slaughter residents within compounds in Riyadh and elsewhere. Here the term denoted an area of elite and privileged existence, in contrast to its use in developed countries where fenced-in areas are used to keep dogs, cars, etc.

counterterrorism   As distinct from **anti-terrorism**, the struggle against existing terrorist threats and groups and policies designed to prevent, if necessary by anticipatory action, future or possible terrorist acts. Has become an all-purpose excuse for unconstitutional procedures.

CSO   Chief Security Officer. By analogy with CEO, Chief Executive Officer, a corporate term introduced after 9/11 for an official with the overall responsibility for a firm's security.

culture of forced consensus   See Chapter 11, also **groupthink**.

Customs–Trade Partnership against Terrorism   US programme established after 9/11 to prevent terrorist attacks via cargo entering America through land borders, seaports and airports. Although 8,000 importing companies signed up to the deal, and thus qualified for reduced scrutiny by customs officials, many did not comply with the new regulations ('Gaps in Cargo Security Continue, Inquiry Finds', *IHT*, 28 May 2008).

D

defensive filings   See **suspicious activity reports**.

Denver Three   Deemed a major security threat, the treatment of this trio is an example of the use of security by the White House to muzzle political debate within the USA after 9/11. In March 2005, Alex Young, Leslie Wise and Karen Bauer went to an open political meeting, a taxpayer-funded Bush Social Security event in Denver, sporting a bumper sticker saying 'No More **Blood for Oil**'. As soon as they entered the event a 'mystery man', with an earpiece and acting like a Secret Service agent, told them to leave. Subsequently, they and their lawyers filed numerous freedom-of-information requests to obtain the identity of the 'mystery man', winning support from eight of Colorado's nine members of Congress. With headquarters in a Denver coffee shop and a loft apartment, they contacted reporters, produced regular news items and fed in questions at White House briefings. There was talk of a lawsuit. The man was not a security agent, it eventuated, but, as the Denver Three concluded, someone acting on behalf of the White House. The case unearthed other instances of White House–sponsored harassment of critics, e.g. a 42-person blacklist used at a Bush event in North Dakota and the fact that, during a campaign in New Hampshire and Arizona, event participants were required to sign loyalty oaths for admission (Dana Millbank, 'The Tenacious Trio', *The Washington Post*, 22 June 2005; Elisabeth Bumiller, 'Bumped at Bush Event, Denver Three Hit Back', *IHT*, 27 June 2005).

de-radicalise   A latter-day, US and allied, variant of what in communist states was termed 're-education' or 'brain-washing'. Part of overall analysis of Islamism that, focussing purely on behaviour and outcomes, and ignoring possible causes of political radicalism, seeks to change opinions and practice of suspected opponents. This verb appeared as part of the Pentagon's efforts in the information war against **Al-Qa'ida**. Selected religious leaders met with American-held detainees before their release to 'de-radicalise' them, after which the American media team publicised their rejection of a violent past (Michael Moss and Souad Mekhennet, 'From American Prison to the Heights of Al Qaeda', *IHT*, 4 April 2008). See **radicalisation/radicaliser**.

Director of National Intelligence   Post created after 9/11 to ensure, or seek to promote, greater collaboration between the many different sections of the US 'intelligence community'. The first director was John Negroponte.

dirty bomb   Not a nuclear weapon, but a conventional explosive device combined with radioactive material. See **nuclear terrorism**, **radiological dispersal device**.

dysfunctional   Medical term normally applied to families, or other social institutions, that failed to work, or work sufficiently together. Used by the US 9/11 *Commission report* to refer to Congressional oversight of intelligence activities. See **Babel of war assessments**.

E

egregious even by Washington standards   Description of money claimed by local bodies for security measures post-9/11. See **Glennville**.

elevated security concern   Increased surveillance of airline passengers, public buildings, etc. in light of information or intuition concerning possible terrorist actions.

equal opportunity destroyer, with no respect for boundaries Graphic description of terrorism, from a speech by President Clinton in 1996, following bombings at Khobar, Saudi Arabia.

***Espacio de Palabras* ('Space for Words')**   Electronic screen erected on 9 June 2004 in the Atocha station, Madrid, to substitute for the altar with candles commemorating victims of the 11 March attack. It was removed three months after the attacks at the request of people working in the station who were, among other things, affected by the smoke. Seven thousand messages were left in the first two days, and the daily number did not drop below 200 in the following four months (messages could be left on online at www.mascercanos.com). As of early August 2004, almost 30,000 messages had been left. Among them was the following:

> *How easy it is to kill, and how difficult to live.*
> *Amhara and Andrea, nine and five years old, send a kiss to all the*
> *people who are in heaven, Mua',*
> *I do not know nor do I want to know the reasons that give the right*
> *to kill.*
>
> (*El País*, 'Palabras que llenan espacios', 4 August 2004)

F

failure of imagination   Exculpatory euphemism for political and intellectual weaknesses of the US intelligence community. Compare it with the application of the term 'human frailty' as the explanation for the 2008 banking crisis (Richard Thaler and Cass Sunstein, 'Human Frailty Caused

This Crisis', *FT*, 12 November 2008). The **9/11 Commission Report**, apart from criticising the grave failure of information sharing between the CIA and the FBI and within these agencies, observed a 'failure of imagination' in response to the warning signs agency members did observe but failed to act upon, in particular a 1998 report warning that **Al-Qa'ida** might carry out a suicide attack with hijacked planes ('Can Spies Be Made Better?', Special Report, *The Economist*, 19 March 2005).

fanatic   From Latin *fanus*, temple, hence someone who is an extreme believer in religion and not open to reason. Term of last resort used by students of terrorism to denote 'new' or religious terrorists of the twenty-first century. A remarkably weak term on which to hang a general theory of this form of violence.

Far Enemy   Arabic *al-adu' al baíd*, designation of the USA and Europe as targets of attack by Islamists, especially by **Al-Qa'ida**, in contrast to previous, more conventional, targeting of states in the Muslim world, the **Near Enemy**, such as Egypt, Algeria, Tunisia and Saudi Arabia.

fifteen squabbling baronies   Description of the American intelligence system. See also **failure of imagination**, *Terrorist Threat Integration Center* ('Can Spies Be Made Better?', Special Report, *The Economist*, 19 March 2005).

food fight   Bureaucratic infighting, term used by Greg Treverton, former vice chairman of the US National Intelligence Council, to describe the 'turbulence and jostling for turf' that resulted from a sweeping reorganisation of intelligence agencies in 2005. Treverton described the battle between the CIA's Counterterrorist Center and the **National Counterterrorism Center** as something that sounded more like the law of the jungle – a 'food fight' (Scott Shane, 'US Spy Overhaul Sinks in Bureaucratic Swamp', *New York Times*, 28 February 2008).

footpad   Term used by British journalist Henry Porter to denote surreptitious, sly and implicitly illegal activities by officials of the Gordon Brown government as it extended counterterrorist surveillance powers without meaningful public or parliamentary debate. Traditionally, a **footpad** is a lowly form of thief, inferior to the more romantic, mounted 'highwayman'. The Liberal Democrat spokesman on Home Affairs, Nick Clegg, pointed this out: '…the **footpads** from the Home Office media department rushed around saying that a full consultation had taken place under the Regulation of

Investigatory Powers Act. Something is very stealthy here' (Henry Porter, 'The Government Trumpets Free Speech While Trampling on It', *The Observer*, 7 October 2007).

Foreign Intelligence Surveillance Court (FISC)   Secret US government body that vets requests from other governments for surveillance warrants against suspected foreign intelligence agents inside the country. Established in the USA by the Foreign Intelligence Surveillance Act of 1978. FISC hearings are closed to the public and its judges have 'greater latitude' in their use of classified material. On 16 December 2005, the *New York Times* reported that the Bush administration had since 2002 also been conducting surveillance operations against *US* citizens, and this without the knowledge of the FISC or any other judicial body. Some Senate Judiciary Commission lawyers also proposed giving new powers to the FISC in an attempt to overcome objections to the use of military tribunals for trying 'terror suspects'. Critics argued that these tribunals were created by the President without congressional approval (Michael Isikoff and Mark Hosenball, 'Got Him. Now What?', *Newsweek*, 16 May 2005).

franchise   Term used to denote decentralised terrorist organisations like **Al-Qa'ida**. Cf. *mouvance*.

G

Gang of Eight   Initially, a group of senior US Congressional leaders who abetted President Bush in a breach of US law. A variant on '**Gang of Four**', the factional termed used in 1976 by Chinese government to denounce and imprison four prominent Communist Party leaders, including the widow of the recently deceased Mao Tse-tung. The 'Eight' were a set of leaders of the US Congress, including the heads of each of the two parties along with the chairs and ranking members of the intelligence committees of both Houses of Congress. The President is required by law to 'ensure that the congressional intelligence committees are kept fully and currently informed of the intelligence activities of the United States.' However, he can elect to report only to the Gang of Eight when he feels 'it is essential to limit access' to information about a covert action. The 'Gang of Eight' was placed in the spotlight with coverage of the Bush administration's warrantless domestic spying programme, of which only the Gang of Eight members were informed: they were 'forbidden' to divulge information about it to other members of Congress.

In January 2003, another 'Gang of Eight' appeared when Tony Blair and Prime Minister José María Aznar of Spain published a controversial joint statement calling for Europe to stand united behind the USA in the looming war with Baghdad. This declaration broke EU ranks after its foreign ministers had agreed on a policy of demanding that Iraq disarm, backing the UN route and supporting weapons inspectors. The Blair–Aznar 'Gang of Eight' consisted of EU members Britain, Denmark, Italy, Portugal and Spain, along with three would-be members of the EU: the Czech Republic, Hungary and Poland ('House Democrat Slams Spy Program Briefings', *IHT*, 6 January 2006; Michael White, Ian Black and Patrick Wintour, ' "Gang of 8" Provokes EU Rift', the *Guardian*, 31 January 2003).

general level of arrogant incompetence   Thus stated the British Member of Parliament, Gwyneth Dunwoody, in regard to the application of airport security measures in US airports, after having been subjected to them three years after the 9/11 attacks. Other passengers had been arrested or deported because their names had somehow appeared on 'no-fly' lists, and some journalists were detained in shackles because no one had informed them that they needed a special type of visa. Giovanni Bisignani, head of the International Air Transport Association, described the lack of coordination as 'inexcusable', noting that requirements in one country can break the laws of another. This was especially so after an agreement was signed between the USA and EU governments in May 2004 requiring European airlines to share data on arriving air passengers, including names, addresses, itineraries, telephone numbers and credit card details. See *Secure Borders and Open Doors,* **passenger name recognition** (Don Phillips, 'Airlines' Representative Deplores Security "Mess" ', *IHT*, 10 December 2004).

Glennville   Small rural town in the southeast US state of Georgia (population about 4,000 with some 28.7 per cent below the poverty line) which, in receipt of funds for anti-terrorist **homeland security**, erected a large billboard advertising a government website telling people how to prepare for a terrorist attack, hence coining the phrase **egregious even by Washington standards**. The case of **Glennville** inadvertently illustrates some problems with the funding allocations for **homeland security** (not to mention its violations of the Constitution and international law). New York's allocation of homeland security funds was $25 per person, while the rural state of Wyoming (Vice-President Dick Cheney was a Congressman from Wyoming) received $61, prompting the California (Democratic) Congresswoman Ellen Tauscher to remark, 'Pretty much everyone in Wyoming has a fire engine'. **Glennville** has only a volunteer-based fire department. Apart from rural politicians that seized upon this **new windfall in homeland security spending**, enterprises related with government members also did a brisk business. See **Halliburton, Homeland Security**.

global counterinsurgency   A somewhat less abrasive alternative to **Global War on Terror/Terrorism** ('Don't Mention the GWAT', *The Economist*, 7 July 2007).

global intelligence failure   Term used by the 9/11 Commission Report to describe failure to anticipate **Al-Qa'ida** attack. Unclear if 'global' means covering the whole globe, or world, or involves all the branches of the Washington intelligence community or if it refers to a failure right across the range of intelligence activities. Perhaps 'all of the above'.

Global Threat Reduction Initiative   Programme established in 2004 by the US Department of Energy as a policy of international collaboration to 'consolidate and accelerate' tracking down, destroying and relocating of 'vulnerable materials' that could be used for making crude nuclear devices. Another, central, part of its mission was securing nuclear fuel, the initial goal (not met) being to repatriate all fresh fuel of Russian origin before the end of 2005. On the other hand, around two-thirds of US-made fuel left abroad was not targeted for removal (Sam Nunn and Pierre Lellouche, 'Now in Rehearsal, the Unthinkable', *IHT*, 31 May 2005).

Global War against Terror/Terrorism (GWAT)   Inflated, open-ended and geographically scatterbrained term used by the Bush administration for post-9/11 campaigns. Term abandoned in 2009 by the Obama administration. See **global counterinsurgency, long struggle, long war, War on Terrorism**.

glocal phenomenon   That is, something that combines 'global' with 'local' issues and causes. Also *glocalisation*. According to Professor Rik Coolsaet, director of the Department of Security and Global Governance Department of the Royal Institute for International Relations (Brussels), *jihadi* terrorism was an example of this, a melange of different sources of real and perceived local discontent stitched together by a radical and puritanical interpretation of Islam and flourishing in its global momentum (Rik Coolsaet, *Between al-Andalus and a Failing Integration. Europe's Pursuit of a Long-term Counterterrorism Strategy in the Post-Al-Qa'ida Era*, 2005, Egmont Institute).

glorifying, exalting or celebrating terrorism An offence in draft British anti-terrorist legislation announced in September 2005 by the Home Secretary Charles Clarke. The provision enabled police to hold terror suspects for three months without charge. The offences carried a jail sentence of up to seven years and covered statements published on the Internet that could constitute 'direct or indirect encouragement' of terrorist acts or that 'glorify, exalt, or celebrate' such acts. The Home Secretary was reported to be preparing a list of events in history, acts whose 'glorification' in contemporary statements would be considered a criminal offence. 9/11 was 'listed', the 1916 Easter Rising in Dublin is not (Nigel Morris, 'Outcry over Plan to Detain Suspects for Three Months', *The Independent*, 16 September 2005).

Ground Zero 'The point on the surface of the earth or water directly below, directly above, or at which an atomic or hydrogen bomb explodes' (from Webster's *Encyclopaedic Unabridged Dictionary of the English Language*, 1989), commonly used for the site of the World Trade Center attacks on 9/11. The term seems to have been first used with the Manhattan Project and the bombing of Japan. It is also used to refer to other large bombs, earthquakes, tsunamis and other catastrophes to designate the hardest-hit point. A less controversial synonym is 'hypocentre'. After 2001, the term and site became the object of different uses and abuses. Thus, on 27 August 2006, Ray Nagin, mayor of New Orleans, answered criticisms in a CBS *60 Minutes* programme about his leadership after Hurricane Katrina, saying: 'That's all right. You guys in New York can't get a hole in the ground fixed and it's five years later. So let's be fair.' His term 'hole in the ground' raised a lot of dust, leading Mayor Nagin to retract: 'I wish I would have basically said that it was an undeveloped site, which it is.' Whatever it is, it is not a rose. However, others came to use the term differently: in an article headed 'Ground Zero Becomes Backdrop for Fashion Show', journalist Christine Kearney reported, 'As much of the 16-acre (6.5-hectare) World Trade Center site remains a dusty pit, plagued with political squabbles over its rebuilding and plans to attract companies back downtown, some fashion designers have decided it's the next hip thing as the scene for their runway shows' (Reuters, 7 February 2007). In an earlier use, the journal *Golf Digest* wrote in May 2000, before the 9/11 attacks, that golf pants were 'ground zero for fashion victims'.

groupthink In the words of the 9/11 Congressional Report, 'collective groupthink' accounted for failure to anticipate attacks (from Irving L. Janis, *Groupthink. Psychological Studies of Policy Decision and Fiascoes*, Boston: Houghton Mifflin, 1972, second edition 1982). Janis, whose work covers the disciplines of social psychology, history and political science, looked at what he termed foreign policy 'fiascos': cases of spectacular misjudgement by US administrations, from the failure to anticipate the Japanese attack on Pearl Harbor (1941), through to the mismanagement of the Korean war (1950–3), to the failed CIA-run Bay of Pigs invasion of Cuba (1961), and the escalation of the war in Vietnam (1965). In each case he ascribed the failure to the dynamics of group psychology, whereby individuals were reluctant to break from the assumptions of the group: 'I use the term "groupthink" as a quick and easy way to refer to a model of thinking that people engage in when they are deeply involved in a cohesive in-group, when the members' striving for unanimity override their motivation to realistically appraise alternative courses of action . . . Groupthink refers to a deterioration of mental efficiency, reality testing, and moral judgment that result from in-group pressures' (Second edition, p. 9). Ironically, there are strong reasons for arguing that the very reports produced by investigative committees in the USA and in the UK after 9/11 and the Iraq War, which were designed to identify the workings of **groupthink**, were, in their usually bland and unanimous conclusions, themselves evidence of this process.

H

hell of a mess   Term applied by the former US solicitor general Theodore Olson to the situation created by detention of 'terror suspects' by the US government as a result of the many unconstitutional aspects of their situation. One problem was the question of whether evidence obtained in secret custody by questionable methods could be admissible as evidence in court (Michael Isikoff and Mark Hosenball, 'Got Him. Now What?', *Newsweek*, 16 May 2005).

hindsight effect   People believing in retrospect that an event, e.g. the collapse of European communism in 1989–91, 9/11 or the 2008 banking crisis, was far more predictable than reality indicated (Stefan Stern, 'A Very Timely Warning', *FT*, 2 December 2004). See **groupthink, Truthers**.

Homeland Defense   A curious reprise of Cold War language – perhaps because it is redolent of the comforting word *homestead*, a term taken from Soviet usage in World War II and applied to US defence policy in the late 1990s – to justify the National Missile Defense Programme. After

9/11, it was used to denote US bodies responsible for internal security in general.

Homeland Security   The broad term popularised after 9/11 to include biodefence, border security, immigration control, infrastructure protection, streamlining effectiveness and coordination of government bodies. Distinct from *national security*, a term conventionally used to denote protection from hostile acts, and espionage by other states. See also **Glennville**.

honey traders   Unlikely group of suspects identified after 9/11. Following 9/11, it was claimed that **Al-Qa'ida** had infiltrated the honey trade and was using it as a cover for moving funds. Severe controls were, for a time, imposed by the relevant states on the trade. The cultivation and sale of honey are a historic and to this day important part of life in the Red Sea region, particularly in Ethiopia and Yemen. The Bible speaks of Israel as 'a land of milk and honey'. There are streets in the Yemeni capital, Sanaa, devoted to the sale of honey. In Ethiopia honey consumption was, prior to the revolution of 1974, limited only to certain classes.

hostage-filled cruise missiles   Metaphorical term for hijacked passenger planes (Thom Shanker, 'For Navy, Gulf Incident Offered a Vision of 9/11 at Sea', *IHT*, 12–13 January 2008).

Humint, Sigint, Imint   Human Intelligence, Signals Intelligence, Imagery Intelligence, respectively, three main traditional forms of information gathering by the US military. Backed up with Techint (Technical Intelligence) and CI (Counter Intelligence). All five methods are considered to be significant elements of Psyop (Psychological Operations). The *Special Operations Forces Intelligence and Electronic Warfare Operations* Field Manual (No. 34–36, published on 30 September 1991 by the Department of the Army Headquarters in Washington, DC) states that the objective of Psyop is to influence humans and that the most effective source for this information is **Humint**.

I

inordinate number of individuals of investigative interest
Part of the warnings sent to FBI headquarters prior to 9/11 which were not taken seriously enough. According to authors Max Bazerman and Michael

Watkins (see **predictable surprises**), a memo was sent to FBI headquarters by an agent concerned about the 'inordinate number of individuals of investigative interest' being trained in Arizona flying schools (Stefan Stern, 'A Very Timely Warning', *FT*, 2 December 2004).

intellectual authorship   'Autoría intelectual', also translatable as *intellectual responsibility*, Spanish criminal law term, akin to 'mastermind', implying that a criminal act had a plotting brain, or author, behind it. Used by Mariano Rajoy, Secretary General of the opposition People's Party (PP) in Spain, to assert links between Arabs involved in 11 March 2004 bombings in Madrid and the Basque separatist group ETA. Rajoy, as Minister of the Interior in the PP government at the time of the explosions, drew on the authority of his personal experience to say that while it was Arabs who carried out the actual attacks, 'these men do not have the intellectual capacity to prepare this type of action'. This argument was in line with the general claim made by the PP government immediately after the Madrid attacks in which they sought to place the blame on ETA. The – false – analogy drawn by investigators of the March 2004 bombings, according to which these actions could be investigated *and* understood using the techniques of a traditional criminal investigation were, of course, replicated in the FBI investigations of 9/11 in the USA.

intelligence   'Intelligence' is one of the most abused words in the whole 9/11 story as it is used to apply to unreliable, poorly analysed, often inaccurate information: thus supposedly secret information, often rumour, conjecture, innuendo or invention were passed off, justified and excluded from assessment or criticism, as 'intelligence'. Shrewdly contrasted by American journalist Jonathan Randal to 'knowledge' (*Osama. Making of a Terrorist* [New York: Knopf, 2004]). In its original, precise, Latin sense, *interlegere*, literally 'to read between', hence to decide on what is significant or not in information, a faculty of judgement, discernment, akin again in the original sense of the term to Greek *istoria*, from *istor*, the skill or science of discerning what is and is not significant. From the late seventeenth century, also secret gathering, as well as assessment, of information related to state security (first usage in English: 1697). Later English usage mixes up the earlier sense of intellectual faculty, judgement, with the quality of superior mental power, supposedly 'cleverness', 'mental ability', and with the security services sense of secret information. Significantly, Middle Eastern languages and official terminology tend not to use words with etymological similarities to 'intelligence', something of which, in the literal sense, most states are afraid, preferring the more direct terms 'security' (Arabic *amn*, Hebrew *aman*, Turkish *imniyet*) and 'information' (*ittila'at, mokhabarat, istikhbarat*). The Pakistani military, on the other hand, true to its post-colonial culture, has its 'Interservices Intelligence', ISI. Israel has three major services: *Mossad*, the organisation of intelligence and special operations (*hamasod limodiín lleteflidim meyujadim*), which operates internationally; *Shabak*, which operates within Israel and the occupied territories (*sherut bitadon klali*); and *Aman*, military intelligence. The three main Hebrew names – *mossad, sherut, aman* – have the same Semitic roots as their Arabic counterparts.

intelligence data   Otherwise '**raw intelligence** data' or 'solid intelligence', often poorly assessed information passed off as special by dint of being acquired in an unorthodox manner. Apart from the abuses of the 'intelligence' world, the very assumption that there are bare, straightforward 'facts' or 'data' which are then in some separate operation liable to interpretation or analysis is an elementary epistemological mistake. The same applies to supposedly direct sensual data. See **raw intelligence**. Certain very specific military secrets aside, the whole idea that there is 'secret' information which, unchecked and taken in isolation, provides 'the truth' about another country or its leaders' plans, is absurd.

intelligence management center   See **sit room**.

investigative shortfalls   One of many US euphemisms for failures in intelligence gathering and analytic failures.

L

layering   Sloppy, when not spurious, method of analysis, used by the CIA for reaching ambiguous conclusions by means of cobbling together scraps of intelligence ('Can Spies Be Made Better?', Special Report, *The Economist*, 19 March 2005). Cf. **multiple intelligence sources**.

little guy   As in Donald Rumsfeld's reported reference to bin Laden after 9/11, 'Why go after the little guy?', the big guy being Saddam Hussein.

long struggle/long war   Somewhat evasive, but also more accurate and measured, alternative to **war on terror**, as the description of military and political conflict, across different continents, between the West and Islamist militants. The adjective 'long' serves rightly to denote the open-ended nature of the conflict, but also the fact that there may be no clear final moment. It is thus designed to divest the illusion that the conflict would have a quick, or clearly definable, end, or even goal. US President Ronald Reagan spoke of a '*long battle* against terrorism' in 1986, while George W. Bush spoke of a '**long war** against a determined enemy' in his State of the Union address in January 2006.

Similar terms were used during the Cold War decades. Ironically, but irrelevantly, the term 'Cold War', meaning a drawn-out, multidimensional and for long inconclusive conflict, as opposed to 'Hot War', was originally used in the fourteenth century by Don Juan Manuel (1282–1348), a Spanish writer, to denote the conflict between Christianity and Islam. The term arises in his *Libro de los Estados*, where a wise man gives advice to a young prince on how to conduct war against the Muslim enemy. The modern, late 1940s usage is ascribed to two American writers, the journalist Walter Lippmann, who wrote a series of influential articles, and later a book, on this subject, and the philanthropist Bernard Baruch, who claims he met a man on a bench in Central Park, New York, who let slip the phrase in conversation about the state of American–Russian relations. Cf. **planetary enemy**.

M

mastermind   Favourite term in criminal investigations, assuming the traditional hierarchical organisation of violent groups (e.g. the *Mafia*) applied erroneously to modern terrorist movements. With Osama bin Laden and 9/11, or *el Egipcio* and 11 March for example the term implies that acts of terror can be understood like bank robberies. It suggests not only that there is one major organiser, but that the act can be seen as a manipulation of other participants, thus avoiding the unwelcome reality that there is considerable support for and willingness to participate in such activities among young radical Muslims. See also **intellectual authorship**.

message force multipliers   Retired US military personnel used by the Pentagon to promote favourable news about its performance in the 'War on Terror'. The 'analysts' were classed as a 'rapid reaction force' to rebut media criticism of the Iraqi and other campaigns. The job of these 'message force multipliers' or 'surrogates', often presented as 'defence specialists' or 'security experts', was to repeat and diffuse administration 'themes and messages' to Americans 'in the form of their own opinions.' Some advised the Pentagon on how to outmanoeuvre media networks, while others warned of planned stories and even sent the Pentagon copies of their correspondence with news executives. The Pentagon claims, 'The intent and purpose of this is nothing other than an earnest attempt to inform the American people'. One of the 'analysts', John C. Garret, described the job as '**psyops** on steroids' (David Barstow, 'Behind TV Analysts, the Pentagon's Hidden Hand', *The New York Times*, 20 April 2008).

Meyssan, Thierry   French writer, author of best-selling book denying part of the 9/11 story, *11 septembre 2001: l'efforyable imposture* (11 September 2001: The Terrible Imposture'), a book whose publishers claimed it had been translated into 26 languages. Meyssan's main claim was that there had been no plane attack on the Pentagon. See **Truthers**.

mouvance   Neologism, a fusion of French words for 'movement' and 'tendency', used of **Al-Qa'ida**, to denote a group that is not organised on a traditional centralised basis, but is more fluid and decentralised. Cf. English word **franchise**, used to try to capture the same sense of a decentralised terrorist group. See also **intellectual authorship, planetary foe**.

multiple intelligence sources   US government term of basis for particular security judgement, implying supposedly strong characterisation, confirmation from different sources, or analytic triangulation. Often reflects multiplication of chaff, or failure to evaluate the varied importance of intelligence sources. See **fifteen squabbling baronies, intelligence data, layering**.

N

National Commission on Terrorist Attacks upon the United States   Report commissioned by the US Congress, issued in July 2004, subsequently becoming a US bestseller. More popularly known as the **9/11 Commission**. The report cited 'failures of imagination, policy, capabilities and management'. Listed multiple '**Operational Failures**' of the US intelligence community prior to 9/11, including the failure of intelligence bodies to share information, failure to check false information in visa applications and passports, losing track of two known terrorists who had entered the USA in the summer of 2001, and failure to include names of known terrorists on no-fly lists. For all its wealth of detail, and critical reflections, the report was seriously flawed by being framed in terms of a classic criminal investigation, thus assuming a hierarchical command and organisational structure for terrorist operations, and excluding consideration of the historical, political and ideological factors that explained 9/11 and other operations.

National Counterterrorism Center   See *Terrorist Threat Integration Center.*

National Terror Alert   After 9/11 the *National Terror Alert Response Center* (www.nationalterroralert.com/) offered updated information about the US **state of terror**. For example, a bar with moving colours showed that the general US risk on 7 November 2007 was yellow (elevated) and that for 'US aircraft' was orange (high). Headlines included, *inter alia*: Pakistans [sic] Nuclear History Worries Insiders; University of Washington Law School on High Alert After Threats; Terror Experts Warn of Increased Threat Due to Pakistan Crisis; Crew Members Fall Ill on US Airways Flight 2022; New York Suspect Causes Terror Concern; Students and Parents Concerned Over Twitching, Mystery Illness at Roanoke High School; US Capitol Police Investigate 7th Suspicious Fire in Senate Office Building.

new tools to monitor terrorists   One of the achievements, along with the creation of the Department of Homeland Security, which President George W. Bush listed in his farewell address of 16 January 2009 (*IHT,* 17–18 January 2009). See **Special Registration Program, suspected terrorists**.

new windfall in homeland security spending   See **Glennville**.

NSA   US National Security Agency, tasked with electronic, now satellite and Internet, espionage, possessing a larger budget than the CIA. Created secretly, at the height of the Cold War in 1952. At the time, there was 'no news coverage, no congressional debate, no press announcement, not even the whisper of a rumour', as James Bamford wrote in his book *The Puzzle Palace.* Such was the secrecy that it was said that NSA stood for 'No Such Agency' (H. D. S. Greenway, 'The Limits of Global Eavesdropping', *IHT,* 14 April 2005).

O

on the offensive   Contrasted to **on the defence**, frequently intoned adrenalin- or testosterone-stimulating description resorted to by the Bush administration (Daniel Benjamin and Steven Simon, 'Unleash the CIA', *IHT,* 25 July 2007). See also **1 per cent doctrine, counterterrorism, paradigm of prevention**.

Open Source Center   New US 'intelligence agency', set up in 2005 in wake of the examination of 9/11 intelligence failures, to gather and analyse information from open sources (including t-shirt slogans) around the world. Established as part of the new intelligence chief John Negroponte's restructuring project. At a news briefing, General Michael Hayden, Negroponte's chief deputy, said, 'Just because information is stolen, that doesn't make it more useful' (Scott Shane, 'No Snooping Necessary', *IHT*, 11 November 2005).

Operation Able Danger   Secret investigative effort based in the Pentagon from 1999, authorised by Joint Chiefs of Staff, using data-mining techniques to identify possible terrorist threats. By 2000 it had information on the 9/11 action leader Mohammad Atta and others. Subject of much later controversy about whether 9/11 attacks could have been avoided.

operational US   Governmental adjective used in a variety of contexts to suggest that some policy, or unit, is active in more than just principle, or to give strength, often tendentiously, to intelligence reporting. This word was used, for example, by EU officials to lend unwarranted reality to their *Common Security and Defence Policy* even when all it meant was that an institutional structure had been set up to bring the planned 60,000 strong rapid reaction force into being (*FT*, 21 November 2001).

opportunity   Term through which the Bush administration, and more generally neoconservative opinion in Washington, viewed 9/11 attacks, as giving them the pretext, and public support at least within the USA, for launching military operations that had been advocated, in vain, for some years previously. Contrasts with public emphasis on a *terrorist threat, danger to America*, etc. According to Bob Woodward and Robert Draper, President George W. Bush told his staff that they should view the 9/11 attacks as an 'opportunity' (*Bush at War* [Simon and Schuster, 2002], p. 32). Karl Rove's version of this was, 'Sometimes history sends you things, and 9/11 came our way'. The 'opportunity' was taken in the form of the massive response of invading and occupying Iraq (David Bromwich, 'Euphemism and American Violence', *NYRB*, 3 April 2008). The analysis implicit in the above use of the word served to support the view that, in the period before the 2003 invasion of Iraq, for all that other factors (oil, Israel, Saudi Arabia, filial revenge for attempt to kill the father) may have played a role, the key factor was that the attack on Iraq fulfilled a long-standing, and ideologically driven, aspiration of US neoconservatives, one that 9/11 enabled them to realise.

Other Governmental Agency   Usually shortened to OGA, a widely-used name for the CIA (*FT*, 27 October 2005). Cf., another often-used insider term, '*The Company*', or just plain '*The Agency*', in British parlance, '*The Firm*', '*The Friends*'.

P

paradigm of prevention/preventive paradigm   Counterterrorism strategy of the Bush administration, particularly Attorney General John Ashcroft, contrasted with policy of remaining *on defense*. Justification for detention, special attention to, and mandatory registration of, thousands of Muslim and Arab immigrants in the USA. Part of broader strategy of *anticipatory state violence*, including **rendition, warrantless wiretapping, preventive war** that followed in a 12 September 2001 meeting in the White House that set the response to 9/11 (David Cole and Jules Lobel, 'We're Losing the War on Terror', *The Nation*, 24 September 2007). Cf. **pre-emption, terrorism suspects**.

passenger name recognition   Part of post-2001 US requirements for any traveller entering the USA from Europe. The 34 pieces of personal information were unspecified: they could be supplied by airlines to the US authorities, who, in turn, demanded the right to hand over the information to other countries (Nicholas Watt, 'Legal Limbo As Air Passenger Data Talks Fail', the *Guardian*, 2 October 2006). Cf. **OMEA**.

Patriot Act   More properly **USA Patriot Act**, *Public Law 107-56*, enacted by 107th US Congress and signed by the President in October 2001, following the 9/11 attacks, and made a permanent part of US legislation through further Congressional votes in March 2006. Much criticised by civil rights specialists and some Congressmen. The words '**USA Patriot**' are an acronym for the law's full title: *Uniting and Strengthening America by Providing Appropriate Tools Required to Intercept and Obstruct Terrorism Act*. The law greatly strengthened the powers of the US security agencies to intercept domestic communications, detain suspects and limit immigration. In effect, it removed the clear distinction that had hitherto existed, and had in some considerable measure been respected during the Cold War, between foreign and domestic intelligence and security operations.

planetary enemy   Term used by former British Prime Minister Tony Blair to denote the enemy he had been fighting: according to Blair, the

West had no choice after 9/11 but to engage, and he joined the fight against this enemy because he believed it was right (Martin Amis, 'The Long Kiss Goodbye', the *Guardian*, 2 June 2007). Presumably the term **planetary** was meant to sound even more pervasive than the more normal synonyms *global, international, transnational, world wide.*

poor tradecraft   See Chapter 11.

predictable surprise   Characterisation of 9/11 in a book of this title by Max Bazerman and Michael Watkins. This and other events were, in this view, predictable as 'the data needed to predict the events of September 11 and the fall of Enron was available in advance'. Such evidence, they argue, was 'so overwhelming that responsible leaders should have acted upon it' (*Predictable Surprise. The Disasters You Should Have Seen Coming and How to Prevent Them*, cited in Stefan Stern, 'A Very Timely Warning', *FT*, 2 December 2004). See **hindsight effect**.

pre-emption   Anticipatory self-defence, conceptually and legally distinct from, but easily confused with, *prevention*. **Pre-emption** is justified in international law, but only when an imminent danger exists. While considered as a possible US policy of prior attack against the Soviet Union in the early days of the Cold War, when America had a clear advantage in nuclear delivery, **pre-emption** was abandoned once the USSR acquired sufficient retaliatory capability, leading to the doctrine of *Mutually Assured Destruction*. With the end of the Cold War, and the appearance of new threats, **pre-emption** became a guiding principle of the Bush administration. It is enshrined in the September 2002 *National Security Doctrine* of the USA. Failure in the early months of 2002 to clinch the case of a direct link between Baghdad and **Al-Qa'ida** led the US and UK governments to lay greater stress on the Iraqi possession of **Weapons of Mass Destruction** as the basis for military action. The policy had a precedent in the reaction of the Reagan administration to the attacks on US forces in Lebanon, 1982–3. Here the commission headed by Admiral Robert Long called for 'an active national policy . . . to deter attack or reduce its effectiveness', thus leading to National Security Decision Directive 138, signed by President Reagan on 3 April 1984, which called terrorism a threat to US national security and called for taking the offensive against terrorism (for an authoritative account, see Michael W. Doyle, *Striking First. Preemption and Prevention in International Conflict* [Princeton: Princeton University Press, 2007]). See also **war of choice/war of necessity**.

Prevent, Pursue, Protect and Prepare   British counterterrorism policy as evolved after 9/11.

protective state   Term applied after 2001 to British government and in particular new policies being implemented on security and anti-terrorism. In 2005 a Special Report in *The Economist*, speaking of the intelligence community, which it referred to as the 'secret part of Britain's new **protective state**', stated that the British government knew 'it is pitted now against a threat with no geography, whose consequences (as in Parliament's recent bitter debate on anti-terrorist legislation) often play directly into the political issues of the hour. The nature, provenance, analysis and use of intelligence have never before had such a central or prominent place in British politics' ('Cats' Eyes in the Dark', Special Report, *The Economist*, 19 March 2005).

R

radicalisation/radicaliser   Apparently neutral, academic, behavioural terms produced post-9/11, present mostly in British counterterrorism literature, to deal with the ideological impact of radical Islam on young people, **radicalisation**, and in particular the factors, generally admitted to be many, that serve as **radicalisers**. Hence also process of changing the mind of such people, **deradicalisation**. The problem with these apparently neutral psychological and sociological terms were the same as those with all such behavioural explanations of cognate activities, e.g. madness, conversion to extreme religious cults, crime, propensity to revolution. It was noted (i) that once an attempt was made to list factors causing the behaviour, and correlate with the likelihood of such behaviour, in this case **radicalisation**, so many factors became involved that any sensible or practical connections were lost; (ii) that the emphasis on *behaviour* removed from the actors, in this case the militants, any motivation, belief, ideological commitment and, in casting such behaviour as intrinsically irrational, precluded discussion of what may well have been real, and political, causes, e.g. solidarity with Palestine, Bosnia, Chechenya, dislike of corrupt elites, etc.

radiological dispersal device   Technical term for **dirty bomb**.

raw intelligence   Apparently clear term used for information obtained by intelligence services prior to its being analysed or presented in a report to political leaders. As any student of the philosophy of social science knows, there is no such thing as a 'pure' fact, or 'raw' intelligence. See also **multiple intelligence sources.**

reconnaissance plans Term used in counterterrorism to denote actions by suspected or known terrorists, involving reconnoitring possible targets, collection of photographs, maps, videos and other relevant information. Also associated with forms of intimidation practised by such groups as the IRA, when not actually intending to carry out armed actions.

responsible co-operators programme Recruitment by US military and intelligence agencies of enemy personnel and suspects for intelligence, often leading to bogus reporting and analysis (*International Herald Tribune*, 30 November 2001). See **Curveball, George Washington of Iraq.**

'R' function Where 'R' stands for 'requirement'. British intelligence department set up to challenge distorted intelligence collection and reporting. In the wake of the 2004 *Butler Report* on weapons of mass destruction, MI6, the foreign intelligence arm of the British government, restored a separate 'Requirements Department'. The new head of the **'R' function** had a 'licence to be awkward' ('Cats' Eyes in the Dark', Special Report, *The Economist*, 19 March 2005).

S

safe haven Tautological term (since a **haven** should, by definition, be safe) applied in the 1990s to areas of countries in conflict (Bosnia, Iraq) where, without a proclamation of formal secession or independence – the power of the enemy – central government was deemed not to run and the inhabitants were entitled to international, often UN, protection. Later, post-9/11, used as depreciating reference to legally protected rights of US citizens: thus William E. Moschella, US Assistant Attorney General and a supporter of a proposed – and subsequently defeated in the House of Representatives – **US Patriot Act** provision that made it easier for federal investigators to review the records of libraries and bookstores on national security grounds stated: 'Bookstores and libraries should not be carved out as **safe havens** for terrorists and spies, who have, in fact, used public libraries to do research and communicate with their co-conspirators' (Carl Hulse, 'House Blocks a Provision for Patriot Act Inquiries', *The New York Times*, 16 June 2005).

Sahel Plan US training programme, initiated in 2004, to combat terrorism in North Africa, the latter including adjacent, southern regions of the

Sahara – hence use of the term *Sahel*. Originally Arabic for 'coast', then for countries bordering a region, in this case the desert, in modern parlance, derived from French usage, it is a loose term covering countries bordering the Sahara, including Chad, Mali, Mauritania and Niger. The **Plan** also involved the participation of Morocco, Tunisia and Algeria, a somewhat complex operation given that Morocco and Algeria had been in a state of near war since the mid-1970s: the aim was to build preventive barriers across Africa. The plural form of *sahil, suwahil*, is the origin of the word for the East African language Swahili, a hybrid of Arabic and African tongues.

Second World War Language   Vocabulary used to justify Western policies, derived from global conflict, 1939–45. Source of several terms used, or revived, in later conflicts, e.g. 'appeasers', 'the Allies', 'home front', 'blitz', 'Churchillian'. See also the US War of Independence symbolic battle, **Snows of Valley Forge**, and related use of World War II battles, *Guadalcanal, Omaha Beach*. Comparable invocation/instrumentalisation of past battles, heroic sacrifices, victories and heroes to give meaning to the often inchoate world of the post-9/11 conflict was made by many other participants in the conflict, including Muslim, Jewish, anti-Islamic and other groups across the world.

Secure Borders and Open Doors   Name of policy introduced in the USA in 2006 to ease entry procedures for visitors. After the introduction of tighter controls in 2001, complaints by foreign businessmen and leisure travellers led the Department of State and the Department of Homeland Security to introduce this programme in February 2006. Another factor was doubtless the WTO data that showed a 17 per cent increase in worldwide travel after 2001, while data from the US Office of Travel and Tourism Industries showed a decline of the same percentage in the USA for the same period. Tom Ridge, the first Secretary of Homeland Security, later employed by the *Discover America Partnership*, declared that 'the welcome mat has a little dust on it right now', adding, 'We have to spruce it up a bit' (Sara J. Welch, 'Welcome to America: Hope You're Not in a Rush', *IHT*, 19 September 2007). See also **general levels of arrogant incompetence**.

secure flight   US flight-monitoring programme intended to identify possible terrorists. In November 2004, the US government ordered 72 airlines to turn over computerised data about passengers that had travelled on domestic flights the previous June. While top European officials claimed that both Europe and the USA had gone to great lengths to protect passenger privacy, airline representatives were not informed of the top-level meetings to discuss security issues. See **general level of arrogant incompetence, OMEA, passenger name recognition, skimming** (Don Phillips, 'Airlines' Representative Deplores Security "Mess" ', *IHT*, 10 December 2004).

sensitive security information   All-purpose pretext enabling governments to withhold information. To all intents tautological, since virtually all, if not all, 'information' relating to security is, by definition, 'sensitive', because its applicability would be prejudiced if those challenging the security, in this case of the state, were to know about it. With government secrecy at an all-time high in the USA after 9/11, federal departments were classifying documents at a rate of 125 a minute, or a total of 15.6 million documents in 2004 (at a cost to taxpayers of $7.2 billion). Thus the need to invent new and imprecise categories, of which **sensitive security information** was one. Meanwhile declassification of documents, and general compliance with the Freedom of Information Act, had slowed from 204 million pages in 1997 to 28 million in 2004 (Scott Shane, 'Official Secrecy Reaches Historic High in the US', *IHT*, 4 July 2005). See **Congressional meddling**.

serious doubts   British official term, as cited in report by the *Butler Committee*, denoting MI6's disquiet with the agents it had in place in Iraq prior to the invasion of March 2003.

sexed-up   See Chapter 4.

skimming   Danger of unauthorised reading of new electronic passports; one of several problems in the attempt to introduce high-tech passports. These could be vulnerable to high-tech reading because of the embedded radio chip holding a digitalised photograph and biographical information. Privacy advocates suspected that the passports may have been vulnerable to 'skimming' from a greater distance – about a metre – than officials asserted (8 centimetres), something confirmed by US government tests. New security measures, including locking the radio chip, encrypting personal data and a protective mental layer, were also being considered. The 27 **visa-waver nations**, mainly in Europe, were given until 26 October 2005 to introduce **tamper-resistant biometric data**, so as to enable their citizens to continue visiting the USA (Eric Lipton, 'US to Alter Passport Design because of Privacy Fears', *IHT*, 28 April 2005).

Special Collection Program   A US intelligence gathering operation, run by the **National Security Agency**, in which the communications of suspected terrorists in the US were monitored. After the 9/11 attacks, President Bush secretly authorised the **National Security Agency** to eavesdrop on American citizens and others inside the USA, under an **executive order** signed in 2002, to search for evidence of terrorist activity without the court-approved warrants ordinarily required for domestic spying. **NSA** monitored without warrant the international telephone calls and international e-mail messages of hundreds, perhaps thousands, of people inside the USA in an effort to track possible 'dirty numbers' linked to **Al-Qa'ida**. Some US officials did consider that *warrantless eavesdropping* inside the USA was unlawful and possibly unconstitutional (James Risen and Eric Lichtblau, 'Bush Let's US Spy on Callers without Courts', *The New York Times*, 16 December 2005).

Special Registration Program   US-wide campaign of ethnic profiling, requiring that all male immigrants from Arab and Muslim countries – around 80,000 people – report to the immigration authorities, to be fingerprinted, photographed and interviewed. Policy introduced by Attorney General John Ashcroft after 9/11 (David Cole, 'The Grand Inquisitors', *NYRB*, 19 July 2007). Contrast with **suspected terrorists**.

specifics-free warning   Announcement by US or other government of imminent terrorist attack, but without specification as to place or form.

state sponsorship   Term used to assert, or imply, responsibility of states, usually anti-Western Middle Eastern states or, during the Cold War, the USSR and its allies, for actions of terrorist groups. Used to discredit political, and national, credentials of groups concerned. Much used after **9/11** by those wishing to argue that **Al-Qa'ida** had the backing of significant Middle Eastern states beyond Afghanistan, notably Iran and/or Iraq and Syria. The reality is that in the Middle East, and elsewhere, the degree of such **sponsorship** varies enormously and may change over time; there is no simple correlation of terrorist or guerrilla action and state involvement: a group such as the **PKK** in Turkey has operated, since 1984, with negligible foreign state support, as did the *IRA* for decades in Northern Ireland. Even in cases where external state support is evident, and acknowledged, such as in the case of **Hezbollah** in Lebanon, the degree of autonomy and local implantation of the group may be considerable. A much-mangled issue during the Cold War, since in a significant number of cases there was state backing, or at least facilitation, for terrorist acts: in some cases, such as the German

Democratic Republic, we were later to learn of support for left-wing guerrillas in Europe itself as of CIA support for right-wing paramilitary forces in Italy in the late 1940s, not to mention the Afghan *mujahidin*, UNITA in Angola and the Nicaraguan **contra** in the 1980s. However, any balance sheet of state support for terrorism in regard to the Middle East and other parts of the Third World over the two decades from 1980 would, however, have to include not only the role of the US's enemies (including Libya, which sent hundreds of tons of weapons to the IRA after the US bombing of Tripoli in 1986) but also the role of US allies, Saudi Arabia and Israel, in backing illegal military and guerrilla groups (in Afghanistan and Lebanon) and that of the USA itself, which, in the 1980s, under the guise of the 'Reagan Doctrine', funded right-wing terrorists in Angola and Nicaragua, as well as in Afghanistan.

steganography   Concealment of secret messages in computer graphics or text, as allegedly practised by **Al-Qa'ida**. From Greek *steganos*, 'water proof', and *graphi*, 'writing'. Just before Christmas in 2003, the US Department of Homeland Security ratcheted up the **national terror alert** system to 'high risk': thirty flights were immediately grounded, including long hauls, because CIA analysts thought they had detected hidden terrorist messages in *al-Jazeera* television broadcasts that identified flights and buildings as targets. Perhaps the earliest account of steganography is Herodotus's story of Histiaeus who, in the sixth-century BC, shaved the head of his most trusted slave, tattooed a message on his scalp and let his hair grow again. The slave then travelled to Aristagoras, who was instructed to shave the slave's head, whereupon he discovered the message urging him to revolt against the Persians. Today matters are more complex: after 9/11, the **steganography** expert Peter Honeyman investigated 'credible sources' suggesting that **Al-Qa'ida** was hiding messages in images on the Internet by analysing millions of images. 'We hunted and hunted and hunted, but we found zero, nothing, not even a "meet me at the Starlight Lounge at 11"' (Ian Sample, 'Messages of Fear in Hi-Tech Invisible Ink', the *Guardian*, 11 August 2005).

superterrorism   Pentagon term for terrorism organised on a massive scale, e.g. a nuclear explosion by a hostile or 'rogue' state as contrasted with the 'normal' terrorism of underground groups. An unacknowledged reference to the fact that most acts of terrorism, i.e. violation of the rules and norms of war designed to intimidate an opponent, have indeed been committed by states.

suspected terrorists/terror suspects   People detained by US authorities after 9/11 on suspicion of involvement in terrorist activities. Around 700 people were so detained, many of them suffering brutal beatings. The Justice Department rules allowed continued detention even when a court had ruled that they be released, or when they had agreed to leave US territory. None of the detained was ever convicted of a terrorist offence. Later, when challenged in the US Congress about this policy, Attorney General John Ashcroft replied: 'We make no apologies' (David Cole, 'The Grand Inquisitors', *NYRB*, 19 July 2007).

suspicious activity reports   Mandatory reporting by banks and other public and commercial bodies, part of a campaign to promote **Homeland Security** in the USA. Companies fearing large fines or criminal indictment for failing to report suspicious transactions were zealous in producing **defensive filings** aimed at protecting themselves from future liability. One of the consequences was that, following the example of the Los Angeles Police Department, police across America were urged to question people who 'use binoculars, count footsteps, fake notes, draw diagrams, change appearance, speak with security staff, and photograph objects "with no apparent aesthetic value"' (*The Economist*, 27 September 2008). Another problem was that this policy led to an information and reporting overload, exactly the kind of confused situation that lay behind the failure to anticipate and prevent 9/11: four years on, reports suggested that the US government was swamped with these reports. They cost billions of dollars and obstructed government efforts to clamp down on money laundering. See also **Glennville** and **homeland security** (Edward Alden and Andrew Ward, 'Washington Tries to Staunch Wasteful Flow of Anti-terrorist Funds to Rural Backwaters', *FT*, 11 May 2005).

T

tamper-resistant biometric data   Element in biometric passports, see **skimming** (Eric Lipton, 'US to Alter Passport Design because of Privacy Fears', *IHT*, 28 April 2005).

terror/terrorism experts   Media-cultivated individuals who profess to know about the arcane world of **terrorism**, usually bereft of any historical, political, local or comparative moral sensibility. The former White

House official and academic Zbigniew Brzezinski referred to them as *terror entrepreneurs*, noting that they 'are necessarily engaged in competition to justify their existence'. The US academic James Petras described their style as 'self-righteous, highly moralistic, vitriolic, hyperventilating and yet slippery with euphemisms when it comes to dealing with the violence of their partisan states' (Zbigniew Brzezinski, 'EE.UU: el terrorismo y la cultura del miedo', *El País*, 4 April 2007; James Petras, 'The Anatomy of "Terror Experts"', *Counterpunch*, 7–8 August 2004).

terror suspects   See **suspected terrorists**.

***Terrorist Threat Integration Center* (TTIC)**   Multi-agency counterterrorism think-tank created inside the CIA's headquarters in January 2003 by presidential executive order in response to recommendations by the *National Commission on Terrorist Attacks upon the United States* (**9/11 Commission**), and in particular their criticism of the lack of collaboration and effective exchange of information between different intelligence and criminal forces within the US government prior to 9/11. Later, under *The Intelligence Reform and Terrorism Prevention Act* of 2004, the TTIC became the **National Counterterrorism Center** (NCTC) and was placed under the newly created **US Director of National Intelligence**, John Negroponte, now the overall in-charge of the intelligence community budget of $40 billion. According to the 9/11 Commission, Negroponte inherited 'a broken corporate culture' ('Can Spies Be Made Better?', Special Report, *The Economist*, 19 March 2005).

terrornomics   Pseudo-scientific, newly concocted, field of study analysing the flow of funds to terrorist organisations, and how they raise, store, move and disburse money, especially groups supporting Islamic fundamentalists. One of the most time-wasting ideas to come out of the study of **terrorism**, since the flows of money involved in what were usually highly decentralised operations was very small, and the motivation of those involved was based on belief, ideology and rage. See *hawala*, **honey traders**.

ticking bomb   Situation where information has to be extracted very quickly, often justification for torture. Cf. TV series *24*.

too sensitive for the public to see   Description by the Bush administration of material deleted from the full classified version of a report from the **9/11 Commission** that criticised the government's failure to heed warnings of aviation threats before the 2001 attacks on the World Trade

Center and the Pentagon (Eric Lichtblau, 'Critics Want 9/11 Panel's Full Report on Threats', *IHT*, 12–13 February 2005).

torque up intelligence   A way of getting attention, possibly career advancement, in Washington. Thus independent-minded columnist Maureen Dowd, after considering the careers of Condoleezza Rice, Paul Wolfowitz, Stephen Hadley and Bob Joseph, wrote that they 'torqued up intelligence to fit the White House's theological beliefs' (Maureen Dowd, 'U. N. Leash John Bolton', *IHT*, 28 April 2005). See **sexed-up, threat inflation**.

Total Information Awareness (TIA)   A typical, overrated, overstated and oversold pseudo-scientific Washington project, ridiculous, if not dangerous, in its pretensions, starting with the obvious fact that there is no such thing as 'total information'. As unreal as the Islamist call for a global **Caliphate**. The Defense Advanced Research Projects Agency (DARPA) of the US Department of Defense set up the **Information Awareness Office** (IAO) in January 2002, bringing together several DARPA projects with the brief to 'imagine, develop, apply, integrate, demonstrate and transition information technologies, components and prototype, closed-loop, information systems that will counter asymmetric threats by achieving total information awareness'. IAO funding was withdrawn by Congress in 2003 following public alarm about a mass surveillance system, but several IAO projects continued with different sources of funding. The IAO logo, combining an eye, a pyramid and a globe, sought to convey its own acronymic message: the eye above the pyramid represented 'I', the pyramid represented 'A' and the globe represented 'O'. In the detail, the eye scanned the globe for evidence of terrorist planning and focused on the part of the world that was the source of the attacks on the World Trade Center and the Pentagon. See www.information-retrieval.info/docs/IAO-logo-stmt.html. The IAO motto: *Scientia est potentia*, 'Knowledge is power' – but only if you are smart enough to know what to do with it. Cf. **intelligence**.

Truthers   Members of a post-9/11 US-based 'truth movement', active on the Internet and through campaigning, who blame the events on the Bush administration. In this version the twin towers of the World Trade Center were brought down by a controlled, pre-organised demolition, set up by the US government to justify their invasions of Afghanistan and Iraq. **Truthers** reject alternative views and reports, referring to these as *neo-Operation Mockingbird*, this last term referring to a CIA operation in the

1950s that sought to influence the media (Peter Barker, 'The Plot Thickens', *FT Weekend*, 20–21 December 2008). Similar views circulated widely in and among other countries such as France and throughout much of the Middle East. **Thierry Meyssan** had become a best selling in Europe. See also Chapter 6, **Fallaci, Oriana**. A similar strain of conspiracy was disseminated in Spain after the 11 March 2004 bombings, above all by COPE, the Catholic Bishops' Conference radio, according to whom the Spanish Socialist Party, PSOE, had cooperated with the bombers. By 2007 it was reported that up to a third of all Americans did not believe the official story on 9/11.

U

unlawful passenger behaviour   Term used by Russian aviation authorities to denote the possible cause of the twin airline crashes on 24–25 August 2004.

V

villains' charter   Where 'villain' is British colloquial for a criminal, description by British Home Secretary Jack Straw of the European Human Rights Act and the protection it gave to suspects.

visa-waver nations   See **skimming** (Eric Lipton, 'US to Alter Passport Design because of Privacy Fears', *IHT*, 28 April 2005).

W

war against terror/terrorism   All-purpose strategic umbrella for US defence and foreign policy since 9/11, more formally termed **Global War against Terrorism (GWAT)**. The use of the word 'war' overstates the rendering of a campaign, policy or commitment, as if there could be a 'war' against something such as **terrorism**, which is in itself a tactic, not an organisation, state or ideology. Analogous, in US political parlance with the misuse of the term 'war', with 'War against Drugs' and 'War against Poverty'. In January 2009, within days of President Bush leaving office, the British Foreign Secretary David Miliband characterised this strategy as 'dangerously counterproductive, misleading and mistaken' (the *Guardian*,

15 January 2009). See **global counterinsurgency, global war on terrorism, long war, World War III, World War IV, worldwide insurgency**. The exaggerated and generic categories used reflected not so much the geographic incidence, or spread of incidents, but as much as anything the many-layered, often inchoate, nature of the conflict.

warrantless wiretapping   US domestic counterterrorist programme that circumvented legal controls and was operated by the National Security Agency.

whatever it takes   (1) After an appeal by firefighters at the World Trade Center to George W. Bush on his visit after the 9/11 attack, often cited by him in campaign speeches, he promised to *do* this by making the American nation safer. Also (2) prevailing sentiment in the Fox Emmy-award-nominated television series '*24*', in which 'terrorist suspects' were tortured. See **24-Jack Bauer,** *The Terrorist Next Door* (Tara McKelvey, 'We Were Torturing People for No Reason', *IHT*, 29 March 2007).

World Trade Center cough   Illness which, after 9/11, affected hundreds of New York firemen involved in the rescue operation. Symptoms included respiratory and gastrointestinal problems.

World War III   See Chapter 12.

World War IV   See Chapter 12.

worldwide insurgency   Former US Defense Secretary Donald Rumsfeld asked his aides to investigate whether this term for the battle his administration was engaged in might not be more rousing than **war against terrorism**. He seemed to suggest that the country was fighting nothing less than a worldwide movement which had the specific aim of challenging the power of the USA: the ultimate goal of such an insurgency was to challenge the government for control of all or part of its territory, or force political concessions in sharing political power. See also **global counterinsurgency, insurgency, long war, snowflakes** (Robin Wright, 'From the Desk of Donald Rumsfeld', *The Washington Post*, 1 November 2007).

'Counterterrorism': Top Ten

1. Binladengate
2. Patriot Act
3. inordinate number of individuals of investigative interest
4. radiological dispersal device
5. specifics free warning
6. suspicious activity reports
7. ticking bomb
8. torque up intelligence
9. warrantless wiretapping
10. whatever it takes

CHAPTER 2

Motifs of *Jihad*: Terrorist Groups, Armed Actions and the Imagery of Osama bin Laden

> Lord, this is one of your days, so take the hearts of the youth of Islam and commit them to jihad for Your sake.
>
> Lord, keep them, to their belief and make them stand firm. Guide their fire and unite their hearts in harmony.
>
> Lord, bring victory to Your servants, the holy warriors, wherever they may be, in Palestine, Iraq, Chechenya, Kashmir, the Philippines, and Afghanistan.
>
> Lord, give comfort to our brothers who are imprisoned in tyrants' jails, in America, Guantánamo, in Occupied Palestine, in Riyadh, everywhere. You have power over everything.
>
> Lord, give us patience, make us stand firm and help us struggle against the infidels. 'God is victorious, although most people do not know it'.
>
> —Osama bin Laden statement of 19 October 2003, 'Quagmires of the Tigris and Euphrates', in *Messages to the World*, p. 211

A

Abu Abdullah   Literally 'father of Abdullah', alternative name of Osama bin Laden, whose eldest son was called Abdullah. Earlier, he was also known as *Abu Qaqa*.

Abu Elias   Alias of Abdelkarim Mejjati, one of the leaders of the *Groupe Islamique Combattant Morrocain* (GICM), which aims to establish an

Islamist state in Morocco. Mejjati was killed in a clash with Saudi Arabian security forces in April 2005, and, according to the Rabat secret services, was involved in the 11 March 2004 attack in Madrid. He figured on the FBI website as 'a possible threat to the United States of America'. Son of a French mother and Moroccan father, he attended the Lycée Française in Casablanca before going to study in France and apparently spoke better French than Arabic. He held a French passport (Ignacio Cembrero, 'Un terrorista del Liceo Francés', *El País*, 7 April 2005).

Abu Hafs al-Masri Brigades   Name of group. Named after the **Al-Qa'ida** leader killed in Afghanistan in late 2001, the group, which has a presence in several countries, claimed responsibility for the 11 March 2004 Madrid bombings, the August 2003 attack on the UN headquarters in Baghdad, the November 2003 attacks on Istanbul synagogues and 10 August 2004 Istanbul blasts involving four bombs that left two dead and 11 wounded, some of whom were foreign tourists. It also threatened in mid-August 2004 to 'burn' Italy if Premier Silvio Berlusconi did not withdraw Italian forces from Iraq.

Abu Hilala, Yusuf   Jordanian poet, member of Muslim Brotherhood. Given to romantic evocation of medieval Arab warriors and much cited by Osama bin Laden, he even dedicated the poem 'The Fighting Eagle' to the latter.

Abu Jahl   The father of ignorance', where *jahl/jahil* serves as a term of Islamic abuse. The Quranic and today Islamist term *jahiliyya*, the age of ignorance, is applied to rulers deemed disrespectful of Islam and oppressive of Muslims. Masood Azhar, leader of **Jaish-e-Mohammed** (Mohammed's Army), had threatened to eliminate former Indian Prime Minister Atal Bihari Vajpayee, whom he refers to as **Abu Jahl** (the father of ignorance).

Abu Sayyaf   Brutalist nom de guerre of Muhammad Shalabi, from Ma'an, Jordan. Literally 'father of the swordsman', from Arabic for sword, *saif*, hence *sayyaf*, 'swordsman'. Sayyaf's arrest in connection with the 2002 murder of the USAID employee Lawrence Foley led to street battles in the town. The name is also used by one of the separatist Islamist groups operating in and around the southern islands of the Philippines, which split in 1983 from the **Moro Liberation Front**, after the latter signed a peace agreement with the Manila government. The name **Saif al Islam**, literally 'Sword of Islam', is often used by sons of monarchs and other rules, e.g. the elder son of President Muammar al-Qaddafi of Libya.

according-to-their-intentions argument   Moral justification used
by some Islamists for terrorist actions.

Ahmed, Rabei Osman Sayed   Thirty-year-old Egyptian former explosives expert, later trained in **Al-Qa'ida** camp in Afghanistan, arrested
outside Milan on 7 June 2004, also known as 'Mohamed the Egyptian' or
just, in Spain *el Egipcio*, 'the Egyptian'. Well connected with Islamist groups
across Europe, alleged to have played important role in 11 March 2004
Madrid bombings, having arrived in Spain in 2003, but exonerated, on a
technicality, in the October 2007 Madrid trial of bombers. Said by some to
have been plotting further attacks at the time of his arrest, possibly against
the Paris Metro using 145 kilos of explosives and mobile phones as detona-
tors (*El País*, 3 August 2004).

Al-Qa'ida   Arabic for the 'base', or the 'foundation', the loose organisation headed by Osama bin Laden. Origins lie in body, the Office of Services,
maktab al-khidmat, established in 1984 in Peshawar, Pakistan, to coordi-
nate volunteers arriving from Arab and other countries for the Afghan War.
According to bin Laden and as confirmed by some other reports, the term
was first used at a meeting in August 1988 held in Peshawar to discuss training
and coordination of Muslim fighters who came to Afghanistan. Originally
taken from the generic name for training camps, *Al-Qa'ida Al 'Askariyya*, or
'the military base', the group, of which Osama bin Laden was an organiser
and leader, uses it (Steve Coll, *The Bin Ladens: An Arabian Family in the
American Century* [New York: The Penguin Press, 2008], pp. 336–8). The
existence of this organisation was announced on 23 February 1998 as part
of a **World Islamic Front to fight Jews and Christians** founded at a meeting in Peshawar comprising groups from Egypt, Pakistan and Bangladesh.
Osama bin Laden himself has on several occasions stressed that **Al-Qa'ida**
is at once a training and fighting organisation, but also a loose network (see
entries *mouvance* and **franchise** in Chapter 1). The term has no apparent
antecedents in Islamic or Arabic political history. Other explanations range
from it being an allusion to the bin Laden family's construction company,
which provided financial and logistical support, via Osama bin Laden, to
fighters in Afghanistan, to the title of a 1951 Isaac Asimov novel, *The Foundation*, translated into Arabic as *Al-Qaída*, a book that describes the destruction
of a mighty empire, *Trantor*.

anfal   Plural of *nafl*, Arabic for 'booty', name of a campaign launched
by the Ba'thist government against the Iraqi Kurds in 1988. Also the title

of a Quranic verse often invoked by suicide bombers in preparation for action.

AQ   Or **AQ Central** abbreviation for **Al-Qa'ida** used by Western intelligence officials.

AQT   Al-Qa'ida and former **Taliban** (see Chapter 4) fighters' US military abbreviation Afghanistan 2001.

aspiring martyrs   Candidates for 'suicide bomb' attacks. After 2003, the Iraqi insurgents were said to have plenty of these along with an abundance of lethal explosives. In the words of Tom Donnelly, a military analyst at the American Enterpriser Institute, 'The insurgents can keep car bombs going forever' (Scott Johnson and John Barry, 'A Deadly Guessing Game', *Newsweek*, 16 May 2005).

Asir   Birthplace of many of the 9/11 hijackers, dissident region of Saudi Arabia, formerly part of Yemen, briefly independent after World War I, relatively deprived area within the Saudi kingdom.

B

Belhadj, Youssef   European spokesman of **Al-Qa'ida**, considered the bombing attacks of 11 March 2004, in which 191 people were killed and several injured, as *'no big deal'*. His justification was that 'If Muslims keep dying in Iraq, people in Spain must die' (Luis Izquierdo and Juan Carlos Merino, 'La portavoz europeo de Al-Qa'ida consideraba que lo sucedido el 1-M había sido poco', *La Vanguardia*, 23 April 2005).

bin Laden, Osama   Self-appointed leader of **Al-Qa'ida**. Born in Saudi Arabia c. 1957, one of over 50 children of Yemeni millionaire building contractor Muhammad bin Laden. Attended Thagh elite secondary school in Jeddah, then studied management, economics and Islamic studies at the King Abdul Aziz University in Riyadh. By his own claim, associated with the 1982 Sunni uprising in Syria, and with the funding and organisation of Arabs in Afghanistan in the 1980s. Visited London in 1986, spending several weeks in the Dorchester Hotel, negotiating with arms dealers on behalf of the Afghan *mujahidin*. Returned to Saudi Arabia in 1990; however, following a dispute with Saudi rulers over their response to the Kuwait Crisis in 1990, moved in 1991 to Sudan and from there, in 1996, back to Afghanistan. Stripped of Saudi citizenship in 1995 (Steve Coll, *The Bin*

Ladens: An Arabian Family in the American Century [New York: The Penguin Press, 2008]; *Messages to the World. The Statements of Osama bin Laden*, edited and introduced by Bruce Lawrence London: Verso, 2005).

Black September   Arabic *aylul al-aswad*. Refers to attack on Palestinians in Jordan in September 1970 by forces loyal to King Hussain. Later, name of extreme Palestinian military group, loosely linked to Al-Fatah, responsible for a number of terrorist actions in Europe and elsewhere. Cf. **Black Tamils, Black Widow.**

Black Tamils   Branch of Sri Lankan 'Tamil Tiger' guerrillas, specialising in suicide bombing missions.

Black Widow   Chechen woman guerrilla and/or suicide bomber, as in near-simultaneous explosions on two Russians planes, in August 2004, days before the Chechen presidential elections.

blind *sheikh*   The name by which *sheikh* Omar Abdel Rahman, Egyptian Muslim leader imprisoned for his role in the attempted 1993 bombing of the World Trade Center, was commonly known. Sightless as a result of childhood diabetes, Rahman has been serving a life sentence in Colorado since 1996 for 'seditious conspiracy,' a charge that required that a crime only be planned and not that it necessarily be attempted. Rahman was one of the main operatives the CIA utilised in its 1980s war against the Soviets because of his influence over the *mujahidin*: it was in these years that he became closely associated with Osama bin Laden. The CIA subsequently brought him into the USA on a CIA-sponsored visa. While the *sheikh* was eventually convicted for conspiracy to bomb targets in the USA, prosecutors encountered resistance in pursuing him and other World Trade Center bombing suspects because of their ties to the Afghan *mujahidin*, and thus to US intelligence. However, according to Stephen Kohn, a lawyer who interviewed a number of current and former counterterrorism officials at the FBI in connection with a lawsuit against the bureau, senior officials, including the FBI director Robert Mueller III, were 'not aware' of the connections between Osama bin Laden and *sheikh* Omar Abdel Rahman. FBI officials informed Kohn that 'no expertise in counterterrorism is needed to be a senior manager in the field' (David Johnston, 'Questions Arise over FBI Leadership in War on Terror', *IHT*, 20 June 2005).

Boko Haram   Literally 'Educated is prohibited', name of extreme northern Nigerian group, centred in Maidaguri and Kano, modelling themselves on the Afghan Taliban and seeking to impose rigid interpretation of *Shari'ah* (see Chapter 5). In late July 2009, hundreds of members of the group, including their leader Mohamed Yusuf, graduate of a theological school in Medina, Saudi Arabia, were reported killed.

Brigade 005   Special military unit, allied to bin Laden, composed of Arab militants, used for operations in support of the Taliban inside Afghanistan. Notorious for the violent suppression of opponents of the Taliban, especially **Shi'i**.

C

cavalry of Islam   Term used by bin Laden to appeal to the Muslim world.

Christian Atrocities   Title of video film used in Afghanistan to train Taliban recruits, portraying killing of Muslim by Christians in Poso, Indonesia.

coffee/coffee houses   Example of prohibition in some interpretations of Islam. The introduction of coffee, and of coffee houses, into the sixteenth-century Ottoman Empire provoked the hostility of some clergy, who claimed that as a result of such houses, the mosques were now empty and that, on the basis of the Quranic prohibition of charcoal as unclean and *haram*, coffee – because it was produced by a process of burning – was prohibited in Islam and considered worse than alcohol (Božidar Jezernik, *Wild Europe: The Balkans in the Gaze of Western Travellers* [London: Saqi, 2004], pp. 157ff). During the sixteenth century, and on some later occasions, such as in the Sultanate of Oman of the mid-nineteenth century, similar attacks took place. See **objectionable and obscene anti-Islamic practices**.

corruption   Arabic *fisad*, from which *mofsid*, a corrupt person, or a person who spreads corruption. Common term of denunciation by, among others, Ayatollah Khomeini and Osama bin Laden for political opponents and rulers of Muslim states, which combines anti-Islamic behaviour with more general forms of corruption, e.g. luxurious living, embezzlement or bribery. In the revolutionary courts of the Islamic Republic of Iran, many former officials of the Shah's regime were tried in summary proceedings and then shot for being *mofsidin fi al-arz*, 'Spreaders of Corruption upon Earth', a hard charge to refute, see Chapter 5. Contrast with **austerity**, Chapter 5.

Crusader Alliance   Term used by Osama bin Laden to denote USA, British and other forces fighting in Iraq in 2001.

cultural aggression, cultural invasion, cultural imperialism
Common terms, developed originally in the 1960s and 1970s by secular intellectuals, later taken up enthusiastically by Islamists in Iran and by militants out of power in the Arab world. Used to attack Western ideas, associated in polemical attacks with **cosmopolitanism** and **liberalism**.

D

Dots of the Letters   Title of a video released at the end of 2007 by As Sahab ('The Cloud'), **Al-Qa'ida**'s nebulous media organisation, in which Abu Yahya al-Libi, the **man for all seasons for AQ**, assessed the state of Islamic militancy worldwide, dwelling *inter alia* on 'defectors' who have renounced violence (see **de-radicalise**, Chapter 1), and discussing US psywar (see **truthful messages**, Chapter 12) tactics.

E

East Turkestan Islamic Movement/Liberation Front   Islamist movement operating out of Pakistan and Central Asian states against Chinese presence in the province of Sinkiang, the latter inhabited largely by Muslim speakers of Uighur.

El Egipcio ('the Egyptian')   See **Ahmed, Rabei Osman Sayed**.

G

Gadahn, Adam   Also known as Azzam al Amriki, a US-born Al-Qa'ida spokesman presumed to be in Pakistan, and the first American to be charged with treason since 1952. Gadahn, who grew up in rural California, was a passionate fan of death metal music before his conversion to Islam. He is thought to have left the USA in the late 1990s. From 2004 he began appearing in a series of videos calling for attacks on US targets. In one message, he used his knowledge of American culture, specifically, the board game Monopoly, to appeal to his audience, saying, 'If you die as an unbeliever in battle against the Muslims, you're going straight to hell, without passing Go' (*The New Yorker*, 22 January 2007).   *(Entry not written by the author – Ed.)*

Gucci muj   Ironic American term for Afghan guerrillas who, in 1980s, dressed in fashionable clothes when out of the country.

H

handful of foreign terrorists   See **small group of dead-enders**.

Hizb al-Tahrir   Arabic for 'The Party of Liberation'. A Sunni fundamentalist group founded in 1953 in Jordan by the Palestinian *sheikh* Taqiuddin al-Nabhani, which aims to restore the Caliphate, with following in the Arab world, Central Asia and Western Europe, especially Britain.

Hezbollah   'The Party of God', see p. 155.

Hizb-ul Mujahidin   Literally 'Party of the Holy Warriors', founded in 1989 in Muzaffarabad, in Pakistan-administered Kashmir. The biggest militant group operating in Kashmir and considered to be the most widely supported. It has vowed to 'put India on its knees'. It is on the terrorist organisations' list of both Europe and the USA ('Los Guerreros del Partido de Dios', *El País*, 29 December 2007).

Hubal of the Age   Osama bin Laden's term for the USA. Hubal was the chief deity of pre-Islamic polytheism in Arabia, whose destruction was one of the main missions of the Prophet Mohammad.

I

Islambouli, Khalid   Egyptian soldier, assassin of President Anwar al-Sadat at military parade, October 1981. He later had a street named after him in Tehran, along with Bobby Sands, the IRA hunger striker, and Mirza Kuchik Khan, earlier Islamist guerrilla and opponent of Soviet influence in northern Iran; one of many new Iraqi guerrilla units, also so named, is responsible, *inter alia*, for the massacre of 12 Nepalese contract workers in August 2004.

Islamic Army in Iraq   Arabic *al-jaish al-islami fi iraq*. Underground group that emerged in 2004, killing Italian journalist and anti-war campaigner Enzo Baldoni in August, and demanding an end to the French ban on Islamic headscarves. Militantly Sunni and close to Wahhabism and **Al-Qa'ida**, it was strongly critical of the Iranian role in Iraq and of Shi'ism more generally.

Islamism Western term used as an alternative to 'fundamentalist' and the French *intégriste*, to denote a movement that used a return to a supposedly traditional Islam as the basis for a radical political programme. Hence, distinct from terms 'Muslim' and 'Islamic', which denote either a believer in the faith of Islam or something generally associated with the faith, but not necessarily with political or social consequences. Examples would include the Iranian Revolution, the Muslim Brotherhood, Deobandism and the Taliban.

J

Jackson, Robert Forty-four-year-old American kidnapped and shot in Riyadh, Saudi Arabia, in June 2004. His captors stated that they had killed him for working with American arms firm Vinnell, manufacturers of the Apache helicopter used against rebels in Iraq.

jahiliyya Arabic for 'ignorance'. Therefore, generic Quranic term for the time, also culture and society, before the arrival of Islam in the seventh-century AD. It is used in modern times by fundamentalists to denote the non-Muslim, specifically Western, world; also in the language of Egyptian fundamentalist Sayyid Qutb to denote 'infidel' Arab regimes. Arabic *jahil* is the origin of the Spanish *gilli*, prefix of a common vulgar expression for rubbish in that language, *gillipollas*, also the adjective *gillipollesco*.

Jaish-e-Mohammed Literally 'the Army of Mohammed', name of the group launched on 31 January 2000, by religious leader Maulana Masood Azhar in Karachi after his release from prison in India with the terrorists-for-hostage swap of 31 December 1999 following the hijacking of the Indian Airlines Flight IC 814. The group, deemed by some branches of the Islamic media to be a creation of the Pakistani secret services, vowed to 'liberate' Kashmir and also take control of the *masājds* (mosques) in Ayodhya (Babri Masjid), Amritsar and Delhi. It is also considered responsible for the kidnapping and murder of the American journalist Daniel Pearl in 2002 ('El ejército de Mahoma', *El País*, 29 December 2007).

jihadi **jet set** Otherwise known as 'flying *jihadis*', term for 'second generation of Arab-Afghans' that appeared in the 1990s. Transnational in activity and engagement, they were sometimes more Westernised than their predecessors and had few links with any particular Muslim country.

Jihadi, jihadist   Recently coined Western term, derogatory in import. In contrast to *mujahid/mujahidin*, term applied with positive import to, e.g. Afghan guerrillas, also termed 'freedom fighters', and 'holy warriors' in the 1980s; since 2001, ***jihadist*** has become virtually synonymous with **fanatic, terrorist** and **Islamo-fascist**, usually sympathiser with **Al-Qa'ida** or other Islamic extremists. In a speech of October 2005, President George W. Bush, referring to 'terrorism', used three religious terms: 'Some call this evil Islamic radicalism; others militant *jihadism*; still others, **Islamo-fascism**.' Timothy Garton Ash prefers ***jihadist*** as an adjective: 'So what should we call the suicide mass murderers and would-be mass murderers? The best answer I have found so far is "jihadists", especially in the form "jihadist extremists" or "jihadist terrorists"' (Jonathan Rauch, 'A War on Jihadism, Not Terror: Defining an Enemy and an Ideology', *Reason Magazine*, www.reason.com/news/show/117337.html; Timothy Garton Ash, 'In Identifying Those Who Are Trying to Kill Us, We Should Choose Our Words Carefully', the *Guardian*, 22 November 2007).

K

kafir   Generic term of abuse in Islam, covering 'infidel', 'non-Muslim', 'blasphemer'. See ***kufr.*** Later, by borrowing from Arab sailors in the Indian Ocean, used by white settlers in South Africa as term of abuse against blacks.

Karzai of Riyadh   Where '**Karzai**', the name of the Afghan president installed and backed by the USA, is synonymous with traitor, or Quisling, derogatory name used by Osama bin Laden for the King of Saudi Arabia. Apart from implying that the Saudi monarchy are clients/puppets of the West, use of this term also suggests that the original Saudi seizure of power, in 1902, from the then ruling al-Rashid dynasty and in opposition to the Ottoman Empire, was aided and financed by Western imperial powers.

killing, ritual   See *nahr.*

kufr   General Arabic and Islamic term for disbelief, used in the Quran for enemies of the faith, non-Muslims, apostates, who are then *kafir/kuffar.* Not a precise equivalent of the Christian term 'blasphemy', as the latter, from Greek *blaptein* + *pheme*, 'to harm in word', is used in the New Testament to refer only to insult to God. Now used as a generic term of abuse against anyone whose views the speaker disapproves of. One who practises *kufr* is a *kafir*, generally an unbeliever. *Global Kufr* is one of the common Islamist terms of abuse applied to the USA.

L

Lashkar-e-Taiba   'The Army of the Virtuous/Virtue', extremist Pakistani group, committed to fighting to 'liberate' Kashmir from Indian occupation, initially supported openly by Pakistani intelligence services, ISI, with training camps in the Pakistani part of Kashmir, banned under US pressure after 9/11. Responsible for the 2001 attack on Indian Parliament in New Delhi and the 2008 attack on Mumbai. Loosely associated with **Al-Qa'ida**. Based near Lahore, Pakistan, and operating several training camps in Pakistan-administered Kashmir, where it strives to achieve its objective of ending Indian rule in *Kashmir*. Capable of motivating fierce loyalty and spirit of self-sacrifice among followers; thus, after a sermon given by its leader, Hafiz Muhammad Saeed in August 2003, he was reportedly approached by a veiled woman, carrying her young son. She handed him a note that read, 'I am highly impressed by Hafiz Muhammad Saeed's lecture on the holy war against anti-Muslim forces. In this scenario, it is my obligation as a staunch Muslim to offer everything I have for the cause of Islam and to fight the infidels. Therefore, I offer my son for this sacred mission.' ('La Armada de los Puros', *El País*, 29 December 2007; Tashbih Sayyed, 'Complicity and Silence', *Pakistan Today*, 22 August 2003) Cf. **Jaish-e-Mohammed**.

liquid bomb   Carry-on liquids that can be used to blow up planes. The transatlantic aircraft plot of August 2006 was an alleged terrorist plan by 24 British citizens of Pakistani origin to detonate liquid explosives carried on board airliners travelling from the UK to the USA. The media reported that targets – involving from 3 to 12 airliners – included American Airlines, British Airways, Continental Airlines and United Airlines flights from London Heathrow and London Gatwick airports to US destinations. Unprecedented security measures were immediately put in place, causing chaos and delayed flights for days. The transatlantic aircraft 'plot' was later doubted and even ridiculed when arrests were made without prior discovery of evidence, and it was soon revealed that there was no money trail and only one suspect had an air ticket, although the destination was not revealed by police. Eleven people were charged, eleven others held without charges and two were released. The charge of 'possessing articles useful to a person preparing acts of terrorism' is difficult to uphold given the fact that supermarkets are full of these items. Nonetheless, 'The Liquid Bomb Threat' (Editorial, *IHT*, 14 August 2006) remains. In the wake of the alarm came a series of reports on the ease of making a liquid bomb out of per se innocent and easy-to-find chemicals. One involves the highly explosive but not-so-readily-available and difficult-to-handle nitroglycerine gel, which could be disguised in shaving or hair gel and set off using a detonator hidden inside electrical devices such as an iPod/MP3 player or cell phone. Then there was the potent explosive acetone peroxide, compound triacetone triperoxide, or TATP (a 'favorite of terrorists', known as 'Mother of Satan' to some terrorist groups according to *The Washington Post* (11 August 2006), which is usually found in the form of a crystalline powder. This powder can be dissolved into an innocent-looking liquid that could be carried aboard a plane, or two chemicals making up TATP could be carried separately and mixed aboard the aircraft. Other devices that could be used, it was claimed, to create a fire or explosion aboard aircraft are oxidisers used to clean swimming pools or even a combination of ammonium nitrate (used as fertiliser) and diesel fuel (www.indiaabroad.com/video/player.php?url=http://video.tv18online. com/cnnibn/flvstore/08_2006/cnn_liquid_explosive.flv). Other writers doubted the claims of 2006 and, more generally, the ability of plotters to detonate such devices (Thomas C. Greene, 'Mass Murder in the Skies: Was the Plot Feasible?' *The Register*, 17 August 2006, www.theregister.co.uk/2006/08/17/flying_toilet_terror_labs/).

lyrical terrorist   Name applied by a Heathrow Airport shop assistant, Samina Malik, to herself in 2007. Malik was the first woman in Britain to be found guilty of terrorist offences. She called herself the 'lyrical terrorist' and wrote poems about indoctrinating children from an early age and killing heathens. Her lines included: 'Kafirs your time will come soon, and no one will save you from your doom'. Malik had been cleared for work in the airport by the airport security services (Duncan Gardham, ' "Lyrical Terrorist" Wanted Children to Carry out Jihad', *Daily Telegraph*, 9 November 2007).

M

man for all seasons   Originally title of play (staged London 1960), later films (1968, 1988). Written by English playwright Robert Bolt, the first two dealt with the life of the sixteenth-century English philosopher and politician Sir Thomas More. In original usage, a 1520 quote by More's contemporary Robert Whittington, the term did not imply opportunism, or fair weather alliances, but rather flexibility and diversity in life, mood and opinions. In a contemporary usage, Jarret Brachman, research director of the Combating Terrorism Center at West Point, thus described the militant preacher and **Al-Qa'ida** strategist, Abu Yahya al-Libi, adding: 'He's a warrior. He's a poet. He's a scholar. He's a *pundit.* He's a military commander. And he's a very charismatic, young, brash rising star within **AQ**, and I think he has become the heir apparent to Osama bin Laden in terms of taking over the entire global *jihadist* movement' (Michael Moss and Souad Mekhennet, 'From American Prison to the Heights of Al Qaeda', *IHT*, 4 April 2008).

martyr Arabic *shahid.* Like its Greek equivalent, the word signifies 'witness' (hence the Muslim proclamation of faith in one God, *shahada,* also root of Iranian pilgrimage town, *Mashad*), the general word used in modern Arabic for those who sacrifice their lives in struggle, be it for national liberation (as in the Algerian War of Independence) or in the war against 'infidels', as with European counterparts not necessarily with any religious overtones. Cf. **Perfect Soldiers**.

martyrdom operations Arabic *'amaliat istishadia.* Conventional Islamist term for what in Western coverage are called 'suicide bombings'.

mochila bomba Spanish, 'rucksack/satchel bomb', used in regard to 11 March 2004 Madrid bombings. Related to *camión bomba* (truck bomb), *coche bomba* (car bomb). Term with particularly sinister resonance as *mochila* is also the conventional word for child's school satchel, whereas a *mochila portabebés* is a baby carrier.

muqawama Arabic for 'resistance'. All-purpose legitimating term for everything from widespread popular mobilisation to unrepresentive murderers. Used for French armed opposition in World War II, then for Afghanistan and Palestine (as in the name **Hamas**, see Chapter 7), from 1990s term of choice across third world, avoiding 'national liberation', 'revolution', 'armed struggle', etc.

muscle hijacker Member of hijack group, tasked with subduing passengers rather than seizing controls of the plane

N

nahr Arabic for 'neck'. Hence used to denote the act of killing/butchering animal by cutting its throat, later applied to ritual killing of infidels in terrorist actions (see Chapter 5).

new terrorism Used to distinguish **Al-Qa'ida** and other groups from earlier forms of terrorism, e.g. the IRA, where means more limited and some prospect of political negotiation existed. While the Islamist violence of **Al-Qa'ida** was in some respects 'new', there are certain continuities that were missed in the reaction to 9/11, not least the fact that terrorist acts, be they a bomb in Belfast or Bilbao of the 'old' type, or the attack on Manhattan, had essentially *political* not *military* ends. Both were conceived of, and executed, in terms of the logics of **asymmetric warfare**.

New York operation Arabic '*amaliat niu york*,' bin Laden's term for 9/11 attacks, also *yaum niu york*, 'The Day of New York'

nuclear terrorism Form of threat whereby terrorist groups gain possession of nuclear material, to detonate either nuclear explosion or a **dirty bomb**. Not seen as plausible before 9/11 but taken more seriously thereafter. The standard antidote to exposure to nuclear material is potassium iodide, but stocks of this in the USA and Western Europe were, as of 2001–2, very low. In the original sense of the word 'terrorism', as coined in the French Revolution and later used, and justified, in the Russian Revolution, meant the use, or threatened use, of violence by those with state power. The whole 40 years of the Cold War, when the USA and the USSR threatened an all-out nuclear war, a conflict that would have affected the whole world, was a time of such **nuclear terrorism**.

O

objectionable and obscene anti-Islamic practices Intolerant, Islamist, term for what were long-established Pakistani, and, before that, South Asian, social practices, such as kite-flying and mixed gatherings at parties, which the *Muttahida Majlis-e-Amal (MMA)*, Pakistan's major Islamic political party, wished to ban ('Thou Shalt Not Have Fun', Lahore correspondent, *The Economist*, 16 April 2005). In Bahrain, the local fundamentalists' targets included sending cards on St. Valentine's Day and the holding of Formula 1 car racing events. By contrast, on an issue on which patriotic feeling indeed runs high, Pakistani Islamists have been strong supporters of cricket matches. For an earlier example of Islamic intolerance, see **coffee/coffee houses**.

Ode of Imru' al-Qays   Pre-Islamic Arab poem about the lives and struggles of nomads. From this classic text, one taught in many Arab schools, Osama bin Laden derived much of his imagery, about *campsites, flashing lances, steeds, strirrups,* etc.

P

Perfect Soldiers   From the book *Perfect Soldiers. The Hijackers: Who They Were, Why They Did It,* by *Los Angeles Times* reporter Terry McDermott. In it, McDermott wrote that the 9/11 hijackers were, rather than **evil geniuses, wild-eyed fanatics** or cardboard cutouts of evil, quite unexceptional individuals with their own complicated stories. The conclusion he drew was that **Al-Qa'ida** had found and could continue to find willing recruits among run-of-the-mill, middle-class and apolitical young men within the Islamic world. It is likely, McDermott wrote, that 'there are a great many more men just like them'.

Pharaoh   Rulers of Ancient Egypt, used in Quran and subsequent Muslim discourse to denote tyrannical ruler. Thus, Egyptian fundamentalists denounced Presidents Abdel Nasser and Anwar al-Sadat in these terms. The word was applied, by extension, to those fighting Egyptian forces in the Yemeni civil war of the 1960s, so that news reports spoke of attacks by *Pharaonic aircraft.*

portable homeland   Term applied to the way the Internet is used by Islamic fundamentalist groups as a 'portable homeland', one that allows them to communicate with one another, to strengthen their global ties and also to communicate with the connected world at large. Hence Islamic fundamentalism is not an 'inward-looking resistant force that opposes globalisation but . . . a glocal force in itself' (Lina Khatib, 2003, 'Communicating Islamic Fundamentalism as Global Citizenship', *Journal of Communication Inquiry,* Vol. 27, No. 4.). See also **glocal phenomenon** (Chapter 1), *umma* (Chapter 5).

punishment of God   Arabic *'uqub Allah,* phrase used by Osama bin Laden to refer to the 9/11 attacks in the USA, and then taken up by protesting crowds in the Arab world. From the same Arabic root, *'uqaba'*, meaning 'to follow', 'to have consequences' as the word for 'sanctions' (*'uqubat'*). Also the root for name of Jordanian port at the top of the Red Sea, Aqaba.

Q

qawwali   Traditional form of Islamic song, much denounced by Islamists for sensuality, religious pluralism and cultural flexibility, bridges the divide between India, Persia and Pakistan. From the Arabic root *qwl* (speak) meaning 'axiom' or 'dictum', or 'art of saying the word well'. The *qawwali* – thought to predate the birth of Muhammad – is closely linked to the mystical Sufi tradition, which strives to attain truth and divine love by direct personal experience. The Quran instructs man to remember God and this remembrance, known as *dhikr*, may be either silent or vocal as in *qawwali* (Miquel Cuenca, 'Voces para reducir distancias', *La Vanguardia*, *Culturas*, 21 September 2005). See **objectionable and obscene anti-Islamic practices, Salafi.**

R

raid   Arabic *ghazu*, hence Arabic and Turkish word *gazi*, a 'military leader', such as Ataturk. Originally associated with nomadic warfare, later used for attacks on the West, e.g. 9/11.

Rakan bin Williams   Title of an online story propagated by Islamic media about a group of Christian coverts to Islam. 'They are a group of your sons who were born in Europe from two European parents, and were Christians who studied in your schools, and enter your places, and know your psychology, and they go to your churches and celebrate mass on Sunday' and they promise to 'carry the flag of their distant brothers and seek vengeance on the evil doers'. Rakan was a hairy medieval warrior in Mesopotamia (Michael Moss and Souad Mekhennet, ' "Islamic Jihadi Media" with American Accent', *IHT*, 16 October 2007).

S

saddle straps   As in injunction by Osama bin Laden to his followers '*tighten your saddle straps*', a poetic appeal to struggle by the faithful, harking-back to romantic medieval Arabic poetry of the **Ode of Imru' al-Qays**. Equivalent to such English language imagery as 'Gird Your Loins'.

Salafist Group for Preaching and Combat (GSPC)   Name of main fundamentalist armed group in Algeria, result of split in 1998 in the other main force, the *Armed Islamic Group*, or GIA. In 2003, the *Salafi Group* proclaimed itself affiliated with **Al-Qa'ida** and called for *jihad*, with the aim of establishing an Islamic Republic in Algeria. While the GIA attacked indiscriminately civilian and military targets, the **GSPC** focussed on military targets initially, but then took to kidnapping foreigners working in Algeria. An estimated 150,000 people are believed to have died in Algeria after the outbreak of fighting between Islamists and the military government in 1991. The group suffered a possibly major blow when in June 2004 the supposed leader Nabil Sahrawi and five other leaders were killed by government forces in the Kabyle region.

Sassanian–Safavid conspiracy   Radical Sunni and Iraqi Arab nationalist conception of Iranian/Shi'i plot to destroy Iraq/Islam to resuscitate Persian imperial rule over the Middle East and eventually the world. **Sassanian** refers to a pre-Islamic Iranian dynasty and to the *Safavids* who ruled Iran and some of Iraq from 1501 to 1736 (Bernard Haykel, 'Al Qaeda Takes a Back Seat', *IHT*, 27 July 2007). See *magus* (Chapter 5), *safawi* (Chapter 5). The predilection for alleging the existence of composite international conspiracies is found in many forms of modern politics, e.g. Spanish dictator Franco's obsession with *judaeo-masonic conspiracy*, the rhetoric of Serbian officials in the 1990s about a *CIA-Vatican-janissary* conspiracy against the Balkans (where *janissary* is synonym for Turkish), and numerous cases of Stalinist regimes in the 1940s and 1950s linking 'Trotskyism', 'Titoism', the CIA, the Gestapo, German 'revanchism', the Vatican in various preposterous and abusive combinations. See also American **traditional values coalition** (Chapter 12) and its fantasy of a *Marxist/Leftist/Homosexual/Islamic coalition*.

Shaykh   Also Arabic *sheikh*, literally 'old man', then head of a tribe, but also, in political and social life, a term of respect for an older man. Commonly used of Osama bin Laden by his followers.

shoe bomber   Term applied to Richard Reid, detained after attempting to blow up a Paris–Miami flight on 22 December 2001. Reid had hidden a powerful explosive, *triacetone triperoxide*, in his shoes. Reid said he had paid $1,500 for the materials and had learnt how to make the bomb from the Internet. *Triacetone triperoxide* was used by the CIA in training Afghan *mujahidin*. French experts said Reid could have prepared the materials on his own. Israeli security officials insisted the explosive was similar to one used by Palestinians and showed a level of sophistication that suggested a co-conspirator. Reid himself, a British Muslim, came from London.

SOS 'Save Our Souls', a traditional maritime distress signal, more recently used as 'Supporters of Shari'ah' by preachers at the London Finsbury Park Mosque.

suicide bombing Term applied to tactic used by terrorist and military groups in a number of countries during the twentieth century, notably kamikaze ('divine wind') airplane pilots in World War II, Tamil Tiger guerrillas in Sri Lanka, **Hezbollah** in Lebanon and Islamists in Palestine. Inaccurate term insofar as *purpose* of action on part of perpetrator not to commit suicide as such but to inflict damage on an enemy by exploding a bomb in such a manner that the carrier of the bomb loses his/her life. Also, distinction needs to be made between cases where this tactic is used against the soldiers of an enemy state (Japan 1940s, Lebanon 1980s/1990s) and where it is used against civilians associated with that state (Sri Lanka, Palestine, 11 September). The Arabic expression *'amaliyya istishhadiyya'* (sacrificial operation) became commonly used in the 1990s. Those who dissented referred to such actions as *'amaliyya intihariyya'* (suicidal mission). The Quran prohibits suicide but not an individual's willingness to sacrifice life in the cause of a just struggle – a position all other major international religions and moral systems share. The Jewish **zealots** at **Masada** are reported to have committed suicide.

T

taghut Quranic term for 'idol', object of pagan worship, to be destroyed by the faithful. Applied by modern Islamists, notably Khomeini, to describe political opponents (the Shah, Bani Sadr, Jimmy Carter, Saddam Hussein). Hence, the generic term *taghuti* for secular elite and their associated lifestyle. Wrongly confused by many Arab writers with the etymologically distinct word for tyrant *taghin*.

taqwa Islamic term for piety, usually born of good deeds and prayer. Often used by fundamentalists as name for organisation.

tatarrus 'Human shield' argument, from *turs* a shield, or body armour. Precedent invoked by some *jihadis* to legitimate civilian deaths in military or terrorist actions. The *tatarrus* principle is drawn from prophetic traditions permitting the use of siege-breaking machines, such as giant catapults, against an enemy that holds Muslims as a shield (*turs*). They base their argument on the claim that Islamic laws sanction suicide (see **suicide bombing**) in operations in which Muslim civilians are killed, on this *tatarrus* principle and on the **according-to-their-intentions** argument. The latter is based on the story of Muhammad telling his wife Umm Salama that innocent people killed along with an entirely destroyed evil army will be resurrected on judgement day and judged 'according to their intentions' (Bernard Haykel, 'Muslims and Martyrdom', *The World Today*, October 2005).

tawhid Oneness (of God), literally 'asserting the singularity, oneness, of something', in this case, Allah; in general a call for return to purity in the face of modern corruptions and accretions. Common name of political and social organisation of contemporary Islamists, in early days of Iranian Revolution much talk of *iqtisad-i tawhidi*, literally 'Unitary Economics'. Cf. ***muwahhidun*** (Chapter 5), those who proclaim the unity of God, also the alternative Muslim proclamation of belief in one God, *la thani*, 'there is no second one'. The opposite of *tawhid* is ***shirk***, 'polytheism', literally 'sharing'. In medieval Islam, the word *thaluthi*, 'trinitarian', served as an abusive term for Christians.

tawhid wa jihad Militant anti-Western and anti-Shi'i Islamist group, active in Iraq in 2004, believed to be controlled by **al-Zarqawi**. In particular, denounced Arab and Muslim states such as Saudi Arabia and Pakistan that were considering sending forces to help stabilise the situation in Iraq.

terrorism Arabic *irhab* (literally, 'intimidation'); Persian *terorizm*. While a core, practical and moral definition of the term is possible, in modern times, and especially since the 1970s, **terrorism** as a legal, moral and military concept has been surrounded with much confusion and verbiage. In essence, it refers to any use of violence, on an indiscriminate basis, that is deemed to be illegitimate, or illegal, in terms of normal understandings of the rules and norms of war. It is, therefore, not a special ideology, political movement or form of psychotic or criminal behaviour, or the practice of any particular religion. Rather it is a tactic used by a range of political actors in conflict situations, and, by extension, a widely used term of political abuse and delegitimation; hence, there can no more be a special 'study' or 'science' of terrorism than there can be of mashed potatoes or holes in the ground. First used in 1795 to denote the terror of the French revolutionary state against its opponents and later in a similar way by the Bolsheviks, notably Leon Trotsky, in his book *Terrorism and Communism*, to legitimate their actions. **Terrorism** has come in the second half of the twentieth century to refer almost exclusively to acts by opposition groups: assassinations, kidnapping and hijacking of planes (occasionally ships and buses) involving civilians as well as bomb attacks on buildings and civilians in public places.

The Mission   Arabic *al-risala*, often used in Islamic vocabulary for work of the Prophet Mohammad, who was, literally, 'The Messenger', *al rasul*, name of a popular Lebanese game show, sponsored by **Hezbollah**, in which contestants have to answer questions that gain them 'virtual steps' towards Jerusalem. When the winner gains the 60 points necessary to 'enter' Jerusalem, the **Hezbollah** parade song, containing the words 'Jerusalem is ours and we are coming to it', is rousingly played. The successful contestant wins 5 million Lebanese pounds (US$ 3,300), 25 per cent of which goes to the 'Palestinian people'. Some questions are about men who carried out suicide operations, for example: 'The martyr Amar Hamoud was nicknamed "The Sword of All Martyrs?" – true or false?' True. The programme host then describes his exploits (Neil MacFarquhar, 'On Game Show, Arab Drumbeat: Remember Jerusalem', *The New York Times*, 19 April 2004).

travellers to heaven   The Saudi writer Turki Al-Hamad dedicated his book *The Winds of Paradise* (published in Arabic in 2005) to all members of the young generation – '**travellers to heaven**' – who were considering suicide missions, urging them to 'put your luggage aside and think'. Four *fatwas* were issued against him by Saudi Arabian clerics and he was named an 'apostate' in an **Al-Qa'ida** communiqué (Neil MacFarquhar, 'For Saudis Promised Liberalizations, a Snail's Pace', *IHT*, 9 June 2005).

trench   A favourite word of Osama bin Laden in regard to forces of Islam fighting the West. From same strategic mental framework as 'the base', **Al-Qa'ida**.

Trenes de la Muerte   'Trains of Death'. Spanish term for commuter trains blown by terrorists in Madrid on 11 March 2004. Those killed were mainly poorer people, many of them immigrants, from the southern suburbs of the city going to work. The term has sinister echoes, to a European ear, of the trains used to transport Jews to the Nazi death camps.

U

usury   Taking of excess interest or profit, profiteering. Islam prohibits this, but does not, despite current fashions for 'Islamic banking', prohibit interest as such. Part of the confusion on this question may result from the similarity of the Arabic/Quranic words for usuary (*riba*) and interest (*ribh*).

V

vassals of Osama bin Laden   The Sunni Islamist militia organisation, the *Salafist Group for Preaching and Combat*, the **Al-Qa'ida** organisation in the Islamic Maghreb, has sworn to overthrow the Algerian government and establish an Islamic state, besides attacking American and French targets. In September 2006, its members declared themselves 'vassals', i.e. loyal servants, probably Arabic *khadimin*, of bin Laden (Ignacio Cembrero, 'Al Quaeda mata a 30 personas en su ataque al corazón de Argel', *El País*, 12 April 2007).

Voice of the Caliphate   Arabic s*awt al-khilafa*. Al-Qa'ida television news programme that also promotes the recruitment of new agents worldwide, part of the *Global Islamic Media Front* (GIMF). The GIMF public relations director, Sayf al-Din al-Kinani, defines *sawt al-khilafa* as 'a self-standing organization of the Islamic Nation, designed for the sons of the *mujahideen*, and impartial vis-à-vis the *jihadi* groups that conduct themselves according to the correct way, and that it is fighting against the domination of the Zionist American media.' He looks to the day when the media wing of the *jihad* reaches its full potential. 'The day will come when anything that does not offer something to the Nation, the Faith and the Brothers, will be expelled ... It is high time for the *jihadi* forums to become a beacon of continuity, and a support for the jihad and its exponents' (Fawaz A Gerges, 'La guerra mediática de Bin Laden', *La Vanguardia*, 11 November 2005; Stephen Ulph, 'The "Voice of the Caliphate" looks Beyond Iraq', *Terrorism Focus*, Vol. 2, No. 22, 29 November 2005).

W

war against Islam   'Campaign' or 'aggression' to which Muslim world, in general, and Arab world, in particular, are said to be subject. A paranoid fantasy. In his June 2009 speech in Cairo, US President Barack Obama stated that the USA was not 'at war with Islam', nor could it ever be, not least because Muslims had been part of American life for many decades.

World Islamic Front to Fight Jews and Christians Name of organisation announced by Osama bin Laden and associates in 1998, alternative name for **Al-Qa'ida**.

Z

al-Zarqawi, Abu Musab Leader of especially brutal insurgent campaigns in Iraq, through *Tawhid wa Jihad* and other organisations. Laced anti-Western rhetoric with incitement to violence against Shi'i. Responsible for bombing of hotels in Amman, Jordan, in November 2005, as a result of which support for his actions reportedly ebbed. Originally from town of Zarqa in Jordan (hence name '*Zarqawi*'), was long such a shadowy figure for the US intelligence community that, one senior official stated, 'We don't even know how many legs he's got' ('Special Report: Iraq', *The Economist*, 18 June 2005). Killed in US bombing attack in Diyala Province, Iraq, on 7 June 2006, after which the **Al-Qa'ida** website announced 'the joyous news of the martyrdom of the mujahed *sheikh* **Abu Musab al-Zarqawi**'.

Language of Osama bin Laden: His Favourite Words

1. cavalry of Islam
2. Crusader Alliance
3. Hubal of the Age
4. *kafir*
5. martyrdom operation
6. Pharaoh
7. punishment of God
8. raid
9. saddle straps
10. World Islamic Front to Fight Jews and Christians

CHAPTER 3

Extraordinary Renditions: Abduction, Abuse and Torture

If the detainee dies, then you're doing it wrong.

—CIA counterterrorism specialist Jonathan Fredman, in a talk with military personnel, Guantánamo Bay, 2002 (quoted in Spencer Ackerman, 'The American Way of Spying', *The Nation*, 14 July 2008)

Our government authorized the use of torture, approved of secret electronic surveillance against American citizens, secretly detained American citizens without due process of law, denied the write of *habeas corpus* to hundreds of accused enemy combatants and authorized the procedures that violate both international law and the United States Constitution.

—Eric Holder, US Attorney General (as cited in David Cole, 'What to Do about the Torturers?', *The New York Review of Book*, 15 January 2009)

The B vocabulary consisted of words which had been deliberately constructed for political purposes: words, that is to say, which not only had in every case a political implication, but were intended to impose a desirable mental attitude upon the person using them ... No word in the B vocabulary was ideologically neutral. A great many were euphemisms. Such words, for instance as `joycamp' (forced labour camp) or `Minipax' (Ministry of Peace, i.e., Minister of War) meant almost the exact opposite of what they appeared to mean. Some words, on the other hand, displaced a frank and contemptuous understanding of the real nature of Oceanic society. An example was `prolefeed', meaning the rubbish entertainment and spurious news which the Party handed out to the masses.

—George Orwell, 'Appendix: The Principles of Newspeak', *Nineteen Eighty-Four* (London: Penguin Classics, 2000), pp. 319–20

> ... all correspondence relating to the matter was subject to rigid
> `language rules', except in the reports from the Einsatzgruppen,
> it is rare to find documents in which such bald words as
> `extermination', `liquidation', or `killing' occur. The prescribed
> words for killing were `final solution', `evacuation' (Aussiedlung),
> and `special treatment' (Sonderbehandlung)... Moreover, the very
> term `language rule' (Sprachregelung) was itself a code name; it
> means what in ordinary language was called a lie.
>
> —Hannah Arendt, *Eichmann in Jerusale. A Report on the Banality of Evil*,
>   London: Penguin Twentieth-Century Classics, 1994, p. 85

24 Hugely popular fictitious series on **Fox TV**, launched in 2001 before
9/11 and continued for at least eight years thereafter, created by Robert
Cochran and Joel Surnow, with unexpected plot twists, suspense and split
screens, and nominated for 57 Emmy Awards. Starring **Jack Bauer**, played
by Kiefer Sutherland, as member of the Los Angeles *Counter Terrorism Unit.*
Bauer is a federal agent who, in the words of the **Fox TV** website, cannot
'afford always to play by the rules', i.e. on the *ticking bomb principle* of the
need to break imminent terrorist action by mistreating suspects. In the
series **Bauer** helps to prevent many terror attacks, and in his endeavours,
torture and even killing are justifiable: almost every episode has a torture
scene in which extremely **aggressive interrogation techniques** are used.
Bauer breaks kneecaps, breaks fingers, kills his boss, chops off his partner's
hand, electroshocks his enemies, withholds medication, threatens 'Russian
gulag towel torture' and fakes the murder of a suspect's child live on video.
His methods always work, even if with only seconds to spare. According to
different reports, *24* has unwittingly served as model for acts of abuse and
torture by US military personnel after 9/11: the fictional figure of **Bauer**
was greatly admired by prison officers working at **Guantánamo** and has
provided a lot of ideas on how to mistreat inmates. One torture-technique
brain-stormer 'believed the series contributed to an environment in which
those at Guantánamo were encouraged to see themselves as being on the
frontline – and to go further than they otherwise might' (Richard Kim, 'Pop
Torture', *The Nation*, 26 December 2005; Philippe Sands, 'Stress, Hooding,
Noise, Nudity, Dogs', the *Guardian*, 19 April 2008).

A

accountability programme   US government claim that it can monitor treatment of prisoners sent to other countries under a **rendition** programme. Thus, according to Porter J. Goss, CIA director from September 2004 to May 2006, the CIA had an **accountability programme** to monitor 'rendered prisoners', i.e. those sent to other countries, such as Egypt, adding that 'of course, once they're out of our control, there's only so much we can do'. Another unnamed official said cryptically, 'For example, in some cases, the US government is allowed access and can verify treatment of detainees', but declined to give more information. The former Attorney General, Alberto Gonzalez, was not much more forthcoming: 'We obviously expect a country to whom [*sic*] we have **rendered** a detainee to comply with their representations to us. If you're asking me "Does a country always comply?" I don't have an answer to that'. Michael Scheuer (see **Anonymous**), a **rendition** supporter, is realistic: 'These are sovereign countries. They are not going to let you into their prisons.' See also **CID treatment, connect the dots, extraordinary rendition, less squeamish governments, outsourcing torture, this government does not torture people** and **third-country dungeons** (Dana Priest, 'CIA Assurances Are Doubted', *The Wall Street Journal Europe*, 18–20 March 2005).

actionable information   Where 'actionable' means 'leading to action', material extracted from interrogation that led to prevention of a terrorist threat.

Addington, David   Adviser to Vice-President Dick Cheney, first as 'counsel', i.e. legal adviser, up to 2005, then as chief of staff; former CIA lawyer, reclusive, sometimes referred to as 'Cheney's Cheney'. One of the main influences behind the August 2002 Office of Legal Counsel **torture memo**. Addington had a record of seeking to overthrow, or bypass, international law, and its attendant constraints on US actions, as 'a tool of the weak'. Like Cheney, he is a strong believer in the **unitary** nature of US government, i.e. removing controls on the executive (David Cole, 'The Man Behind the Torture', *New York Review of Books*, 6 December 2007).

Ali Baba   Classical name of hero of Middle Eastern story; then offensive name used by American soldiers and their allies in Iraq to describe individuals suspected of offences related to theft and looting. It is now used as a general term for the Iraqis, similar to 'Hajji' or 'Charlie' for the NLF in the Vietnam War or 'Gooks' in the Korean War. Also the name of a British military operation against looters in Basra on 15 May 2003, when Major Dan Taylor ordered that the captives should be 'worked hard': photos of the resulting abuses showed sexual humiliation, with prisoners being forced to simulate sodomy and oral sex. One man was strung up in a cargo net that was hung from a forklift truck and another photo showed a soldier standing on an Iraqi man curled in a foetal position. Three soldiers were court-martialled. Taylor, who had destroyed records relating to the illegal punishment of the Iraqi prisoners, was exonerated by the army on the basis that he had acted with 'well-meaning and sincere but misguided zeal' (Press Association, 'Army Major "Destroyed Iraqi Abuse Records"', the *Guardian*, 25 January 2005).

alternative set of procedures   Phrase used by President George W. Bush in a speech in September 2006 to denote new forms of interrogation licensed by his administration. According to a report by the International Committee of the Red Cross, these included: continuous solitary confinement and incommunicado detention, suffocation by water, prolonged stress standing, beatings by use of a collar, beating and kicking, confinement in a box, prolonged nudity, sleep deprivation and use of loud music, exposure to cold temperature/cold water, prolonged use of handcuffs and shackles, threats, forced shaving, and deprivation/restricted provision of solid food, among other 'procedures' (Mark Danner, 'US Torture: Voices from the Black Sites', *New York Review of Books*, Vol. 56, No. 6, 9 April 2009).

American gulag   Cruel and unaccountable elements of American prison system; an analogy of the Soviet term for concentration camp and forced labour system, GULAG, the compacted version of *Generalni Upravlenie Lagerov*, the General Camps Administration. First used to refer to immigration prisons inside the USA (as in the book by Mark Dow entitled *American Gulag: Inside US Immigration Prisons*) or the complex of **third-country dungeons** used for 'terror suspects' after 9/11.

American Taliban   20-year-old American John Walker Lindh captured with Afghan forces in November 2001. Brought up in a middle-class Californian household, he had converted to Islam as a teenager, and his parents had not seen him since February 2000.

***Animal House* on the night shift**   One of several euphemistic phrases used by US military officials, used to imply that the personnel who carried out abuse of prisoners at the **Abu Ghraib** prison in Iraq were an unrepresentative and unauthorised minority (Michiko Kakutani, review of *The Torture Papers. The Road to Abu Ghraib, IHT,* 16 February 2005). *Animal House,* a 1982 feature film based on a cartoon series in the magazine *National Lampoon,* is about a group of misfits in an early 1960s US college. Available evidence suggests that whatever the characters in the original film got up to, it did not include torture and gross humiliation of detainees. See **few bad apples.**

B

Baghdad Correctional Facility   Notorious setting for torture committed by US troops, otherwise known as **Abu Ghraib**. See **ghost detainee, Gitmo-ize**.

biscuits   Short for 'Behavioural Science Consultation Teams', units that included psychologists and/or psychiatrists, deemed to be an 'essential part' of interrogations of suspected terrorists. The first **biscuit** was introduced into **Guantánamo** by Major General Geoffrey **(Gitmo-ize)** Miller, who considered them so successful that he urged their use in **Abu Ghraib**. **Biscuit** members were trained in Fort Bragg's SERE (*Survival, Evasion, Resistance and Escape*) School where – theoretically – American soldiers were also taught to resist their captors by means of exposure to abusive techniques, some amounting to torture, delivered by fellow soldiers (Jonathan H. Marks, 'The Silence of the Doctors', *The Nation,* 26 December, 2005).

Black Hole of Calcutta   1756 incident when British prisoners incarcerated by a Bengali ruler died of heat and dehydration. Often used metaphorically to denote a place where prisoners are forgotten or neglected. Noteworthy that, although the ruler responsible was a Muslim Indian prince, the term carries no overt anti-Muslim connotations, being, rather, a byword for barbarous behaviour in general and the abuse of prisoners, and captured Europeans by native captors in particular.

black site   Secret and extraterritorial US prisons where detainees were maltreated, and sometimes tortured, without record or accountability. True to original association with **Black Hole of Calcutta,** contrast with **black hole state.**

blunt force trauma   Official term used by military coroners for cause of death when two prisoners died after being struck by guards in Bagram,

Afghanistan, in December 2002. Military guards had repeatedly struck the shackled men's thighs. However, agents of the army's Criminal Investigation Command reported to their superiors that they 'could not determine any clear responsibility for the detainees' injuries', a view also expressed by military lawyers at Bagram. In apparent mitigation, a defence lawyer described one of the dead detainees as 'the most combative detainee ever' (Tim Golden, 'US Army Inquiry Slow to Act on Abuse', *IHT*, 23 May 2005).

C

chameleon effect   Description by Guantánamo prison officials of journalists who are allowed to visit the detention 'facility' but who, after being hosted by the US military, then 'churlishly' refuse to say nice things about the place (Karen Greenberg, 'Guantánamo Is Not a Prison: 11 Ways to Report on Gitmo without Upsetting the Pentagon', *TomDispatch*, 9 March 2007).

CID treatment   Not, as in widespread English language usage, the implicitly reassuring Criminal Investigation Department, nor Care in Detention, but 'cruel, inhuman or degrading treatment', a term used in international legal conventions, colloquially and indulgently referred to by a number of phrases widely used and repeated in the media in the aftermath of controversy over Guantánamo Bay, Abu Ghraib and other prison's **harsh treatment**, **stress positions** and **torture lite**. 'Lite' includes interrogations lasting 18 to 20 hours a day, blasting prisoners with strobe lights and music, snarling dogs, threats against their families and humiliation such as leading them around on a leash and stripping them naked in front of women. Former Attorney General Alberto Gonzales argued at his confirmation hearing that the Supreme Court has held in other unrelated contexts that the Constitutional prohibition of CID does not apply outside US territory (David Luban, 'Torture, American-Style. This Debate Comes Down to Words vs. Deeds', *Washington Post*, 27 November 2005).

Cocktail no. 4   Defined as 'a mixture of urine, faecal matter, semen and spit that, it has been claimed, some Guantánamo Bay inmates throw at their guards' ('*Schott's Almanac 2007*: Words of the Year', the *Guardian*, 18 December 2006).

conditioning techniques   Forms of brutality used by British soldiers in Basra against Iraqi detainees, including kicking, punching, beating with rifle butts, depriving them of sleep, denying them food and water, making them remain for long periods in **stress positions** (the *Guardian*, 11 December 2008). See **Ali Baba**.

connect the dots   Sinister phrase used to justify identification, detention and mistreatment of individuals suspected, or accused, of being terrorist contacts or suspects. Used when US authorities were under fire for having failed to 'connect the dots' before the 9/11 attacks – a rather quaint way of describing a refusal of the country's top officials to heed serious warnings by their highest intelligence people. The zealous search for suspects began furiously to wag the dog and determine practice. The use of the term **connect the dots** in regard to someone who has not, at the time of 'connection', i.e. arrest and coercive interrogation and intimidation, been convicted of any crime is, of course, to presume guilt and deprive the person of fair treatment or unbiased news coverage. One such victim of this was Maher Arar, a Syrian-born Canadian citizen who, according to a Justice Department document, was a 'member of Al-Qa'ida'. He was seized in 2002 as he changed planes in New York and was **outsourced** to Syria, where he was badly tortured, although his tormentors had to conclude there was 'nothing there'. An anonymous 'former official' explained this treatment simply by saying, 'We wanted more information . . . This was a pragmatic decision. People's lives were at stake' (Scott Shane, 'Storm over Deportation to Syria', *IHT*, 31 May 2005).

control technique   One of many military euphemisms for torture and abuse, in this case forcing prisoners to lie, or stand, on top of each other for long periods of time. Making 'human pyramids' of prisoners in Abu Ghraib was no more than this according to Guy Womack, defence lawyer for a US soldier who was court-martialled in the Abu Ghraib detainee abuse scandal: 'It's not torture. Pyramids can be used as a *control technique* . . . Don't cheerleaders all over America form pyramids six to eight times a year?' (Cited by Weasel Words, www.weaselwords.com.au/language.htm).

controversial interrogation techniques   Journalistic euphemism for abuse and torture.

crafting legal fictions   Work of lawyers justifying torture.

D

dark art   Interrogation techniques that are 'excruciating for the victim' but 'leave no permanent marks and do no lasting physical harm' (Mark

Bowden, 'The Dark Art of Interrogation', *Atlantic Monthly*, October 2003). This article was said to have influenced US interrogators working in Abu Ghraib and elsewhere (Tara McKelvey, 'We Were Torturing People for No Reason', *IHT*, 29 March 2007).

dark side   As in 'dark side' of the moon, a region we know exists but can never see; term used after 9/11 by US Vice-President Dick Cheney in reference to counterterrorism policies that were done without comment or accountability, 'quietly, without any discussion'. General rubric under which the use of **torture** was authorised. British and earlier Caribbean slang uses *dark* as a term for violent, ugly behaviour, but this is unlikely to have resonated in US usage.

detainee   Euphemism for prisoners, someone coercively and illegally held against their will, often in an unknown place, and forcefully removed to a country other than their own.

detention facility   Like 'cabin attendant' to describe 'stewardess', 'body lotion' to describe 'soap', and 'arrangement fee' to describe a bank rake-off, a euphemism to conceal and/or embellish more mundane words, in this case 'jail' and 'prison'. Guantánamo was, thus, not a 'prison', but a 'detention facility' (Karen Greenberg, 'Guantánamo Is Not a Prison: 11 Ways to Report on Gitmo without Upsetting the Pentagon', *TomDispatch*, 9 March 2007).

dogs   Apart from being traditionally held in the English-speaking world to be 'man's best friend' and being used to terrify prisoners, dogs were held up as an example of humiliation in Guantánamo interrogations. Thus, an extract from the interrogation of prisoner 063 on Day 28 goes as follows: 'Told detainee that a dog is held in higher esteem because dogs know right from wrong. Began teaching the detainee lessons such as stay, come, and bark ... Detainee very agitated' (Philippe Sands, 'Stress, Hooding, Noise, Nudity, Dogs', the *Guardian*, 19 April 2008). Apart from the fear that dogs can be trained to instil, there are cultural differences in regard to this animal. In much of Islamic tradition, dogs are held to be impure animals, as in the *hadith*, or saying attributed to the Prophet, that an angel will not enter a room where there is a dog. In conventional English, while it is considered an insult to use the feminine form, *bitch*, the word 'dog' applied to men can imply affection and roguishness. In other languages and cultures, e.g. the Spanish *perro*, it is a term of insult, analogous to English *bastard*. Arabic *kalb* and Persian *sag* are, in modern political vocabulary, more assimilated to the populist and radical term of abuse, 'running dog', a slave or obsequious follower of, e.g. imperialism. Thus the last Shah of Iran was denounced by his opponents in the 1978–9 revolution as *sag-i amrika*, a 'running dog of America'. Yet in an example of the flexibility and polysemic potential of words, the diffusion during the Cold War of the pejorative communist term *running dog*, where the word is negative, coexisted quite happily with that of the American fast food *hot dog*, where the word has positive associations.

E

enemy combatant   Prior to 9/11 in international law, specifically the **Geneva Conventions**, a category of prisoner captured in war that is entitled to **prisoner-of-war** status. Distinct from **unlawful combatant**, someone who is not entitled to that status. After 9/11 the distinction between **enemy** and **unlawful** disappeared in US military and legal discourse, and both terms were used by US forces to denote prisoners suspected of involvement in terrorist activity. They were thus denied the legal status, under the 1949 Geneva Conventions, of being 'prisoners-of-war', and, in practice, even the guarantee of **human treatment** which the Fourth Convention prescribes for those who are not **prisoners-of-war**.

enhanced interrogation techniques   One of several US euphemisms for **torture**, see also **CID treatment**, **waterboarding**. Analogous to, and possibly derived at least indirectly from, the Gestapo term, *verfschärfte Vernehmung*, 'sharpened' or 'enhanced' interrogation.

environment adjustment   Altering the environment in which a prisoner is held, e.g. by applying noise, changing temperature. See **frequent flyer program**.

excesses of human nature that humanity suffers   Explanation by then Defense Secretary Donald Rumsfeld for torture by American soldiers at the Iraqi prison Abu Ghraib, an observation immediately followed by a reassurance to his audience at a Defense Department Town Hall Meeting on 1 May 2004 that 'our military justice system is working' (findarticles.com/p/articles/mi_m0PAH/is_2004_May_11/ai_n6110833). See also **few bad apples**.

extradition   Legal practice, governed by bilateral treaty between states, and based on the principle of 'double criminality', whereby the action of which the person so extradited is accused is considered a crime in *both* countries. In the case of the European Union it was replaced, after 9/11, by the principle of *surrender*, which required only that the person so transferred was accused of something that is a crime in the country requesting the move. In the mid-2000s an estimated 400–500 people were so moved, many of them on charges other than terrorism.

extraordinary   With all the calls upon this word, e.g. **extraordinary rendition** below, in the War against Terror to justify whatever measures the Bush administration considered necessary, *FM 3-24*, the US military's counterinsurgency field manual, recalled the French experience in Algeria to use the word **extraordinary**. In the Algerian War of Independence (1954–62), French leaders decided to permit torture against suspected insurgents, arguing that since it was a new kind of war, the old rules did not apply, that the enemy represented such a great evil that 'extraordinary means' were justified, while claiming that torture applied to **insurgents** was 'measured' and 'non-gratuitous'. The manual concluded that the use of torture had negative consequences: 'It empowered the moral legitimacy of the opposition, undermined the French moral legitimacy, and caused internal fragmentation among serving officers that led to an unsuccessful coup attempt in 1962. In the end, failure to comply with moral and legal restrictions against torture severely undermined French efforts and contributed to their loss despite several significant military victories.' The heading of the section is 'Lose Moral Legitimacy, Lose the War' (Kristen Williams, 'Counterinsurgency 101', *In These Times*, March 2007).

extraordinary rendition   Euphemism for state kidnapping and deportation, used for the US practice of detaining terrorism suspects and, in circumvention of normal criminal and wartime justice systems, coercively sending them to other countries. First authorised in President Directive 39 of 1995 and used much more widely by the Bush administration. Contrast with **legal rendition**, deportation in accordance with international treaty and law, and **erroneous rendition**, where detainee turns out to be innocent. See **black sites, Ghost Plane, *Il Iman Rapito*, rendition**.

F

Fear Up Harsh   Title of book by Tony Lagouranis, a man who worked as a torturer in Abu Ghraib, Al Asad Airfield and other places in Iraq in 2004.

His book (co-authored with Allen Mikaelian) was called *Fear Up Harsh: An Army Interrogator's Dark Journey through Iraq*. In an interview, Lagouranis stated, 'I started realizing that most of the prisoners were innocent . . . We were torturing people for no reason. I started getting really angry and really remorseful and by the time I got back I completely broke down'. In his book he writes, 'I didn't know I would discover my own evil. . . . And now that it has surfaced, I fear it will be my constant companion for the rest of my life' (Tara McKelvey, 'We Were Torturing People for No Reason', *IHT*, 29 March 2007).

few bad apples   Claim that prison guards were out of control. Attempt to disown higher-up responsibility for torture and abuse in US-run detention centres. See ***Animal House* on the night shift**.

finest traditions of valour   Term invoked on 2 December 2002 by President George W. Bush: he told a large and enthusiastic audience that terror was one of the unprecedented challenges the USA had to face but it would respond to these challenges in the 'finest traditions of valour'. He was at that time secretly authorising the use of torture in Iraq and Afghanistan, and the covert surveillance of American citizens (Philippe Sands, 'Stress, Hooding, Noise, Nudity, Dogs', the *Guardian*, 19 April 2008).

force drift   Another euphemism for torture, this one referring to the situation where interrogators start believing that if some application of force is good then more will be even better (Philippe Sands, 'Stress, Hooding, Noise, Nudity, Dogs', the *Guardian*, 19 April 2008).

forced grooming   Military euphemism for forcible shaving of a prisoner's body hair, a violation of his/her right to personal dignity. This tactic was included in the US government's Haynes Memorandum approving new and aggressive torture techniques: shaving off of body hair is deemed to be especially effective against Muslims for whom hair is, in some cases, sacred. An extract from the interrogation of Guantánamo prisoner 063 on Day 50 relates: 'Source received haircut . . . Detainee stated he would talk about anything if his beard was left alone. Beard was shaven . . . detainee began to cry when talking' (Philippe Sands, 'Stress, Hooding, Noise, Nudity, Dogs', the *Guardian*, 19 April 2008). A cognate practice was that of shaving obscene and culturally insulting patterns in the hair of the prisoner.

freelance counterterrorist   Overenthusiastic mercenary, as used by US government in conflict zones, notably Afghanistan and Iraq to detain, interrogate and abuse local people. Made famous by the case of Keither Idema, a US civilian who detained and allegedly tortured Afghans at the request of US officials by keeping a private jail. Press comment speculated whether he was a **deluded mercenary** or **misled crusader** (*FT*, 24 August 2004). See also **private security contractor, security contractor**.

frequent flyer program Term used by prison guards in Guantánamo to refer to the practice of tormenting, in effect torturing, inmates by going into cells and waking, and often moving, them from place to place, sometimes for as much as two months at a stretch. (See *sleep deprivation* interview by correspondent Daniel Sandford with former prison guard Chris Arendt, on *BBC News* website, 10 January 2009). According to Arendt, who was 19 years old when he was sent to Guantánamo, for some of the guards it was 'just doing a job', whereas others were 'genuinely psychotic' who saw their assignment to the detention centre as 'the chance in a lifetime to mistreat people'. Another tactic involved playing loud music for hours on end to detainees who were shackled to the ground. In 2004, according to US records, one teenage prisoner, Mohammad Jawad, was moved from cell to cell 112 times in a two-week period in order to maintain his state of sleepless disorientation.

G

Geneva Conventions   Agreements drawn up in 1949 by the International Committee of the Red Cross, regulating the treatment of prisoners of war. All four have a common Article 3, which prohibits 'cruel or degrading treatment' and insists on the 'basic humanity' of the prisoner.

ghost detainee   Term officially used by the Bush administration to designate a person held in a detention centre and whose identity is kept secret by keeping them unregistered and hence anonymous. It was used for the same purposes by the *Joint Interrogation and Debriefing Center* (JIDC) at the Abu Ghraib prison in Iraq. The USA was estimated in 2005 to have about a hundred such **ghost detainees** apart from people who have been subjected to **extraordinary rendition**.

Ghost Plane   Covert aviation network of CIA planes used, under the **extraordinary rendition** programme, to send hundreds of prisoners to foreign jails, where they ran the risk of being tortured or detained indefinitely.

Described in Stephen Grey's *Ghost Planes: The Inside Story of the CIA's Secret Rendition Programme* (London: Hurst, 2006). Derived from the older film title *Ghost Ship* (original version 1952, remake by Steven Beck 2002). The term has at least three meanings: a ship, like the *Marie Celeste*, found abandoned, without its crew; a ship that sails the seas for ever, without finding a port, as in the legend of *The Flying Dutchman;* a ship that operates without apparent state controls, carrying out illegal and menacing activities, such as in one cinematic case, a vessel with Nazi concentration camp personnel cruising the world and seeking new victims. The post-9/11 term **ghost plane**, with its overtones of danger, secrecy, invisibility and apparent lack of accountability, is an adaptation of these meanings. See also **rendition, third country dungeons**. In a cognate linguistic manoeuvre, during the Bosnian War of the early 1990s, planes with arms supplied by Turkey and Iran for the Bosnian Muslim forces were permitted to land at night by the UN and, indirectly, US authorities, despite a formal embargo on arms shipments to both sides. No reports on these landings were filed by the international forces then in Bosnia: from the name of the airport they used, these were known as *the flying saucers of Tuzla*.

Gitmo   Abbreviation derived from GTMO, the *Guantánamo Bay Detention Camp*. See **CID treatment**, **Gitmo-ize** ('Gitmo: A National Disgrace That Must Be Ended', *IHT*, 7 June 2007). A play on the colloquial word for gadget, *gizmo*.

Gitmo-ize   To follow the interrogation practices already carried out in the Guantánamo detention centre. In August 2003, the then Commander of Guantánamo Bay and subsequent Commander of all US detention operations, including Abu Ghraib, Major General Geoffrey Miller, visited Baghdad, where he insisted that the Abu Ghraib prison had to be 'Gitmo-ized': Iraqi detainees had to be subjected to the same aggressive techniques being used to extract information from Guantánamo detainees – forced nudity, hooding, shackling men in 'stress positions', the use of **dogs**. Miller told the Abu Ghraib military police commander, Brigadier General Janis Karpinski, 'You have to treat these detainees like dogs'. When reports of abuse, torture, sodomy and homicide of prisoners appeared in 2004, Karpinski denied knowledge of torture, claiming that the interrogations were authorised by her superiors and performed by subcontractors. A report in *The New York Times* dated 12 January detailed some of the abuses of which Karpinski was 'unaware', even though Miller had told her, 'You have to have full control'. These included urinating on detainees, jumping on a detainee's bullet-wounded leg, pouring phosphoric acid on detainees, sodomisation of detainees with a baton, tying ropes to the detainees' legs or penises, dragging them across the floor. At his retirement service in 2006, Miller was awarded the Distinguished Service Medal, and was praised as an 'innovator' (Jeff Jacoby, 'The Silence on the Right', *IHT*, 18 March, 2005).

gloves off   As in the phrase 'now the gloves are off': a euphemism for, *inter alia*, violation of the rights of prisoners, used by CIA official at Congressional hearings after 9/11. Implications include not only greater budgetary and political authority in Washington, but also greater licence in treatment of detainees and in choice of who to work with in undercover organisations. Richard Clarke, former head of security in the White House, asked why, given the history of attacks inspired by Osama bin Laden going back to 1993, the 'gloves' were ever 'on' in the first place.

golden shield   Used by CIA interrogators and their supervisors of the August 2002 Office of Legal Counsel **torture memo** to justify abuse, in effect **torture**, of prisoners (David Cole, 'The Man Behind the Torture', *New York Review of Books*, 6 December 2007).

Guantánamo Bay   Geographic area and hence name of US base in eastern Cuba, the oldest such base in the world. Its 45 square miles of land and water were first leased by the USA in December 1903 for use as a coaling station. The territory was then unilaterally seized by the USA in 1911 and used as a military base: crucially, for later use, the area was never formally annexed to the USA, as was the neighbouring Caribbean island of Puerto Rico, and thus remained outside US legal jurisdiction, with the protection this would have given to prisoners. Chosen as a site for detention of nearly 600 people captured during the Afghan War of 2001 and later because, falling outside US territory, it was not subject to US prison law. One of 13 such secret or extra-legal detention centres worldwide. Subsequently, for many Muslims, **Guantánamo** became a potent symbol, standing for the low regard in which they believed they were held by the USA. The name is of Arauaco native American origin. When Christopher Columbus sailed into Guantánamo Bay on 30 April 1494, he was reportedly warmly received by the Arauaco people with fruit and salt fish. The well-known Cuban song *Guantanamera*, composed in 1928 by José Fernández Díaz for a poem by José Marti, is about Guantánamo: the words in the refrain '*Guajira Guantanamera*' are sometimes said to refer to a 'Guantánamo girl', but they could also mean 'Guantánamo song'. Whatever the case, it is a song of compassion. See also **Gitmo**.

guilt and innocence   Basic principles of judicial procedure and basic justice, thrown overboard in regard to detention of suspects in **Guantánamo**. In 2007 the commanding officer Rear Admiral Harry B. Harris, Jr., was quoted as saying: 'Today, it is not about guilt or innocence. It's about unlawful enemy combatants' (Karen Greenberg, 'Guantánamo Is Not a Prison: 11 Ways to Report on Gitmo without Upsetting the Pentagon', *TomDispatch*, 9 March 2007, www.antiwar.com/engelhardt/?articleid=10644).

H

habeas corpus   Latin 'you shall have your body' right of a person to be released from jail, dating back to the fourteenth century and later enshrined in international law. Fundamental right denied in war on terror.

habeas **lawyers**   That is defence lawyers who plead for the right of *habeas corpus* release on the assumption of innocence until proven otherwise. Treated with great suspicion by US military officials in **Guantánamo**. According to the latter, they could be 'unwitting pawns of terrorists' because the al-Qa'ida training manual that was discovered in Manchester, England, in 2000 encouraged terrorists to 'take advantage of visits with *habeas* lawyers to communicate and exchange information with those outside' (Karen Greenberg, 'Guantánamo Is Not a Prison: 11 Ways to Report on Gitmo without Upsetting the Pentagon', *TomDispatch*, 9 March 2007, www.antiwar.com/engelhardt/?articleid=10644).

hanging gestures   That is suicide attempts of varying degrees of seriousness by US prisoners. There were 120 of these among the 350 'incidents of self-harm' in Guantánamo in 2003, according to US Army spokesman Colonel Leon Sumpter (BBC News, 25 January 2005, news.bbc.co.uk/2/hi/americas/4204027.stm).

Happy Mohammed mask   Form of humiliation used in interrogation of Muslim prisoners in Guantánamo. Thus reports of the interrogation of 'Detainee 063' on Day 27 mentions this form of treatment: 'Happy Mohammed mask placed on detainee and he was yelled at when he tried to speak' (Philippe Sands, 'Stress, Hooding, Noise, Nudity, Dogs', the *Guardian*, 19 April 2008).

hard facts   Like **rights**, these were thin on the ground in Guantánamo, as a 'security measure'. The journalist Karen Greenberg gives an example: Question: 'How long has the lieutenant been here?' Answer: 'Since she got here' (Karen Greenberg, 'Guantánamo Is Not a Prison: 11 Ways to Report on Gitmo without Upsetting the Pentagon', *TomDispatch*, 9 March 2007, www.antiwar.com/engelhardt/?articleid=10644).

harsh interrogation techniques   Euphemism often deployed to avoid use of the word 'torture' (David Cole, 'The Man Behind the Torture', *New York Review of Books*, 6 December 2007).

high-value terrorism suspects   US detainees believed to have important information, so more liable to be abused by their captors.

I

Il Iman Rapito   Italian media term for the 'kidnapped Imam', in reference to Hasan Mustafa Osama Nasr, also known as Abu Omar, an Egyptian citizen who was kidnapped in Milan on 17 February 2003 after being grabbed by two men, sprayed in the face with chemicals and shoved into a van. He was taken by private jet to the US air-force base of Aviano, in Italy, then to another US base at Ramstein in Germany and finally to Cairo, where he 'disappeared' in May 2004. He was released in February 2007 and stated that he had been tortured. Abu Omar was apparently the target of a CIA-sponsored operation known as **extraordinary rendition**. Prosecutors and judges in Milan later issued arrest warrants charging 22 alleged CIA operatives, including the head of the CIA substation in Milan, with kidnapping and other crimes. Italian investigators said they believed the abduction was orchestrated by the CIA's station chief in Rome and by officials assigned to the US Embassy there. The case is notable for being the first time that a foreign government has filed criminal charges against US operatives for their role in a counterterrorism mission (Enric González, 'Italia busca a 13 agentes de la CIA por el secuestro de un integrista egipcio', *El País*, 25 June 2005).

interrogation guidelines   Instructions drawn up by the US military, with support from administration lawyers, in effect authorisation for abuse and, in some cases, torture of suspects. See, in particular, **torture memo**.

interrogation techniques   Term used to describe forms of interrogation and torture authorised by the US General Roberto Sanchez, later commander-in-chief of US forces in Iraq. These techniques included manipulation of the prisoner's diet, isolation for more than 30 days, inflicting humiliation, withholding painkilling medicines, deploying dogs, keeping in a 'pressure posture' for 45 minutes, denying the use of religious symbols. Such practices were among the techniques used by US interrogators in the Baghdad prison of Abu Ghraib, site of some of the greatest violations of prisoners' rights during the US occupation of Iraq. See **mild non-injurious physical contact**.

K

knowing   Testifying before a Senate Panel in April 2007 on the dismissal of eight attorneys from his office because of their political views, Attorney General Alberto Gonzalez, a master of the evasive and the tawdry denial of responsibility, and one of the architects of the use of torture in Guantánamo and elsewhere, answered a question by Senator Edward Kennedy thus, 'Senator, I have in my mind a recollection as to knowing as to some of these United States attorneys. There are two that I do not recall knowing in my mind what I understood to be the reasons for the removal' ('Gonzalez Testifies before Senate Panel', *The Washington Post*, 19 April 2007). See, below, **loyal Bushies**.

L

lawyers justifying torture   The 28 March 2009 investigation by Spanish courts, under the practice of 'universal jurisdiction', of lawyers responsible for 'devising the legal architecture that allowed torture to become official US policy, were: Office of Legal Counsel lawyers Jay Bybee and John Yoo, White House lawyers Alberto Gonzales and David Addington, and Defense Department lawyers Douglas Feith and William Haynes ('Bush Torture on Trial?', *The Nation*, 20 April 2009).

legal limbo   Status and whereabouts of dozens of prisoners held in custody in secret CIA prisons or **third-country dungeons**. See **Limbo**.

less squeamish governments   The 'hosts' of the US' 'terror suspects', people detained and deported without judicial overview or conviction. See also **outsourcing torture**, **rough ally**, **surrogate jailer**, **third-country dungeons** (Michael Isikoff and Mark Hosenball, 'Got Him. Now What?', *Newsweek*, 16 May 2005).

Limbo   From Latin *limbus*, 'border' or 'shore', in traditional Christian theology, a place that is supernatural, i.e. not on Earth, but neither heaven nor hell, a place of temporary lodging for souls that had to purge their sins before being admitted to heaven. In contemporary political parlance, as in the term '**Legal Limbo**', no such temporary or transient status is implied, rather a sense, as with those held by the USA after 9/11 in undocumented detention centres across the world, of being outside any judicial or accountability system. More recent Catholic doctrine has declared the concept of **Limbo** to be without theological validity. Traditionally considered as the place to which souls of babies born before baptism went: following the abandonment by the Catholic Church of the 'Limbo' doctrine, the Vatican felt compelled to set up a special theological commission to determine 'the fate of babies born without baptism'.

looked the other way   Mawkish term for failures of the US media, politicians and military to protest sooner about practices of prisoner abuse and torture.

loyal Bushies   Members of the US legal procession deemed to be uncon-ditionally loyal to the US President, especially on matters relating to treat-ment of suspects in regard to the **war against terror**. Three emails released on 15 March 2007 reveal that, early in 2005, the US Justice Department rec-ommended removing up to 20 per cent of the country's attorneys who were deemed to be 'underperforming' while retaining **loyal Bushies**. They also show that presidential adviser Karl Rove asked the White House counsel's office in January 2005 whether it was going to fire all 93 federal prosecutors. The plan to remove a large number of federal prosecutors was well advanced just before the Senate hearings on the nomination of the ultra-loyal **Bushie** Alberto Gonzales as attorney general. Gonzales, it transpires, spoke 'briefly' with D. Kyle Sampson, his soon-to-be chief of staff at the Justice Depart-ment, about the plan. Sampson wrote to the White House counsel's office, '[W]e would like to replace 15–20 percent of the current US Attorneys – the underperforming ones ... The vast majority of US Attorneys, 80–85 percent, I would guess, are doing a great job, are **loyal Bushies**, etc., etc.' And though he opposed the idea of firing *all* the attorneys, he wrote, 'That said, if Karl thinks there would be political will to do it, then so do I.' One **loyal Bushie** prosecutor, Gordon D. Kromberg, was asked by Salim Ali, the defence lawyer of a Falls Church student Ahmed Abu Ali (no relative), held without charge in a Saudi Arabian prison since June 2003, about bringing Abu Ali back to the USA to face charges. In an affidavit, Salim Ali stated that Kromberg 'smirked and stated that "He's no good for us here, he has no fingernails left"' (Dan Eggen and Paul Kane, 'Justice Dept. Would Have Kept "Loyal" Prosecutors', *The Washington Post*, 16 March 2007; Caryle Murphy, 'Official Allegedly Hinted at Saudi Torture of Virginia Man', *The Washington Post*, 19 November 2004; Editorial, *IHT*, 19 September 2007).

M

medical personnel   Often attached to interrogation and advising on how best to break suspects. In one incident, a medical officer told the prisoner, 'I look after your body, only because we need you for information' (the *Guardian*, 8 April 2009).

mild non-injurious physical contact   US military term used in official memo of 8 January 2003, updating 1987 army field manual and detailing 17 permissible **interrogation techniques**.

Military Tribunal System   Military courts set up by the US military to assess and try terrorism suspects, criticised by many as denying legal rights to detainees.

moral scruples   Term of derogation for legal and moral principles.

more sugar in your tea where you're going   Phrase used by British intelligence investigator of Binyam Mohammad, in regard to prospective transfer to a third country where torture was anticipated (cited in Timothy Garton Ash, 'British Torture?', TGA Weekly article, 13 March 2009, using British High Court reports on hearings relating to Binyam Mohammad in regard to the British intelligence officer, named in court as 'Witness B', who interrogated him in Pakistan in 2002).

N

new   Apparently low-key, innocent and welcome term used to conceal substantial and sinister developments in a state's policy. Thus the post-9/11 US *new tools to monitor terrorists' movements* (term used by George W. Bush in farewell interview, *IHT*, 17–18 January 2009) included, and sought to conceal from public and Congressional scrutiny, a range of unconstitutional practices. See also **new thinking on the laws of war, outmoded, quaint**. Also chimera of 'new form of warfare' – RMA 1990s, Af 2001.

new agenda   Amnesty International characterisation of the post-9/11 legitimation of torture by the US administration. Thus, at the launch of the *Amnesty International Report 2005*, the organisation's Secretary General Irene Khan said that governments are betraying their promise of a world order based on human rights and are pursuing a dangerous 'new agenda . . . A new agenda is in the making with the language of freedom and justice being used to pursue policies of fear and insecurity. This includes cynical attempts to redefine and sanitise torture' (Pere Rusiñol, 'Amnistía denuncia que EEUU está redefiniendo la tortura', *El País*, 26 May 2005). See **new thinking on the laws of war**.

new normal (the)   The term – with its noun – adjective grammatical problems (cf. *the new black, the new must-have, New Labour*) – was first used to denote life in the USA after 9/11, with its associated security concerns and pervasive public fear. Later it came to acquire connotations of normalising the state of legal and political exception introduced by the Bush administration. Thus, a 2003 report by the US Lawyers Committee for Human Rights noted, 'The expansion of executive power and abandonment of established civil and criminal procedures have become part of a "new normal" in American life' (Jess Whyte, 'The New Normal', *On Line Opinion*, 18 March 2005, www.onlineopinion.com.au/view.asp?article=3263).

new thinking on the laws of war   Euphemism for abandonment of basic principles of prisoner protection, and respect for human rights of the enemy, enshrined in the Geneva Conventions. Term used by George W. Bush in regard to laws governing interrogation of detainees by US forces. That there were elements of the 1949 Conventions which were outdated (the favourite target of US scorn were the provisions on the right of prisoners to smoke cigarettes) and while the very development of warfare itself, and of the legal and moral framework (e.g. on gender), has required revision of international law, the disdain for, and erosion of, basic protection, on the grounds, implied in the term 'new', that this is 'outdated', amounted to an apology for abuse and torture. See **new agenda, new tools to monitor terrorists**.

non-judicial punishment   That is not published at all; term taken from the US Code of Military Justice, Article 15, used to lessen or cancel verdicts handed down to US personnel charged with torture and abuse of prisoners.

non-lethal torture   Interrogation methods justified, in CNN interview with Wolf Blitzer, 3 March 2007, by US lawyer Harold Dershowitz, in the case of the **ticking bomb scenario**. Cf. **uncivilized means**. Among practices Dershowitz regarded as legitimate in such circumstances were the insertion of a sterilised needle under the nails of the detainees.

not off the table   Euphemism for a policy remaining in place without official confirmation. Thus, turning 'terror suspects' over to **less squeamish governments** was 'not off the table' according to an unnamed 'administration source' in 2005 (Michael Isikoff and Mark Hosenball, 'Got Him. Now What?', *Newsweek*, 16 May 2005).

not recall key details   Favourite tactic of Bush administration officials when later questioned about authorisation of torture.

novel ways of extracting information   Another euphemism for circumventing legal and moral norms of interrogation.

O

outsourcing torture   The US practice, not far removed from contract killing, of sending 'terror suspects' to friendly henchmen in countries like Syria, Jordan, Egypt, Morocco and Uzbekistan in the secret programme known as **extraordinary rendition** so that they could be held, interrogated and, potentially, abused away from the jurisdiction of US law in order to extract information (Bob Herbert, 'Outsourcing Torture', *IHT*, 12–13 February 2005). The term 'outsourcing', which became part of the business lexicon in the 1980s, means subcontracting a process to a third-party company, usually in order to cut financial, energy, labour and technological costs. It is frequently accompanied by off-shoring – using third world countries where workers are paid very low wages. In the security field, it also correlates with large increase in the use of mercenaries. See **private military contractors, private security contractor.**

P

painful stress positions   Another euphemism for torture, one version of **CID treatment.**

philosophical guidance   High-sounding term for authority, when not incitement, to torture. Retired US Army colonel Larry Wilkerson, who served as former Secretary of State Colin Powell's chief of staff, stated that torture was practised in US 'facilities' and 'There's no question in my mind where the **philosophical guidance** and the **flexibility** in order to do so originated – in the Vice President of the United States' office'. The 'implementer' was Donald Rumsfeld and the Defense Department (Editorial, *The Nation*, 26 December 2005, 166; CNN Online: http://edition.cnn.com/2005/US/11/20/torture/). See also Chapter 1, **intellectual authorship**.

prisoners   As the word 'prisoner' was associated with, at least minimal, legal status and rights, as under the 1949 **Geneva Conventions** and US domestic law, this category did not exist in detention centres such as Guantánamo. These places contained only 'detainees', enemies or, in the legal invention much used by the Bush administration to circumvent existing protective laws and norms, '*unlawful enemy combatants*' (Karen Greenberg, 'Guantánamo Is Not a Prison: 11 Ways to Report on Gitmo without Upsetting the Pentagon', *TomDispatch*, 9 March 2007, www.antiwar.com/engelhardt/?articleid=10644).

prisoner abuse   One of the most common US euphemisms for war crimes, not always equivalent to torture, but often used as a euphemism for it. Term much used after revelations of US treatment of Iraqi prisoners in the Abu Ghraib prison. See in particular **enhanced interrogation techniques**.

provided inaccurate information   That is, lied. Used in relation to Monica Goodling, White House liaison for the Justice Department, in regard to answers to questions given in a lawsuit brought by a rejected job applicant. In the words of an editorial, 'An internal investigation released Monday found that the department's top staff routinely took politics and ideology into account in filling nonpolitical positions – and lied about it' (*IHT*, 30 September 2008).

pump and dump   Originally the name of a CIA torture programme in the 1970s – to **pump** prisoners for information and then **dump** their bodies. Though widely used in Vietnam, where many Vietnamese prisoners were tortured to death and their bodies secretly disposed of, it was more overt in the Philippines. There the torturers did not hide evidence of their work but left the bodies in the street as an arbitrary-terror warning that would traumatise the whole society (See Alfred McCoy, *A Question of Torture: CIA Interrogation from the Cold War to the War on Terror* [New York: Henry Holt and Company, 2006]). More recently, in a recycling of a sinister military term into civilian usage, this term mainly refers to a form of Internet fraud involving the use of false or misleading statements to **pump** up the value of stocks, which are then **dumped** on the public at inflated prices. Such schemes involve telemarketing and Internet fraud.

Q

quaint Along with *obsolete* terms used by White House lawyers Alberto Gonzales and David Addington in regard to the **Geneva Conventions** and as part of their preparation for decisions authorising torture (*The Nation*, 20 April 2009). The – in psychoanalytic terms – projection of outdatedness on to realities, or constraints, that the speaker now wishes to discard is recurrent: Cf. the description of weapons systems as *ageing*, when the speaker wants to justify new military appropriations, and the use by Israeli speakers of the term *new realities*, thereby questioning UN and other international agreements limiting settlement and occupation on the West Bank.

R

redefine the law Euphemism for suspension of previous US and international prohibitions of abuse and torture. Cf. **new thinking on the laws of war**.

rendition One of the most important post-9/11 US euphemisms: the sending of suspected terrorist prisoners to third world countries without judicial process and with the knowledge that those countries routinely use torture in interrogation. The noun, **rendition**, is derived from the verb **to render**, i.e. to give or send something to an appropriate destination, to repair, interpret or correct, and hence carries an implicit – and in this context quite spurious – suggestion of something orderly, correct, just being done. This implication is also reinforced by the use of the word in the conventional English variant of the phrase about the obligation of Christians to obey the temporal state, *render under Caesar what is Caesar's, and unto God what is God's.* Prior to 9/11 the only normal English language usage of the term was as a noun denoting the interpretation by an actor or an equivalent of a theatrical work, or the *rendering/rendition*, i.e. translation of a work into another language. Some dictionaries, e.g. Webster's *The New International Dictionary of the English Language*, also give a secondary meaning, 'to extradite'. However, this etymology is itself apologetic, as *extradition* implies an act conducted by two states under an existing law or statute, and hence within an appropriate, and visible, legal framework. More pertinent is the mention by the *Oxford English Dictionary* of the early-nineteenth-century American usage, '**rendition** of fugitive slaves' from the Northern states of the USA, where slavery had been abolished, to the slave-owning South: this brings out the key elements of the post-9/11 practice, one that is coercive, without legal framework or guarantees, and of a generically punitive, and racist, character. The root is from Latin *reddere*, vulgarised as *rendere*, 'to give back', 'to deliver', 'to hand over'. For CIA claims that it monitored the fate of detainees so *rendered*, see **accountability programme**. Also **extraordinary rendition, reverse rendition**. Compared to French *refoulement*, from *refouler*, 'to step again (on a person's native soil)' (*fouler* is to step or treat on something), the word which gained common usage in the European Union for involuntary repatriation of immigrants. Although not applied to people judged guilty of a criminal offence (other than violation of immigration laws), the French term was also a monstrous euphemism, since what defined the action was not the deported individual's ability to set foot again on their native soil, something which by seeking to emigrate they had clearly wished to set behind them, but the coercive nature of the action. According to the international legal expert Scott Horton, who helped prepare a report on renditions for NYU Law School and the New York City Bar Association, it was estimated that between 2001 and 2005, 150 people were **rendered** by US military and security officials to other countries. It was generally assumed that on being sent to other countries, such as Syria, Egypt and Uzbekistan, the detainees would be subject to brutal treatment and often to torture. See **outsourcing torture** (Jane Myer, 'Outsourcing Torture: The Secret History of America's "Extraordinary Rendition" Program', *The New Yorker*, 14 February 2005; Bob Herbert, 'Outsourcing Torture', *IHT*, 12–13 February 2005).

restraint chairs   Chairs that were sent to Guantánamo in order to enable force-feeding of prisoners who were on hunger strike in an attempt to commit suicide in protest at their indefinite confinement. According to the manufacturer's Web advertisement, they are 'like a padded cell "on wheels"'. Detainees were strapped into the chair, sometimes for hours on end, so as to be fed through tubes and were prevented from vomiting afterwards. One prisoner told his lawyer that more than half of a group of 34 long-term hunger strikers had abandoned their protest after being strapped into such chairs and having their feeding tubes inserted and removed so violently that some bled or fainted. Hunger strikers were also deprived of 'comfort items', such as blankets and books. A report by an American law firm (Robins, Kaplan, Miller & Ciresi), investigating abuse or injury of inmates through the use of **restraint chairs** in the USA, stated: 'Since the beginning of 2000, at least four inmates have died in the USA after being subdued in a **restraint chair** – a metal-framed chair in which prisoners are immobilized in four-point restraints securing both arms and legs, with a strap across the chest. In 2001, three prisoners died within the space of three months while confined to these **restraint chairs**. These cases are the latest in a disturbing increase of **restraint chair**-related deaths that have occurred in prisons and jails nationwide. There are also numerous reports of prisoners being subjected to verbal, physical or mental abuse while in restraint chairs. Moreover, although designed to be used as temporary restraint devices, there are reports of prisoners being inhumanly held in these restraint chairs for long periods of time – even days' (Tim Golden, 'Tough US Steps in Hunger Strike at Camp in Cuba', *The New York Times*, 9 February 2006, 181; http://www.rkmc.com/Restraint-Chairs-Cause-Unnecessary-Pain-Injury-and-Even-Death.htm [last accessed 21 March 2008]). In his classic analysis of the origins of World War I, based on the willingness of members of the German officer corps to obey orders, kill and die, Freud attributed much to the workings of the *Schreberstuhl*, a punitive or restraining chair designed by a Dr. Schreber in the 1870s, for disciplining young boys.

retro/reverse engineering   In manufacturing, the reconstruction of the general model of a product on the basis of one already manufactured example. Applied to the use of US Army training of pilots and others to resist interrogation to construct new interrogation techniques post-9/11. See **SERE**.

return to the fight   Continuation of *jihad* against USA after release from custody, the danger of which is often used to justify the continued detention of suspects without trial.

reverse rendition   Transfer of non-combatants who have been arrested by foreign authorities and returned to US territory without the basic protections that are afforded by law to criminal suspects. Such was the case of the Yemeni businessman Abd al-Salam Ali al-Hila who was handed over to US authorities and 'disappeared' for 18 months before being sent to Guantánamo. In essence a form of state-sponsored kidnapping. See also **extraordinary renditions, outsourcing torture, rendition.**

rough ally   Indulgent and collusive US term applied to Uzbekistan after 9/11. Similar to British terms such as *they do not play by the Queensbury rules.* After becoming a **surrogate jailer** for the USA, the Tashkent regime received more than $500 million for 'border control and other security measures'. It is estimated that dozens of 'terrorism suspects' were sent to Tashkent even after a State Department human rights report on Uzbekistan noted that police routinely tortured prisoners, noting that the most common techniques were 'beating, often with blunt weapons, and asphyxiation with a gas mask'. Moreover, human rights groups had reported 'boiling of body parts, using electroshock on genitals and plucking off fingernails and toenails with pliers'. See **less squeamish governments, outsourcing torture, rendition, third-country dungeons, this government does not torture people** (Don Van Natta, 'US Recruits a Rough Ally as Jailer', *IHT*, 2 May 2005).

rubberhose cryptanalysis   Form of torture – beatings, frequently on the soles of the feet – with a rubber hose. Euphemism for the extraction of cryptographic secrets (e.g. the password to an encrypted file) by torture, in contrast to a mathematical or technical cryptanalytic attack.

Rumsfeldians   Term invented and applied by LSE Professor of Human Rights Connor Gearty to officials of Western governments who agree to accommodate torture. Such accommodation, Gearty wrote, 'is not as difficult as it ought to be. At the centre of any such normalisation process, driving forward the acceptability of such conduct in an entrenched democracy, there is invariably to be found a particular category of persons, the **Rumsfeldians**' (Connor Gearty, *Index*, 11 February 2005, cited in *News & Views*, LSE, 28 February 2005).

S

Secret Detention Centres   In July 2004, the USA was accused by the NGO *Human Rights First* of having at least 13 secret centres around the world where prisoners were held in violation of the Geneva Conventions. These include Guantánamo in Cuba, Abu Ghraib in Iraq, Bagram in Afghanistan, the Indian Ocean island of Diego Garcia, sites in Jordan and Pakistan and at least two naval vessels off the US coast. Between 1,000 and 3,000 people were believed to be held in these places. See **American gulag, Ghost Plane**.

SERE Survival, Evasion, Resistance and Escape School at Fort Bragg, where USA trained servicemen to resist capture and/or enemy interrogation. Experiments on extraction of information, and how to resist this, had been conducted since the 1950s: some of these techniques were then **reverse-engineered** after 9/11 to serve as new interrogation techniques. Those who had been involved in training US servicemen to *resist* interrogation were now redeployed to advise on how to *abuse* enemy prisoners (Jane Mayer, *The Dark Side* [New York: Doubleday, 2007]).

shucking and jiving An inconvenient practice, attributed to 'terror suspects', whereby, in communications that may be subject to interception, they use slang, obscure references, code words and speak in such awkward languages as Baluchi. The US 'intelligence community' (**fifteen squabbling baronies**) is not noted for **cosmopolitanism** or linguistic skills (H. D. S. Greenway, 'The Limits of Global Eavesdropping', *IHT*, 14 April 2005).

Special Removal Unit Name adopted by the crew of CIA aircraft. See **Ghost Plane**, which transported abducted prisoners to third world countries in 2002.

strategy of the weak Derogatory term for tactics used by opponents of US policy, associating human rights groups and independent media with terrorism. Cf. *habeas* lawyers. Thus, according to Secretary Donald Rumsfeld in the 2005 *National Defence Strategy of the United States*, the **strategy of the weak** involved 'using international fora, judicial processes and terrorism'. Implicitly a play on other demeaning phrases such as *weapons of the weak, poor man's nuclear bomb*, etc. The juxtaposition of the three elements – media and law being bracketed with violence – is revealing (Karen J. Greenberg, 'Secrets and Lies', *The Nation*, 26 December 2005).

stress position Forced sitting or squatting for up to four hours. One of 'permissible' interrogation techniques authorised by the US Army in January 2003. See **mild non-injurious physical contact, torture lite**.

surrogate jailer Name for other countries used by the USA to house prisoners after 9/11 under **rendition** programmes. By May 2005, it was estimated that the USA had transferred between 100 and 150 prisoners to its **rough-ally** partners in Egypt, Jordan, Syria, Morocco, Saudi Arabia, Pakistan and Uzbekistan (Don Van Natta, 'US Recruits a Rough Ally as Jailer', *IHT*, 2 May 2005). See also **ghost detainee, less squeamish governments, outsourcing torture, rough ally, third-country dungeons**.

Swan Arr Shin   Intimidatory euphemism from another conflict, in this case Burmese for 'masters of force': the name of the civilian clothes-clad group trained by Burma's military regime to beat up demonstrators. Not too remote cousin of **Shock and Awe**.

T

tabloid terror   Title of work by Florida International University professor François Debrix (*Tabloid Terror War: Culture and Geopolitics* [London: Routledge, 2007]). An account of how the mass media in the USA helped promote George W. Bush's policies by increasing the level of public fear. Essential precondition for general acceptance of violation of prisoner rights.

Talon   Sinister name of the US Defense Department's database of information on 'potential' threats to military facilities and personnel. By January 2006, it had 13,000, including 2,821 reports involving American citizens, 186 of which dealt with 'anti-military protests or demonstrations in the US'. The American Civil Liberties Union attorney Ben Wizner protests, 'The US military should not be in the business of maintaining secret databases about lawful First Amendment activities' (Walter Pincus, 'Protesters Found in Data Base', *Washington Post*, 17 January 2007; 'ACLU Sues Pentagon Over Talon Database', Fox News, 14 June 2006, www.foxnews.com/story/0,2933, 199471,00.html).

telegraphing weakness   Description by Republican critics, such as former Vice-President Dick Cheney, of disclosure by President Obama of documents and reports on torture under the Bush administration.

third-country dungeons   'Secret locations' outside the USA where 9/11 suspects were held and, reportedly, also tortured.

This government does not torture people   Reaction of President George W. Bush, at a rapidly called press conference on 5 October 2007, to a Congressional uproar over the disclosure of secret Justice Department legal opinions permitting the harsh interrogation of terrorism suspects. In two separate legal opinions written in 2005, the Justice Department authorised the CIA to subject terror suspects to an onslaught combining painful physical and psychological tactics, including head-slapping, simulated drowning and frigid temperatures. The deputy White House press secretary criticised *The New York Times* for publishing the stories, saying it was 'chipping away at the safety and security of America with the publication of this kind of information'. Democrats and some Republicans are said to have been 'furious at the way the administration has kept them out of the loop' (Sheryl Gay Stolberg, 'Bush Says Interrogation Methods Aren't Torture', *The New York Times*, 6 October 2007).

torture   To subject to systematic and extreme ill-treatment, with the intent to extract information, punish or otherwise ill-treat, from Latin *torquere*, to twist, or turn. This root is perhaps associated with the medieval use of a *rack*, to which prisoners were tied and put over fire, as a means of extracting information or forcing them to renounce religious beliefs. Defined by the UN 1987 *Convention Against Torture* as 'any act by which severe pain or suffering, whether physical or mental, is intentionally inflicted on a person for such purposes as obtaining from him, or a third person, information or a confession, punishing him for an act he or a third person has committed or is suspected as having committed, or intimidating or coercing him or a third person, or for any reason based on discrimination of any kind'. In international law, and even under the Fourth Geneva Convention which exempts some detainees from the rights of prisoner of war, there is an injunction to treat such people 'with humanity', thus constituting an implicit, and unqualified, prohibition of the right of states, or others, to torture.

torture crowd   US troops who routinely indulge in torture. The *International Herald Tribune* correspondent Bob Herbert described this as a group that 'somehow loosed their moorings to humanity and began behaving as sadists, perverts and criminals' ('Rumsfeld and the Degradation of the US Military', *IHT*, 24 May 2005). See **frequent flyer program**.

torture lite   A smirking phrase, one of the nastiest to come out of the whole post-9/11 experience.

torture memo   Legal opinion, August 2002, by the Office of Legal Counsel lawyers Jay Bybee and John Yoo, justifying the use of **harsh methods** to interrogate suspected terrorists. The memo argued that **torture** occurred only when pain inflicted was *such as to cause organ failure or death*; hence all other forms of mistreatment were justified (David Luban, 'The Defense of Torture', *New York Review of Books*, 15 March 2007). While the 2002 memo was only a legal opinion, and was later rescinded, the 2006 **Military Commissions Act** granted immunity to CIA interrogators, removed *habeas corpus* protection from detainees, allowed military tribunals to hear evidence gathered by force and denied protection to foreign nationals of the Geneva Conventions.

Torture Team   Title of the book on Donald Rumsfeld and the circumvention of legal constraints on torture by British lawyer Philippe Sands (Basingstoke: Palgrave Macmillan, 2009).

torture warrants   Mechanism suggested by US right-wing lawyer Alan Dershowitz as a means of 'bringing it within the law', by which he means breaking the law to permit torture. See **uncivilized means** (David Bromwich, 'Euphemism and American Violence', *New York Review of Books*, 3 April 2008).

U

uncivilized means   Euphemism used to legitimate torture. Thus, in an essay entitled 'Torture, Terrorism and Interrogation' published in *Torture: A Collection* (ed. Sanford Levinson), Richard Posner, a judge on the US Court of Appeals for the Seventh Circuit and senior lecturer at the University of Chicago Law School, wrote: 'Torture is uncivilized, but civilized nations are able to employ **uncivilized means**, at least in situations of or closely resembling war, without becoming uncivilized in the process'. In a similar vein, Michael Levin, professor at City University of New York, argued in an essay titled 'The Case for Torture' (1982) in favour of torturing not only suspects but their infant children if it would make them talk. Another supporter of 'harsh interrogation techniques', Harvard Law School professor Alan Dershowitz, classified 'a wide range of (historically) practiced techniques, which can range from the **mundane** (e.g. food deprivation) to the **creative** (e.g. removal of fingernails)'. Mirko Bagaric, head of Deakin University Law School (Australia), argues that since, according to Amnesty International, 132 countries use torture it might as well be regulated (Tara McKelvey, 'Rogue Scholars', *The Nation*, 26 December 2005).

unlawful combatant   Term used in some legal literature, but not in any international convention, before 9/11, then popularised by the US government after 9/11 to denote individuals captured by a military force, as in Afghanistan, or Iraq, but not qualifying for protection of the Geneva Convention or even basic recognition of rights. Formalised in the 2006 **Military Commissions Act**. Confused by American government with the term **enemy combatant**, both becoming in effect synonyms for people accused of being members of **Al-Qa'ida** or supporters of the Taliban. Such people were often sent to detention centres such as **Guantánamo**. A modern equivalent of the term *outlaw*, someone who was not only themselves operating outside the law, i.e. a criminal, but who could be treated outside any legal framework. The standard debate on combatants captured in war has revolved around the two categories of *civilian* and *prisoner of war*, the latter being owed full protection under the four 1949 *Geneva Conventions*. However, the Fourth Geneva Convention does state that those deemed to have been involved in fighting, but not accorded POW status, still enjoy legal protection, and should 'be treated with humanity and, in case of trial, should not be deprived of the right of fair and regular hearing'.

unleash   Purports to convey a playful sense of sadism and cruelty, as if those so to be released, were wild animals, or attacker dogs, a somewhat nauseous association given the use of dogs to harass and torture detainees in **Guantánamo** and **Abu Ghraib**. Hence, **unleash John Bolton** (Maureen Dowd, 'Unleash John Bolton', *IHT*, 28 April 2005). Also **unleash the CIA** in 2007, when *International Herald Tribune* writers Daniel Benjamin and Steven Simon called on the Bush administration to **unleash the CIA** as 'the paramilitary capacity America profoundly needs'. Intelligence experts themselves deemed the Pentagon incapable of carrying out **what needs to be done**, giving as an example the failed operation to capture or kill **Al-Qa'ida's** Number 2, Ayman al-Zawahri (Daniel Benjamin and Steven Simon, 'Unleash the CIA', *IHT*, 25 July 2007). In such Washington circles, the failures of the USA in intelligence and counterterrorism owed much to the unjustified constraints imposed on the agency by Congress in the 1970s, these, be it recalled, after a series of reports on the torture and killing of detainees in Vietnam, and reports of attempted assassination attempts.

unsign   What the Bush administration did in April 2002 to Bill Clinton's endorsement of the 1998 Rome Statute establishing the International Criminal Court: they **unsigned** it (Eric Reeves, 'Darfur and the International Criminal Court', *Middle East Report Online*, 29 April 2005).

V

Vice-President for Torture   Description of **Vice-President Dick Cheney** in headline on the lead editorial of the *Washington Post*. The paper accused him of seeking to exempt CIA interrogators from anti-torture legislation: '...this vice-president has become an open advocate of torture' (Guy Dinmore and Alex Barker, 'Controversy Grows over Fate of Iraq Detainees', *FT*, 27 October 2005). Cheney himself always denied that he or the Bush administration had sanctioned torture, telling an interviewer at the end of his period in office: 'Torture – that word gets thrown around with great abandon' (interview with Fred Barnes and Bill Kristol of *The Weekly Standard*, cited in *International Herald Tribune*, 14 January 2009). When it became known, in May 2009, that Cheney was working on his memoirs, President Obama remarked that they should be titled *How to Shoot Friends and Interrogate People*, a variant on the bestseller of earlier decades by Dale Carnegie, *How to Make Friends and Influence People*. In 2003, just some months after the invasion of Iraq, Cheney and his wife sent a Christmas card with the quote: 'If a sparrow cannot fall to the ground without his notice, is it probable that an empire can rise without His aid?'

W

walling   Practice of slamming a prisoner against a wall, often using a collar or towel held around the prisoner's neck. One of the 12 basic techniques documented by the International Committee of the Red Cross in a report submitted to the US Government in February 2007, on treatment of prisoners in CIA custody. After initially bashing the prisoner against a concrete wall, a plyboard screen was installed, apparently to avoid the risk of serious physical damage. This had, however, the further effect of enhancing the process with loud and disturbing banging noises (Mark Danner, 'The Red Cross Torture Report: What It Means', *The New York Review of Books*, Vol. 6, No. 7, 30 April 2009).

waterboarding   Form of torture used by US armed forces in interrogation especially after 9/11; euphemism given a superficially innocuous veneer by association of name with the sports of *surfboarding* and *waterskiing*. Involves strapping a prisoner down, placing a cloth over his face and dousing him with water to simulate the sensation of drowning. Despite the fact that two laws passed by Congress after 2001, and a Supreme Court ruling on the treatment of detainees, were generally interpreted to have banned the CIA's use of this interrogation method, the White House itself declared that it was legal and that President Bush could authorize the CIA to resume using the simulated-drowning method under 'extraordinary' circumstances. In support of this position, CIA Director Michael V. Hayden stated that depriving the CIA of **enhanced techniques** would place 'America' in greater danger, while 'a senior US intelligence official' argued that waterboarding should not be considered torture because the US military had subjected its own personnel – 'tens of thousands of American Air Force and naval airmen' – to the method to prepare them for the possibility of being captured (Greg Miller, 'Waterboarding Is Legal White House Says', *Los Angeles Times*, 7 February 2008). Yet in a 2007 letter to Senator Patrick Leagy, four retired military lawyers, led by Rear Admiral Donald J. Guter, stated, 'waterboarding is inhumane, it is torture, and it is illegal' (Moustafa Bayoumi, *In These Times*, October 2008). Cheney, when asked on TV about waterboarding, had said that for him it was a 'no-brainer', 'a dunk in the water' (Nicholas Kristof, *New York Times*, 20 March 2007).

water cure   Form of torture used in the US war in the Philippines over a hundred years ago, later evolved into **waterboarding**. In the presence of a doctor, recipients are held beneath a water tank and were forced to swallow the gushing water or choke to death, or water is siphoned into a person's nostril: medical personnel are there not to restrain the torture but actively to heighten it if the 'patient' is not cooperative (Jonathan H. Marks, 'The Silence of the Doctors', *The Nation*, 26 December 2005).

with one hand tied behind the back   Phrase much used in debate on whether democratic countries, and the USA in particular, were entitled to use coercion and torture when dealing with terrorism suspects. Implication of unfair, and hence dispensable, legal and moral constraints in a war situation. Cf. **unleash**.

worked hard   Euphemism for mistreating prisoners, as in the instruction of a British military commander in Basra in 2004 that captured Iraqis should be worked hard. See **Ali Baba**.

worst of the worst   US military term for detainees held at Guantánamo. In the event, the majority were freed without any charges, or an evidence-based case, being made against them.

Abduction, Abuse and Torture: The Worst Euphemisms

1. *Animal House* on the night shift
2. black site
3. enhanced interrogation techniques
4. environment adjustment
5. extraordinary rendition
6. forced grooming
7. frequent flyer program
8. novel ways of extracting information
9. outsourcing torture
10. unlawful combatant
11. waterboarding
12. worst of the worst

CHAPTER 4

The Wars in Afghanistan and Iraq

There are a lot of things if I could go back and do them differently, I would. But the one I would not do differently is, we should have liberated Iraq. I'd do it a thousand times again. I'd do it a thousand times again.

—Secretary of State Condoleezza Rice, quoted in Bob Woodward, *The War Within. A Secret White House History*

Mission Accomplished.

—Slogan on US warship forming the backdrop to President George W. Bush's 'victory' speech after the invasion of Iraq, May 2003

You can get rid of me as President but, if you do, you will need at least seven Presidents to hold this country down.

—Saddam Hussein, President of Iraq (1979–2003)

If a problem cannot be solved, enlarge it.

—President Dwight D. Eisenhower

3161s US civilians working in the 'provincial reconstruction teams' in Iraq. The State Department described them as 'fully qualified for their highly technical jobs' but diplomats demurred, saying that many of them were incompetent and had been hired only for their loyalty to the Republican Party (Guy Dinmore, 'US Twists Civilian Arms to Fill Its Fortress Baghdad', *FT*, 8 January 2007). See **right-thinking Americans**.

A

Abu Ghraib Prison in Baghdad used by Saddam Hussein and American occupiers for torture and mass detention of opponents. See *Animal House* **on the night shift**.

accommodation without reconciliation   Phrase popular among the US military in 2007–8 to describe the post-**surge** situation in Iraq, where the parties accepted the formal imbalance of power with Shi'i on top and Sunnis and Kurds sharing some of the power, while the political struggle is crucially played out with violence at the excluded levels (Thomas L. Friedman, 'Debating Iraq's Transition', *IHT*, 22 November 2007).

Afghaniscam   Corrupt and inflated post-2001 consultancy system in Afghanistan. Susanne Koebl, using this term, outlined how the West's need for a quick success story and abundant cash flows – at least $4 billion, rising to $15 billion by 2009 – attracted an invasion of 'gold-digging consultants and aid workers'. The daily rate of pay offered by the globally operating USAID was $840, while a British consultant from the firm Crown Agents was paid $207,000, plus expenses, for his 180 days' placement in the Aid Coordination Office. Another aid worker in the office submitted a bill for $242,000 for 241 days' work, more than ten times what the Afghan minister responsible for development projects earns in a year (Susanne Koebl, *Der Spiegel*, 30 March 2005).

Af/Pak   Abbreviation for 'Afghanistan and Pakistan', term popularised around 2005–6 in Washington to denote – much belated recognition of – links between combat and Taliban/radical Islamist activity in both countries. The term was resented by many Pakistanis.

Al-Horra   Literally 'the free one', pro-US and US government-funded Arabic-language TV station broadcasting since February 2004 from Virginia in the USA. Operated by a non-profit organisation, *The Middle East Broadcasting Networks, Inc.*, itself funded by the Broadcasting Board of Governors (BBG). The latter, which formerly came under the United States Information Agency (USIA), operates and funds Voice of America and Radio Free Europe as well as the Prague- and Washington-based *Radio Farda* ('Tomorrow') in the Persian language and the Arabic-language *Radio Sawa* ('Together') broadcasting from Washington and Dubai. *Al-Horra* copies the *al-Jazeera* formula of instant news but offers its own interpretation of the events.

allies of convenience   President George W. Bush, in a speech to the National Endowment for Democracy on 6 October 2005, denounced Syria and Iran as **outlaw regimes** that acted as 'allies of convenience' to Iraqi insurgents (Guy Dinmore, 'US "Seeks New Syrian Leader" as Pressure Mounts', *FT*, 9 October 2005).

Al-Thawra   Literally 'the Revolution', 24-hour satellite television station known as *Muj TV* by Iraqis, began as a song-and-dance channel but, after the occupation began in 2003, became a mouthpiece for the Ba'thist-dominated insurgent group Islamic Army. Transmitting from an unknown location, it showed repetitive loops of car bombs and mortar attacks from *jihadi* websites along with images of prisoner abuse from **Abu Ghraib**, while also attacking members of the Shi'a-led government as 'Iranian stooges' (Michael Howard, 'Insurgent TV Channel Turns into Iraq's Newest Cult Hit', the *Guardian*, 15 January 2007).

America's nouveau Tet   The battle in early 2005 for the Iraqi town of Fallujah, by analogy with 'the Tet offensive', spectacular set of coordinated attacks by NLF forces in Vietnam in the month of February ('Tet' in the Vietnamese month system) 1968, which, though militarily very costly to the Vietnamese insurrectionaries, undermined political support within the USA for the war and led then President Johnson to announce he would not stand again as president (Frank Rich, 'A Quagmire for the MTV Attention Span', *IHT*, 29–30 January 2005).

Anonymous   See *Imperial Hubris* below.

Arabisation   In Iraq, the policy of Saddam Hussein in Kirkuk, which led to the expulsion of many Kurds and their replacement by Arabs from elsewhere in Iraq (Vincent Boland, 'Turks Fear Civil War if Kurds Win Kirkuk Victory', *FT*, 27 January 2005). In Gulf states, it denotes employment policy that favours employment of local Arabs, and reduction of dependence on immigrant workers. Also broken down into *Saudisation, Omanisation*, etc.

ATM peace   A peace based on cash, as from an ATM cash dispenser. In the words of columnist Thomas Friedman, the **surge** of 2007–8 prepared Iraq not for formal political reconciliation but for an '**ATM peace**' in which the Baghdad government became a cash machine 'supporting the army and local security groups and dispensing oil revenues to the provincial governors and tribal chiefs from each community'. Could **ATM** also refer to 'Asynchronous Transfer Mode'? (Thomas L. Friedman, 'Debating Iraq's Transition', *IHT*, 22 November 2007).

avert failure   Scaled-down goal of President Bush in Iraq (*IHT*, 11 April 2008). See **sustainable stability**.

awakening   Arabic *sahwa*, movement, also *majalis al sahwa*, 'Awakening Councils', in Iraq: a predominantly Sunni Arab armed force of some

65,000 to 80,000 members recruited in 2007–8 to fight Islamic extremist groups, seen as a linchpin of the US strategy to pacify Iraq. For some commentators this experiment in counterinsurgency warfare was leading to a civil war in which the USA effectively helped to organise some of the Sunni forces arrayed against the mainly Shi'i central government. An Iraqi intelligence official calculated that '[h]alf of the Awakening movement is infiltrated by Al Qaeda' (Solomon Moore and Richard A. Oppel, 'Attacks Imperil US-backed Militias in Iraq', *IHT*, 24 January 2008). In another report, it was stated that American commanders operating with such groups divide their leaders into 'fake sheiks, little sheiks and big sheiks' (Alissa J. Rubin and Damien Cave, 'Iraq Forces Builds Calm and Worry: US-paid Sunni "Awakening" Hold Seeds of Possible Conflict', *IHT*, 24–25 December 2007). Similar initiatives, such as the 'Strategic Hamlets' programme, marked US policy in the Vietnam War.

B

Babel of war assessments   In 2005 America's top brass were unable to say how the Iraq War was going because the different US services ('intelligence community') had never agreed on a unified system of gauging successes and failures, hence 'the Babel of war assessments' (Scott Johnson and John Barry, 'A Deadly Guessing Game', *Newsweek*, 16 May 2005).

backdoor draft   Term used by Democratic opponents of President Bush in 2004 election to describe extensive use of non-regular army, mainly the National Guard and reservist forces, to garrison Iraq. See **stop-loss**.

bait   Part of a classified programme in which the Pentagon's Asymmetric Warfare Group urged US military snipers in Iraq to drop 'bait' – such as electrical cords and ammunition – and then shoot Iraqis who picked up the items. This from evidence given in the case of army sniper Jorge G. Sandoval, Jr., acquitted by a US military court in Baghdad on 28 September 2007 after being accused of the murders of two unarmed Iraqi men on 27 April and 11 May. The jury accepted defence arguments that the killings were within the 'approved rules' (*Washington Post*, 24 September 2007).

bargain   'One of the biggest **bargains** of all time', according to President George W. Bush, was war-on-terror saving in Afghanistan, where the US Operation **Enduring Freedom** of 2001 used only about 110 CIA officers and 316 Special Forces personnel. The cost of the rest of the operation consisted of the distribution of 70 million dollars worth of hundred-dollar bills to the regional **commanders** of private militias (Pankaj Mishra, *Temptations of the West* [London: Picador, 2006], pp. 273–4). The problem was, however, that the quick victory of October–November 2001 proved illusory, and Afghanistan, like Iraq, was to draw in many more troops, and cost much more money, as the years unfolded.

benchmark   Along with ('flexible' or 'artificial') 'timetable', 'deadline' and 'target date', this word was much bandied around with reference to the Iraq War. But there are nuances. For example, according to Vice-President Dick Cheney, 'deadline' indicated 'legislation that ... would guarantee defeat'. The word 'benchmark', in the conveniently flexible sense of 'point of reference', made things easier: hence in his January 2007 speech announcing the troop **surge** in Iraq, President Bush declared that 'America will hold the Iraqi government to the **benchmarks** it has announced', even while Prime Minister Nuri Kamal al-Maliki's view was that it would take 'a miracle' to pass the legislation America required. In Iraq *thawabit* (approximately 'principles') is seen as one translation of benchmark, while another is *iltizamat* (commitments or obligations) but, in Washington, perhaps commitments and obligations in Iraq were not prominent on the agenda (William Safire, 'Benchmark and Timetable', *IHT*, 28 May 2007; Frank Rich, 'They'll Break the Bad News on 9/11', *IHT*, 24 June 2007). In late 2008, when the US and Iraqi governments signed an agreement envisaging a complete US troops withdrawal by the end of 2011, it was the USA which was now apparently being subjected to a **benchmark**.

Blackwater   One of the most important, and controversial, **private military contractors** working in Iraq after 2003, founded in 1997 by Erik Prince and Al Clark and based in the US state of North Carolina, where it trained more than 40,000 people a year from US or foreign military and police services, as well as other government agencies. It was the largest of the US State Department's three private security contractors: at least 90 per cent of its revenue came from government contracts, two-thirds of which were no-bid contracts. On 31 March 2004, four Blackwater Security Consulting (BSC) employees were ambushed and killed in Fallujah, and their bodies were hung on a bridge. US forces attacked the city in retaliation. On 16 September 2007, Blackwater employees in Nisour Square, Baghdad, shot and killed 17 Iraqi civilians. Erik Prince was an intern to the first President Bush, was a former Navy SEAL and is from a well-connected Republican family from Michigan, with close ties to conservative Christian groups.

Maureen Dowd called this kind of relationship the **mercenary-evangelical complex**, while Henry Waxman, chairman of the House Oversight and Government Reform Committee, called the State Department a 'Blackwater's enabler'. In December 2006, a drunk – off-duty and at a Christmas party – Blackwater employee killed the guard of Iraqi Vice-President Adil Abdul Mahdi and within 36 hours the culprit had been transported out of Iraq with State Department's permission. A report on the incident noted that the State Department chargé d'affaires 'suggested a $250,000 payment to the guard's family, but the Department's Diplomatic Security Service said this was too much and could cause Iraqis to "try to get killed"'. They agreed on $15,000 in the end, although 'the State Department requested only a $5,000 payment to "put this unfortunate matter behind us quickly"' (Maureen Dowd, 'Sinking in Blackwater', *IHT*, 4 October 2007).

blithe insouciance   Term applied by British writer Al Alvarez to the unconcerned frivolity (not to mention callousness) of those who predicted that invading Iraq would be a **cakewalk**. He originally used the term to describe the 'blithe insouciance' with which British naval officers sailed through the Northwest Passage in cocked hats and insignia of rank, refusing furs so as not to be mistaken for Inuit (Al Alvarez, 'S&M at the Poles', *NYRB*, 27 September 2007). See Bush's disdain for the **reality-based community**.

Blood for Oil   Slogan used to denounce wars over Kuwait, Afghanistan and Iraq in 1990 and in subsequent years. Implicit is the claim that no humanitarian, or strategic, concerns lay behind the decision to launch these campaigns. Usually accompanied by facile denunciation of Western violence without any reference to the violence of terrorists and militaristic Middle Eastern states.

Blue Dog Coalition   A group of moderate and conservative Democratic Party members of Congress, fiscal and military 'hawks', who criticised the Bush administration's approach to financing the Iraq and Afghanistan military operations. The name is said to come from the 'Blue Dog' paintings by Cajun artist George Rodrigue that were on the walls of the offices of Louisiana representatives where the original coalition members used to meet. It is also suggested that it is an ironic counter to the 'Yellow Dog' label, applied to Southern Democrats who would vote for a yellow dog before a Republican. The two 'Blue Dog' representatives in whose offices the meetings were held, Billy Tauzin and Jimmy Hayes, later switched to the Republican Party (Eric Schmitt, 'Bush Asks for an Extra $81.9 Billion', *IHT*, 16 February 2005).

BRAC for Iraq   BRAC is an acronym for '**Base Realignment and Closure**' programme, a sweeping plan to close or reduce forces at 62 major bases and nearly 800 minor facilities in the USA, out of a total of over 6,000 military bases. As designed in 2004–5, the Iraqi-rhyming-variant, '**BRAC for Iraq**', appeared to be based on the assumption that American forces were likely to remain in the country for some years, even after their numbers began to drop, and that the planners envisaged that they probably would continue to face danger. 'Camp Victory' at the Baghdad International Airport was a vast Vietnam-style encampment with an aura of permanence.

bull's-eye   An American warship docked in Qatar was mysteriously decorated with this target sign in spring 2007. Some Iranian Revolutionary Guards hinted that they might have been the artists (Seymour M. Hersch, 'Shifting Targets: The Administration's Plan for Iraq', *The New Yorker*, 8 October 2007). Ever since the missile attack by **Al-Qa'ida** affiliates or members in Aden Harbour in October 2000 on the *USS Cole*, a missile-carrying ship, in which 17 people died as a result of the attack, the US Navy has been concerned at such targeting of its vessels.

Butler Enquiry   The 196-page official British enquiry by five people headed by Lord Butler, former head of the UK civil service, published on 14 July 2004, into whether the Labour government had deliberately misused intelligence information in the run-up to the war with Iraq in 2003. A bland and evasive oeuvre. See **bill of goods, raspberry, sexed-up, threat inflation, Weapons of Mass Destruction**.

C

Camp Exxon, Camp Shell   Forward military bases set up by US invasion forces in 2003, named after oil companies. Eventually the Pentagon staff, seeing that this might be a public relations gaffe, ordered their renaming. An Exxon spokesman, Tom Cirigliano, claimed, 'This has absolutely nothing to do with the war being about oil … Anyway, I'm certain of this: that the restrooms in Camp Exxon are much cleaner than the restrooms in Camp Shell' (Oliver Burkeman, 'US Army's Desert Filling Stations Add Fuel to Fire', the *Guardian*, 29 March 2003).

Camp Victory   Complex of five bases, housing up to 20,000 US troops in suburbs of Baghdad, but, while lying on both sides of city boundary, classified as *outside* city boundaries to exempt it from commitment to withdraw troops from city by 30 June 2009. Other Baghdad bases included **Camp Prosperity**, next to the Green Zone, and **Forward Operating Base Falcon**.

casualty intolerance/force protection fetishism   Lawrence Freedman, *A Choice of Enemies. America Confronts the Middle East,* London: Weidenfeld and Nicolson, 2008, p. 380.

cats' eyes in the dark   In the context of public controversy over the role of British intelligence services in the run-up to the 2003 invasion of Iraq, Sir Colin McColl, former chief of the British Secret Intelligence Service, MI6, remarked that this is the most intelligence services can provide ('Cats' Eyes in the Dark', Special Report, *The Economist,* 17 March 2005). **Cat's Eyes** is UK terminology for reflectors placed in the road. Not clear if McColl literally meant two shining points that give sense of where the animal is, or reflectors running down the middle of the road.

Central Front   Term originally applied in Cold War to line of confrontation between Western and Soviet forces in Europe, expected to be the area of major warfare if hostilities broke out. For the Bush administration, Iraq played this role in the 'war against terror'. A CBS survey in 2006 showed that the public did not agree. Only 9 per cent felt that America's involvement in Iraq was helping to decrease terrorism (Frank Rich, 'Five Years after 9/11, Fear Finally Strikes Out', *IHT,* 21 August 2006).

Chaldeans   From 'Chaldea', ancient word for Mesopotamia, contemporary Iraq, also name of sixth-century BC dynasty. Eastern Christians of Iraq, affiliated since sixteenth century to the Roman Catholic Church, with substantial communities in Baghdad, Basra and Mosul. Estimated in 2004 to be around 700,000. Protected under monarchical and nationalist regimes, but in 2004 subject to systematic arson attacks on churches by Sunni radicals, leading to mass exodus. With long-term emigration from Iraq, the largest Iraqi Christian city has long been Detroit, USA. The most prominent member of Chaldean community was Tariq Aziz, deputy prime minister and long-term foreign minister of Iraq under Saddam Hussein.

channel with a reputation   Term used by US media officials of *al-Jazeera* to exclude them from press briefings at military HQ, or ban them from entering conflict zones, such as Fallujah, in Iraq, even when they had the correct press credentials (Steve Tatham, *Losing Arab Hearts and Minds: The Coalition, Al Jazeera and Muslim Public Opinion* [London: Routledge, 2007], p. 124). According to the Internet search engine Lycos, the word *al-Jazeera* received more hits than 'sex' or 'war' (Tatham, p. 197). Tatham was head of the British Royal Navy's Media Operations in the Northern Arabian Gulf from November 2002 to May 2003 and served as the British Navy's spokesperson in the months leading up to, during and after the invasion of Iraq. He was responsible for war correspondents **embedded** with British troops. Compare this to the abuse of CNN, as **Chicken News Network**, by rivals such as Fox News.

cleanup phase   Donald Rumsfeld, US Secretary of Defense, on the situation in Afghanistan in May 2003.

Coalition Provisional Authority   Transitional government in Iraq after the government of Saddam Hussein was demolished in 2003. Under UN Security Resolution 1483 (2003), the **CPA** was vested with executive, legislative and judicial authority in Iraq from 21 April 2003 to its dissolution on 28 June 2004. Its forerunner, the **Office for Reconstruction and Humanitarian Assistance**, was established by the Bush administration two months before the invasion as a future caretaker administration until the formation of a democratically elected civilian government. See also **financial irregularities** and **protecting the Development Fund for Iraq** (James Drummond, 'Dispatches from Iraq's "Frontlines"', *FT*, 26–27 February 2005).

commanders   After the Soviet withdrawal from Afghanistan in 1989, the *mujahidin*, now bereft of the US support they had enjoyed in the anticommunist **jihad**, turned to brutal violence to maintain their authority in the territories they controlled. In Afghanistan, *mujahidin* **commanders** are men with guns and bands of supporters who set up toll-tax checkpoints on roads and engage in other kinds of extortion and crimes such as arbitrary arrests, killings, kidnapping and rape (Pankaj Mishra, *Temptations of the West* [London: Picador, 2006], p. 273).

communal struggle for power   US military term designed to minimise import and scale of Iraq war. A Joint Strategic Assessment Team seeking to define the conflict in Iraq in 2007, as a means of producing a new strategy, determined that what scholars were calling one of the world's worst civil wars in 60 years (on par with Bosnia and Burundi) was a mere domestic squabble, a 'communal struggle for power'. The implication of the use of the word 'communal' is that the conflict is of a lower order than a 'civil war' let alone 'national uprising', and, even less so, the result of 'an invasion' or act of war by an outside power ('US Plan for Iraq Has 2-year Horizon', *IHT*, 24 July 2007; *IHT*, Edward Wong, 'Scholars Say Iraq Meets Definition of "Civil War"', 27 November 2006).

contractors   See **Blackwater**.

Curveball   Codename of Rafid Ahmed Alwan, Iraqi defector, alcoholic cousin of one of Ahmed Chalabi's (see **George Washington of Iraq**) most trusted lieutenants, fed hundreds of pages of information containing 'first-hand' descriptions of Saddam Hussein's supposed mobile biological weapons factories into US intelligence dossiers. These factories were, so it was claimed, disguised as agricultural plants, such as that at al-Hakem, south-west of Baghdad. Secretary of State Colin Powell used the information in his UN presentation to garner support for the war, despite warnings from German intelligence that Curveball was fabricating claims. The CIA later admitted that the defector made up the story, and Colin Powell apologised for using the information in his speech. One report noted that there were problems with Curveball from the start, but the intelligence community was willing to believe him 'because the tales he told were consistent with what they already believed'. By early 2001, the CIA was receiving reports from US Foreign Services that Curveball was 'out of control' and was also warned by his handlers in the German intelligence services that some aspects of his behaviour 'strike us as typical of individuals we would normally assess as fabricators'. But the warnings were overridden and analysts who expressed concern were blocked by spy chiefs and obliged to leave the unit that assessed his claims so that their warnings never reached the ears of policy makers (Edward Helmore, 'US Relied on "Drunken Liar" to Justify War', *The Observer*, 3 April 2005; Maureen Dowd, 'The Latest Intelligence Study: 601 Empty Pages', *IHT*, 4 April 2005). For baseball origin of the term, see Chapter 9, **curveball**.

D

DCIEDs   'Dog-concealed improvised explosive devices' or **IEDs** hidden inside dead Iraqi dogs (Roger Cohen, 'Iraq's Intricate Theater of Dawning Democracy', *IHT*, 12–13 February, 2005).

DDR   Not, as it was for decades of the Cold War, East Germany, or the *Deutsche Demokratische Republik*, but an internationally funded, and almost totally ineffectual, programme in Afghanistan, 'Disarmament, Demobilisation and Reintegration', designed to redeploy former Taliban fighters. Most of those so processed took the money offered and went on supporting their original leaders.

deBa'thification   Removal of members of formerly ruling Ba'th Party from public positions in Iraq. Modelled on post-1945 term 'denazification'.

defense contractor   In post-Ba'thist Iraq, a firm or company carrying out work, of military or civilian character, for the US armed forces, such as **Halliburton**, also a mercenary. See also **Blackwater**.

deliberate and careful misrepresentations   That is, official lies. The term was used after an official cover-up of the death in Afghanistan in 2004 of US football star Pat Tillman, who had caused a sensation when he turned down a huge offer to join the Arizona Cardinals in order to enlist in the US Army after 9/11. His death was presented as a result of heroic engagement with the enemy, but he was in fact killed by his own side, i.e. in **friendly fire**. His brother accused the military of 'intentional falsehoods' and 'deliberate and careful misrepresentations' to 'deceive the family and the American public', and added that, '[r]evealing that Pat's death was a fratricide would have been yet another political disaster in a month of political disasters so the truth needed to be suppressed' ('Army Lied, US Athlete's Brother Says', *IHT*, 25 April 2007). See **Rambo from West Virginia**.

Desert One   Originally the improvised landing strip and operations centre in the central Iranian desert set up during the disastrous 1980 attempt to free American hostages in Iran. Later a term for any overambitious special operation being advocated by political officials, as by senior military officials to dismiss requests in the late 1990s by the Clinton administration for ground troops to hunt and destroy terrorists in Afghanistan (Daniel Benjamin and Steven Simon, 'Unleash the CIA', *IHT*, 25 July 2007).

doddering daiquiri diplomats   Characterisation used in July 2004 of retired Australian diplomatic and service personnel who wrote letters critical of Prime Minister John Howard's policies in Iraq.

dodgy dossiers   See **sexing up Iraq**.

Downing Street memo   Document written within the office of the British Prime Minister in Downing Street stating that British officials believed that 'intelligence facts were being fixed' in Washington in 2002 in order to justify an attack on Iraq ('The War Debate Opens', Editorial, *The Nation*, 4 July 2005).

dumb luck   Perverse and cruel term used by US intelligence officials who regarded bombings of Iraqi police stations and military posts by opponents

of the US occupation as a 'positive sign'. Perhaps resonant of American collo-
quialism *dumb cluck*, term derived from aimless noise of farmyard chickens,
also of *touch luck*. Such attacks were 'dumb luck' they said and the high
casualty figures 'merely' reflected the fact that increasing numbers of Iraqis
were pitting their lives against the **insurgency**. One unnamed US official
commented, 'The administration can stomach television images of Iraqis
getting killed', whereas images of American dead in similar circumstances
would be quite unacceptable (Scott Johnson and John Barry, 'A Deadly
Guessing Game', *Newsweek*, 16 May 2005).

E

Enduring Freedom   The official name used by the US government for
its military response to the 9/11 attacks on the USA. The original name was
'Operation Infinite Justice,' but since this 'Infinite Justice' had previously
been used to describe God (by several faiths), it is thought to have been
changed to avoid offending Muslims. The main focus was Afghanistan,
where the aim was to capture Osama bin Laden and overthrow the Taliban
regime. Despite initial military success, in occupying Kabul and driving
out the Taliban, this proved in many ways an illusory victory: bin Laden
was not captured, and, by 2005, the Taliban were resurgent, placing the
Kabul government and its Western allies under greater pressure. The subsequent March 2003 attack on Iraq only worsened the situation; ironically,
the one thing that did 'endure' was not 'freedom', but 'war'. See also *Mission
Accomplished*.

Explosively Formed Penetrators   Bombs used by Iraqi insurgents
which discharge a semi-molten copper slug that can tear through the armour
of a US **Humvee** armoured car. According to the second-ranking US commander in Iraq, Lieutenant Raymond Odierno, these came into increasing
use with 'surging support' for Shi'i militia from Iran (Seymour M. Hersch,
'Shifting Targets: The Administration's Plan for Iraq', *The New Yorker*,
8 October 2007).

F

Fallujah effect   News of the casualty rate in the Iraq War that served
to lower enlistment rates in the USA, named after the town of Fallujah in
western Iraq, scene of some of the heaviest fighting between US and Iraqi

insurgent forces in 2005. The steady stream of news of US casualties in Iraq had an inhibitory consequence on Marine Corps recruitment. In 2005 Marines made up 21 per cent of the 150,000 military personnel in Iraq and suffered 31 per cent of the military deaths there. New re-enlistment bonuses of up to $35,000 were then being offered (Eric Schmitt, 'US Marines Face Concerns in Recruiting', *IHT*, 26 February 2005).

fiery cleric   Euphemistic word, like 'sage' or 'faith community', for demagogic religious leaders, e.g. Ayatollah Khomeini in Iran, Muqtada al Sadr in Iraq.

financial irregularities   Major feature of US administration of Iraq after occupation. At the end of the Iraq invasion in 2003, vast sums of money were made available to the US-led provisional authorities. Under Security Council Resolution 1483, of 22 May 2003, the funds were transferred into an account at the Federal Reserve Bank in New York, called the Development Fund for Iraq (DFI). The money was to be spent by the Coalition Provisional Authority (CPA) 'in a transparent manner . . . for the benefit of the Iraqi people'. In charge of the funds was CPA director Ambassador Paul Bremer. When Bremer left the post eight months later, $8.8 billion of that money had disappeared. The CPA spent up to $20 billion of Iraqi money, compared with $300 million of US funds. The 'reconstruction' of Iraq was paid for by the Iraqis themselves, largely out of their oil revenues. Among the **financial irregularities** described in audit reports produced by US government agencies and auditors working for the international community were nearly $600 million in CPA cash for which there was no paperwork, truckloads of dollars being handed out for which neither the CPA nor the recipients were accountable, dozens of contracts involving billions of dollars paid to American personnel and corporations and $3.4 billion appropriated by Congress for Iraqi development that were later siphoned off to finance 'security' (Javier del Pino, 'Una auditoria revela el descontrol de la reconstrucción', *El País*, 6 May 2005; Ed Harriman, 'So, Mr Bremer, Where Did the Money Go?', the *Guardian*, 7 July 2005). See also **no-bid contracts**.

flexibility   Euphemism for imprecise and easily expandable instructions, i.e. refusal of commanders and political leaders to give clear rules of engagement to expeditionary forces, as desired by US Secretary of Defense Donald Rumsfeld for NATO troops in Afghanistan. See **national caveats**.

flypaper effect   The attraction of potential terrorists from other countries to Iraq, thus decreasing the chances of their acting elsewhere. According to columnist Jacob Weisberg, 'Mr. Bush's poorly judged, dishonestly sold and incompetently executed war in Iraq' had this advantage: it 'created a convenient target of opportunity, drawing terrorists who would otherwise ply their trade elsewhere, including possibly in the US' (Jacob Weisberg, 'Bush (and Luck) Have Shielded America', *FT*, 7 September 2006).

Fortress Baghdad   The name given by critics to the planned US Embassy in Baghdad, scheduled to be the largest in the world. The embassy, in the 'Green Zone', covers 104 acres; i.e. it is six times larger than the UN compound in New York and is to be 'a city within a city for more than 1,000 people'. Its walls are built to be 15-feet thick, and it is expected to cost $592 million. When asked why the government was sending so many diplomats into a war zone when these conditions would lead to closure anywhere else, the State Department replied that such comparisons were 'inappropriate' (Guy Dinmore, 'US Twists Civilian Arms to Fill Its Fortress Baghdad', *FT*, 8 January 2007).

Fourth-Generation Warfare   Term used by Lieutenant Barnon, a commander in the US forces in Afghanistan 2003–5 to describe a supposedly 'new' form of **asymmetric warfare** and counterinsurgency that 'uses all available networks – political, economic, social, and military – to convince the enemy's political decision makers that their strategic goals are either unachievable or too costly for the perceived result' (quoted in Antonio Giustozzi, *Koran, Kalashnikov and Laptop* [London: Hurst, 2007], p. 98).

fox in charge of the henhouse   See **George Washington of Iraq**.

freedom is untidy   US Secretary of Defense Donald Rumsfeld's response to the looting that devastated ministry buildings in Baghdad after the fall of Saddam Hussein. Among his other, exculpatory responses was '**stuff happens**' (Roger Cohen, 'Picking up the Pieces in a Looted Ministry', *IHT*, 9 February 2005).

FREs   In Iraq, Former Regime Elements (Roger Cohen, 'Iraq's Intricate Theater of Dawning Democracy', *IHT*, 12–13 February, 2005).

fusilocracy   From French *fusil*, 'rifle', political system based on the rule of the rifle, e.g. 2000s Afghanistan.

G

gated communities   US military euphemism for urban areas, such as in cities of Iraq, that are forcibly cordoned off with blast walls, watchtowers and concertina wire, and are isolated, subject to forcible house entry at night, mass roundups and detentions (*The Nation*, 24 September 2007, p. 20).

George Washington of Iraq   The name given to Ahmed Chalabi by US neocons (including contacts in the **Project for the New American Century**, Paul Wolfowitz and Richard Perle) before he fell out of favour and was investigated by several US official bodies. Chalabi was also wanted for embezzling almost $300 million from a bank he had earlier founded in Jordan. Chalabi was part of a three-man executive council of the opposition Iraqi National Congress (INC), formed in 1992 with the aim of overthrowing Saddam Hussein, and was helped by considerable funding and assistance from the USA. Through Chalabi and the INC, the USA received most of the falsified information concerning alleged weapons of mass destruction and Iraqi ties with **Al-Qa'ida** with which the 2003 invasion of Iraq was justified (see **Curveball**). Although Chalabi was later said to have little influence in post-2003 Iraq, he was appointed by Prime Minister Nouri al Maliki in October 2007 to head the Iraqi Services Committee, covering eight service ministries and two Baghdad municipal posts that were to restore electricity, health, education and local security services to Baghdad's neighbourhoods as part of the **surge**. He has also played a leading role in the controversial deBa'thification process. Other titles attributed to Chalabi include **neocons' con man, charlatan, Thief of Baghdad, fox in charge of the henhouse** (Maureen Dowd, 'The New Iraq Comes Ethics-free', *IHT*, 3 May 2005).

ghost ship   Term, implying invisibility and silence, applied to low-profile US policy in Iraq in 2005: 'America's Iraq policy is like a ghost ship . . . ', wrote two journalists after the administration had tried to lower its profile and so avoid giving the impression that the Iraqi assembly was a tool of the USA. See also **Babel of war assessments, not uplifting** (Scott Johnson and John Barry, 'A Deadly Guessing Game', *Newsweek*, 16 May 2005).

glide path   Official British euphemism for surreptitious withdrawal of troops from Iraq. In October 2007, when newly appointed Prime Minister Gordon Brown announced plans to halve the British troop's presence in Iraq by April 2008, a 'senior government official' was reported as saying, 'I think what we would want to get ourselves getting on to is a progressive

glide path' (Stephen Fidler, Security and Defence Editor, 'British Troops on "Glide Path" out of Iraq', *FT*, 9 October 2007). Analogous to the term used of US forces in Lebanon after the 1983 bombing of their barracks, in which over 200 died, according to which the remaining forces would be **redeployed on ships** – the, unstated, corollary being that these same ships would then sail away. As they did.

go massive   Phrase used by US Secretary of Defense Donald Rumsfeld in response to the **opportunity** that the attacks represented for the Bush administration to launch military operations anywhere it wanted in the world. In his words: 'Sweep it all up. Things related and not' (David Bromwich, 'Euphemism and American Violence', *New York Review of Books*, 3 April 2008). See also **little guy**.

granularity   Reference to the 'granular' images that characterise US military night-time vision equipment. Explaining why Abu Musab al-Zarqawi, the Al-Qa'ida leader in Iraq, survived a coalition assault in Mosul in November 2005, Major General Bill Caldwell said, 'Obviously, the other five in the building did not, but he did for some reason. And we do not know ... as to whether or not it was because he might have been right outside (the targeted building) or whatever. We just don't have that granularity' (www.weaselwords.com.au/language.htm).

gratitude level   According to US President George W. Bush, 'the Iraqi people owe the American people a huge debt of gratitude' while he wondered 'whether or not there is a **gratitude level** that's significant enough in Iraq'. The same sentiment is illustrated in the words of vocal war supporter, journalist Charles Krauthammer: 'We midwifed their freedom. They chose civil war'. Perhaps more accurately, Zbigniew Brzezinski, a former White House National Security Adviser, called the Bush policy one of **blame and run** (Frank Rich, 'Operation Freedom from Iraqis', *IHT*, 28 May 2007).

H

Halliburton   Private US contracting firm that, as of August 2004, had earned $3.2 billion for services to US forces in Iraq. Total **Halliburton** contracts in Iraq at that time were estimated at $18.6 billion. At Congressional hearings, former employees reported multiple malpractice, including failure to keep records of expenditure, dismissal of employees who spoke up, abandoning US$80,000-worth of new trucks on account of flat tyres and housing employees in five-star hotels in Kuwait. See also **sole source contracts**.

hearts and minds   Term used in counter-insurgency operations of the 1950s and 1960s, by the British in Malaya and the Americans in Vietnam, to denote attempts to win over the often brutalised and terrified local population. Euphemism for propaganda, bribery and intimidation. Notably absent in response to 9/11 and the run-up to the March 2003 invasion of Iraq, where emphasis was on the use of military power (see **Shock and Awe**). It reappeared in the face of widespread Iraqi opposition to US presence in 2003–4. This is reflected in the statement (July 2004), of some historical condescension, by then Presidential National Security Adviser (later Secretary of State) Condoleezaa Rice: 'The **hearts and minds** issue is back'. See **Human Terrain Teams/System, public diplomacy**.

hell no   Stock answer by Senator Joe Biden, later Vice-President under Barack Obama, when asked if he was auditioning to be the next Secretary of State; yet if asked whether his **soft-partition plan** for Iraq was close to fruition he dispensed with the 'hell' (Helene Cooper, 'A Plan to Heal Iraq by Splitting it Apart', *IHT*, 31 July 2007).

historic sense of responsibility   This, according to President Bush in the transcript of his meetings with other pro-invasion leaders in Crawford, Texas, in 2002 guided his plan to invade Iraq, with or without UN approval. The same document showed that he was more guided by a tormenting impatience to invade, which he calls **Chinese water torture** (Mark Danner, ' "The Moment Has Come to Get Rid of Saddam" ', *NYRB*, 8 November 2007).

Hulagu   Mongol leader who sacked Baghdad, and destroyed the Abbasid Empire, the second of the two great Arab Islamic empires, in 1258. A term used by Saddam Hussein, in 1991, to describe George W. Bush senior. Saddam did not at that time use the term 'Crusader', as the European 'Crusaders' operated far to the West, along the Mediterranean coast and the Levant.

human terrain anthropologists   Experts 'embedded' with, i.e. working alongside, US troops operating in Iraq and Afghanistan. Used ethnographic knowledge to advise and inform troops in the field. Travelled with armed escorts and were, in some instances, themselves armed and wearing uniforms (David Price, 'Pilfered Scholarship Devastates General Petraeus's Counterinsurgency Manual', *Counterpunch*, 30 October 2007; www.counterpunch.org/price10302007.html). See next entry.

Human Terrain Teams/System   System used, above all in Afghanistan, to recruit anthropologists to work alongside counter-insurgency troops and gather information on 'operationally relevant cultural information'. Extraordinary inversion of normal usage, where *people* become objectified as **human terrain**. The **Teams** consisted of three military personnel and three civilians. According to the HTT website: 'The role of the HTTs is to help the troops to better understand who is NOT the enemy' and to help the US Army 'influence the population through non-lethal means'. Deployed in Afghanistan in 2007, one of the first casualties was a doctoral candidate from Oxford University, Michael Bhatia, and a social scientist attached to the 4th brigade of the 82nd Airborne Division. Denounced by many anthropologists as dishonest and fraudulent, and cynically described by one of its leaders, David Kilkullen, an Australian who had served with the Indonesian army in repressing the guerrillas in East Timor, as 'armed social work', the HTS programme was administered by BAE systems, a British-based arms firm, on a contract for $160 million (Bill Stamets 'Anthropologists at War', *In These Times*, July 2008). An example of this 'cultural context' concern was offered by a SEAL commander who remarked that nowadays US special operations teams in Afghanistan were 'sipping a lot of tea' (Austin Bay, 'We Can Overdo "Culture" Piece of War and Peace', *Houston Chronicle*, 5 October 2007; /www.chron.com/disp/story.mpl/editorial/outlook/5192091.html). Cf. **hearts and minds**.

Humvee   Four-wheel-drive US military vehicle, a form of what in other armies is termed an Armoured Personnel Carrier (APC). Full name *M998 High Mobility Multipurpose Wheeled Vehicle* (HMMWV or **Humvee**). First saw combat in 'Operation Just Cause', the US invasion of Panama in 1989. Over 10,000 were used during 'Operation Iraqi Freedom' in 2003. With improvements in guerrilla weaponry, it became increasingly vulnerable to attack, especially by **explosively formed penetrators**.

Hussein, Saddam   Former Iraqi leader detained by US forces in 2003. Born near Takrit, northern Iraq, in 1937. Joined underground Ba'th Party in the 1950s. Wounded and fled country after the attempt on then President Abdel Karim Qasim's life in 1959, and then lived as a refugee in Cairo, where he is believed to have had contacts with the US Embassy. Already an important figure in the Ba'th seizure of power in July 1968, he was in effect the most powerful person in Iraq from the early 1970s onwards. He was formally appointed President in 1979. Led his country into two disastrous wars with Iran (1980–8) and Kuwait (1990–1). Careful student of Soviet dictator

Stalin. Believed to be author of novels. Said, prior to his fall, 'You may get rid of me as President, but, when you do, you will need seven presidents to hold this country down'. Also remarked to a Kuwaiti visitor, in regard to the strong Iraqi response to the border incident with Kuwait, 'When a cat annoys you, you do not pull its tail, you chop off its head'. Despite his arrest, he was popular in much of the Arab world, where he was known as *al-rais al'asir*, 'the Prisoner President'. He was sentenced to death by hanging and was executed on 30 December 2006 (See Said Aburish, *Saddam Hussein: The Politics of Revenge* [Bloomsbury: London, 2001]; Kanan Makiya, *Republic of Fear: The Politics of Modern Iraq* [University of California Press, 1998, new edn; first edn. published in 1989 under pseudonym Samir al-Khalil]).

I

IED   Acronym for **improvised explosive device**, a bomb constructed and deployed in non-conventional military action, often in terrorist operations or by guerrillas or commando forces in Iraq and then, extensively, by the Taliban in Afghanistan. In Iraq, IEDs were used extensively against the US and other occupation forces, causing some 40 per cent of deaths. A car or truck bomb, generally used by suicide bombers, was known in military circles as a **VBIED** or vehicle-borne IED. The fuel of the vehicle could also act as an incendiary weapon. See also **DCIEDs, vehicle-based insurgency** ('Heroes Wanted', Special Report on Iraq, *The Economist*, 18 June 2005).

iffy drafting   Description used by UK intelligence staff to describe a dossier put out by the British government to justify the invasion of Iraq. See **raspberry, sexed-up**. At one point an official, in response to a claim that Saddam Hussein has 'assembled specialists to work on its nuclear pro-gramme', writes: 'Dr Frankenstein, I presume? Sorry, it's getting late ... ' (the *Guardian*, 13 March 2009).

illusionists   Name given to Paul Bremer's team in Iraq, earlier post-invasion administrators, by the 'hard-headed diplomats' that replaced them (Roger Cohen, 'Iraq's Intricate Theater of Dawning Democracy', *IHT*, 12–13 February, 2005). The word originally means either someone who creates 'illusions', such as a magician, or someone who believes in the theory of illusionism, according to which material reality does not exist.

Imperial Hubris   Title of book published by ex-CIA official in the sum-mer of 2004 under the name 'Anonymous', arguing that the US was losing the war against terrorism and that the invasion of Iraq had strengthened the terrorists' hands. 'Hubris' is the classical Greek term for pride leading inevitably to a fall. The dust jacket referred to the author as 'a senior US intelligence official with nearly two decades of experience in national security issues related to Afghanistan and South Asia'. 'Anonymous' turned out to be Michael Scheuer, an intelligence official with indeed 22 years of experience. He had been ordered to conceal his name by his employers, the CIA, as a precondition of publishing the book.

infinitely more important than Northern Ireland   Term used in his farewell tour to cheer on his men in Iraq, as Tony Blair informed British troops in Basra that their struggle was of such significance because it would 'shape the future of the world' (Martin Amis, 'The Long Kiss Goodbye', the *Guardian*, 2 June 2007).

Inside Iraq   News service run by McClatchy Newspapers, the third-largest newspaper company in the USA, questioning the accuracy of mainstream, Bush-line stories about Iraq. By early 2008 the *Inside Iraq* operation in Baghdad had had three bureau chiefs who were young Arab-American women with some fluency in Arabic. Early in 2007, it set up a blog exclusively for contributions from its Iraqi staff (at washingtonbureau.typepad.com/iraq). The bureau chief in early 2008, 26-year-old Leila Fadel, was reported as stating: 'It's an opportunity for Iraqis to talk directly to an American audience'. One contributor on 29 January wrote under the header, 'method of corruption', 'Corruption is the disease that corrodes Iraq's body from the inside . . . Any terrorist can join to any ministry if he has amount of money and that what made the ministries moan of corruption aches' (Michael Massing, 'As Iraqis See It', *New York Review of Books*, 17 January 2008).

insurgency   The word generally used to describe the uncontained violence in Iraq after the American-led occupation. According to the US Department of Defense Joint Publication (JP) 1-02, *Dictionary of Military and Associated Terms*, an insurgency is 'an organized movement aimed at the overthrow of a constituted government through use of subversion and armed conflict.' Thus, the term denotes armed rebellion and avoids connotations of 'revolution', 'revolt', 'rebellion', all of which are potentially positive, but also **civil war**, a term that the USA and allies sought to avoid after 2003. There are also problems with the word 'uprising' as it tends to question the legitimacy of the authority the people are rising against: it never appeared in US discussion of Iraq. See also **worldwide insurgency**.

intelligence study   In February 2003 President George W. Bush announced that that he was forming a nine-member independent commission to look at US intelligence capabilities, especially intelligence about weapons of mass destruction. The commission's co-chairman, Laurence Silberman, quickly declared, 'Our executive order did not direct us to deal with the use of intelligence by policy makers, and all of us agreed that that was not part of our inquiry'. In the words of feisty Washington columnist Maureen Dowd, the 601-page report, which cost $10 million, was 'yet another investigation into the chuckleheaded assessments on Saddam's phantom weapons of mass destruction that intentionally skirts how the $40-billion-a-year intelligence was molded and manufactured to fit the ideological schemes of those running the White House and the Pentagon' (Maureen Dowd, 'The Latest Intelligence Study: 601 Empty Pages', *IHT*, 4 April 2005).

international legitimacy   What José María Aznar, then Prime Minister of Spain, declared he needed in a conversation with President George W. Bush on 22 February 2003. Millions had been marching in angry opposition to the imminent invasion of Iraq in Spanish cities and Aznar pleads, 'We need your help with **our public opinion**.' Bush replied that he could get the necessary UN Security Council resolution – international legitimacy – by exerting economic and diplomatic pressure on its members. And if they did not comply, '**we'll go** . . . anyway'. The second UN resolution in favour of the invasion was never achieved; hence Aznar did not get his necessary backing, and, on 15 March, a year after the invasion of Iraq that began on 19 March 2003, he was voted out of office by the Spanish electorate. For Bush's feelings of impatience at the time, see **Chinese water torture** (Mark Danner, 'The Moment Has Come to Get Rid of Saddam', *NYRB*, 8 November 2007).

Iraqi face   Denotes the 2005 Pentagon **public diplomacy** policy of putting an 'Iraqi face' on the war, in other words that Iraqi commanders, and not Americans, should be the ones seen to be talking to reporters. Initially the policy backfired when Iraqi commanders failed to step forward, leaving a news vacuum that allowed the insurgents' successful attacks, not their failures, to dominate news coverage (John F. Burns and Eric Schmitt, 'Generals Offer a Sober Outlook on Iraqi War', *The New York Times*, 19 May 2005).

Iraqi Media Network   In 2003 the Coalition Provisional Authority (CPA) in Iraq set up this radio and television network with Dr Ahmad

Al-Rikabi, a former London bureau chief of the US-funded Radio Free Iraq, as its head. On his resignation two years later, Al-Rikabi said, 'I accepted [the job] with the dream of creating, as the Americans had promised, a free and high-quality mass media but the whole project was in the hands of one company that was only concerned about raking in money. The corruption was huge. It began with an initial investment of 60 million dollars and what it ended up doing wasn't even worth a million. There were Americans charging 800 or 1,000 dollars a day and the Iraqi who risked his life by appearing on the screen was only paid 120.' Al-Rikabi speaks of the CPA period as the time 'when there were American tribes in Baghdad'. See **Radio Dijla**. The seasoned American journalist Don North also quit, saying that the IMN was being used as an organ of **public diplomacy** and was as such an 'irrelevant mouthpiece for Coalition Provisional Authority propaganda, managed news and mediocre programs.' Closing an article explaining his resignation, North quoted John Milton, speaking before the British Parliament in 1644, 'Let truth and falsehood grapple. Who ever knew truth put to the worse, in a free and open encounter?' ('Iraq: One Newsman's Take on How Things Went Wrong', *Television Week*, 15 December 2003; Luis Prados, 'Bagdad al habla', *El País*, 14 April 2005; 'US Journalist Quits Pentagon Iraqi Media Project Calling It US Propaganda', *Democracy Now*, 14 January 2004, www.democracynow.org/2004/1/14/u_s_journalist_quits_pentagon_iraqi).

Iraq Survey Group   Military unit, drawn from US and British personnel, set up to analyse large quantities of documents and other material found in Iraq after the 2003 war and relating to a possible Weapons of Mass Destruction (WMD) programme. Based in a US military base in Qatar, the ISG was much referred to immediately after the war, as a possible source of evidence for the existence of WMD, but it soon slid into obscurity. One reason is believed to be that many of its personnel, translators and others, were sent to Iraq to deal with the deteriorating security situation there. On a visit to Qatar in February 2004, the author asked the British Embassy to arrange a visit for him to the ISG: 'I am sorry I cannot help you on that one', the senior diplomat in question replied, professing never to have heard of the unit.

Iraqi National Congress   Coalition of Iraqi exiles set up in 1992, in the Kurdish region of Northern Iraq, with the aim of encouraging US invasion, a term modelled, without much real similarity, on the African National Congress of Nelson Mandela. Following the 2003 invasion, and the emergence of new, and some old, political parties and factions within Iraqi politics, the INC faded from view.

irresistible sweeteners   One of many sudden reverses in US policy in Iraq after 2003, carrot-instead-of-stick attractive policies, designed to win back hitherto alienated and disregarded Iraqi Sunnis, part of Senator Joe Biden's **soft partition plan** for Iraq. The word 'irresistible' has, however, a subcurrent of menace, and coercion, redolent as it would be to any English speaker at that time, of the expression taken from the film on the mafia, *The Godfather*, 'an offer he cannot resist'.

J

jirga   Pashtu for tribal council, used for some of the more formal elected bodies in post-2001 Afghanistan.

K

Karbala moment   The US Ambassador to Iraq Ryan Crocker, commenting on Prime Minister Nuri Kamal al-Maliki's ill-conceived attempt to 'restore order' in Basra (where 'He went in with a stick and poked a hornet's nest', according to one coalition official), said, 'I think for him it was a Karbala moment'. He was suggesting that Maliki was impetuously outraged by militia violence in Basra and had rushed there, hoping for the success he had had in the Shi'i city of Karbala in central Iraq several months earlier. However, an unnamed 'US intelligence officer' opined that the Iraqi leader was more concerned with weakening the **Mahdi Army** and political party of the Shi'i cleric Muqtada al-Sadr before provincial elections to be held in January 2009 (Michael R. Gordon, Eric Schmitt and Stephen Farrell, 'As Iraq's "Defining Moment" Unravels, US Cites Poor Planning', *IHT*, 4 April, 2008).

Kharshi   Town in Uzbekistan used after 9/11 by US forces for operations in Afghanistan and Central Asia. Generally held to be the reason for US indulgence of the dictatorial activities of Uzbek President Karimov's regime in the name of the war against terrorism.

known unknowns, unknown unknowns   Terms used in an uncharacteristic moment of epistemological speculation by former US Secretary of Defense Donald Rumsfeld. Thus, in a statement in February 2002 he said: 'Reports that say that something hasn't happened are always in-teresting to me, because as we know, there are known knowns; there are things we know we know. We also know there are known unknowns; that is to say we know there are some things we do not know. But there are also unknown unknowns – the ones we don't know we don't know' ('Rumsfeld in His Own Words', BBC News, 8 November 2006, http://news.bbc.co.uk/2/hi/americas/6130316.stm). Had Rumsfeld or any of his advisers done the most elementary course in philosophy, they would have been aware of the elementary principle that you cannot prove a 'negative existential'; i.e. you cannot be sure something like pink elephants, or cheese on the moon, does not exist.

L

Little America   Emblematic, but short-lived, area of intense US devel-opment efforts after 2001: with the fall of the Taliban, the town of Lashkar Gah became the focus of the US-led stabilisation effort and Afghans called it 'Little America.' By 2005 it was an epicentre of the Taliban resurgence (David Rohde, 'Afghanistan's "Little America" Unravels', *IHT*, 5 September 2005).

little more than aggressive camping organisations   Charac-terisations of other European armed forces by British officer Colonel Tim Collins (*BBC Radio*, 'The World Tonight', 12 January 2007). Collins also referred to his European counterparts as a *Home Guard*, this being the name of a ramshackle militia of older men, unofficially known as 'Dad's Army', established in Britain in 1939–40 to offer resistance to a possible German invasion, object of many jokes, satirical TV series, etc.

livin' the dream   Sardonic summary of the British military mission in Afghanistan. Painted in two-feet-high letters on the mess hall wall of the British base in Lashkargar, Helmand Province, southern Afghanistan, this became the unofficial motto of the troops stationed there. 'I'm just **livin' the dream**' is given as an answer to almost any question a journalist asks (Richard Westmacott, 'We're Living the Dream, Joke Soldiers Stretched to Limit', *The Daily Telegraph*, 4 September 2006).

local power brokers   Term used in a 2005 British survey of opium pro-duction in Afghanistan to designate Afghans who bribed local farmers in Nangahar to abandon poppy cultivation with promises of lots of aid. How-ever, while US$300 million had been allocated for eradication of poppies, only $120 million was earmarked for alternative livelihoods: consequently, the British report saw 'a strong potential' for a resurgence of cultivation in the province ('Fewer Poppies, for the Present', Jalalabad correspondent, *The Economist*, 16 April 2005). Reports from three years later, in 2008, more than confirmed this latter prognosis.

M

Mahdi Army Arabic *jaish al-mahdi*, 'the army of the *Mahdi*'. Irregular Iraqi force, mainly recruited from unemployed youth in Baghdad and core Shi'i cities such as Najaf and Kufa, by clerical leader Muqtada al-Sadr, from 2003. Used to stage high-risk theatrical seizure of Imam Ali mosque in Najaf in July 2004, later mobilised for political and, sometimes, military confrontation with US forces.

mainlining Originally term for injection of narcotics into the blood, used in the run-up to the 2003 Iraq War by US officials to denote inclusion of suspect Iraqi opposition material in the official intelligence process. See, in older idiom, **threat inflation**.

Mayor of Kabul Derogatory term for Afghan President Mohammad Karzai. See also Chapter 2, **Karzai of Riyadh**.

Mayor of Ramallah Ironic term for Palestinian President Mahmoud Abbas, used by Palestinians and Israelis alike. See **Ramallah model** (Henrique Cymerman, 'Mahmoud Abas declara illegal el brazo armado de Hamas en Cisjordania', *La Vanguardia*, 18 June 2007).

Mayor of the Green Zone Derogatory term for Iraqi Prime Minister Nuri Kamal al-Maliki.

Medal of Freedom The highest civilian medals the US President can give, awarded to Coalition Provisional Authority head Paul Bremer, 2003 invasion commander General Tommy Franks and CIA Director George Tenet for their 'contributions' in Iraq.

metric Pseudo-scientific US method for evaluating the success of the troop **surge** in Iraq in 2007–8. When the Bush administration had to account for its policy on 11 September 2007, a White House spokesman wriggled clear with the excuse that only 'a little bit of metric' was available for measuring success. For his part, Peter Pace of the Joint Chiefs of Staff argued that the rise in troop deaths was the 'wrong metric' for this exercise (Frank Rich, 'They'll Break the Bad News on 9/11', *IHT*, 24 June 2007).

Miles Davis of the war   Eccentric and frivolous characterisation of Shi'i militia leader Muqtada al Sadr by *International Herald Tribune* writer Edward Wong. The use of the famous jazz trumpeter's name does not refer to anything musical but to the Iraqi flexibility in policy and action, Wong characterising al Sadr as 'a great improviser' (Edward Wong, 'Rhetoric aside, Sadr Needs US – for Now', *IHT*, 25 April 2007).

military promenade   English version of French *promenade militaire*, term initially used of a 1667 campaign that captured Lille, Douai and other towns, where *promenade* refers to a leisurely walk. More accurate translation might be 'armed stroll'. See **cakewalk**, equivalent term used prior to 2003 invasion of Iraq by neoconservatives.

Millennium Challenge 2002   Large-scale and, even in simulated terms, seriously misconducted US war manoeuvres, designed to prepare for real action in the Gulf, against Iraq and/or Iran. This was the biggest war game of all time – $250 million worth – planned for two years and involving integrated operations by the US army, navy, air force and marines. The exercises were partly real, with 13,000 troops spread across the USA, supported by actual planes and warships, and partly virtual, generated by sophisticated computer models. It used Hollywood blockbuster techniques (as in *Gladiator*) with real soldiers in the foreground and digital legions. The retired marine playing the role of Saddam Hussein, Lieutenant General Paul Van Riper, won the battle in a few days using surprise tactics that sank most of the US expeditionary fleet in the Persian Gulf, bringing the US assault to an inglorious halt. Faced with the embarrassing situation of having lost 16 warships to swarming tactics by enemy speedboats, the Pentagon pretended it had not happened. They ordered their dead troops back to life, 'refloated' the sunken fleet and instructed the enemy forces to let their marines go ahead with amphibious landings. Van Riper, objecting to the cheating, refused to play any more. 'Nothing was learned from this', he says. 'A culture not willing to think hard and test itself does not augur well for the future.' The exercise, he says, was rigged almost from the outset. Officially, America won and a rogue state was liberated from an evil dictator (Thom Shanker, 'For Navy, Gulf Incident Offered a Vision of 9/11 at Sea', *IHT*, 12–13 January, 2008; Julian Borger, 'Wake-up call', the *Guardian*, 6 September 2002).

Mission Accomplished   Triumphalist banner erected by the crew of the US aircraft carrier *Abraham Lincoln*, off the California coast on 1 May 2003 as a backdrop to the Iraq victory speech by George W. Bush, who, no doubt for added triumphalist effect, arrived on deck clad in an airman's flight suit. Many more Americans were to die in Iraq after this date than in the preceding war itself.

mission accomplished first   According to one platoon leader in Iraq, referring to military command's concern to manipulate the news, in the Marines 'it's mission accomplished first, troop welfare second' (Sue Halpern, *NYRB*, 18 December 2008).

Missouri moment   Imagined final and formal surrender of the enemy, never attainable in either Afghanistan or Iraq, in reference to the Japanese formal surrender on the deck of the *USS Missouri* at the end of World War II, invoked at the end of Kuwait War in 1991 and other wars as a model for concluding hostilities.

moral idealism   See **projects of a missionary style**.

most dangerous five kilometres of road in the world   The drive into town from the Baghdad airport. In the words of John Garratt, managing director of *Erinys*, a British security company with over 1,000 employees in Iraq, 'the worst operating environment as far as safety goes anywhere I've ever known' (Roger Cohen, 'Iraq's Intricate Theater of Dawning Democracy', *IHT*, 12–13 February, 2005).

N

nation-building   US political term that confuses 'nation' with 'state'; should be called 'state-building' or 'state-construction'. Originated in the 1960s and 1970s to denote the positive process of building the state and its core institutions – armed forces, civil administration, judiciary – in newly independent countries. Revived in the late 1990s under the George W. Bush administration, first as a term of contempt for preceding President Bill Clinton's policies in Bosnia and Haiti (as the fashionable neo-con phrase had it, 'We do not do nation-building'); then, after the wars in Afghanistan in 2001 and Iraq in 2003, it was used to describe the US occupation policies in these countries with the suggestion that the military effort was being matched by a serious political commitment. Thus, initially, the Bush administration was opposed to this project, regarded as associated with the liberal idealism of the Clinton period: George W. Bush notoriously remarked, 'I don't think our troops ought to be used for what's called **nation-building**. I think our troops ought to be used to fight and win war.' After 2005, however, US soldiers were being used to promote 'democracy in the Middle East', and Bush then claimed that America has 'the ultimate goal of ending tyranny in our world'. See also **do**.

national caveats   Limits imposed by participant countries on their military forces operating under multilateral command. Often expressed reservations by sending states at real intentions of US commanders. General James Jones, NATO's Supreme Commander, objected in 2005 to 'national caveats' on troop movements in Afghanistan, prompting former US Defense Secretary Donald Rumsfeld to call for more **flexibility**, meaning freedom from the national rules of engagement and restrictions on operations to which forces under NATO command are subject (Demetri Sevastopulo and Peter Spiegel, 'Rumsfeld Calls for More Flexibility from Nato Troops', *FT*, 13 September 2005).

National Intelligence Estimate   US government evaluation, as in October 2002 a 93-page NIE of Iraq, of an intelligence issue, or specific country. The Iraq report was a rushed job, written under considerable pressure, and was later discredited. In the words of one intelligence analyst, Thoms Fingar, in a speech in February 2008, 'It was requested. We were given a two-week period in which to produce it. And it was bad. It was really bad ... The percentage of analysts who participated in the production of that hurry-up, get-it-out-of-the-door-in-two-weeks product was tiny compared with the larger set, all of whom were tarred with the same brush of incompetence' (Spencer Ackerman, 'The American Way of Spying', *The Nation*, 14 July 2008). At one point, when the CIA did not produce material supporting the White House's claims on weapons of mass destruction in Iraq, they were told to '*re-look*' at the evidence.

negative attitude/positive attitude   Options for UN Security Council members, as defined by President Bush, in the days preceding the invasion of Iraq. See **Chinese water torture** (Mark Danner, 'The Moment Has Come to Get Rid of Saddam', *NYRBs*, 8 November 2007).

neo-Taliban   Taliban forces involved in the post-2001 war with the US and other troops in Afghanistan. Contrasted to the 'old Taliban' of the

1990s in adopting a more international *jihadist* rhetoric and in actively using new military and informational technologies (Antonio Giustozzi, *Koran, Kalashnikov and Laptop. The Neo-Taliban Insurgency in Afghanistan* [London: Hurst, 2007], p. 236).

next round   Pre-2003 reference to anticipated, and, by use of term from boxing ring, supposedly inevitable and legitimate, relaunch of a war already commenced with Iraq.

nightmare with no end in sight   General Ricardo Sanchez, commander of US forces in Iraq for a year after 2003 and in command when the Abu Ghraib prisoner abuses occurred, has described the US mission in Iraq in these terms. He described the invasion as a '**catastrophically flawed plan**' and the 2007 **surge** of additional troops as a 'desperate attempt by the administration that has not accepted the political and economic realities of this war' (*Los Angeles Times*, www.latimes.com/news/nationworld/world/la-na-sanchez13oct13,0,5708908.story?coll=la-home-center). The use of the word **nightmare**, like other exculpatory words such as **mess** and **quagmire**, obscures the responsibility of the USA for creating the difficulties in the first place.

Northern Alliance   In Afghanistan, a loose group of non-Pashtun guerrillas opposed to the Taliban, and comprising *mujahidin*, mainly Tajiks and Uzbeks, who held power in Kabul from 1992 to 1996. Their leader, Ahmad Shah Masud, was fatally wounded in an assassination attack two days before 9/11. It is reasonable to surmise that these events were connected. They formed a part of the post-2001 Kabul regime, with a special presence in the intelligence services.

not idyllic but very good   Characterisation of the situation in Iraq on the fifth anniversary of the invasion of Iraq, by former Spanish Prime Minister José María Aznar, one of the **Gang of Four** Western leaders who had endorsed the March 2003 action at a meeting in the Azores. When Aznar spoke, recent surveys had shown that between 80,000 and 90,000 Iraqi civilians had lost their lives since the invasion, that four and a half million people had abandoned their houses, that there was at least 60 per cent unemployment, that more than 40 per cent of the population was at the extreme poverty threshold and that 70 per cent of the population did not have access to drinking water. Nonetheless, Aznar said that the situation was 'less difficult' than in the times of Saddam Hussein as 'there is freedom in the country, with the possibility of establishing a democracy and more security'. One day after Aznar's assertion, 56 people were killed in an attack by a female suicide bomber on Shiʻi worshippers in the city of Karbala ('Aznar asegura que "la situación in Irak es muy buena"', *El País*, 19 March 2008). See **public diplomacy**.

not uplifting   Evasive term for depressing, not to say disturbing. Thus an 'unidentified source' described in these words a classified report on the **Babel of war assessments** in post-occupation Iraq (Michael Isikoff and Mark Hosenball, 'Got Him. Now What?', *Newsweek*, 16 May 2005).

O

Office for Reconstruction and Humanitarian Assistance   Ironically named administrative body tasked with running post-invasion Iraq, later **Coalition Provisional Authority**.

Office of Special Plans   Soviet-sounding unit set up within the Pentagon and intelligence community by US Secretary of Defense Donald Rumsfeld and his assistant Paul Wolfowitz to push the case for a link between Iraq and **Al-Qa'ida** and to plan for the post-conflict situation in Iraq. Bypassed regular defence and intelligence bodies.

off-message   Conventional US, later UK, government **news management** term for journalists, or political figures, who do not repeat the official line, and either wander from or contradict official policy, hence are not *on message*. After the 2003 invasion of Iraq, the US-led coalition in that country generally excluded journalists who were not American or British, in particular those, such as the correspondent of *al-Jazeera* TV, who were deemed to be 'off-message'. See **Channel with a reputation** (Steve Tatham, *Losing Arab Hearts and Minds: The Coalition, Al Jazeera and Muslim Public Opinion* [London: Routledge, 2007]).

oil for food   Programme introduced by UN Security Council in 1996 by which Iraq was allowed to export stipulated quantities of oil and in turn, under supervision, import food and other necessities. Later associated with large-scale corruption within UN monitoring, purchasing and administration systems, and with systematic Iraqi circumvention of rules by use of a practice known as 'the coupons of Saddam', whereby oil was given to foreign associates of Iraq and they were able to take a percentage of the sales in return for providing Iraq with unmonitored revenue.

oil stain approach   Apparently technical term in counter-insurgency, derived from French 1950s application to Algeria, *tache d'huile*, involving concentration of forces in particular areas and then spreading control out from these. Thus, in 2006 the Washington think-tank, the Brookings Institution, called for the USA to change its counter-insurgency strategy in Iraq, advocating what it termed the 'oil stain approach' of shifting forces away from western Iraq and into major urban centres and 'economically sensitive areas' (Holly Yeager, 'Disunity on Iraq Could Hit Democrat Poll Hopes', *FT*, 27 February 2006).

Old Rumsfeld   At the 41st Munich Conference on European Security Policy in February 2005, Rumseld attempted a 'seduction offensive'. Asked about his derogatory reference to 'old Europe' two years earlier when countries including Germany and France opposed the invasion of Iraq, he replied, 'That was the old Rumsfeld' (Marc Bassets, 'Rumsfeld intenta seducer a Europa', *La Vanguardia*, 13 February 2005).

Operation Enduring Freedom   Term finally given to the US campaign against its opponents, after abandonment of earlier versions, such as *Infinite Justice* (this latter was said to be offensive to Muslims, since Allah is the only source of such an action). See **bargain, Enduring Freedom**.

Operation Telic   Codename for British participation in the 2003 invasion of Iraq (and afterwards). One of the largest deployments of British forces since World War II, with an original total of 46,000 troops from all the British Services committed. In the planning phase around Christmas 2002, it was said that the letters of the name stood for 'Tell Everyone Leave Is Cancelled' (Steve Tatham, *Losing Arab Hearts and Minds: The Coalition, Al Jazeera and Muslim Public Opinion* [London: Routledge, 2007]). The official position on operational codenames for the British armed forces is that they are chosen, at random, and are without inherent meaning or message. For what it is worth, **Telic** could mean 'having a *telos* or goal', i.e. being directed or tending towards a purpose, 'purposeful'.

optimist/at peace with myself   How President George W. Bush described himself to Spanish Prime Minister José María Aznar in the days just prior to the US invasion of Iraq. Aznar had just ventured, 'The only thing that worries me about you is your optimism'. See **Chinese water torture** (Mark Danner, 'The Moment Has Come to Get Rid of Saddam', *NYRB*, 8 November 2007). For his part, Aznar was to declare years after the invasion that he was **not worried** by the situation; he, in assisting Bush, had helped create in Iraq.

P

package   VIPs protected by **private security contractors**, such as **Blackwater**, in Iraq.

Pakhtu/Pashtu/Pushtun   Linguistic community organised into tribes comprising over 40 percent of the Afghan population, and that of the neighbouring North-West Frontier Province in Pakistan. Its main cities are Kandahar and Jalalabad in Afghanistan and Peshawar in Pakistan.

pariah   Tamil for a caste whose members perform unclean activities, particularly leatherwork and shoemaking; later 'outcast'. In international relations of the 1990s, it was a term used for states with which the USA has major security conflicts: Iran, Iraq, North Korea and Afghanistan.

PDPA   People's Democratic Party of Afghanistan, a communist party founded in Kabul in 1965, probably the last communist party founded anywhere in the world. Persian: *hizb-i dimukrat-i khalq-i afghanistan.* In power from 1978 to 1992: leaders included Nur Muhammad Taraki (1978–9), Hafizullah Amin (1979), Babrak Karmal (1979–86) and Najibullah (1986–92). Taraki was murdered in October 1979 by Amin, who in his turn was killed by Soviet forces in December 1979; Karmal was ousted by Soviet pressure in 1986 and died later in exile in Moscow; Najibullah fell to the *mujahidin* in April 1992, lived for four years in the UN compound in Kabul and was captured, tortured and hung, along with his brother, when the Taliban took Kabul in September 1996. From 1978 to 1979 the party was dominated by the *khalq* (people) faction, and from 1979 to 1992 by *parcham* (flag).

Plame Affair   Scandal involving CIA clandestine operative Valerie Plame, whose professional identity was leaked to the Washington Press by White House officials, in order to discredit and put pressure on her husband, Joseph Wilson, a US diplomat who, sent to the African state of Niger to substantiate a story that Iraq was illegally acquiring uranium from that country, reported that there was no evidence to back up the case.

Plan for Victory   New name for his Iraq policy that was introduced in a major address by President George W. Bush at the end of 2005 in Annapolis, Maryland; the words were written large on a screen. This followed such manifestly failed notions such as 'greeted as liberators' and 'insurgency in its last throes' (Vice-President Cheney). Six months after the **Plan for Victory**

flourish, Bush had to acknowledge that 'the violence in Baghdad is still terrible', while Secretary of State Condoleezza Rice tried a generalising praise-with-faint-damnation gloss, 'confessing' that the USA had made 'tactical errors, thousands of them' (Jim Rutenberg, 'As War Worsens, White House Alters Message', *IHT*, 7 August 2006). Later in 2006 came the **surge**.

poppy palaces   Buildings constructed in Kabul by warlords, government officials and drug traffickers on the basis of profits generated by the heroin trade.

Por el imperio hacia Dios   The motto of Generalísimo Francisco Franco, El Caudillo de España (1939–75), 'Through the empire to God', slogan that found a latter-day echo in President George W. Bush who claimed he was told by God to invade Iraq and attack Osama bin Laden's stronghold of Afghanistan as part of a divine mission to bring peace to the Middle East, security for Israel and a state for the Palestinians. The former Palestinian foreign minister Nabil Shaath says Bush told him and Mahmoud Abbas, now Palestinian President, about his first-name-terms relationship with God: 'I'm driven with a mission from God. God would tell me, "George, go and fight those terrorists in Afghanistan." And I did, and then God would tell me, "George go and end the tyranny in Iraq," and I did.' He then told the two Palestinian leaders, 'I feel God's words coming to me: "Go get the Palestinians their state and get the Israelis their security, and get peace in the Middle East." And by God, I'm gonna do it' (Rupert Cornwell, 'Bush: God Told Me to Invade Iraq', *The Independent*, 7 October 2005).

positive domino theory   Neoconservative US view, popular prior to 2003, that the overthrow of the Ba'thist regime in Iraq would set off a democratic wave elsewhere in the Arab world. By contrast with the *(negative) domino theory* of the Cold War, especially in regard to the Vietnam War of the late 1960s and early 1970s, according to which a communist victory in one state, in this case Vietnam, would lead to the fall of other states, i.e. the *dominoes*. Term derived from speech in 1954 by then US President Dwight Eisenhower in which he spoke of 'the "falling domino" principle' (speech of 7 April 1954, quoted in *The Oxford Dictionary of Quotations*, fourth edition [Oxford: OUP 1992], p. 268).

potential marriage   Term commonly used in American prenuptial negotiations and speculations, applied fancifully by extension by the Bush administration to possible, but not actualised, alliance of Saddam Hussein's

regime with **Al-Qa'ida** prior to the 2003 Iraq invasion. Part of the justification for the policy of **pre-emption**. The **potential** of such an alliance
was one of the arguments used to justify the **pre-emptive/preventive** attack
on Iraq in that year. Much of the argument in favour of this story rested on
a meeting in Prague between an official of the Iraqi Embassy there and an
Al-Qa'ida envoy. The story, which is believed to have come from sources
in Czech intelligence, was without evidential support. Later attempts to link
the Saddam regime to **Al-Qa'ida** rested upon the supposed collaboration of
the two in supporting a small Islamist military group active against the two
main parties in Iraqi Kurdistan. In her analysis of the Nazi extermination
campaign in World War II, Hannah Arendt notes that the Jews of Eastern
Europe were killed for being 'potential enemies' (*Eichmann in Jerusalem*
[London: Penguin Twentieth-Century Classics, 2006], p. 106).

pre-emption Political, and sometimes, legal term used to justify attacking an enemy first, often confused with **prevention**. In conventional English
language parlance, **pre-emption** denotes an attack on an enemy that *is said
to be*, on reasonable (but sometimes fabricated) evidence, about to attack,
whereas **prevention** means attacking an enemy that *might* do something in
the future. Proclaimed as the central plan in US foreign and defence policy by
President George W. Bush in speech to the US Military Academy, West Point,
in January 2002, hence application of the term **Bush Doctrine** to it. The USA
use of the term **pre-emption** in regard to Iraq before March 2003 was thus
a misnomer: in the run-up to March 2003, Iraq was *not*, on any evidence,
about to attack the USA, the UK or, indeed, any of their Middle Eastern Allies. On the other hand, such action, had it been taken in a timely and decisive
fashion, could have prevented the Iraqi invasion of Kuwait in August 1990.
The most famous examples of the **prevention** were the US pursuit of nuclear
superiority in the Cold War, designed to **prevent** the USSR from gaining
strategic nuclear parity, and the outbreak of the Peloponnesian War in 404
BC, when Sparta attacked Athens because it 'feared the rise' of the latter's
power (as famously analysed by the historian Thucydides, in a passage much
cited to justify the US nuclear weapons programme during the Cold War).

private security contractor Commonly used euphemism for **mercenary, soldier of fortune**, especially in the context of the Afghanistan and
Iraq Wars post-2001.

private warrior Euphemism for mercenary, soldier of fortune. See
Blackwater.

progress   Much overused word, repeated at different moments during the initial, deteriorating years of the US occupation in Iraq to support claims of positive military and political development. Thus, speaking of the situation in Iraq in October 2003, President George W. Bush said that the USA was making 'really good progress'; in September 2004, Iraq was making 'steady progress'; in April 2005, the USA was making 'good progress' there. In October 2005, Iraq had made 'incredible political progress', and, one month later, it was 'inspiring progress' (Nicholas D. Kristof, ' "Inspiring Progress" on Iraq?', *IHT*, 13 July 2007). In fact, for the first three years of the US occupation at least, the situation by any criteria continued to deteriorate. Cf. expression much used by comparably overoptimistic Soviet commentators on the situation in Afghanistan after the Red Army entry of December 1979, *the situation is returning to normal.*

Project for the New American Century   Group established in 1997 by the right-wing intellectuals William Kristol and Robert Kagan that advocated a projection of American power and values across the world, by military means, if necessary, in contrast to the prevailing post-Cold War thinking on foreign policy. In 1998 PNAC sent a letter to then president Bill Clinton urging him to topple Saddam Hussein. Among the signatories of this letter were the coterie of neoconservatives and hawks later associated with the 2003 invasion of Iraq: Richard Perle, Paul Wolfowitz, Donald Rumsfeld and John Bolton. A 2006 BBC report claims PNAC has now been reduced to 'a voicemail box and a ghostly website' (BBC Newsonline, 21 December 2006).   *(Entry not written by the author – Ed.)*

promptings   Divine messages, as in claim by George W. Bush that he had been the recipient thereof. See *Por el imperio hacia Dios.*

protecting the Development Fund for Iraq   Phrase covering incompetent, intrusive and massively corrupt US administration of Iraqi oil revenues after March 2003. Formally, the title of *Executive Order 13303* issued by President Bush on 22 May 2003, granting authority to take control of Iraqi oil and oil revenues, officially to ensure they were spent on 'Iraqi reconstruction.' The same day, the *Development Fund for Iraq* was created by UN Resolution 1483, replacing the UN-controlled **Oil for Food** Programme which used Iraqi oil revenues to purchase food and medicine. The new Fund came under the control of the **Coalition Provisional Authority** (CPA) headed by Paul Bremer, who answered to George W. Bush. Even though the Fund was on the books of the Iraqi Central Bank, the money was kept in the Federal Reserve Bank of New York. By October some $5 billion had gone to the fund, of which, according to a report by Christian Aid in the UK, over $4 billion was missing. This 'missing' figure soon rose to $8.8 billion. The first CPA head of finance, David Oliver, resisted bringing in external auditors and ran the fund in a highly idiosyncratic manner. He was unable to explain where the $8.8 billion had gone: 'I have no idea, I can't tell you whether or not the money went to the right things or didn't – nor do I actually think it is important,' he is reported to have said. See **executive orders** (Mark Gregory, 'Baghdad's "Missing" Billions', *BBC News*, 9 November 2006, news.bbc.co.uk/2/hi/business/6129612.stm).

purely by military means   Throughout the first year of the **insurgency** in Iraq, the USA insisted it would be tackled 'purely by military means'. 'Bring them on', said President Bush in July 2003. 'We have the force necessary to deal with the security situation' (Fareed Zakaria, 'Like a Country without Oxygen', *Newsweek*, 16 May 2005).

Q

questioned and unsupported costs   Term applied to some $2,700 million that US Federal investigators found were unaccounted for in US Army contracts held by the contracting company **Halliburton** (known for having US Vice-President Dick Cheney as its chief executive officer from 1995 to 2000) and its government contracting unit KBR in Iraq. See **BRAC for Iraq, Glennville, Halliburton, sole source contracts** (Perry Williams, 'From Houston to Dubai', *MEED*, 16–22 March 2007).

R

Radio Dijla   Otherwise known as *Radio Tigris*, Iraq's first independent talk radio station, founded by Dr Ahmad Al-Rikabi, a former London bureau chief of the US-funded *Radio Free Iraq*. Callers were free to express their opinions as long as they did not incite violence: at its height, it was receiving up to 18,000 calls a day, the majority condemning violence. In May 2007 – World Press Freedom Day – **Radio Dijla** was attacked and completely destroyed by 80 **Al-Qa'ida** supporters. The subsequent station press release stated: 'In spite of being informed and during such a long period, no positive action by the Iraqi authorities was noted. The situation was treated with negligence, and as a consequence, **Radio Dijla** was left a smouldering wreck.' See **Iraqi Media Network** (Luis Prados, 'Bagdad al habla', *El País*, 14 April 2005).

Rambo from West Virginia   Term of approbation coined in 2003 by US armed forces in public relations attempt to portray Private Jessica Lynch, badly wounded in Iraq, as popular hero. Private Lynch was badly wounded in 2003 when her convoy was ambushed in Iraq and was subsequently rescued by American troops from an Iraqi hospital. However, she made a point of rejecting the official story of her heroism, saying that, '... the American people are capable of determining their own ideals of heroes and they don't need to be told elaborate tales'. When she was wounded, she was riding on the back of a truck and not fighting and hence declined to accept her official depiction as a **Rambo from West Virginia**. See **Deliberate and careful misrepresentations** (Michael Luo, 'Army Lied, US Athlete's Brother Says', *IHT*, 25 April 2007).

raspberry   As in the British colloquial phrase '*to blow a raspberry*', meaning to voice considerable scepticism about something, roughly equivalent to the US term 'a Bronx cheer'. Used by British government official John Morrison, adviser to the parliamentary *Intelligence and Security Committee*, to describe his reaction to Prime Minister Blair's claim that Iraq posed a 'serious and current threat' to the Kingdom. Later he was quoted by the BBC as saying: 'When I heard him using these words, I could almost hear the collective **raspberry** going up around Whitehall'. After the broadcast of this programme, Morrison's contract with the ISC was not renewed, and he was given 90 days to leave (the *Guardian*, 26 July 2004).

raw power and victory   Citing *Middle East Quarterly* editor and academic Martin Kramer, neocon journalist Charles Krauthammer proposes that '[t]he way to tame the Arab street is not with appeasement and sweet sensitivity but with raw power and victory.' See **Arab street** (Charles Krauthammer, 'Victory Changes Everything', *Jewish World Review*, 30 November 2001).

Right Man   Title of a 2003 book by David Frum, the man who is attributed with coining the phrase **axis of evil,** *The Right Man: The Surprise Presidency of George W. Bush*. According to Frum, 'George W. Bush was hardly the obvious man for the job. But by a very strange fate, he turned out to be, of all unlikely things, the right man' (Amazon advertisement for the book, www.amazon.com/Right-Man-Inside-Account-White/dp/0812974905).

ripple of change   Purportedly cautious, but optimistic, term, used by prime minister Tony Blair about what he saw in 2005 as positive changes in the Middle East, reminiscent of the *wind of change* speech made by Harold Macmillan in 1960 about Africa. In Blair's usage, it was both celebrating the notion of change and being used as a warning to Syria to comply with international demands. See **democratisation industry** (Ewen MacAskill and Jonathan Freedland, 'Blair Hails "Ripple of Change" in Middle East', the *Guardian*, 2 March 2005). What Blair and/or his advisers seemed not to have noticed was the contrary process, *a tidal wave, tsunami, shock wave or whatever* of violent opposition to the West, and to Britain and the USA in particular, resulting from the 2003 invasion of Iraq.

rules of engagement   Conventional legal and military term for rules governing use of force, in particular opening fire, on the part of armed forces. Often used to remove blame from individuals guilty of abusive behaviour: thus at a military court hearing at Fort Bragg in September 2007, it emerged that two US soldiers had been cleared in an earlier army investigation of shooting and killing an unarmed Afghani man who had offered no resistance when encountered on 13 October 2006, because they had been operating under 'rules of engagement' that empowered them to kill individuals who have been designated 'enemy combatants,' even if the targets presented no visible threat. The soldiers considered that this was a textbook example of a classified mission completed in accordance with the American rules of engagement. See **flexibility** and **national caveats** (Robert Parry, 'Bush's Global "Dirty War"', *Consortium News*, 1 October 2007).

S

saddest acre in America   Section 60 of Arlington National Cemetery, near Washington, where around ten of the US Iraqi War dead were buried. By March 2008, this figure had passed the 4,000 mark.

safe areas/safe havens   1990s term for regions, such as the Kurdish regions of northern Iraq, and the Bosnian enclaves surrounded by Serbian forces in former Yugoslavia, where international forces committed themselves to protecting populations, without declaring formal territorial control, annexation or trusteeship. Maintained, with some Iraqi incursions, in Kurdistan, notoriously not in regard to the enclave of Srebrenica, declared a **safe area** by UN Security Council Resolution 819 of 16 April 1993, where an estimated 8,000 Bosnian men and boys were killed by Serbian troops in July 1995.

sahwa See **awakening**.

Salman Pak Town near Baghdad said to have housed Iraqi nuclear facilities, repeatedly attacked by Western air forces. Named after Salman al-Farisi, 'Salman the Persian', one of the *ansar* (companions) of the Prophet – and the first Persian to convert to Islam – who is buried there.

Salute to the Troops Title of four-day celebration, coinciding with the second Bush presidential inauguration bash in January 2005, a party thrown by the Reverend Lou Sheldon of the **Traditional Values Coalition** at the Ritz-Carlton in Washington. This was a 'four-day bacchanal' resembling 'the martial pageantry broadcast by state-owned networks in banana republics'. According to *The Los Angeles Times*, there was 'nary a mention' of the Iraq war or the price paid by US troops and their families. Judy Bachrach, a *Vanity Fair* writer, who noted on **Fox News** that the 'military ball and prayer service would not keep troops "safe and warm" in their "flimsy" **Humvees**', was quickly told she had been allowed 'more than your time'. At the Red, White and Blue inaugural ball, Nile Rogers and Chic sang 'Clap Your Hands' and 'Dance to the Beat' to a group of soldiers missing hands and legs. A total of $40 million was spent on the celebrations (Frank Rich, 'A Quagmire for the MTV Attention Span', *IHT*, 29–30 January 2005).

sanctions fatigue 1990s term for growing international abandonment of sanctions as a legitimate took of pressure on states, a change from the earlier belief that they were a more humane, and hence preferable, alternative to military action. Twin of exculpatory term *compassion fatigue*, increasing reluctance of Western governments, and publics, to help the needy elsewhere in the world.

SEAL US naval special forces, under Naval Warfare Special Command. Short for *SeaAirLand*.

selling the threat Closely linked to the concept of 'threat inflation', this is a process by which governments seek to mobilise public support for military action by promoting alarmist analyses. In this case, the actions taken by the US and UK governments to mobilise support for the 2003 Iraq War.

Seven Dwarfs US intelligence term for the seven Afghan guerrilla groups funded via Pakistan in the 1980s, also known as 'the Peshawar Seven', after the town in Pakistan from which they operated. The term was also applied in the 1960s to IBM and its six mainframe rivals. Cf. use of term *Seven Sisters* to refer to seven major oil companies of this time. It was these groups that, after the collapse of the Soviet-backed regime in April 1992, attempted to take power but instead plunged Afghanistan into another civil war, which ended only when the Taliban drove them from power in 1996. How, and indeed if, the Afghanistan guerrillas of the 1980s could be reconciled with the original *Snow White* story in which the dwarfs appear is not specified, nor which political forces corresponded to Princess Snow White, the ugly Queen, and, of course, Prince Charming. All seven of the Afghan guerrilla groups could be said to fit the character of the ill-tempered and ungrateful dwarf *Grumpy*. All seven of these groups were drawn from the Sunni part of the population, the two Shi'i groups being supported by Iran. Ayatollah Khomeini, contemptuous of the Peshawar group, and presumably unaware of the *Snow White* story, referred to them as *islam i imrikai*, 'American Islam'.

sexed-up Puerile British official term, used in connection with Hutton enquiry, on threat inflation and exaggeration of intelligence material pertaining to Iraq. Implies that the thing (or person) so treated is, like intelligence data, completely passive, an anthropologically improbable premise. See **selling the threat**.

sexing up Iraq British Prime Minister Tony Blair and his Director of Communications, Alastair Campbell, were accused of this. The term was widely used in particular after an article in the *Mail on Sunday* stated that Campbell had been responsible for adding the claim that Saddam's weapons of mass destruction could be launched within 45 minutes to the dossier that presented the government's case for war against Iraq. See also **gin up** (Maureen Dowd, 'Unleash John Bolton', *IHT*, 28 April 2005).

Shh! Concerned exclamation by Dr Ira Katz, head of mental health services for the US Veteran Affairs Department, in regard to the apparently high incidence of suicide attempts amongst US war veterans. Katz wrote to a colleague: '*Shh!* . . . Our suicide prevention coordinators are identifying about 1,000 suicide attempts per month among the veterans we see in our medical facilities. Is this something we should (carefully) address ourselves in some sort of release before someone stumbles on it?' In November 2007, Katz denied before the House Veterans' Affairs Committee that there was any suicide epidemic among veterans returning from Afghanistan and Iraq, asserting that there had been 'only' 790 attempts in all of 2007 (Editorial, *The New York Times*, 11 May 2008).

shell game   Term used by US officials to describe what they claimed was an Iraqi policy of moving prohibited military equipment and related documentation around from place to place to avoid detection by UN weapons inspectors.

Shock and Awe   US military policy developed as a retrospective counter to mistaken, incremental, 'turning the screw' policy used in Vietnam and later blamed for US defeat there. 1991 'Desert Storm' was an example of this new approach, later applied in 2001 and 2003. The air war in Kuwait 1991 was *Instant Thunder* as opposed to the Vietnam War's *Rolling Thunder* (Lawrence Freedman, *A Choice of Enemies. America Confronts the Middle East* [London: Weidenfeld and Nicolson, 2008], pp. 235–6). It was also believed that the application of overwhelming force would convince the enemy that resistance was hopeless and thus reduce American casualties.

shoe thrower   The 28-year-old journalist, Muntadar al-Zaidi, employee of *Baghdadia TV*, Cairo, who threw both his shoes at President George W. Bush during the latter's farewell press conference in Baghdad, December 2008. 'This is a farewell kiss from the Iraqi people, you dog!' he shouted. Many offers to buy the Turkish-manufactured shoes were then made, including one $10 million bid from a Saudi businessman. In tribute, the American 'Deadline Poet', Calvin Trillin, penned the following lines:

> To most Americans it came as news:
> To show your disrespect you throw your shoes
> Directly at the guy you're disrespecting
> (When shoes are not at all what he's expecting).
> Should this catch on here in the USA.
> It's possible George Bush should stay away
> From, say, New Orleans. Otherwise, I'd posit
> He'd see more shoes than in Imelda's closet
> *(The Nation,* 12–19 January 2009)

In the event, President Bush did not need to go anywhere: within days of the Baghdad protest, demonstrators in Washington, DC, were hurling shoes over the White House fence and into his front garden.

short, sharp war   What, according to Prime Minister Tony Blair, the attack on Saddam Hussein's Iraq in 2003 was going to be, British equivalent of *Mission Accomplished* (David Bromwich, 'Euphemism and American Violence', *New York Review of Books*, 3 April 2008). See **military promenade**.

shout, show, shove, shoot   According to *Time*, an 'easy mnemonic'. US Marine Corps rules of engagement in Iraq required patrol members to observe this four-step procedure, a way to 'distinguish friend from foe'. However, it was acknowledged that 'sometimes emotions take over' and step four becomes step one (Michael Duffy, Tim McGirk, Bobby Ghosh, 'The Ghosts of Haditha', *Time*, 4 June 2006).

Sit Room   Short for *Situation Room*, synonym for a command centre, in this case a 5,000-square-feet conference and **intelligence management centre** in the basement of the West Wing of the White House (Martin Amis, 'The Long Kiss Goodbye', the *Guardian*, 2 June 2007).

small group of dead-enders   Originally seriously underestimated assessment of Iraqi opposition by Washington. According to the Bush administration, the violence in occupied Iraq was caused by these people. Later, it was said to be fuelled by a **handful of foreign terrorists**. Hence there was no political dimension to the **insurgency**, and hence the anger of the disempowered Sunnis was not deemed relevant (Fareed Zakaria, 'Like a Country without Oxygen', *Newsweek*, 16 May 2005).

snowflakes   Informal thoughts and memos of US Secretary of Defense Donald Rumsfeld. Dictated into a hand-held tape recorder and then typed by an assistant, between 20 and 60 of these memos fell every day from Rumsfeld's desk: instructions included the need to 'keep elevating the threat', 'link Iraq to Iran' and develop 'bumper sticker statements' to rally support for an increasingly unpopular war. Against the ropes in April 2006 when op-ed articles by retired generals were calling for his resignation, Rumsfeld produced another snowflake stating: 'Talk about Somalia, the Philippines, etc. Make the American people realize they are surrounded in the world by violent extremists.' Another one announced that people 'rally' to sacrifice and 'Sacrifice = Victory'. In May 2004, Rumsfeld was wondering whether it might be better to rename the war against terrorism a fight against '**worldwide insurgency**': he asked his aides to 'test what the results could be' if the war on terrorism were renamed, while he noted in the same memo that, thanks to their oil wealth, Muslims are detached 'from the reality of the work, effort and investment that leads to wealth for the rest of the world. Too often Muslims are against physical labor, so they bring in Koreans and Pakistanis while their young people remain unemployed'. And he pronounced that '[a]n unemployed population is easy to recruit to radicalism'. The final **snowflake** noted, 'Announce that no matter whatever new approach the USA decides on, the USA is doing it on a "trial basis". This will give us the ability to read-just and move to another course, and therefore not lose.' One long-serving Rumsfeld aide remarked of the **snowflakes**, 'And, oh, by the way – unlike the ones found in nature – two can be alike' . . . 'Two. Sometimes more. Lots more can be alike' (Robin Wright, 'From the Desk of Donald Rumsfeld', *The Washington Post*, 1 November 2007; Thom Shanker, 'Buzzwords', *The New York Times*, 24 December 2006).

Snows of Valley Forge   One of the several, fanciful, historical ana-logues used by US Secretary of Defense Donald Rumsfeld to describe the fighting in the 'sandstorms of central Iraq'. Also invoked, in regard to sur-viving the financial crisis, by President Obama in his Inaugural Address of January 2009. The phrase refers to an incident during the American War of Independence in the winter of 1777–8, when George Washington and his army struggled to survive freezing conditions and snow at Valley Forge, Pennsylvania: they did, and a stronger army emerged. Presumably the con-trast between snow and desert is meant to have some oxymoronic appeal. In portraying the war in Iraq, and seeking to invest it with borrowed histor-ical legitimacy, Rumsfeld also deployed World War II incidents, comparing battles in Iraq with the June 1944 D-Day landings on Omaha Beach, Nor-mandy, and the Battle of Guadalcanal, a protracted battle between US and Japanese forces over an island in the South Solomon islands that lasted from August 1942 to February 1943 (Frank Rich, 'Donald Rumsfeld's Dance with the Nazis', *IHT*, 4 September 2006). The name *Guadalcanal* is in origin the Arabic for a town in Andalusia, north of Seville, the local Pacific Islander name being *Istabu*.

soft-partition plan   Variation, adapted for Iraq, of the blueprint for dividing Bosnia in 1995, devised by Senator, later Vice-President, Joe Biden. Biden envisaged a **loose Kurdistan**, a **loose Shi'astan** and a **loose Sunnistan**, under a big Iraq umbrella. According to Biden, the plan offered **irresistible sweeteners** for the Sunnis to participate (Helene Cooper, 'A Plan to Heal Iraq by Splitting It Apart', *IHT*, 31 July 2007).

solatia   Payments by US forces in Iraq for deaths or physical damage.

sole source contracts   Euphemism for unvetted, often corrupt, alloca-tion by US official agencies of contracts, to friends and cronies. Applies to US defence and services contracted to **Halliburton** in the aftermath of the 2003 Iraq War. According to the Government Accountability Office, war costs for the fiscal year 2004 alone were $12.3 billion above Pentagon estimates.

sparrow   Vice-President Dick Cheney's 2003 Christmas card flaunted a quotation from Benjamin Franklin: 'And if a sparrow cannot fall to the ground without His notice, is it probable that an empire can rise without His aid?' Cheney seemed to be suggesting that God is on the side of the USA and its project in Iraq but Franklin was talking about humility (Nicholas D. Kristof, 'The God Gulf', *The New York Times*, 7 January 2004).

Special Activities Division   Secret unit of the CIA, consisting of small irregular paramilitary groups of about half a dozen men, who do not wear military uniform. As of 2001, when the Division was being used for covert operations in Afghanistan, it was believed to comprise around 150 members, consisting of fighters, pilots and specialists. The **Division** was equipped with helicopters, airplanes and the unmanned Predator drone.

Stability First/Redeploy and Contain   Options remaining for US forces in Iraq, as formulated in late 2006 by Congressional bipartisan *Baker-Hamilton Report*. It ruled out the prospect of establishing a democracy, then considered two option papers: **Stability First** argued that US troops should focus on stabilising Baghdad, while US diplomats negotiated a settlement with insurgents. **Redeploy and Contain** called for a phased withdrawal, although retaining the ability to strike from a distance (Michael Howard, 'Iraq Cancels Peace Talks after Scores More Die', the *Guardian*, 16 October 2006). The *Baker-Hamilton Report*, despite having the support of members of Congress from both parties, was ignored by the Bush White House.

Stone Age   Where Pakistan would be bombed, in a threat made by Richard Armitage, then Deputy-Director of State in the Bush administration, to Pakistan's intelligence director if his country did not help the USA in its struggle against terrorism. President Pervez Musharraf is reported to have said that this was 'a very rude remark' ('Bush Was "Taken Aback" by US Threat to Pakistan', *IHT*, 23–24 September 2006).

stop-loss   US policy, introduced in 1973, after introduction of volunteer army after Vietnam War, of involuntary extension of a soldier's active term of duty, beyond normal combat period of two to four years, with the aim of maintaining combat unit cohesion, applied to over 58,000 US troops in Iraq up to June 2008. Denounced by Democratic candidate John Kerry in 2004 as a **backdoor draft**. In 2007, the *Iraq Veterans Against the War* launched a *Stop the Stop-loss* campaign.

surge   Increase in US troops levels in Iraq in 2007–8, supposedly the cause of the decrease in violence, especially in Baghdad. Largely illusory, as violence continued at levels higher than in any other city in the world, while much of the decrease was due either to the unilaterally declared ceasefire by the Mahdi Army or to the fact that the forcible division of the city into solely Sunni or Shi'i areas had been in large measure completed.

sustainable stability Redefinition of success in Iraq by forces command General Petraeus 2007. See **avert failure**.

T

Talib, **plural: Taliban** The singular is Arabic, plural tullab, the plural form Taliban being Persian and Pashtu: literally a religious student. After 2001, the plural form was increasingly used in press reports as a singular, like *agenda, data:* thus references to 'an American Taliban'. It was taken as the name of the movement and was based on recruits from Deobandi *madrasas* in Pakistan in 1994, which went on to capture Kabul in 1996 and control Afghanistan until 2001. The term has echoes of 'Students (*daneshjuan*) Following the Imam's Line', the group of Iranians who seized the American Embassy in Tehran on 5 November 1979.

the right people Ordinary inhabitants of a conflict-riven country, such as Afghanistan, who were supposed to receive foreign aid but often did not: thus in early 2007 it was estimated that up to half of all aid to Afghanistan failed to reach 'the right people' – i.e. it was stolen on the way (Antonio Giustozzi, *Koran, Kalashnikov and Laptop. The Neo-Taliban Insurgency in Afghanistan* [London: Hurst, 2007], p. 215).

Thief of Baghdad Title of one of the best known stories of the *Arabian Nights* and subject of modern versions in cinema and stage, especially the 1940 Hollywood version; more recently applied to Iraqi exile politician Ahmad Chalabi. See **George Washington of Iraq**.

threat inflation Standard Cold War practice, exaggerating Soviet military capability and intentions, recycled for use against Iraq prior to 2003. For critiques of earlier Cold War distortion, see Andrew Cockburn, *The Threat*, and Fred Halliday, *The Making of the Second Cold War* (London: Verso, second edition, 1986). On the 'Islamic threat', see Fred Halliday, *Islam and the Myth of Confrontation* (London: I.B.Tauris, 1996). That a threat is *inflated, exaggerated*, etc. is not the same as saying it is wholly *invented*: the Soviet Union *did* have nuclear missiles, and some millions of troops, targeted at Western Europe and the USA, and some Islamic militants *do* want to attack the West, kill Christians and Jews, and convert the whole world to their branch of Islam. The issue is one of accuracy as to capability.

three-legged stool argument　Argument that US policy in Iraq had to make progress on three fronts – military, but also economic and political – to succeed. Used to justify the February 2007 'surge' in Iraq, but also taken up by 'moderate' Democrat Representative Tim Mahoney of Florida in explaining his change of heart over Iraq policy, to one of opposition, on grounds of the financial costs of the war. As late as July 2007, after a visit to Iraq, he was quoted by a Republican press release in a Florida newspaper, while attempting to establish himself in a firm centrist position in a traditionally Republican district, as saying that the escalation had really gotten **Al-Qa'ida** 'on their heels'. Later, his, revised, argument was that, while things had improved militarily [*sic*], '. . . everybody I talked to at the beginning of the surge back in February all said the same thing, "**This is a three-legged stool.**" There has got to be economic progress. We haven't seen it. There has got to be political progress – nonexistent.' He added, 'We put the $100 billion in, and two legs of this stool are broken, the two things the army can't solve' (David M. Herszenhorn, 'A Moderate Democrat Hardens His Stance on Iraq', *IHT*, 4 September 2007).

toothpicks　As in the observation by UN weapons inspector Hans Blix that the Iraqi *Al-Samoud 2* missiles, which Baghdad had begun to destroy after 1998, were not 'toothpicks'.

Town Square Test　Slogan of Israeli politician (minister for Jerusalem and Diaspora Affairs) and former Soviet dissident Natan Sharansky, whose book *The Case for Democracy. The Power of Freedom to Overcome Tyranny and Terror* (co-authored by Ron Dermer) was obligatory reading in White House circles. In January 2005, Condoleezza Rice declared that it would guide her policy: 'The world should apply what Natan Sharansky calls "the **town square test**": if a person cannot walk into the middle of the town square and express his or her views without fear of arrest, imprisonment or physical harm, then that person is living in a fear society, not a free society. We cannot rest until every person living in a fear society has finally won their freedom.' The book's arguments may be summarised as follows: freedom is attainable for every person on Earth; it is the best guarantee of global security; fear societies are dangerous because they are always seeking an external enemy; to act on the above requires 'moral clarity' and this means 'recognizing that the great divide between the world of fear and the world of freedom is far more important than the divisions within the free world'. Again, it asserts that, 'When it comes to promoting democracy and human rights across the globe, the values and interests of the free world are one and the same'. Sharansky also describes the Israeli sweep through the West Bank town of Jenin in 2002 as 'one of the finest examples in history of a democracy protecting human rights in wartime', asserting that the widespread condemnation of the Israeli actions as brutal resulted from 'an environment that lacked moral clarity.' George W. Bush declared that Sharansky's thinking is 'part of my presidential DNA' (Elisabet Bumiller, 'White House Letter: Bush Borrows a Page from Natan Sharansky', *IHT*, 31 January 2005; Roger Cohen, 'The View of Democracy Forged in Totalitarian Prisons', *The New York Times*, 12 February 2005). If a different, equally commonsensical, criterion, namely the *second hand car salesman test*, had been applied to the nomination and election of US Presidents, history might have been a bit different. See **positive domino theory**.

true believers   Phrase popularised by 1951 book by social psychologist Eric Hoffer, *The True Believer*, a study comparing, and in considerable measure equating, fascism, communism and religious extremism, including that of early Christians. Denotes positive attitude to belief, faith, unquestioned values. According to US soldiers in Iraq, they went to that country as 'true believers' in their mission, but over time were disabused of their patriotic faith. On 29 April 2007, a patrol in the Shi'i enclave of Khadimiya engaged in a two-and-a-half-hour gun and rocket-propelled grenade fight with insurgents, after Iraqi army and police checkpoints had been abandoned. Among the dead were at least two Iraqi army soldiers who had been armed and trained by American forces. Captain Douglas Rogers called the fight a 'watershed moment', adding, 'Before that fight there were a few **true believers**. After the 29th, I don't think you'll find a true believer in this unit.' Neither, did it appear, were US-trained Iraqi security forces anything similar: one US squad leader, Sergeant Kevin O'Flarity estimated that '[h]alf of the Iraqi security forces are insurgents' (Michael Kamber, 'With Allies in Enemy Ranks GIs in Iraq Are No Longer True Believers', *IHT*, 28 May 2007). Whether the term could be applied to supporters of **Al-Qa'ida** is another matter.

U

unfinished business   Term applied in 1990s by neoconservatives to policy on Iraq, in this case, the need for the complete removal of Saddam

Hussein's regime that was not carried through at the end of the Kuwait War in 1991. Also applied in 2008 by President George W. Bush and his aides to bring six Guantánamo detainees to trial and to seek the death penalty. Explaining this **unfinished business**, the President declared: 'We've gone on the offense [*sic*] against these extremists. We're staying on the offense, and we will not relent until we bring them to justice' (Steven Lee Myers, 'Focus of Sept. 11 Trial Could Suit President's Agenda', *IHT*, 13 February 2008).

ungoverned spaces   Term for countries that, while not 'failed states', in whole or in part lack effective administration in control, particularly the **Federally Administered Tribal Areas** of Pakistan and much, or all, of Afghanistan and Yemen. Since they were also advocating that the Bush administration should **unleash the CIA** especially in Afghanistan and Pakistan, one might also surmise that these two countries come under the same heading (Daniel Benjamin and Steven Simon, 'Unleash the CIA', *IHT*, 25 July 2007). See **Federally Administered Tribal Areas.**

uninvited guests   Description of US and British position in Iraq given by Iranian President Ahmadinejad in an interview with Jon Snow on Channel 4 TV, 12 September 2007. By contrast, and in this case with some reason, the Iranian leader spoke of his country's good relations with Iraq: 'We have historical good relations with the Kurds in Northern Iraq and the President of Iraq is Kurdish and friendly and sincere with us ... We also have a sincere relationship with the Sunni sect in Iraq, the head of the Iraqi Parliament is Sunni and he has a very good relationship with us and also the prime minister of Iraq is Shi'a and has a good relationship with us. Your problem, the problem of British and the USA is that you do not have good relations with any of them. The problem is that you are **uninvited guests**' (www.channel4.com/news/articles/politics/international_politics/full+transcript+ahmadinejad+interview/797347). A somewhat similar observation could, however, be made of the presence in the Kurdish regions of Iran itself of the President and of the organisation he was long involved with, in part in suppressing local Kurdish movements, the Islamic Guards, or *pasdaran*. Early on in his post-revolutionary career, in the early 1980s, Ahmadinejad himself is believed to have taken part in the bloody suppression of the movement for autonomy in Iranian Kurdistan.

unity of effort   Policy, more honoured in the breach than in reality, of co-ordinating different military forces in Afghanistan after 2001. The US forces engaged in fighting the Taliban as part of **Operation Enduring**

Freedom, being often at cross purposes with, and undermining the political and civil goals of, the other international contingents, 36 in all, in the International Security Assistance Force, the most important being from fellow NATO states ('Fatal Errors in Afghanistan', *The Economist*, 23 June 2007).

UN route   One of the options Bush was weighing prior to his 2003 invasion of Iraq was to obtain **international support** via a resolution of the UN Security Council. However, and despite the presentation by US Secretary of State Colin Powell of false intelligence information to the Council, this option was discarded, among other reasons because waiting for the report of the UN weapons inspectors that might have validated the attack on Iraq was, for Bush, like **Chinese water torture**. In other words, the decision to attack Iraq had already been taken, some time in the summer of 2002, and the President did not feel like waiting any longer. In the end, of course, the UN inspectors found no **weapons of mass destruction**, nor did the Western group set up after the invasion to find corroborative evidence, the **Iraq Study Group** (Mark Danner, 'The Moment Has Come to Get Rid of Saddam', *NYRB*, 8 November 2007).

UN's Abu Ghraib   Amateur pornographic videos shot by a French UN logistics expert who worked at Goma airport in the Democratic Republic of Congo – and on sale in the country – unleashed a sex scandal that some observers have described as the **UN's Abu Ghraib**. The case drew attention to rampant sexual exploitation of Congolese girls and women by the UN's 11,000 peacekeepers and 1,000 civilians. Investigators soon had 150 allegations of sexual misconduct by peacekeepers and UN staff despite the UN's official policy of 'zero-tolerance'. There were 68 allegations of misconduct in the town of Bunia alone ('Un Français impliqué dans le scandale des abus sexuels commis par des employés de l?ONU au Congo', *Le Monde*, 14 February 2005).

UNSCR 678   UN Security Council resolution of November 1990, authorising use of 'all necessary means' against Iraq, the legal and political basis for the January 1991 war to drive Iraq out of Kuwait.

V

VBIED   See **IED**.

vehicle-based insurgency   Characteristic of Iraqi actions against US troops, the first insurgency to be so characterised.

venerated cleric   Positive term used by Western media and diplomats to denote favoured Iraqi clergyman Ayatollah al-Sistani, the opposite of the **radical/renegade/wanted cleric**, his opponent and rival, Mortada al-Sadr.

very strong humanitarian package   Political mission accompanying, and in the eyes of the Bush administration justifying, the 2003 invasion of Iraq, and a reason for ratification by other states of a second UN resolution that would give **international legitimacy** to this action. According to President Bush the invading US forces were taking with them a **very strong humanitarian package**. See **Chinese water torture** (Mark Danner, 'The Moment Has Come to Get Rid of Saddam', *NYRB*, 8 November 2007).

W

war of choice/war of necessity   Terms much used in Washington during the second Bush administration to justify attacks, specifically those on Iraq in 2003, that did not respond to an immediate threat, as opposed to the Afghan War of 2001, which was 'of necessity', a direct response to the 9/11 attack. Linked to **Bush Doctrine** and the concept of **pre-emption**. The originating source appears to have been a speech by Israeli Prime Minister Menachem Begin in August 1982, justifying the attack on Lebanon and its goal of eliminating the PLO in that country. Begin, citing religious and historical examples, distinguished between those wars fought by Israel which were unavoidable, 'wars of necessity' and 'no-choice wars', namely 1948–1949 War of Independence, the 1968–1969 War of Attrition and the 1973 October war, from those that were decided upon by Israel in 1956 and 1967. In Begin's argument, the wars of choice involved Israel in much lower casualties than the wars of necessity, a judgement which the subsequent 18 years in Lebanon did something to erode, as did the US experience in Iraq.

weapons of mass destruction-related program activities   Phrase in President George W. Bush's January 2005 State of the Union address, when he asserted that 'the Kay Report identified dozens of **weapons of mass destruction-related program** activities'. The phrase appears to mean that, although the US armed forces had in the end found no evidence of Iraq having *WMD*s, it was still intent on constructing nuclear weapons.

'We'll go'   President Bush himself was clear: with or without a UN resolution – **international legitimacy** – America was, by early 2003, ready to invade Iraq. 'If anyone vetoes, **we'll go**', he declared. See **Chinese water**

torture (Mark Danner, 'The Moment Has Come to Get Rid of Saddam', *NYRB*, 8 November 2007).

we're moving in the right direction   Standard line of US officials on the situation of occupied Iraq at the height of insurrection (Jim McGovern, 'What I Didn't See in Iraq', *The Nation*, 2 May 2005). Cf. repeated Soviet phrase re: Afghanistan in the 1980s, *the situation is returning to normal.*

Whopper   Name given by fellow soldiers to US Marine who, desiring to **get some**, shot two unarmed teenage boys herding camels at a distance. So called because **Whoppers** are sold by the fast-food chain *Burger King*, whose initials, *B.K.*, also stand for 'baby killer' (Sue Halpern, 'The War We Don't Want to See', *NYRB*, 18 December 2008).

Y

Yellowcake   Name given to a type of uranium ore. In the run-up to the invasion of Iraq, both the British and American governments referenced claims that Saddam Hussein had tried to buy uranium in this form from Niger. Joseph Wilson, a former ambassador sent by the CIA to investigate these claims, wrote in an op-ed in the *New York Times* that he had declared them to be unfounded before Bush cited them in his 2003 State of the Union address, leading to a dramatic conflict involving Wilson, the media establishment, the CIA, the Vice-President's Office and a Grand Jury known as the **Plame Affair**. The IAEA later declared that the evidence on which the claim that Iraq was trying to buy yellowcake from Niger was forged. *(Entry not written by the author – Ed.)*

youngest democracy in the world   President Bush's somewhat premature, if well-intentioned, description of Iraq after the elections of January 2005 (Fernando García, 'Bush pasa revista a los aliados europeos', *La Vanguardia*, 21 February 2005).

CHAPTER 5

Some Islamic and Middle Eastern Vocabulary

A

Abadgaran Short name of the alliance of Iranian political parties and organisations *I'tilaf-i Abadgaran-i Iran*, 'The Alliance of Developers of Iran', which elected Mahmoud Ahmadinejad the President of Iran in June 2005. The Alliance was founded just before the local council elections of 2003, embodying a rebellion by younger conservatives against the old guard who were dominating the decisions of the right-wing religious parties. The root of the word ***abadgara*** – *abadi* conveying a sense of rural roots and values – implies work of rural construction; hence the word is best rendered as 'developer', 'promoter of development': the implicit contrast is with the title of the coalition associated with President Rafsanjani, former reformist and main rival of Ahmadinejad in 2005, *kargozaran-i sazandegi*, 'the workers of construction'. The title suggests a populist appeal: Ahmadinejad's grouping is claiming to be closer to the people and the poor than the organisation associated with the established clerical elite, often accused of being corrupt and involved in shady business dealings, associated with Rafsanjani. Despite having considerable political pluralism, and elections and parliamentary votes that exhibit major and shifting differences of policy and leadership, the Islamic Republic of Iran does not recognise the existence of political parties in the proper sense. It is also worth noting that for all the emphasis on Islam, religious values and **Shi'i** symbols in the image of the Islamic Republic, the main political groupings all have secular titles, reflecting developmental, nationalist and populist values. See *hizb*, **Hezbollah**.

Abu Literally Arabic for 'father of', much used in terms of familial affection, political and military pseudonyms, general formulation denoting respect, etc. **Umm**, 'mother', is later also used colloquially to denote special importance or size, similar to English 'super-', e.g. the term used by Saddam Hussein for the war over Kuwait in 1991, **umm al ma'arik**, 'the mother of all battles'. See, for examples, Chapters 1, 2 and 7.

Abu Markub   A curious but engaging historical use of the Arabic patronymic 'Abu', *not* an **Al-Qa'ida** operative, but a large East African bird, found in marshlands from Sudan to Zambia, related to pelicans or storks. Its unusually large, shoe-like bill has given it the English name 'shoebill' or 'whalehead' and in Arabic *abu markub* from the word *markub*. The name **Abu Markub**, applied to a particular bird, was immortalized in a story about the Berlin zoo after the city was captured and largely destroyed in April and May 1945. *The Last Battle*, written some 40 years ago by the American reporter Cornelius Ryan, finishes with an account of the Berlin zookeeper named Schwarz, who had made superhuman efforts to keep the animals alive through World War II. After fighting ended, he walked through the devastation calling for the animal he loved most, the bird with the Arabic name. 'There was a fluttering. At the edge of the empty pool was the rare **Abu Markub** stork, standing on one leg and looking at Schwarz. He walked through the pool and picked up the bird. "It's all over, Abu", said Schwarz. "It's all over." He carried the bird away in his arms' (quoted by Simon Carr, 'Art Means Never Having to Say You've Got Nothing to Say', *The Independent on Sunday*, 3 June 2002). Similar stories were told about the animals in Kabul zoo, some of whom survived the successive Afghan wars of 1978–2001, particularly the lion **Marjan**.

Against Islam   Arabic *dhudd al islam*, all-purpose excuse for Middle Eastern and other Muslim states, as well as for patriarchs, clerics and other defenders of traditional authority, for discrediting critical or independent ideas. Examples: The Saudi government's rejection of calls by liberal citizens for a constitutional monarchy, the Sudanese government's rejections of human rights organisation reports on atrocities in Darfur, the Iranian government's denunciation of calls for freedom of speech in Iran, sundry *fatwas* or other condemnatory rulings by the Egyptian, Saudi, etc. grand **ulema** of views or interpretations of the Quran or Islamic law that they do not like. Similar in intent, and wide application to 'Anti-American', and, before 1991, 'anti-Soviet'.

akhund   Persian term, of popular and often disparaging character, for a Muslim cleric. Hence *akhundism*, term used in post-revolutionary Iran by secular critics of the Islamic clerical regime. Whence *Postakhundism*, below. In English literature, the word occurs in the Edward Lear poem 'The

Akond of Swat', where it refers to the ruler of a district of Pakistan, much more recently, in 2008–9, the scene of a major Islamist insurgency (see Chapter 10). The neutral Muslim terminology for a member of the clergy includes *'alim'*, plural *'ulema'*, literally 'a knowledgeable person', and, in Shi'i countries, *mullah*, 'my master', itself similar to Hebrew *rabbi* (correct transcription *maula*, from which *maulana* 'our master', used of clergy in South Asia and of Arab monarchs).

`alim, **plural:** *ulema*   Arabic normal term for a Muslim clergyman, literally someone proficient in *'ilm*, knowledge or science. In Iran also known as *mullahs*. Formally, Islam does not have an equivalent of the Christian sacrament of ordination, hence no 'clergy' or 'priests' in the Christian sense, or a clear clerical hierarchy, with bishops, cardinals, etc., but in practice the *ulema* perform this role. See *'ilm, mullahs.*

al-Jazeera   Arabic: 'island', 'peninsula'. Since 1996 the name of a popular pan-Arab satellite TV station based in Qatar, later also broadcasting in English. While controversial on some issues, this station was in no sense an independent or free entity, or an emblem of some new 'civil society' in the Arab world, controlled as it was by the country which funded it, Qatar. In Arabic *al-jazira* is the conventional word for the Arabian Peninsula, or what in English, but not in Arabic, is termed 'Arabia'. Also in plural, *al-jiza'ir*, 'the islands', origin of geographic term Algeria, reflecting the geographic reality that, with tracts of desert surrounding them, peninsulas are, to all intents and purposes, like islands. Osama bin Laden often claimed that the Arabian Peninsula, site of the two most holy places in Islam, had been kept pure of external corruption by dint of being 'surrounded by water'.

Arab Tony Blair   Disparaging name for King Abdullah of Saudi Arabia (Martin Amis, 'The Long Kiss Goodbye', the *Guardian*, 2 June 2007).

Arab Pinochets   Term applied by French scholar of the Arab world, Professor François Burgat, to pro-Western regimes seen by **Al-Qa'ida** and others as legitimate targets (Isabel Ramos Rioja, 'Entrevista a François Burgat, experto en islamismo', *La Vanguardia*, 13 November 2007).

asceticism   Arabic *zuhd* quality espoused by some Muslim leaders, who gain legitimacy in contrast with the lavish lifestyles and expenditure of the majority elite. Ayatollah Khomeini, Osama bin Laden and the Palestinian *sheikh* Ahmad Yasin all exemplified this quality. Opposite of all-purpose category of 'corruption', *fisad.*

ayatollah   Arabic for 'Shadow' or 'Sign' of God, high clerical title in Shi'i Islam, widely used in Iran and Iraq. The supreme *ayatollah* may be known as *marja al taqlid*, 'the Source of Inspiration', a title applied to Ayatollah Khomeini, leader of the Iranian Revolution and head of the country from 1979 to 1989, but not to his successor Ayatollah Ali Khamene'i. After the Iranian Revolution, it became a term for an opinionated and dogmatic person, hence 'secular ayatollahs'. See Chapter 7 *Israel's Ayatollahs.*

B

bara'a   Muslim term for 'refutation' or 'denunciation'. While not one of the five core obligations of Islam, this practice, in prayers, sermons and meetings, is considered a religious obligation and forms the justification for the speeches of political denunciation of the West which Muslim clerics are commonly heard to utter. Also used in the 1980s as justification for anti-American demonstrations by Iranian pilgrims in Mecca.

baraka   Arab for 'fortune', 'blessing', from which is derived the first name of the 44th President of the USA, Barack Obama, and the French slang, of North African derivation, for 'good luck', *baraka*.

Ba'thism   From the Arabic word *ba'th*, 'revival', a militant nationalism, drawing on fascist ideas of war, leadership and blood, as well as racial superiority, in this case Arab, but also on communist forms of state and party organisation. Ideology of the *Arab Ba'th Socialist Party*, in power in Iraq since 1968 and in Syria since 1963.

bats   Arabic *khaffash*, in Middle Eastern usage and related political terminology not associated, as in English, with madness, but with birds of the night that are scattered and driven out by the light of, respectively, Islam or **Ba'thism**. Used by Saddam Hussein in 1990 when describing the flight of the Al-Sabah ruling family from Kuwait after the invasion by Iraqi troops.

beating heart   As in the Syrian regime's claim that Damascus is the 'beating heart of Arabism', *qalb nābid lil-'uruba*. In reply, the Lebanese columnist Samir Kassir applied this term to Beirut – the city which had suffered most from Syrian, as well as Israeli, assault in recent decades, after the massive demonstration in that city's Martyrs' Square on 14 March 2005. Kassir, who was soon assassinated by killers assumed to be Syrian agents, stated that the 'Arab nationalist cause has shrunk into the single aim of getting rid of regimes of terror and coups, and regaining the people's freedom as a prelude to the new Arab renaissance. It buries the lie that despotic systems can be the shield of nationalism. Beirut has become the "**beating heart**" of a new Arab nationalism' (David Hirst, 'The Syrian Dilemma', *The Nation*, 2 May 2005).

behind   As in 'Who is behind this?', Arabic *min warā'a*. Frequent response to a particular event, terrorist attack, assassination, with suggestion, sometimes true, of a broader conspiracy or international connection.

Busharraf   Derogatory Pakistani term for pro-Washington President Musharraf. Cf. **Arab Pinochet, Arab Tony Blair,** *mamluk*.

C

Caliphate   From Arabic *khilafat*, itself from *khalifa*, 'a successor' (of the Prophet Mohammad), the form of government enjoined by Islam and continued by Sunni states and empires until the abolition by Turkey in 1924, adopted in reaction by newly emerging Muslim political group in India, the *Caliphate Movement*, more recently revived by groups such as **Al-Qa'ida** and *Hizb al-Tahrir* who call for its restoration. Never precisely defined, the contemporary term denotes an unquestioned authoritarian ruler. The word came to be widely used, in a polemical and negative sense, in Washington circles to discredit the Islamist movement, after Vice-President Dick Cheney used it on the hustings in Lake Elmo, Minnesota, during the 2004 Presidential election campaign. According to former-CIA-analyst-turned-scholar Kenneth Pollack, 'They recognise there's a lot of resonance when they use the word "caliphate"'. In Lake Elmo, referring to bin Laden and his followers, Cheney warned, 'They talk about wanting to re-establish what you could refer to as the seventh-century caliphate' and this will be 'governed by *Shari'ah* law, the most rigid interpretation of the Quran'. For Donald Rumsfeld, 'Iraq would serve as the base of a new caliphate to extend through the Middle East, and which would threaten legitimate governments in Europe, Africa and Asia'. General Abizaid (Commander of the US Central Command, overseeing American military operations in a 27-country region, from the Horn of Africa, the Arabian Peninsula, to South and Central Asia, covering much of the Middle East) declared to the House Armed Services Committee in September 2004, '[t]hey will try to re-establish a caliphate throughout the entire Muslim world', adding that among its goals would be to destroy Israel. 'Just as we had the opportunity to learn what the Nazis were going to do, from Hitler's words in "Mein Kampf" . . . we need to learn what these people intend to do from their own words' (Elisabeth Bumiller, 'Watchword of the Day: Beware the Caliphate', *IHT*, 12 December 2005).

Camel Corps   Originally camel-mounted cavalry, part of British armed forces deployed in the Middle East in the campaign against Ottoman forces during World War I (and of which there is a fine, low-key, group sculpture Victoria Embankment Gardens next to Charing Cross Station, London), later applied to specialists on the Arab world in the British Foreign Office, suspected of pro-Arab sympathies, including a group of British former diplomats who protested, in 2005, at government policy in Iraq (Steve Tatham, *Losing Arab Hearts and Minds, The Coalition, Al Jazeera and Muslim Public Opinion* [London: Routledge, 2007], p. 20). Contrast with *sherpas*, Nepalese climbers and porters used to assist and accompany Western mountaineers on Mt. Everest, later term applied to officials of a head of state or prime minister who prepared ground and negotiations prior to summit meetings.

capitulationist   Arabic *istislami*. Term of nationalist and fundamentalist abuse for agreements that betray national interests, e.g. make peace with Israel.

CENTCOM   US 'Central Command', long based in Florida and set up after the Iranian Revolution of 1979, unit responsible for Persian Gulf security. Base for the *Rapid Deployment Force* of the 1980s. Organising framework for 1991 Kuwait, 2001 Afghanistan and 2003 Iraq wars. Later moved to the Persian Gulf state of Bahrain.

Conservative Democrats   Term used in some Muslim countries, especially Turkey, by analogy with German, and former Italian, 'Christian Democrats', but avoiding explicit 'Muslim Democrats' to present their Islamist parties as reconciling democratic principle and practice with religious affiliation, as the European Conservative Democrats had done with Catholicism in the post-war period. Turkish Prime Minister Recep Tayyip Erdogan told reporters, 'What you write about the AKP [Justice and Development Party] makes me sad'. He rejects the label 'Muslim democrats' for his party because 'it exploits religion', insisting that AKP is a party of 'conservative democrats' (Vincent Boland, 'A Reformer Regardless of Religion', *FT*, 18 September 2007).

creationism   A controversial concept in both Protestantism and Islam, but with different connotations. In the former it is associated with the conservative claim that the world was created by God at a particular time, usually

5000 BC or thereabouts. Otherwise known as 'creation science', see *Discovery Institute* and **intelligent design**. In Islam **creationism** is associated with the liberal view (for example that of the Egyptian writer Nasir Abu Zeid) that the Quran is not an eternal, fixed-meaning document, but was *created* at a particular time and in a particular context and must therefore be interpreted according to different social concerns.

D

da'wa   Arabic, literally 'Call', used of call to Islam, also to daily prayer, and then of political movements or parties, notably *Hizb al-Da'wa*, the Da'wa party in Iraq, an underground Shi'i group opposed to the Ba'thist state, and backed by Iran, and later a participant in the post-Saddam political process.

defeatist   Arabic *inhizami*. Term of abuse for Arab states that negotiate with the USA, try to make peace with Israel, etc. See **capitulationist, tottering, wavering**.

Deobandi   Conservative Islamic movement, named after the town of Deoband in India, where it originated in the nineteenth century. The ideological inspiration for conservative Pakistani groups and, in the 1990s, for the Taliban. Opposed to the liberal trend founded by the college at Aligarh, Pakistan.

donkey   Term frequently used of politicians, other ethnic groups and generally anyone the speaker disapproves of. One of the key cultural fault-lines between Middle Eastern and Western European societies is the incidence of jokes, and insults, related to donkeys. Thus, in Persian the word *khar*, 'donkey', is a very frequent term of abuse, implying stupidity. More generally, an animal with a key role (along with the mule) in Mediterranean cultures, in livestock husbandry, shaping the landscape, appearing in literature and philosophical tracts, raising issues such as, in one academic symposium, the working conditions of the animals and their owners, gender issues in donkey use, religious representation, harnesses and ornamentation, language of donkeys and their drivers, donkeys in song, culinary considerations, donkeys in war, as a transport option, etc. The donkey has also been used in recent nationalist symbolism in Catalonia, as an alternative to the Spanish bull, and can be seen on the back of taxis and cars in Barcelona and other Catalan cities: some rumours suggest that it was the hardy Catalan Pyrenean donkey that the CIA bred and used in Afghanistan in the 1980s, to ferry arms to the *mujahidin*.

E

ebbing   Favourite word of Osama bin Laden in regard to America's global power.

Entity, The   Arabic *al-kian*. Frequently used Arab nationalist term for Israel, avoiding mention of the country name. Comparable to the West German practice during the Cold War of avoiding the name of the German Democratic Republic (GDR) by calling it *die Zone*, the (Soviet Occupation) Zone, its original post-1945 name; *die sogennante*, the 'So-Called', i.e. GDR, or just *Drüben*, 'Over There'. Analogous forms of linguistic denial can be found in everyday speech, e.g. as in affectionate British Isles expressions for close relatives such as 'His Lordship' and 'Her Indoors', and also as a way of expressing religious disapproval, e.g. the Hebrew term for Jesus Christ, regarded as a traitor to Judaism, *ha-shem*, 'the name'.

F

faqih   In Islamic terminology, an interpreter of *fiqh*, or Islamic law, some-times translated by the term 'jurisconsult'. Can be used for any interpreter of the law, or, as in post-revolutionary Iran, to refer to one senior cleric: hence the institutional role description of the supreme religious leader of the Is-lamic Republic of Iran, first Ayatollah Khomeini (1979–89) and then Ayatol-lah Khamene'I (1989–), is that of *velayat i faqih*, literally 'the guardianship of the jurisconsult', i.e. a position of supreme authority held by someone authorised to interpret *fiqh*, in political as well as strictly legal matters. In modern Arabic colloquial usage, the word can also denote a verbose or irresponsibly unrealistic person, also, as in a famous song by the Egyptian singer Umm Kalthoum, mocking a former paramour who dreams of restart-ing the romance, as a *fa'ih*, a wastrel, a dolt. Not to be confused with the Anglo-Indian word *faqir* (originally Arabic *poor*), a beggar or a person who performs tricks in public for payment. The Arabic word is the origin of the Spanish and Catalan for an Islamic holy person, or legal expert, *alfaquí*.

fard   Arabic for 'duty', now much used by Osama bin Laden and other Islamist militants to denote the obligation of all Muslims to wage *jihad*. Islam distinguishes between *fard al-'ain*, 'of the individual', one of the five duties incumbent on all Muslims (prayer, fasting, pilgrimage, charitable giving, profession of faith in one God), also known as the five 'pillars' (*arkan*) of

Islam, and *fard al-kifaya*, a collective obligation – such as *jihad*, returning greetings or attending funerals – which is performed by some on behalf of the community as a whole. The current Sunni fundamentalist interpretation, as in the statements of bin Laden and his associations, is, in effect, a theological and political innovation. See *jihad*.

fatwa   Technically a judgement by an authorised Islamic judge, or *mufti*; more generally, any polemical point of view by a self-proclaimed source of authority. In conventional Islamic legal tradition, *fatwas* are supposed to be formulated according to certain clear presentational rules; hence the famous denunciation by Ayatollah Khomeini of the novelist Salman Rushdie in February 1989 was not strictly a *fatwa*, but only a 'judgement' or *hukm*.

fifteenth sha`aban   Date in Islamic calendar marking day in March 1991 when the Iraqi popular revolt against Saddam Hussein began, following defeat in the Gulf war.

'foreigners without hats'   Arabic *khawajir bidun quba'at*, disparaging characterisation of modern Arab leaders by Egyptian fundamentalist Shaykh Qaradawi.

G

'the going and the coming'   Arabic *el ga'in wa el ra'in*, phrase used by Egyptian President Nasser (d. 1970) to refer to the British and Americans as imperial powers in the Middle East. What would he have said 40 years on?

H

halal   Term used by Muslims for foods, such as meat, or practices that are deemed free, literally 'released' from prohibition. More generally, as synonym for 'permitted'. The similar Hebrew word *kashar* also implies something that is 'fit', 'suitable'. Cf. *Shari'ah-compliant banks*.

hammour   Stout-bodied fish (English name, *grouper*) popular in the Gulf countries, known for swallowing prey whole rather than biting bits off. Now used to refer to the Saudi super-rich who dominate the stock market (Simeon Kerr, 'Gulf Investors Stake Out UK High Streets', *FT*, 22 May 2007).

hawza   Arabic, literally 'holding' or 'defence', Iraqi Shi'i term for senior clerics, a traditional locus of authority in that country. Also a college for the training of Shi'i scholars, religious leaders, teachers of Islam and jurists. Such *hawzas* are found in any country with a large Shi'i population, e.g. Iraq, Lebanon, Iran, Syria, Afghanistan, India, Pakistan, Saudi Arabia, Kuwait and Bahrain.

hijab   Arabic for 'cover', 'curtain'. Conventional word for Muslim woman's veil. See Chapter 6, **voluntary apartheid**. In some Muslim countries, *hijab* was traditionally common, in others not. In origin, any piece of clothing that covers all or part of a woman's head and face, now used to refer to any head covering said to be enjoined by Islam. For all its controversial character, compulsory covering of Muslim women is *not* enjoined by the Quran: Verse 24:31 calls for covering women's 'adornments' from the eyes of strangers, and Verse 33:59 enjoins the wives of the Prophet to cover their hair, but the practice of forcible, total or partial, covering was a later innovation. The word 'veil' denotes, and confuses, at least three distinct kind of head covering: (1) *hijab* (refers to 'modest dress' and differs according to cultural context, although in the UK it usually refers to a headscarf); (2) *niqab* (a veil, worn with a *hijab* and drawn across the face, leaving the eyes visible); (3) the full enveloping of the body in a long loose gown, variously known as *jilbab, litham, burqa, abaya* or *chador*. A veiled woman is, in Arabic, a *mohajjaba*. Islam has traditionally enjoined 'modest' clothing for women *and* men (hence the preference for loose-fitting trousers on men as in the Pakistani *shalwarkhamis,* and the Arabic *jallabia* and *dishdasha*). The Western *pyjama* or loose night garment for men is, in origin, the Persian *paijama,* literally 'foot and leg'. The veil has in recent years come to be the most controversial symbol of Muslim identity, not only in Western Europe but also in countries such as Turkey where it is contested, and to some degree prohibited, by secular states. The practice of partial covering, particularly of the hair, is not, of course, peculiar to Islam. Cf. the head covering, and in some cases wigs, worn by Orthodox Jews, the traditional black headscarf of Mediterranean women and the Catholic practice of women covering their heads as a sign of religious devotion. Western brides, of course, traditionally wear veils on their wedding day. Apart from Turkey, the other country where controversy, and state-directed rigidity, were most evident was France. Among terms used by prominent French politicians and writers to describe this phenomenon were 'a form of aggression', 'a successor to the Berlin Wall', 'a terrorist operation', 'a lever in the long power struggle between democratic values and fundamentalism'. Under pressure from anti-Muslim right and secular left forces, the government of President Chirac in 2003 appointed a commission, chaired by former minister Bernard Stasi, to consider policy on the veil: while the commission itself recommended recognition of the variety of religions in France, the government's response was a one-sided law, enacted in March 2004, and brought into force for the new school year in October 2004, banning all 'conspicuous' religious signs – this category including Jewish skullcaps and large Christian crosses as well as the veil. Medallions, small crosses, stars of David, hands of Fatima and small Qurans were permitted (Laila Lalami, 'Beyond the Veil', review of Joan Wallach Scott's *The Politics of the Veil* [Princeton: Princeton University Press, 2007], *The Nation*, 10 December 2007).The widespread adoption by Muslim migrant women in European cities of extreme, in some cases all black, and head-to-toe covering in the 1990s was a misguided identity statement, often serving as a distorted and masochistic defiance of anti-Muslim prejudice.

hisba   Literally 'balance', term used in a variety of ways within Islamic law and thinking. On the one hand, it refers to the traditional balance of power and influence within Islamic society, but is also revived by conservative Islamic elements in Egypt to promote divorce of thinkers deemed unorthodox, such as Nasr Abu Zayd in 1992, from their wives, on the grounds that the wife, as a Muslim, could not be married to an unbeliever. Thus in this latter case the 'balance' being restored is purportedly that of keeping a Muslim woman free from ties to a heretical man.

hizb   Modern Arabic, secular and, by adoption, religious word for a political party. The word has Quranic precedence, where it means a section – one of 60 – into which the Quran is divided for memorising.

hizb allah   Literally 'The Party of God', taken from the Quran (5:56, 58:22). Term used of pro-Japanese nationalist group in Indonesia in the 1940s, then in Yemen in 1960s, then of irregular pro-Khomeini militants in Iran after the 1979 revolution and best known as the name of the new Lebanese Shi'i Party in 1984. The active participle derived from this root, *mutahazzib*, is the contemporary Arabic for 'biased'.

how to beat a wife   Example of religious endorsement of violence against women. Thus the Saudi Arabian cleric Mohammed Al-Arifi explained on Lebanese television that 'the blows must be soft and not on the face', which 'is prohibited, even for animals', while noting that some religious schools say a women should be 'beaten with a toothbrush'. By way of demonstration he took a toothbrush from his pocket, noting that the 'offended' husband should first try other measures such as warning her, stop sharing the marital bed and conversing with her. If this fails then he may beat her, 'but without going too far' because it is not a question of inflicting pain, but of appealing to her emotions, telling her, 'This has gone too far and I can't take any more' (*El País*, 10 November 2007). In one of its verses, often used by conservative judges in Muslim countries such as Egypt in cases of alleged gender violence within the family, the Quran, in effect, sanctions forcible sexual relations in marriage ('Go unto her, like a furrow – Arabic *hirathun* – in the field', Quran 2: 223).

I

ijtihad   In Islam moral and legal term, from the same root as *jihad*, the Islamic word for 'struggle'. Denotes the ability to exercise, and right to, independent judgement in the interpretation of texts within Islam, especially associated with Shi'as, hence less tied by traditional authority, or *sunna*. The conventional Sunni position is that the 'gate of *ijtihad*' was closed centuries ago.

'ilm   Arabic for 'knowledge', 'science'. Root of conventional term for clergyman, *'alim* (plural *ulema*). In modern usage *'ilm* is applied equally to what in the West would be theology and natural science. Registered in the quotation of the Prophet *'atlub al-''ilm hatta fi al-sin*, 'Seek Ye Knowledge Even in China', a saying often used to promote an open-minded attitude to ideas from the non-Muslim world, where China is taken – as it was in the seventh century – as the most remote area of the known world. In the period when Soviet communism was influential in some Arab states, its official theory, 'scientific socialism', was rendered as *al-ishtirakia al-'ilmia*. See **mullah, ulema**.

imposed   Arabic *mafrudh*, Persian, *mahmul*. Widespread term in the Middle East referring to agreements, compromises, treaties that are said to be 'imposed' from outside, and hence to be rejected, even if formally negotiated and agree to by national governments. Also used by Iranians to refer to the 1980–8 Gulf War, which Iraq initiated in September 1980 (*jang-i mahmul*, 'The Imposed War'), the implication here being not only that Iran was an innocent party, but that in invading Iran the Iraqis had acted at the behest of Western imperialism.

inshallah   Common Arabic and, by extension, Muslim term, literally if (*in*) wills (*sha*) God (*allah*), origin of Spanish word *ojalá*, and broadly equivalent to Irish colloquial 'God willing', in effect 'I hope so', 'I trust it will be so'. Like Spanish and especially Mexican use of term *mañana,* 'tomorrow', taken, by Arabs as well as impatient Westerners, to epitomise lax commitment to time and work of people in the Middle East. Thus the common Arab observation that they themselves have an '*IBM culture*', where I stands for *inshallah,* 'B' for *bukra,* 'tomorrow' (i.e. *mañana)* and 'M' for *mumkin,* 'possibly' or 'maybe', or *mashallah,* 'What God wills'. During the US occupation of Iraq an Iraqi translator was asked to explain the differences he saw between Iraqis and the Americans he encountered in Iraq: he cited the Arabic phrase '*inshallah*' as an example of the difference, saying that Americans respect time, while Iraqis, 'use the word *inshallah,* which means "if God wishes", to postpone things'. Nonetheless, some kind of cross-fertilisation may be blurring these differences as the war in Iraq seems to have offered a new word to match a new sense of American limitations. An American colonel in Iraq, writing to *The Washington Post*'s Thomas E. Ricks, observed: 'The phrase "*inshallah,*" or "God willing," has permeated all ranks of the Army. When you talk to US soldiers about the possible success of "the surge," you'd be surprised how many responded with "*inshallah*"'. However General David Petraeus, commander of US forces in Iraq, sought to maintain American standards: 'This is not an *inshallah* time', he stated (Cullen Murphy, 'Inshallah', *American Scholar,* Autumn 2007). Literally, what Petraeus was saying would have been anathema to the main Evangelical Christians backing the war, starting with the Commander-in-Chief George W. Bush, namely that it did not matter what God wanted.

inshallahshaheed   Literally 'If God wills, a martyr', title of a blog by a 21-year-old American Muslim, Samir Khan, who had joined what **Al-Qa'ida** called the 'Islamic jihadi media' (Michael Moss and Souad Mekhennet, ' "Islamic Jihadi media" with American Accent', *IHT,* 16 October 2007).

intifada   Arabic 'uprising', from *faudha,* unrest or disorder, a level of mobilisation below *thawra,* revolution, and less coordinated and comprehensive than *qiam,* a general revolt. Used of the 1948 and 1952 popular demonstrations in Iraq, and of the 1970–1 state-directed but pseudo-spontaneous, Chinese-style, peasant risings in South Yemen. Mostly associated with the Palestinian movements of 1987–92 and 2000–1 against Israeli occupation.

Islam   Literally 'submission' in Arabic, the religion revealed to the Prophet Muhammad between 610 and 632 AD. Now the faith of well over 1 billion believers, around 90 per cent Sunni and 10 per cent Shi'i, with some smaller groups, such as Ibadhis in Oman. As of early 2009, 57 countries were members of the Islamic Conference Organisation, an inter-state body set up in 1969 after an arson attack on the al-Aqsa mosque in Jerusalem by a deranged Australian tourist, but blamed by much of the Muslim world on the Israeli authorities. The core texts of Islam are the Quran, the word of Allah as revealed to Muhammad, and the *hadith*, or sayings attributed to the Prophet.

Islam forbids such weapons   One argument offered by many Iranians who say the West need not worry about Iran's developing nuclear missiles (Neil MacFarquhar, 'For Many Iranians Nuclear Power Is an Issue of Pride', *IHT*, 30 May 2005). The problem with all such claims is, first, that major religions, Islam included, always permit multiple possible moral and legal interpretations, and, secondly, that many of the other things that 'Islam' supposedly forbids, such as fighting in Ramadan, suicide or killing innocents, have been widespread in modern times.

Islamic Art   Widespread, and historically bogus, curator's term for works of art originating in any Muslim country over the past 14 centuries. As readers of the *IHT* correspondent Souren Melikian's frequent and scholarly articles will know, this is a fictitious term, without historic, artistic or theological basis, invented by museum directors and sales room promoters to cover a wide variety of different cultural and geographic works. Akin to '**Islamic Banking**' as, in effect, a pseudo-religious hype, designed to boost sale room prices.

Islamic banking   Financial services that are compliant with *Shari'ah* law. Much of the propaganda about special 'Islamic' norms and rules for banking rests on a confusion, by Muslims who do not know Arabic or how to pronounce it correctly, between the word for profiteering, or usury (*ribā*), which *is* forbidden, and *ribh* or normal interest, which is permitted and has been part of banks and financial activity in Muslim societies for centuries.

Islamic hospitality sector   Leisure facilities – hotels, restaurants – deemed to be compliant with Islamic laws and custom, e.g. in Dubai. Measures include a ban on alcohol, pork and nightclubs, gender-segregated fitness centres and prayer rooms, indications of direction to pray towards Mecca, avoidance of placing beds or toilets in the direction of Mecca, provision of Quran, prayer mats and prayer beads in each room or at front desk, staff to be predominantly Muslim and in conservative/traditional attire

(Karen Thomas, 'Islamic Hospitality Sector Emerges', *Middle East Economic Digest*, 2–8 May 2008).

Islamic public   Imaginative and analytically fruitful term coined by the German historian Reinhardt Schulze, to denote the growth from the nineteenth century onwards, of an informed, newspaper- and book-reading Muslim intelligentsia, and more broadly a community of people in different countries aware of issues of common concern (see his *A History of the Islamic Peoples* [London: I.B.Tauris, 2000]).

Islam, Yusuf   Greek Cypriot singer once known as Cat Stevens, author of the songs 'Where Do the Children Play?' and 'Peace Train', *inter alia*. After his conversion to Islam, he was active in Muslim education in Britain in collaboration with Pakistani and other associations. Deported from the USA in 2004 as a security threat: according to the Department of Homeland Security there were 'concerns about activities that could potentially be related with terrorism' (Peter Aspden, 'A Very Reluctant Spokesman Makes a Keynote Address', *FT*, 21 March 2005), though has since been allowed to return.

J

Janjaweed   Sudanese term, said to mean 'men on horseback', but not from any evident Arabic root, militiamen in the Darfur region of Sudan and neighbouring region of Eastern Chad, mostly members of nomadic tribes who had old grievances with settled darker-skinned African farmers in Darfur and Eastern Chad. Until 2003, the conflicts were primarily over scarce water and land resources. The *Janjaweed* became much more aggressive in 2003 against two non-Arab groups, the Sudan Liberation Army and the Justice and Equality Movement which had taken up arms against the Sudanese government. The *Janjaweed* militias pillaged towns and villages, especially of the Zaghawa, Masalit, and Fur tribes. Many observers believe that the *Janjaweed* were encouraged, if not equipped and recruited, by the Khartoum-based government, a claim that the government vehemently denied (Eric Reeves, 'Darfur and the International Criminal Court', *Middle East Report Online*, 29 April 2005).

jihad   Normal Arabic word for 'effort', comprising military, political and spiritual activities. Normally used by Islamists for 'struggle', in contrast to the Arabic secular term *nidal*. From this root come both *mujahid*, one who struggles for Islam in one way or another, in modern terms a political and military activist, and *ijtihad*, independent judgement within Islam. After 9/11, enormous amounts of academic and historical effort went into identifying the religious origins and meanings of this term, most of it a waste of time: the modern meaning and usage, as in the statements of Osama bin Laden, according to which *jihad* is the duty of all Muslims, is really an Islamic rendering of the populist third world concept of 'armed struggle', or 'legitimate self-defence'. Also used in the Iranian Revolution for mass mobilisations such as that to promote development of the countryside, *jihad i sazandegi*, the 'Construction Campaign'. See Chapter 2, **jihadi**. Strictly speaking all Muslims are 'jihadis', in the sense of believing in making various forms of spiritual and social effort.

K

Kongra-Gel   Formal title of Kurdish guerrilla group the **PKK**, Congress of the People of Kurdistan, name adopted, but not widely adopted, after attempted change of policy in the 1990s. A ceasefire instituted in 1999 was ended by this organisation in June 2004, and was followed by extensive fighting in eastern Turkey and northern Iraq. However, despite the Turkish government's claims to the effect that it was the **Kongra-Gel/PKK** that was responsible for the August 2004 hotel bombings in Istanbul, and later attacks in that and other Turkish cities, most evidence suggested these were the work of Islamists, or even part of a war between different Turkish criminal groups.

L

Land of the two Holy Places   Arabic *bilad al haramain*, Saudi Arabia or, in some renderings, the Arabian Peninsula as a whole. The two 'Holy Places' are the cities of Mecca and Medina. In recent times the term **Holy Land** has been applied by Islamists to Palestine, but this has no historical or canonical basis and is a straight, nationalist, borrowing from the Christian usage. On a few occasions the founder of Saudi Arabia, King ibn Abdel Aziz, referred to the Hijaz region of Arabia, where the cities are located, as the 'Holy Land', but this usage was not sustained, in part because of the Saudi conqueror's desire not to give prominence to the historical distinction of this area.

leeches   Also 'blood suckers', Arab nationalist term for US and British forces in Iraq.

liberal, liberalism   Term of abuse by both the Islamic Republic of Iran and American neoconservatives. In the case of Iran, used by right-wing leaders of the Islamic Republic to justify attacks on supposedly 'foreign' ideas, in particular closing of opposition press in 1979 (when, in response to demonstrations in support of press freedom, women's rights and secularism, under the slogans *marg bar irtija*, *marg bar fascism*, 'Death to Reaction, Death to Fascism', crowds organised by the regime marched through the streets of Tehran shouting *marg bar liberalism* – 'Death to Liberalism'). Meant to denote any pro-Western, secular or dissident thinking and activity. The Islamist term was taken directly from the vocabulary of Stalinist communism, just as were the Islamist concepts of imperialism, revolution and party. In the US case, the term is often found in set clichés such as 'East Coast **liberals**', '**liberal** press' and even '**liberal** fundamentalists'.

M

magus   Ancient Persian, Zoroastrian priest, later practitioner of obscure skills, particularly astrology, hence 'magic'. *Magian* is an alternative Western term for Zoroastrian and Parsee. In modern Arabic, an anti-Persian term of abuse, e.g. by Saddam Hussein of Khomeini during the Iran–Iraq war. In what is a striking example of the 'invention of tradition', the term is used in Christian lore to refer to three wise men, *magi*, Spanish *Los Reyes Magos*, who visited Jesus at his birthplace in Bethlehem, an event celebrated on 6 January as the Epiphany. The original reference in the Gospel of St. Mark uses the Greek word *magoi*, wise persons from the east (not necessarily men) but does not give a number, or names, and sets the visit two years after the birth of Christ. Most of what later became customary belief derives from sources long subsequent to the Gospels: the belief in *three* **Magi** was popularised by Pope Leo the Great (440–64 AD) and the names attributed in Western tradition to the three 'Kings' – Balthasar, Gaspar, Melchior – derived from an eighth-century chronicle, *Excerpta Latina barbari;* Eastern Christians give different names. The very rendering of Matthew's *magoi* as 'Kings' is based on the fourteenth-century translation of the New Testament into English by John Wycliffe, while the phrase 'wise men' is from the King James Bible. That they came from Persia also remains supposition, Matthew only mentioning that they came 'from the east'.

Mahdi   Arabic: literally 'rightly guided' person or being, Muslim equivalent of Judaic and Christian 'the Messiah'. In Shi'ism, sacred figure who will come, or return, to Earth at the end of history to save humanity (but *not* claiming divinity, as in Christian tradition), in Sunni cultures often a figure claiming divine authority and inspiration, e.g. the late-nineteenth-century political leader in the Sudan who resisted British forces and killed General Gordon at Khartoum in 1886.

Majetski (His)   Combination of 'Majesty' and 'water ski', ironic name by which the Moroccan king Abdullah has been called by some of his subjects because of his playboy tastes, which include water sports. A related coinage is **Marock**, the title of a film on the sex-drugs-and-rock-'n-roll hedonism of the children of Casablanca's elite (Jason Burke, 'Morocco's Turning Tide', *The Observer Magazine*, 22 April 2007).

mamluk   Arabic: literally 'owned'. Historically a term for the special corps of Turkish soldiers and administrators brought in by the Abbasid Empire – a process leading to the gradual weakening of Arab control and the rise of the Ottomans. In contemporary usage, often applied to Arab state reliance on Western advisers and specialists, this taken as a fateful weakening of initiative and independence.

martyr   Christian concept of a person who sacrifices their life for their faith, often leading to later canonisation. From Greek *martiros*, 'witness'. In Islam **shahid/shuhada**, literally a 'witness'. As Islam was not, like Christianity, persecuted in the first centuries after its emergence, 'martyrs' play a less important role in its history and sacral self-narrative. Sunni Islam, insisting on the sole sanctity of God above all in its more orthodox variants, does not have the Christian equivalent of 'saint's days', or the naming of places of worship after saints. Shi'i yield somewhat on this, in regard to their founders, Ali and Hussain, whom they do consider as martyrs, and the names of the subsequent **Imams**.

Mecca   Arabic title *makka al-mukarrama* (blessed Mecca). An ancient trading and pilgrimage city in the Hijaz, western Saudi Arabia, population 700,000 (in 2000). Site of the *Ka'ba* (Arabic, literally, 'cube' – hence the Egyptian Arabic for 'mumps,' 'the father of lumps'), a stone covered with a black cloth which stands at the centre of the Great Mosque, allegedly built by Adam and later rebuilt by Abraham and Isaac as a replica of God's house. The pilgrimage to Mecca, *hajj*, at least once in a lifetime, is one of the five duties or pillars (*arkan*) of Islam. The city has an exclusion radius of around 30 kilometres, beyond which access is now limited to Muslims. As a positive figure of speech in English, a place or goal which people aspire to visit (e.g.

tourist sites, dance halls), first used in 1823. In the past Mecca had a very diverse population, with Muslim communities from West Africa, Sudan, Central Asia, China and Indonesia.

Ministry for the Promotion of Virtue and Prevention of Vice

Name of institution created by the Taliban during their rule in Afghanistan, 1996–2001, name taken from words of the Quran, see *mutawwi'un* below. The Ministry punished men whose beards were not the prescribed eight centimetres long, not to mention those that did not observe prayer times and fasts, while zealously working to ensure that male minds were not contaminated by the thoughts that could be occasioned by the proximity of unveiled women. The punishments for offenders were more than harsh. Adulterers were stoned to death and, in some cases, women had the tips of their thumbs cut off for wearing nail polish (Pankaj Mishra, *Temptations of the West* [London: Picador, 2006], pp. 269–70). See *Mutawwi'un*.

misguided individuals   Saudi press term for terrorists. Those detained were subject to re-education programmes, a kind of official Islamic brainwashing.

mofsid fi al'arz   Persian legal term, literally 'spreader of corruption on earth'. Generic term used to discredit and, in court cases, sentence to death those opposed to the Islamic regime in Iran after 1979. See also Islamic *moharib bi khoda*, and cognate Judaic terms, *moser*, *rodef*.

moharib bi khoda   Persian legal term, literally 'waging war on God'; like *mofsid fi al'arz*, a moral and legal term used in Iran to condemn opponents.

muhajirun   Arabic literally 'emigrants', those followers of Islam who fled from Mecca to Medina with the Prophet in 622 AD. In contrast to the *al-ansar* (the Prophet's companions), who were from Medina itself. Term used in modern times by a range of Islamist groups. The word **muhajir** and its cognate *mughtarib* are the normal contemporary Arabic words for a 'migrant worker'. In arguments by Muslim writers opposed to nationalism, much is made of the centrality of migration, *hijra*, in the life of the Prophet, the implication being that attachment to particular place or location is not consistent with Islam; hence Muslims should reject modern forms of territorial nationalism.

mujahid   Arabic, plural *mujahidin*. One who wages *jihad*, used in modern political discourse to denote nationalist and Islamist fighters, e.g. during the Algerian War of Independence (1954–62), the anti-monarchical resistance against the Shah (1971–9) and the Afghan anti-communist war (1978–92). See *ijtihad, jihad, jihadist* and Chapter 2, **Gucci muj.**

Mujahedin-i Khalq/Mujahidin-e Khalq   Literally 'Fighters of the People', Iranian guerrilla group, also known by initials *PMOI, People's Mujahidin Organisation of Iran*, and *MEK*, espousing radical interpretation of Islam mixed with elements of Marxism, first active against the Shah in the 1970s. They supported the 1978–9 Iranian Revolution, then went into opposition against the Islamic Republic in 1980. Hence the derogatory rendering of the organisation's title by Ayatollah Khomeini as *Munafiqin-i Khalq*, for which see *munafiqin*. Once blacklisted by the US government as a terrorist group, it was offered a base in Iraq by Saddam Hussein, and, by dint of very active publicity campaigns in Europe and North America, won support of some parliamentary and other officials. After the fall of Saddam, it became a leading source of claims, all unverifiable, about Iran's nuclear capability. In time, the group won the support of many Washington neocons, including White House officials in Vice-President Dick Cheney's office (Juan Cole, 'Combating Muslim Extremism', *The Nation*, 19 November 2007; 'MEK Providing Dubious Intelligence about Iran's Nuclear Capabilities, *Cooperative Research History Commons*, October 2006, www.cooperativeresearch.org/entity.jsp?entity=mujahedeen-e_khalq). Subject of much indulgent, when not inaccurate, reporting. For corrective, see excellent study by Ervand Abrahamian, *The Iranian Mujahidin* (London: I.B.Tauris, 1989) and the autobiographical account by a former leader Masoud Banisadr, *Masoud: Memoirs of an Iranian Rebel* (London: Saqi, 2004).

mullah   Arabic and Persian 'Master' or 'lord', similar to Hebrew *rabbi* ('my master' or 'my teacher'). General term in Shi'i Islam for a Muslim clergyman, or *'alim*, plural *'ulema.*. The South Asian term *maulana* signifies a respected clergyman. See *'ilm, ulema*. In modern times it is often used in a disparaging context, thus referring to the government of the Islamic Republic of Iran as 'the mullahs'.

munafiq, plural munafiqin   Islamic term of abuse, first attributed to the Prophet Muhammad, for those who pretended to espouse Islam but were insincere in so doing; usually translated as 'hypocrites'. From *nifqa*, flattery, hence practice, common in Arab Gulf countries, of *shi'r al nifqa*, literally 'poetry of flattery', verbose eulogies, amounting to sycophancy, read out at public gatherings or printed in press, praising Princes, Amirs and sundry other members of the elite.

Muslim   Literally 'some who submits', hence a person who adopts Islam by accepting the will of God. In more antique versions, *musulman*. The root *slm*, denoting rest or quiet, is also the core for Semitic words for peace (Arabic *salaam*, Hebrew *shalom*) and for personal names, *Salim* and *Suleiman/Solomon*. The archaic term for a believer in Islam, 'Mohammedan'/ 'Mahometan' is incorrect: a mistaken analogy with 'Christian', a follower of Christ, it suggests that Prophet Mohammad was divine. See similar error with regard to the term **Wahhabi**, correctly *muwahhidun*.

Muslim-oriented web projects   Virtual sites aimed at Muslim communities. Began with the Digital.Halal portal (digitalhalal.com), including virtual mosques, a virtual Mecca, mosque social year and articles on the Muslim lifestyle. Promoted by an Egyptian living in Finland, Mohamed El-Fatatry, pioneer of *Muxlim Pal*, a virtual world which Muslims could explore (pal.muxlim.com) (Linton Chiswick, 'In a Virtual World of their Own', the *Guardian*, 11 December 2008).

Mutawwi'un   Literally 'volunteers', enforcers of belief, the religious police known in Saudi Arabia, and in Afghanistan, as the Force for the Enforcement of Good and the Prevention of Evil (a phrase taken from the Quranic phrase, *al 'amr bi al ma'aruf, wa al nahy 'an al mankar*, 3: 109). A brutal, authoritarian and intrusive irregular force used to employ dissident tribesmen and harass women, foreigners and others in public spaces. See **Ministry for the Promotion of Virtue and the Prohibition of Vice**.

Muttahida Majlis-i-Amal (MMA, or United Action Council)
Pakistani electoral coalition of Islamist parties, successful in the 2002 elections, gaining control of two out of the country's four provinces. In return to being allowed to campaign freely, the MMA then voted for an amendment to the constitution allowing President Musharraf to retain dictatorial powers till 2007. See **Mullah-ism**.

muwahhidun   Literally 'those who unite', in this case those (Muslims) who affirm their belief in the oneness of God, and renounce all forms of polytheism, from Arabic *wahid*, 'one'. The Christian term 'Unitarian', of those who deny the Trinity, is analogous. The correct term for what in the West are called 'Wahhabis'. The practice of calling Arabian Hanbali Muslims 'Wahhabis' after the name of Muhammad Abdul Wahhab, founder of this religious tendency in the eighteenth century, is probably akin to the incorrect use of the term 'Mohammedan' to describe a Muslim – a result of the transposition of the practice in Christianity, where the religion is named after its originator, Jesus Christ. (That Christ himself, in his lifetime, could not have been called 'Christ' in any case, because the word is a later Greek term meaning 'the anointed one', does not seem ever to have bothered anyone.) See *vovchik,* **Wahhabism.**

N

nahr Arabic noun, from root verb *nahara,* cutting the throat of or slaughtering sheep, now used by some Islamists to denote ritual throat cutting or beheading of their captives (the *Guardian,* 18 December 2006 – citing *Scott's Almanac 2007*). Thus Mohammad Bouyeri, the assassin of the Dutch film-maker Theo van Gogh in Amsterdam in November 2004, attempted, after shooting his victim, to cut his throat as well. There is also evidence that the hijackers of the planes which hit the World Trade Center towers in New York in September 2001 viewed themselves as engaged in a massive version of ritual killing, in this case of the passengers presumed to be 'infidels'. The Arabic for suicide, *intihar,* i.e. 'self-slaughter', is derived from the same root and, in purely etymological terms, conveys a more negative attitude to this action than the more neutral, Latin-derived, 'suicide'. In Islamist political rhetoric, of course, those who blow themselves up with the bombs they are carrying are termed *martyrs,* ***shuhada'***. See **martyrdom operations.**

Noriba Bank That is 'no-interest', literally a bank which does not charge *ribā'*, which is prohibited by Islam. Name given to 'Islamic bank' in the **Gulf.** See **Islamic banking.**

O

Old Man Arabic *al-khityar,* rendering of Turkish word, term used of PLO leader Yasser Arafat, with mixture of affection and disdain. Cf. use of term *El Viejo* of Argentinean leader Peron, prior to his death in 1974. Such exculpatory, pseudo-familiar, terms serve to exculpate the populist leader of responsibility for his actions, and corruption, these being blamed on younger associates and hangers-on.

P

Postakhundism   From *akhund/akhundism*, derogatory Persian word for a *mullah* or Islamic clergyman and their control of society and politics and from the term invented by Fred Halliday (1995) to denote a possible future, more tolerant and secular, form of Iranian culture drawing on major distinct trends in Iran's culture and politics – the variety of national traditions, cultural and literary; modern international ideas of democracy, individual rights; more open, unorthodox and non-hierarchical interpretations of Islamic identity and culture.

Post-Islamist   Term pioneered by Iranian social scientist Asef Bayat to note social customs, political ideas, architecture, especially in the Islamic Republic of Iran, that reject definition in religious terms (See his *Making Islam Democratic. Social Movements and the Post-Islamist Turn* [Stanford: Stanford University Press, 2007]).

prayer leader   Informal term used to denote a person who leads the faithful at prayer in Islam. Not necessarily someone formally recognised as a member of the Muslim 'clergy', an *'alim* or *mullah*. Technically correct, and capturing the original sense of title word *Imam*, which literally means someone who is 'in the front'. The task of leading the faithful to prayer can, in theory, be assumed by any believing Muslim.

Q

Quran   Sometimes transliterated *Koran*, but renderings which insert an apostrophe, as in *Qor'an*, inaccurate. The 'a' is pronounced long so, most correctly, **Qorān**. Literally, 'recitation', from Arabic root *qaraa*, 'to read out loud', 'recite', hence also injunction to quote from it, **iqraa**. Contrast with the emphasis on written text in the Christian word *Bible*, from Greek for 'book', *biblios*. The sacred book of Islam and the fundamental source for classical Arabic. In total, 6,000 verses, 130 chapters. While Muslim orthodoxy asserts that the text is the word of God, as dictated by an angel to the Prophet Muhammad, and subsequently transcribed (the Prophet himself was said to be illiterate), modern textual criticism indicates that the work is a compilation of oral material from seventh-century Arabia and that, on the basis of available material, there are distinct versions of the text. Orthodox Islam also asserts that, since the Arabic text is the word of God, it cannot be *translated* into other languages, hence the practice of describing what are, in effect, translations as *commentaries*. The claim of the more orthodox Sunni Muslims that the text is an unequivocal and timeless doctrine, or dogma, is at variance with the widespread Islamic practice of 'supervention' (*naskh*), whereby in cases of apparent conflict between verses, one (*nasikh*, 'supervening') is deemed, by suitable authority, to take precedence over the other (*mansukh*). Shi'i tradition also allows for the practice of independent reading, or judgement, **ijtihad**, while modern liberal Muslims challenge the view that the text is a timeless **creation** and argue that, like any other text, the **Quran** has to be read in its time and context – e.g. that verses on slavery, or death by lapidation, do not apply to the modern world. Similarly, the verses in the early part of the book celebrating the joys of wine (promising in paradise *nuhur al khamr*, 'rivers of red wine') are, perhaps regrettably, also considered by most contemporary Muslims to be 'supervened' by prohibitions later on.

R

ra'is   Arabic 'President', often used of head of state in republican regimes – in the 1950s and 1960s of President Nasser of Egypt, then in 1990s of Arafat as 'President', a more honorific title than 'Chairman', of the Palestinian National Authority. Example of common Arabic practice of naming leaders by semi-official titles, thus Qaddafi *al-akh al-'aqid* (the 'Brother Colonel'); Iraqi leader Abdel Karim Qasim (1958–63) *al za'im al awhad*, 'the one and only leader'; President Salim Robe Ali of the People's Democratic Republic of Yemen (1978–86) *muhibb al kadihin*, 'Beloved of the Oppressed'.

Ramadan   Ninth month of the Islamic calendar. A time of fasting and abstinence from sexual activity from dawn to sunset. Associated with family and social visits, at night-time, often with special foods and social gatherings. Despite recurrent claims that Muslims do not fight in Ramadan, also associated with some of the bloodiest battles in early Islamic history, notably that of *Badr*, the October 1973 Arab–Israeli war (the Egyptian offensive was named 'Operation *Badr*'), and with heavy fighting in the Iran–Iraq war of 1980–8.

rejectionists   Term common in Arabic political context, *morafidin/rafdiin*, from *rafd*, 'rejection', for those who *reject*. Historically, term for religious renegade, apostate, including Shi'i sect known as the *rafidiin*. In modern political terminology, has favourable connotations, usually in regard to refusal of any peace negotiations or agreements with Israel, such as the 1979 Camp David Agreement and the 1993 Oslo Accords. Arab states and allied political groups who opposed these agreements, including Syria, Iraq, Libya formed a 'Rejection Front', *jabhat al rafd*. In the 1990s overlapped with movement 'Against Normalisation', *dudd al tatbia*. Later taken up in American political vocabulary: thus in a speech given to the US Naval Academy in late 2005, President George W. Bush defined the enemy in Iraq as 'a combination of **rejectionists**, Saddamists and terrorists'. For Bush, **rejectionists** were resentful but reachable Sunnis who need to be brought into Iraq's new political system (William Safire, 'Insurgent Irresponsiveness', *IHT*, 16 January 2006). In 2007–8 US policy in Iraq began to reach out to such Sunni groups, organising and financing the **Awakening/***sahwa* movement.

religious status   Category included in the new machine-readable Pakistani passport. Initially this was not the case: the first page complied with international standards and had no space for a column on religion. The change was made when General Musharraf's government ceded to Islamist pressure to include this category. As a result, hundreds of thousands of passports were recalled ('Thou Shalt Not Have Fun', Lahore correspondent, *The Economist*, 16 April 2005).

S

safawi   Arabic variant of *Safavi* (there is no 'v' in Arabic), the name of the Iranian dynasty that ruled from 1501 to 1738, with its capital at Isfahan, which re-established the territorial and political integrity of the country after the period of Mongol rule, and which occupied Baghdad in 1508, hence also a traditional term of abuse for Persians and their, supposedly allied, Iraqi Shi'i co-believers. Used in a modern context by Sunni Arabs in Iraq to describe the country's born-again Shi'i religious and political establishment. See also *magus,* **Sassanian-Safavid conspiracy** (Michael Howard, 'Insurgent TV Channel Turns into Iraq's Newest Cult Hit', the *Guardian*, 15 January 2007). Anti-Persian chauvinism was a stock in trade of successive Arab, Sunni regimes in Iraq from the 1940s onwards. Saddam Hussein wrote a pamphlet entitled *Three Things Which God Should Never Have Invented – Persians, Jews and Flies.* This document was made compulsory reading in Iraqi secondary schools.

al-Sakina   Arabic word for 'harmony' and oneness with Allah, suggestive of mystical and, possibly, sacrificial state, used more recently by Islamic youth training groups in the UK.

Salafism   Islamic movement deriving from the Arabic word for ancestor (*salaf*), referring to the earliest Muslims from the time of the Prophet Muhammad. Salafis seek to restore Islam to what they see as its original purity in the Prophet's lifetime, before it was supposedly corrupted by innovations. Often, though incorrectly, used interchangeably with Wahhabism (see **Wahhabism**).   *(Entry not written by the author – Ed.)*

sandbox democracy   Image designed to convey the idea of *make-believe, childish, nursery* political behaviour. Thus in the words of the Ugandan-Canadian writer Irshad Manji, 'Egypt's elected legislators are children fiddling in a sandbox, supervised by profligate and democratically stunted grown-ups' (Irshad Manji, 'Mubarak's **Sandbox Democracy**', *IHT*, 21 June 2007).

Shari`ah   Common, if inaccurate, synonym for 'Islamic law', literally 'the (correct) path', from the same Arabic root as *shari'ah* (street). A generic term for divinely sanctioned Islamic law, now a talisman invoked by fundamentalists without historic or canonical authority: often confuses the 80 out of 6,000 verses of the Quran that are concerned with law and, by dint of being the word of Allah, divinely sanctioned with the broader body of Islamic law (*fiqh*). *Shari'ah* is thereby used to include the Quran, the *hadiths* (sayings of the Prophet), the *Sunnah* (records of the Prophet's deeds) and subsequent jurisprudence: these additions entail, however, that *Shari'ah* is not divinely sanctioned.

***Shari`ah*-compliant banks**   See **Islamic banking**.

Shi'a   Arabic: literally 'faction'. Shi'as were the followers of Ali, the cousin and son-in-law of the Prophet Muhammad, and his two sons Hassan and Hussein, who fell into conflict with Muhammad's successors and formed a separate sect within Islam. They now make up around 10 per cent of the world's Muslim population. Subgroups include Twelvers, Ja'fari, Ismaili and other communities. Shi'ism is the dominant religion in Iran and Azerbaijan. The Shi'i mourning phrase, *Ya Hassan, Ya Hussein*, chanted during the commemoration of Ali's sons, was corrupted in British colonial India into *Hobson-Jobson* – itself the name for the Anglo-Indian argot which rendered regional speech according to English linguistic patterns. In an example of the pluralism, and shifting focus, of identities, it may be noted that the majority of those who arrived in the UK in the 1960s as, in the terminology of that time, *East African/Ugandan Asians* were by origin Gujarati or Marathi *Shi'i*.

Shirt of Uthman   Arab phrase denoting repression, in reference to a harsh political order imposed by Caliph Muawiya after the assassination of his cousin Uthman, the third Caliph, in 656 AD. Used in the Arab world after 9/11 to justify increased suppression of dissent.

sons of monkeys and pigs, people of fornication and vice Abusive terms used to describe Americans on the official Iraqi television channel, Channel 3, prior to the American takeover of the channel on 10 April 2003 (Anthony York, 'Propaganda or Journalism', Salon.com, 23 April 2003, http://dir.salon.com/story/news/feature/2003/04/21/television/index.html).

Sunni   Pertaining to one of the two main branches of Islam, from *sunna* (Arabic: literally 'tradition'). Forming the current majority in Islam, Sunnis number around 90 per cent of its followers. Less receptive to interpretation and innovation, Sunnis strongly adhere to texts and to the revival of political authority, often phrased in terms of a restoration of the **Caliphate**, the supreme Muslim authority established in the seventh century and abolished by Kemal Atatürk in 1924. Of the contemporary Islamist groups, a majority, including the **Muslim Brotherhood, Al-Qa'ida, Salafis** and **Wahhabis**, are all Sunni. See also **Shi'i**.

T

tawhid   Religious term for unity, using same Arabic word for 'one', but in a different rendering as a political term, e.g. for Arab unity, *wahda*. Common, if never defined, concept and slogan of Islamists since the 1970s, including, in early days of the Iranian Revolution, appeals to '*tawhidi* economics' and use of the word in various Islamist and violent groups.

tawhid wa nur   'Oneness' and 'Light', two core Islamist concepts, name of a department store chain established by the Egyptian entrepreneur Ragab Suwirki, who began offering women free 'Islamic dress' if they handed over their Western apparel (Joel Beinin, 'Neo-Liberal Structural Adjustment, Political Demobilization, and Neo-Authoritarianism in Egypt', July 2007).

theocracy   Literally 'rule by God' (*theos* in Greek), in modern politics system of government controlled by clergy and/or allegedly organised on religious principles, e.g. the Islamic Republic of Iran in its early days, when nearly all the most powerful political leaders were Muslim clergy. Technically a government run by clergy should be a *hierocracy*. Word invented by the Jewish historian Josephus at the end of the first century, to describe the system of government he believed was intended by Moses.

tottering   Arabic term of political denunciation, *mutamillmill*. Used of 'regimes' that are denounced by Arab nationalists. See also **capitulationist, defeatist, wavering**.

trusted people   In the run-up to Saudi Arabia's first 'nationwide' elections (from which women and political parties were barred), hundreds of candidates appeared but just before the vote, text messages were sent urging people to vote for the **trusted people**. The Arabic phrase *ahl al thiqa*, 'People of Trust', is often used of the confidential, inner circle, of a Middle Eastern ruler. In the Saudi case the term meant 'candidates endorsed by the religious hierarchy'. The messages suggested that forwarding them would bring blessings (Neil MacFarquhar, 'Some Saudis Fear Complaints May Taint Milestone Elections', *IHT*, 15 February 2005).

U

umma   Arabic word denoting the community, usually 'the community of all Muslims', sometimes any religious community and, in modern times, a synonym for 'nation'. Thus in modern political discourse it can denote the Arab world (*al-umma al-'arabiyya*) or the community of all Muslims. Contemporary usage suggests aspiration to unity of all members into one political community. Broader than the terms 'nation', 'people', 'country'. Mentioned 62 times in the **Quran**, with several different meanings in some passages: using the word to mean 'religious community' in general, the **Quran** suggests that in Paradise the Muslim *umma* will be a minority of all these present. Also gives the Arabic term for 'internationalism' (*al-umamiyya*), nationalisation (*ta'mim*) and the UN (*al-umam al-muttahida*). The same root is found in the Hebrew word *am* (people, nation).

uncovered meat   Misogynistic image propagated by one *sheikh* Taj Din al-Hilali, a Sydney Muslim cleric, who said in a Ramadan sermon that 'immodestly dressed' women, by which he seems to have meant those who do not wear Islamic headdress, are at fault if they are preyed on by men. 'If you take out uncovered meat and place it outside on the street, or in the garden or in the park, or in the backyard without a cover, and the cats come and eat it . . . whose fault is it, the cats' or the uncovered meat?' A variant of well-known phrases of all predators, aggressors and bullies, *they had it coming to them, they asked for it* (Barbara McMahon, 'Sheilas Put the Mockers on Ockers', *The Observer*, 11 November 2007; Richard Kerbaj, 'Muslim Leader Blames Women for Sex Attacks', *The Australian*, 26 October 2006). In a mild, and perhaps misguided, partial defence of the *sheikh*, it should be noted that in most Middle Eastern and South Asian Muslim languages there is no distinction between the English words for *flesh* and *meat*. If he had been reported as talking about 'uncovered *flesh*', the insult to women and their freedom to dress as they chose would have remained, but the crudity of the remark would have been attenuated. It is not clear in what language he was speaking.

V

veil   See *hijab*, above.

W

Wahhabism   Western term used of the official ideology of the Saudi state since its formation in 1902. As with the antique term **Mohammedanism**, a mistaken analogy with Christian religion where the belief system is named after the founder or leading prophet, in the latter's case Jesus Christ. More broadly, movements supported, or allegedly supported, by Saudi Arabia. Founded by Muhammad Ibn Abd al-Wahhab (1703–87). Followers of the strict Hanbali school of Islamic law, Wahhabism is one of the three main components of conservative Sunni Islam, along with the Muslim Brotherhood and the Deobandis. Ibn Abd al-Wahhab branded all who disagreed with him, including other Muslims, especially Shi'as as 'infidels' and declared *jihad* on them. In their 1802 conquest of Iraq, and in their revival in the early part of the twentieth century, they destroyed Shi'i shrines and tombs. The descendants of Ibn Abd al-Wahhab are in Saudi Arabia today called the *Al Sheikh* (the 'Family of the Sheikh'), in contrast to the politically dominant *Al Saud*. Saudis do not call themselves **Wahhabis**, but rather **mowahhidun**, those who proclaim belief in one God, *tawhid*.

wavering   Arabic: *ha'ir*. Familiar Middle Eastern term of derogation for states, classes (e.g. in earlier times the petty bourgeoisie) and individuals deemed to be in contradiction with the speaker. Opposite of **steadfast**, *samid*. See also **capitulationist, defeatist, tottering**.

Y

al-Yamama Massive, secretive and reportedly corrupt arms and oil deal reached between the UK and Saudi Arabia in the 1980s, believed also to have covered coordination of guerrilla activity in Afghanistan. Derived from the ancient name of a region of the Arabian Peninsula which seems to have roughly coincided with today's administrative district of al-Riyadh, centre of a bustling, diverse, local culture and economy from the sixth or seventh century CE until the end of the Umayyad caliphate in 749 AD.

YSP *Yemeni Socialist Party*, target since 1980s of armed attack, and widespread assassination by Islamists inside Yemen inspired, and in some cases organisationally linked to, **Al-Qa'ida**. During the last decade of the Cold War the pro-Soviet, socialist state in former South Yemen – the *Peoples' Democratic Republic of Yemen* – along with the pro-Soviet regime in Afghanistan in the 1980s – the *Democratic Republic of Afghanistan* – was ruled by the **PDPA**, one of the two main targets of the right-wing Islamist armed movement that arose under the tutelage of Saudi Arabia and the CIA. Arabic: *al-hizb al-ishtiraki al-yamani*. Founded in June 1965 as the National Front for the Liberation of South Yemen, it came to power in South Yemen in November 1967 and transformed into the YSP in 1978. The only Arab regime to support Soviet-style 'scientific socialism'. Initially supported revolutionary movements against North Yemen, Oman, Ethiopia and Saudi Arabia. Weakened by factional disputes of 1969, 1978 and 1986, this last involving several thousand casualties. Merged with conservative North Yemen in May 1990, and was defeated by coalition of North Yemeni army and pro-**Al-Qa'ida** militias in the inter-Yemeni civil war of April–July 1994. Retains semi-legal existence within Yemen. Its Secretary General, Jairullah Omar, was himself assassinated by an Islamist gunman in 2002.

Z

zabib Arabic: literally 'raisin'. The mark on the forehead of a devout Muslim male indicating that he prays regularly and hence acquired a mark at the point where his forehead touches the ground. Also known as '*dinar* (coin) of Allah' or *halat al-salah* (the mark of prayer).

zakat   Conventional rendering of word for alms, charitable donation, strictly *zaka*, one of the five 'pillars', i.e. individual obligations, of Islam.

zakat-eligible   category of donation identified by *CAIR*, the *Council of American-Islamic Relations*, as both falling within the Quranic definition of charitable gift for religious purposes (*fi-sabilillah*, one of the eight categories of *zakat* recipients detailed in Chapter Nine, Verse 60 of the **Quran**) and being tax-deductible under US law (CAIR Newsletter, 27 September, 2007).

CHAPTER 6

Images of Muslims: Stereotypes, Insults, Self-Perceptions

Islam is in Danger.

—Ayatollah Khomeini

No to Eurabia.

—Dutch politician Geert Wilders in 2009
European election campaign

As far as I know.

—Hillary Clinton, Democratic Presidential candidate 2008,
in reply to a question as to whether it was proven that her
rival, Barack Obama, was not a Muslim

I'd rather be ruled by a wise Turk than by a foolish Christian.

—Martin Luther King Jnr

A

Aboutama   Popular nickname of Ahmed Aboutalib, here fused with 'Obama', Social-Democratic Mayor of Rotterdam, first Moroccan, or Arab, elected (2008) head of a European city (*El País*, 21 April 2009).

Arabic–English programme   Educational initiative in New York and occasion for outburst of public hostility to Arab culture. This was an attempt to establish joint teaching of Arabic and English in some New York schools in 2007. '[T]he readiness of the post **9/11** American debate to descend into a kind of hate-mongering and hysteria' appeared again when the New York mayor and schools chancellor both supported an Arabic language programme in public schools. With the opening in Autumn 2007 of the *Khalil Gibran International Academy*, an Arabic–English dual language middle school, hostile website *pundits* asserted that Osama bin Laden would be overjoyed, while Rabbi Aryeh Spero claimed that, in supporting the programme, the mayor and school chancellor had become 'part of a program to destroy the American public school system' (Richard Bernstein, 'Back to (Arabic) School: A Debate over Diversity', *IHT*, 10 September 2007).

Arabicide   Term coined by writer Fausto Giudice, chronicler of an estimated 200 cases of killings of Arabs in France in the 1970s and 1980s: see his *Arabicides: Une Chronique Francaise 1970–1991* (Paris: La Decouverte, 1992; see also interview in *Race & Class*, London: Institute of Race Relations, Vol. 35, No. 2, October–December 1993).

Arab street   Term used before the invasion of Iraq in US official circles to mean non-violent Arab public opinion. Somewhat derogatory and spuriously condescending term for Arab public opinion, at odds with reality that most such news is gathered and opinions formed in a living or dining room, while watching TV or listening to the radio. Like **Arab Soul**, as in 'the battle for the **Arab Soul**', the term somehow assumes there is one monolithic public view. The American writer Nancy Snow considers use of this term to imply that the Arab countries are particularly prone to mob rule (Nancy Snow, *Information War: American Propaganda, Free Speech and Opinion Control since 9/11* [New York: Seven Stories Press, 2004]). The Jordanian commentator Rami Khouri notes that this term should be distinguished from the more important *Arab basement* where small groups of hard-core ideologues retreat to mix fertilizer, C-4 plastic explosives and gasoline to make bombs (*The New York Times*, 23 October 2002). Cf. **Muslim Rage, soul of Islam**.

Asian   In modern English usage, a multipurpose ethnic term. Literally, anyone from the continent of Asia, from Turkey to Japan, and comprising all of the Middle East, South Asia, Southeast Asia and East Asia. Since the 1980s contemporary British usage, an inhabitant of, or person originating from, South Asia, of indeterminate religion (i.e. Hindu, Muslim, Buddhist, Sikh, Jain or Christian). The term was originally applied in 133 BC to the kingdom of the former ruler of Pergamon, who on his death bequeathed it to the Romans and gave it the name *Provincia Asia*. The word is Greek in origin, and its highest religious official was known as an *Asiarch*.

ayatollahs of secularism   Abusive description by religious fundamentalists in the USA and France of their, secular, opponents. Similar in its twisting of logic to the term *the Liberal Inquisition* to tarnish the opponents of religious thinking in education and public life in Western Europe.

B

Barry Soetoro   Abusive right-wing American name for Barack Obama, with 'Barry' the name he was known by as a child and Soetoro the surname of his mother's second, Indonesian, husband (the implication being that she had not been married to her first husband, a Kenyan academic also called Barack Obama, at the time of the birth of their son).

bigness   A vainglorious and provocative attribute of the Christian God. Lieutenant general William G. Boykin (former US Deputy Undersecretary of Defense for Intelligence), and evangelical Christian, offended Muslims by his account of a meeting with a warlord in Somalia: 'Well you know what I knew, that my God was bigger than his' (http://news.bbc.co.uk/2/hi/americas/3202690.stm [last accessed 21 March 2008]). Not clear if this remark was meant to contradict the claim of Muslim call to prayer, 'God is the Greatest', *allahu akbar*. Cf. **superior**.

binladens   Term for €500 notes, the largest denomination, so called in Spanish as they were widely used in criminal and illegal activity, and are never seen. Half of all the €500 notes in circulation in the countries of the Eurozone were believed to be in Spain ('Words of the Year', the *Guardian*, 18 December 2006).

Binliner   Derogatory popular British name for Osama bin Laden.

Binners   British military term for Osama bin Laden.

black arses   See *chernishopi*.

C

caid   With the French *banlieue* riots in November 2005, the then French Interior Minister Nicholas Sarkozy called the older brothers of rampaging adolescents *caids*, French slang for a gang leader, deriving from the Arabic word for a leader, *qa'id* (this also being the root of the word **Al-Qa'ida**). Sarkozy (*Sar-co-co* to his critics) also inflamed feelings by vowing to *Kärcheriser*, 'to clean the city with a Kärcher', after the name of a high-powered pressure cleaner, and referring to rioters as *voyous* and *racaille* (thugs and riff-raff) (Isabel Ramos Rioja, 'El Bálsamo del hermano mayor', *La Vanguardia*, 10 November 2005).

Chhatrapati Shivaji   Hindu warrior king, symbol of anti-Muslim prejudice in India. He was based in Maharashtra, with capital at Bombay (today factitiously retitled *Mumbai*), and fought against Mughal emperors in Delhi. The right-wing nationalist party Bharatiya Janata Party retitled a large park in Bombay in his name.

chernishopi   (Literally 'Black Arses'). Generic Russian term of abuse for peoples of the Caucasus, particularly Muslims, first and foremost Chechens, but also applied to Christian peoples of that region.

Chirac, Jacques   See *le bruit et l'odeur*.

Christophobia   Recent equivalent of more traditional *anticlericalism*, an adaptation of the 1990s concept of **Islamofobia** used by defensive Christian clergy and others to denote criticism of influence of Christian churches by secular representatives, also Mahatma Gandhi: 'I like Christ, but not the Christians'. According to the Spanish lay theologian Juan José Tamayo, **Christophobia** is 'at the end of the day, a form of self-hatred' ('Cristofobia episcopal', *El País*, 12 December 2008). Compare **self-hating Jew**.

Clash of Civilisations   Term originally coined by historian Bernard Lewis in regard to relations between the Muslim world and the West (e.g. see his 1990 essay 'The Roots of **Muslim Rage**'). Lewis was careful to use the phrase with the indefinite article, *a clash of civilisations*. Later popularised and vulgarized by American political scientist Samuel Huntington, first in a 1993 article of that name, later in a book, *The Clash of Civilisations and the Remaking of World Order* (New York: Simon & Schuster, 1996). Thus in this book he wrote: 'Culture and cultural identities, which at the broadest level are civilisational identities, are shaping the pattern of cohesion, disintegration, and conflict in the post-Cold War world ... A civilisation-based world order is emerging: societies sharing cultural affinities cooperate with each other; efforts to shift societies from one civilisation to another are unsuccessful; and countries group themselves around the lead or core states of their civilisation' (p. 20). Although Huntington applied the theory globally, to all seven of the 'civilisations' he identified, the thesis was particularly directed at the Muslim world and was redolent, as well as readily put to use in the service, of anti-Muslim prejudice. Apart from grossly simplifying the history, and present state, of relations between Muslim societies and the West, this 'theory' also served as a way to avoid facing up to any of the real political and economic issues involved. The underlying fallacy in the whole work, and in other explanations of this issue, was that it took a frozen, and one-dimensional, conception of culture, in this case 'Islam', and used it as an explanatory variable.

croissant   French term for crescent, literally something, as in regard to the half-moon, which is 'growing', by extension a symbol of Muslims, and, in celebration of defeat of the Ottomans in 1683 outside Vienna, applied to half-moon-shaped sweet pastry. Good example of the anti-atavistic point that the *origin* or etymological *root* of words is often irrelevant to explaining contemporary usage and definition. See, for a comparable case of etymological wandering, *kafir*.

crusade   From the French *croix*, 'cross', a campaign by Christians to defeat Muslims and reoccupy the Holy Land of Palestine in the eleventh to thirteenth centuries. First used in English in 1577. Associated at the time, as in the occupation of Jerusalem in 1099, with the massacre of Muslim *and* Jewish inhabitants. First used in 1786 to denote, more generally, aggressive movements against a public enemy: the right-wing British newspaper *Daily Express* has, as its emblem on the front page, a drawing of a crusader. This is intended not primarily as a statement of Christian aggressiveness, but of the paper's 'crusading' mission in general. The Arabic/Muslim term *salibi*, 'crusader', from the Arabic for cross *salib*, has been used in recent times, but rather less frequently before, as a term of invective against Western states. Its use by Muslims outside the Mediterranean is a product of activism in the late 1990s. See also Chapter 4, **Hulagu**, for a contrary historical analogy. The history of this word may serve as a reminder, at a time when all attention is fixed on the aggressiveness of Islam, of the belligerence long associated with Christianity, summarised in the common hymn *Onward Christian Soldiers*.

D

del Valle, Alexandre   Pseudonym of anti-Islamic and far right French journalist Marc d'Annal, author of verbose denunciations of Islam and Arabs, all supposedly in league with the USA to destroy Europe in some global pincer movement based on Puritanism, belligerence, etc. Proponent of theory of Islam as, after communism and fascism, the **third totalitarian system** of modern times.

Deutschkei   A merging of the German words 'Deutschland' and 'Türkei', German for 'Germany' and 'Turkey', to denote the 'transnational connections between Turkey proper and Turkey in Germany' (Betigul Ercan Argun, Turkish writer, in her *Turkey in Germany: The Transnational Sphere of Deutschkei*, [London: Routledge, 2003], p. xi). **Deutschkei** takes up Jürgen Habermas's concept of the 'public' sphere saying that, in occupying a space between Germany and Turkey, it is a 'transnational public sphere' in which 'ideas about national identity, citizenship, social integration and democracy in the native setting' (p. 30) can be expressed and shaped.

dhimmitude   Pejorative term for subordination of non-Muslims within Muslim society, from *dhimmi*, a protected, but second-class, non-Muslim inhabitant of earlier Muslim empires. In earlier Muslim states, the people of the *dhimma*, or pact of protection, are non-Muslim subjects of a state governed by *shari'ah* law. The state protects the individual's life and rights in exchange for subservience and loyalty, and the payment of a tax known as the *jizya*. The recently coined term **dhimmitude** is used differently. It is said to have been coined in 1982 by the Lebanese Maronite militia leader Bachir Gemayel to describe perceived attempts by the country's Muslim leadership to subordinate the Christian minority. Bat Ye'or (Gisele Littman), author of *Islam and Dhimmitude. Where Civilizations Collide*, defines **dhimmitude** as 'behavior dictated by fear (terrorism), pacifism when aggressed, rather than resistance, servility because of cowardice and vulnerability'. A recent example is found in an article entitled 'Dhimmitude in Practice' by American conservative academic and Middle East specialist Daniel Pipes. Pipes writes: '[w]herever Muslims form a plurality of the population, the life of non-Muslims tends to be grim. In some part, this results from the laws of Islam, which disdain and purposefully oppress the non-believer.' He gives examples: a demolished church in Malaysia, an order by the Mahdi Army in Baghdad that women should veil themselves, Christian Assyrians in Baghdad being obliged by Muslims to pay protection tax ... and, of course, the '**Teddy-Bear** *Intifada*' in Sudan (http://www.danielpipes.org/blog/568 [last accessed 6 January 2008]).

E

'Eye-rack'   US military pronunciation of 'Iraq', standard process of verbal denigration of enemy people and country, with perhaps subliminal association of the word 'rack' with torture. Cf. pronunciation of 'Iran' as '*Eye-ran*', with comparably subliminal association of Iranians as cowards. Also earlier pronunciation of 'Italians' as 'Eye-ties', also in Kuwait war of 1990–1 of

Saddam as *soddom*, ditto **Binliner, Binners**. Cf. **World War II** British army slang for Egypt (*Egg-whipped*) and for an Italian (*Eye-tie*).

F

Fallaci, Oriana   Spirited and widely travelled Florentine journalist (d. 2007), one of the first to confront Ayatollah Khomeini in 1979 over his insistence that women cover their heads, later author of an ill-judged, and in many respects inaccurate, diatribe against the Muslim world, the Arab world, *i figli di Allah* ('the sons of Allah') and, above all, those in Italy who sympathised with them, *La rabbia e l'orgoglio* ('Anger and Pride') (Milan: Rizzoli, 2001). This book was reprinted eight times in two years. Among its many mistakes is the claim (p. 61) that there are 24 million Arab-Muslims in the USA – the figure for all Muslims is approximately 4–5 million, the majority being South Asians or African-Americans. In line with other purveyors of conspiracy theories (see **Truthers**) she also claims (pp. 55–6) that the casualty figures given for the 9/11 attacks concealed a much larger number. An unworthy end to a great and courageous career.

fasting deaths   In a notorious anti-Muslim slur Thaksin Shinawatra, Prime Minister of Thailand (February 2001–September 2006), and self-described as 'I am not very tolerant', alleged that 78 Islamic protestors who had suffocated to death after being hogtied and thrown into military trucks had died because of weakness caused by Ramadan fasting (Seth Mydans, 'Thaksin's Tough Tactics Arouse Tough Criticism', *IHT*, 11 March 2005).

feuding Muslims   US term for sectarian conflict between Sunnis and Shi'i in Iraq and elsewhere in the Middle East with the implication (i) that the conflict has no reasonable basis and (ii) is endemic to the groups involved, and is in no way a consequence of US action or policy. In fact, the eruption of fierce violence between Sunnis and Shi'i in Iraq in 2006 was a direct consequence of the US invasion in 2003, and of the favouring by the US occupiers of Shi'i as against the hitherto dominant, but minoritarian, Sunnis. Later attempts, in 2007 and 2008, to try to correct the pro-Shi'i balance and to arm Sunni groups in the 'Awakening' or *sahwa* (see Chapter 4) tribal units may only have stored up more trouble for the future. Cf. use by early Bolsheviks of the term 'petty nationalist squabbling' to refer to ethnic disputes in the Caucasus.

fuzzy-wuzzies   British colonial term for fights loyal to the *Mahdi* during the invasion of the Sudan in 1886; allusion to hair of Horn of Africa peoples.

G

goat fuckers   Original Dutch word *geiteneuker* applied to Muslims by Dutch film-maker Theo van Gogh. Analogous to abusive English language term *camelfucker*. Van Gogh once included a goat on the set of his television chat show so that Muslim guests, or 'goat fuckers', as he called them, could 'have a go'. Weeks after showing Ayaan Hirsi Ali's 11-minute film *Submission* (August 2004), showing women's bodies with verses from the *Quran* projected on them as they described the beatings, rapes and ostracism they had endured from their own families for having boyfriends, van Gogh was murdered by 26-year-old Mohammed Bouyeri, a Dutch citizen of Moroccan descent. According to Bouyeri, 'The story that I felt insulted as a Moroccan, or because he called me a goat fucker, that is all nonsense. I acted out of faith' (Pierre Tristam, 'Theo and the Goat-Fucker: Enlightenment's Assassins', *Candide's Notebooks*, 28 December 2007, www.pierretristam.com/Bobst/07/cn122907.htm). Van Gogh was an exponent of the self-indulgent and, in modern legal and customary terms, unacceptable Dutch practice of outrageous insults, *scheldkritieken*. He did not confine his bile to Muslims but also insulted Jews. On one occasion in an essay published in 1988 in the cinematic journal *Moviola*, and in words reprinted in a later book, he taunted a pro-Israeli Dutch writer, Leon de Winter, with sarcastic remarks about the smell given off by the burning of diabetic Jews, the Gestapo 'soap' (the human fat left behind in the gas chambers was used to make this), 'lampshades' (the skin of dead Jews was used to make these). For this article, and its later republications, van Gogh was prosecuted in Dutch courts, being fined on one occasion (100 guiders or 20 days in prison), on the second acquitted. Ironically, and almost certainly unknown to nearly all his viewers, the Dutch colloquial word for 'fuck' that he drew on, *neuken*, is in fact of Arabic and indeed Quranic origin, being derived from the classical Arabic word for married or sexual relations, *nakaha*. Similar slang words derived from this origin are to be found in French, English and Spanish. In the case of Dutch, the word, like the generic abusive term *kafir*, to mean an African, but originally a Muslim for 'infidel', probably came through South Africa, where Afrikaans absorbed many words from Arab traders along the East African coast.

H

***halal* hippy**   European term for European youth, e.g. in Denmark, affecting Islamic lifestyle, wearing Palestinian or Afghan headgear, smoking *nargilehs*.

Hirsi Ali, Ayaan   Somali-born former Dutch MP, known for her controversial anti-Islamic views, now working for the conservative think-tank, the American Enterprise Institute. Having sought asylum in the Netherlands in 1992, she rose to prominence with her denunciation of Islam in the wake of 9/11. In 2004 Ali wrote the film *Submission*, portraying her views on the treatment of women in conservative Islamic cultures. The film drew both praise and outrage, and after it was shown on Dutch TV, the director, Theo van Gogh, was murdered by a radical Islamist, and Ali went into hiding. She has since written several books, including *The Caged Virgin* (New York: Free Press, 2006), *A Muslim Woman's Cry for Reason, Infidel* (New York: Free Press, 2007), *My Life* and *Nomad* (New York: Free Press, 2010), Nomad, From Islam to America: A Personal Journey Through the Clash of Civilizations (New York: Free Press, 2010). She later left Holland following a controversy over her asylum application, and now resides in the USA. *(Entry not written by the author – Ed.)*

hostile image   Negative stereotype, translation from German *Feinbild*. Concept much used in the analysis of racism, hostility to other peoples and religions. Cf. **Islamofobia, other**.

I

Irish *fatwa*   Fanciful application of original Islamic judicial term: according to journalist Eilis O'Hanlon, the Irish language radio station *Radio na Gaeltachta* had hatched a 'cunning plan' to reverse the downwards slide in its ratings. 'They're going to reverse a 30-year-old *fatwa* and start playing songs in the language of the hated colonial oppressor' (Eilis O'Hanlon, 'Fatwa Ends at RnaG', *The Independent*, 10 May 2005).

Islam-bashing   American Muslim term for hostility to Muslims, speeches and media with such content. Cf. European term **Islamofobia**.

Islam des caves   French: 'Islam of the basements'. In reference to informal networks and meeting places in poorer suburban districts of French cities.

Islamo-fascism, Islamofascism   Neologism widely and carelessly applied after 9/11 to imply that all Muslims, or at least all who espoused political and social goals defined in Islamic terms, were 'fascists', hence proponents of irrational violence, to be fought unconditionally. Protean term of abuse, also relying on inversion of usually semantic structure of such terms in English, e.g. *cryptofascism, Eurocommunism* in which key substantive is preceded by adjective, so that, in this case, while the main odium falls on the 'Islamo-' section, it is not the main noun. Originally applied by critics of violent and authoritarian **Islamist** movements, particularly the *Islamic Republic of Iran* after its establishment in 1979, later used more widely, and indiscriminately, to apply to all **Islamists**, and by attention, in post-2001 USA, to all Muslims. Thus, the right-wing Freedom Center, run by the once-intelligent and open-minded writer David Horowitz (for thus he was when I knew him in the early 1970s as editor of *Ramparts* magazine), organised 'Islamo-Fascism Awareness Week' in October 2007 to 'break through the barrier of politically correct doublespeak that prevails on American campuses, if you want to help our brave troops, who are fighting the Islamo-Fascists abroad'. Pamphlets distributed by the group included 'The Islamic Mein Kampf', 'Why Israel is the Victim' and 'Jimmy Carter's War Against the Jews'. This campaign was backed by, among others, Rudy Giuliani, former mayor of New York then running for nomination as Republican candidate for President and a champion of anti-Arab rhetoric: of his attitudes, the report said, 'Rudy would probably only take the hand of an Arab leader to throw him down a ravine, or a wadi' (Maureen Dowd, 'Rudy Roughs up the Arabs', *IHT*, 18 October 2007). The word appears in the *New Oxford American Dictionary* (2005) as 'a controversial term equating some modern Islamic movements with the European fascist movements of the early twentieth century'. The origins of the term are debated. In the 1940s and 1950s, Arab Communist Parties, especially in Egypt and Sudan, faced with violent, extreme right-wing hostility from the **Muslim Brotherhood**, would refer to the latter as 'fascist'. More recently, in 1979, in a debate with Michel Foucault in the pages of *Le Monde* over the nature of the 1978 Iranian Revolution, the great French Middle East expert Maxime Rodinson described the Khomeini regime and other organisations like the Muslim Brotherhood as '*une type de fascisme archaique*'. In my own reports from Tehran published in the London *New Statesman* (17 and 24 August 1979) on the repression of left-wing groups, I used the phrase 'Islam with a fascist face', while around 1990 the historian of Islamic movements, Malise Ruthven, writing in the newspaper *The Independent*, applied the term to various Muslim states. The critical, and morally as well as analytically, dubious extension of the term to cover opposition movements, and then by implication all Muslims, came after 9/11. Thus the term – an emotional pointing to old enemies, Italian fascism and German Nazism, which also sit uneasily together under this single heading – became ubiquitous, mainly in neocon-speak, conflating into one category a wide variety of states, organisations and movements, from the relatively secular nationalist regime of Saddam Hussein to the stateless, fundamentalist **Al-Qa'ida** and the backward-looking Taliban. Some British writers, such as Martin Amis, also used the term carelessly: the aim of such usage was not to achieve political or ideological clarity, but to denigrate, for example, the labelling of Bush critics as being like 'those who enabled Hitler' (Katha Pollitt, 'Wrong War, Wrong Word', *The Nation*, 11 September 2006 and 25 September 2006). As George Orwell noted in his major 1946 essay, 'Politics and the English Language', 'The word Fascism has now no meaning except in so far as it signifies "something not desirable".'

Islamofobia, Islamophobia   Termed coined in the early 1990s, aiming to provide a concept comparable to **Anti-semitism** to identify, and counter, widespread prejudice in Western societies. In some ways, a mistaken term, as the prejudice involved is not, in the main, one of hostility to a religion or set of beliefs ('Islam') but rather to antagonism to, and propagation of negative stereotypes about, a people or community, *Muslims*. The more appropriate term would be *Anti-Muslimism*. The conceptual sleight of hand involved appealed, however, to conservative Muslim leaders who, with the collusion of ill-informed Western liberals, such as the Runnymede Trust in the UK, gave the concept official status (for a critique of the term, see Fred Halliday, 'Antimuslimism and Contemporary Politics: One Ideology or Many?', *Islam and the Myth of Confrontation* [London: I.B.Tauris, 1996], Chapter 6). Such a critique was, of course, ignored by those promoting the concept and it has now passed into general, and normally uncontested, usage.

K

Karcheriser   From *Kärcher*, brand of powerful steam cleaner, used by then Minister of Interior Nicholas Sarkozy in a threat to immigrant regions of Paris. See also his use of ***caid*, racaille**. The originator of this name, the very-much-alive German entrepreneur Herr Kärcher was, understandably, indignant at the misuse of his name in this way.

Kilroy-Silk, Robert   Oleaginous former Labour Member of Parliament, popular host of BBC TV discussion programme and promoter of prejudice. After earlier bouts of insults against the Irish, he rose to particular prominence in January 2004 for chauvinist and inaccurate remarks about the

Arab and Muslim worlds. At first treated indulgently by BBC and politicians of all parties, he was dismissed with some delay by BBC in return for compensation reported to be over £600,000, later became leading candidate for *United Kingdom Independence Party* in the June 2004 European elections. **Kilroy-Silk** represented the more polite, if completely ignorant, face of British anti-Muslim prejudice, all masked in words about 'not ashamed to be British', 'speaking his mind', dislike of 'political correctness'.

Kingdom of Heaven *Twentieth Century Fox* film, shot in 2004, and budgeted for US$130 million, on the twelfth-century Crusades. Characters include historic figures such as the Muslim leader Saladin (a Kurd) and Balian of Ibelin, the Crusader who defended Jerusalem in 1187. The Arab Anti-Discrimination Committee spokespeople protested the film as reinforcing anti-Arab prejudice, while an interfaith educational expert said it was 'stirring up a hornet's nest'. Director Ridley Scott denied this saying, 'There's no stomping on the Quran, none of that' (*International Herald Tribune*, 19 August 2004).

L

le bruit et l'odeur French for 'noise and smell', title of the best-known song of the pop group *Zebda* ('butter' in Arabic, a reference to *beur*, meaning 'Arab born in France', which sounds like *beurre* [butter]). The title of the song is a reference to anti-immigrant comments made by Jacques Chirac in 1991, when he was Mayor of Paris. Speaking of the problems of a French worker living next-door to 'a father with three or four wives and twenty kids who gets 50,000 francs from welfare without having to work', he went on to remark: 'If one adds the sound and the smell to this, the French worker goes crazy' (Rafael Jorba, 'Los "intelectuales" del Otoño francés', *La Vanguardia*, 12 November 2005).

Londonistan See Chapter 10.

M

Manchurian Candidate In Cold War mythology, a brainwashed person despatched to carry out a political mission to the detriment of the USA, one of the abusive characterisations to which Democratic Presidential candidate Barack Obama was subjected to in the early part of the 2008 Presidential campaign: detractors made this charge because of his middle name of Hussein, his schooling in Indonesia; his pastor's embrace of Louis Farrakan, the founder of the Nation of Islam; and his calls for dialogue with Iran. Or in the words of one Southern radio chat show host, 'Well, his name isn't "Smith" is it?' *The Manchurian Candidate* (1959) was a novel written by Richard Condon and adapted into films in 1962 and 2004, about the son of a prominent political family who was brainwashed as a POW in Korea into becoming an assassin for the Communist Party (Roger Cohen, 'No Manchurian Candidate', *IHT*, 11 February 2008). See also **Barry Soetoro, Jihadi Candidate**.

man in pajamas   US military term for Iraqi civilians. Also see Chapter 4, **Ali Baba**.

Maurofobia   'Hatred of Moors and Moorish culture', Spanish term for anti-Muslim and anti-Arab prejudice, a historic equivalent of **Islamafobia**.

minarets   From Arabic *minar/manara*, literally a 'light-house' such as that at Alexandria in Egypt, then by extension applied to towers of Muslim mosques, used to proclaim the call to prayer. From *nur*, light. Architecturally similar to, and originally borrowed from, belfries of Christian churches that the Arab armies encountered on their conquests of the Middle East in the seventh century AD. More recently the focus of public and often anti-Muslim controversy in many Western European cities, including Cologne (Ian Traynor, 'The Rise of Mosques Becomes Catalyst for Conflict across Europe', the *Guardian*, 11 October 2007). Thus, in the Swiss Alpine village of Wangen, the local inhabitants tried to prevent the construction of such a tower: the controversy began with a house belonging to the region's Turkish immigrant community, the basement of which was used by Muslims for their Friday rites. 'I've got nothing against mosques, or even against minarets. But in the city. Not in this village. It's just not right. There's going to be trouble', said Roland Kissling, a perfume buyer. In an unprecedented case, the Turks of Wangen then won the right to erect a six-metre-high minaret. In retaliation, an MP from the right-wing Swiss People's Party, Ulrich Schlüer, launched a campaign for a new clause in the Swiss Constitution stating, 'The building of minarets in Switzerland is forbidden'. Switzerland has over 300,000 Muslims. In Austria, the far-right leader Jörg Haider wanted to make his province Carinthia 'a pioneer in the battle against radical Islam for the protection of our dominant western culture.' The Bishop of Graz was also forthright: 'Muslims should not build mosques which dominate towns' skylines in countries like ours'. The root of the word, *nur*, Arabic for 'light' has many religious and cultural applications: thus the city of Medina, the second pilgrimage city for Muslims after **Mecca**, is often given the title *al munawwara*, 'the Enlightened City', while Arab Christians refer to the Virgin Mary as *umm al nur*, 'the Mother of Light'.

mlecche   Hindu chauvinist term for Muslims, literally 'half-penis'.

moro   The modern Spanish equivalent to Arab *and* Muslim, hence its application to the Muslim minority in the Philippines. From classical Greek *mauros*, 'black', term for (at that time pre-Arab and pre-Muslim) inhabitants of North Africa, later applied to Arabs. In early modern English, as in Shakespeare's play *Othello* the word *moor* has tended to mean someone of mixed Berber, Arab and/or African descent. The geographical term *Mauritania* was used in classical and medieval times to denote larger areas of North Africa, encompassing what are today parts of Algeria and Morocco, but, in modern times, denotes a separate Arab-African state, with its capital at Nouakchott, south of Morocco. In contemporary Spanish, the expression *hay moros por la costa*, literally 'there are Moors (Arabs) off the coast', a reference to hostile naval or pirate forces that raided Spain in the sixteenth and seventeenth centuries, is a colloquial way of telling someone that you are not free to speak at that moment. Crowds demonstrating against the importation of season labour from Morocco in the southern town of El Ejido during the early 2000s often shouted '*Moros* Go Home!' Such negative association did not, however, prevent the guerrilla movement that rebelled against the Philippine government in the 1970s on Mindanao and adjacent islands as the *Moro National Liberation Movement*.

Mullah-ism   Pejorative – *and accurate* – word used in Pakistani politics by critics of the *Jamiat-Ulema-Islami* party, which was backed by the Taliban in Afghanistan, and of other clerical forces. The term was popularised decades earlier in the writings of the liberal Muslim writer Mohammad Iqbal. Analogous to Persian *akhundism*. But see **Muttahida Majlis-i Amal**. European Christian countries had, in the past, generated some similar terms, such as 'priest-ridden', 'priest-infected', 'clerico-fascist' or the fine Spanish term of abuse *meapilas*, literally 'someone who urinates holy water'.

Muslim headbangers   Newspaper columnist Richard Littlejohn's reference to British Muslims who protested at parades for soldiers returning from combat duty in Iraq and Afghanistan. Also termed *Islamic nutjobs* ('Put These Toytown Talibandits on the First Flight Home', *Daily Mail*, 13 March 2009).

Muslim Rage   Demeaning, culturally reductionist, term for hostility to US policies in the Middle East and Muslim world. See 'The Roots of Muslim Rage' in Bernard Lewis, *From Babel to Dragomans. Interpreting the Middle East* (London: Weidenfeld & Nicolson, 2004), Chapter 33, first published in *The Atlantic Monthly*, September 1990.

Muslim smear   Also **madrasa smear**, generic term for use by opponents of Presidential candidate Barack Obama of his Muslim family background, childhood residence in Indonesia (his mother's second husband was from there), attendance at age six at a Muslim school or **madrasa** and the Islamic character of both his first and second names. Some made a point, contrary to normal American usage, of always mentioned his second name, *Hussein*, no doubt redolent to many Americans of that of Iraqi leader Saddam Hussein, just as his family name to that of 'Osama' bin Laden, and used this Muslim background to claim he was acting on behalf of extremist interests: thus right-wing commentator and Cold War veteran Frank Gaffney argued that Obama aimed to use 'the Jihadist vote' to get elected, and was relying on 'between $30m and $100m from the Mideast, Africa and other places Islamists are active' (the *Guardian*, 28 October 2008). Others portrayed him as brainwashed, perhaps '*madrasa-indoctrinated*' from his childhood in Indonesia, and thus the Muslim equivalent of the communist-indoctrinated politician portrayed in *The Manchurian Candidate*. A more extreme claim was that, if elected, he would invite speakers to the White House to broadcast the Muslim call to prayer. Other attacks were cruder, such as that of the radio chat show host Rush Limbaugh, who referred to him as Barack Hussein *Odumbo*, or the demonstrators who addressed him as **Barry Soetoro**. However, the very fact that he might be, or had been, a Muslim or from an Islamic father was in some cases enough for his critics: thus in a televised meeting with an audience in Minnesota on 10 October 2008, with Republican candidate John McCain, a woman in the audience shouted that Obama was 'a terrorist, an Arab and a traitor'. McCain, who in general behaved decently on this matter during the campaign, and more so than Obama's Democratic rival Hillary Clinton (see quote at the top of this chapter), could not bring himself to refute the implications of his questioner's remarks, replying: 'No – he's decent, a family man', by implications inconsistent with being an Arab. Popular voices reported in a *BBC* Radio News programme broadcast on 23 August 2008 included the sentences: 'Well, his name is not Bill Smith, is it?' and 'Obama tries to say he is not a Muslim'.

N

Northern League   In Italy, a chauvinist, anti-southern Italian and anti-Arab political group that developed in northern Italy in the 1990s. One of its leaders, Roberto Calderoli threatened in 2007 to stage a 'day of pork' in order deliberately to provoke Muslims and to take pigs to 'defile' the proposed mosque site. (Ian Traynor, 'The Rise of Mosques Becomes Catalyst for Conflict across Europe', the *Guardian*, 11 October 2007). See **minarets**.

O

Oliver   Banalisation by cartoon strip figure Homer Simpson of Muslim *Allah*, in an episode of *The Simpsons* broadcast in late 2008 in the USA entitled *Mypods and Broomsticks*. In the episode, Homer suspects his neighbour Amid of plotting to blow up the Springfield shopping centre, but, at the end, realises he is mistaken and apologises. Reactions to the episode varied: in the USA the Council on American-Islamic Relations (CAIR) welcomed the episode as a humours rebuttal of anti-Islamic prejudice, whereas in Britain the *Islamic Cultural Centre* and the *Central London Mosque* condemned it as an example of **Islamofobia**.

OMEA   Abbreviation for 'Of Middle East Appearance', term used by US authorities in racial profiling.

orientalism   Literally 'the study of the Orient', the latter something encompassing all of Asia, including India, China and Japan as well as the Middle East, more recently particularly denoting the study of the Arab world and the Middle East. As a scholarly discipline, with many centres and institutes bearing the title, it is the study of the history, law, religion, languages, etc. of these countries. Since the 1970s it has been a term of derogation, linking such study to imperialism, racism and disdain for the peoples concerned. Famously attacked by Columbia University literature professor Edward Said in his book of that name in 1979. Too easily used as an all-purpose category for critiquing conventional study of the region, the term served in many cases, and for many years, to divert the academic study of the Middle East away from substantive study – of states, economies, societies, ideologies, popular movements – into a meta-debate that clarified little (See Fred Halliday '"Orientalism" and its Critics', *Islam and the Myth of Confrontation* [London: I.B.Tauris, 1996], Chapter 7). Those wishing to read an alternative, more measured, informed and creative critique of writing on the Middle East should read Maxime Rodinson, *Europe and the Mystique of Islam* (Seattle: University of Washington Press, 1991).

other/the other   Social–psychological and political term, much used in studies of culture and inter-civilisational relations. Cf. **hostile image, pseudo-speciation**. It received spurious analytic backing from revival of interest, in the 1980s and 1990s among modish Western political theorists, in the second-rate German proto-fascist writer Carl Schmitt. Much used to describe the European, and implicitly Christian, relation to the Islamic world, to support the argument that Europe's identity was historically formed in conflict with the Islamic world. While **other** can be a valid term in the context of developmental psychology, to denote the process by which a child comes to realise its individuality and differentiates itself from parents and family, it is usually misleading in describing relations between states and peoples. First, a theoretical problem: in contrast to individuals, peoples and nations are, by dint of being collective entities, formed mainly by a process of internal growth, conflict and self-definition, within which the external plays a secondary role. Second, an anthropological reality: however, much people, cultures and nations may be opposed to or confront 'other' people, they also etc., for much of the time, trade, exchange food, religions and cultural symbols with each other, rather than live in fixed hostility. Third, in historical terms, it is simply not true that European nations and peoples were formed through some collective confrontation with the Islamic world. Insofar as the external 'other' played a role, it was usually not Muslim countries – Turkey, or, before that, Egypt or Morocco – but *other European states*, as in relations and wars between Britain, France and Germany and, for the colonial powers, such as Spain, Portugal, Britain, France and Holland, and their relation to their non-European empires. Even for countries close to, and sometimes occupied in whole or in part by Arab and Turkish empires, such as Greece, Serbia, Italy and Spain, the Islamic component of their identity and cultural formation is secondary at best. In terms of the history of international, i.e. interstate, relations over recent centuries, the Islamic world was not the 'other' at all, but as with the Ottoman Empire a participant, through shifting alliances, in European diplomacy and, from the nineteenth century onwards, the object of colonial and semi-colonial appropriation.

P

permitted Arabic words   List of Arabic/Islamic terms which prisoners in British jails were allowed to use in verbal communication with their families and lawyers. The unstated implication being that, unless explicitly stated, Arabic words were forbidden: British prison regulations dictate that inmates may speak only in English, but some conventional Arabic terms such as *Assalaamun alaikum* ('Peace be With You'), the regular Muslim greeting, and *inshallah* ('If Allah Wills', somewhat equivalent in usage to the Irish 'God Bless'), were accepted through negotiation between the prison authorities and representatives of the Muslim communities.

plastic *mujahidin* Term applied by UN military sources to young men in Bosnia-Herzegovina who were not very clear about Islam as a religion but were nonetheless impressed with the sincerity and bravery of foreign, often Arab, *mujahidin* fighters who came to fight there in the 1990s and wanted to emulate them. See Chapter 2, **Gucci muj**.

pseudo-speciation Psychological mechanism for naming, and by implication demeaning, another ethnic or religious group. Cf. **hostile image, Islamofobia, other**. A form of stereotyping with the promotion of **enemy images**, often accompanied by incitement to violence and the condoning of killing and territorial expulsion of other people, widely practised by both the Muslim and non-Muslim worlds. Term coined by psychologist Erik Erikson in his *Childhood and Society* (New York: Norton, 1964). The term refers to the practice whereby – as a result of cultural diversity, in itself a potential source of enrichment and enjoyment – human communities (ethnic groups, tribes or nations) come or, more precisely, are led to perceive each other as if they were completely different, and inferior, species. Recent examples include the Islamist denomination of Europeans and Americans as *infidels*, or, in Islamic terms, **Crusaders, *kafir*/kuffar, enemies of Islam, taghuti** and Western terms of abuse of Muslims, such as **camel-jockey, haji, Islamo-fascist, towelhead**. The mechanism is an old one: thus one group, whose name for itself will be some variant of 'the true people/humans' will call others, for example, 'the stutterers' (barbarians), as in the updated version of the ancient Greek term for Persians. Another commonplace way for denying full human status, and hence rights, to 'barbarian' communities is to call them 'slaves' (Slavs), Serbs (from the Latn *servus*) or *dasa*, the Aryan word for the dark-skinned Dravidian speakers in India. Inequality, manifested as domination/subordination, and exploitation follow from this practice where the difference of others is presented as another (lower) plane of existence. Much is made, as in the pseudo-theory **Clash of Civilisations**, of how 'ancient', 'deep structured', 'immanent' and 'atavistic' such conceptions are, but many are either modern inventions or else contemporary revivals, and recycling, of terms that had previously fallen into disuse. The means by which **pseudo-speciation** is promoted include the invention and promotion, often by modern politicians and nationalist writers, of derogatory terms for other peoples, and the diffusion by modern media, including the press, TV, film and more recently the Internet, of hostile images.

R

racaille Abusive French term, 'rabble', applied by Sarkozy to demonstrators in French cities in 2005. See ***caid, Karcheriser***. Right-wing opponents of the anti-racist movement *SOS-Racisme* termed it *SOS-Racaille*.

raghead Abusive term for Middle Eastern, also some South Asian, including Sikh, men, by reference to their wearing turbans and other head coverings. Cf. **Towelhead**.

S

sand-nigger Racist American term for an Arab.

Shaikh Google Network of Islamist websites, including ones such as *Al Sahab*, run by **Al-Qa'ida**.

Shared Values TV series, funded by the US State Department as part of its **public diplomacy** campaign, to the tune of $15 million, organised by Charlotte Beers, a **public relations** specialist hired by the US government to promote better relations with the Muslim world after 9/11. ***Shared Values*** depicted the lives of selected duly adapted US Muslims: it was launched in Indonesia but failed to find outlets in the Middle East, where it was seen as propaganda. The project was abandoned and, in the aftermath, Beers resigned from the State Department in March 2003 (Steve Tatham, *Losing Arab Hearts and Minds: The Coalition, Al Jazeera and Muslim Public Opinion* [London: Routledge, 2007])

sheep in every bathtub French: *un mouton dan la bagnoire*. Derogatory remark about Muslim citizens of France by then Minister of the Interior Nicholas Sarkozy.

Shit of Persia Derogatory rendering in the 1970s of the former *Shah of Iran* by the British satirical journal *Private Eye*.

Sick Man of Europe   Common nineteenth-century term for the Ottoman Empire, a classic anti-Turkish stereotype. First used by the Russian Czar Nicholas I in conversation with the British ambassador, Sir Hamilton Seymour, in 1853, as an argument for collaboration between the two countries in a peaceful partition of Turkish domains. Almost immediately afterwards, the British went to war with the Ottomans against Russia, as they almost did again in 1878. If subsequent international developments are anything to go by, it was two other countries, Russia and Germany, which were by far the sickest in Europe, their internal crises before, during and after World War I precipitating three quarters of a century of war and massacre across the continent. Also a historical corrective to the contemporary argument made against Turkish entry into the European Union, namely that it is **not part of Europe**.

skinnies   US military term for Somalis, during the occupation of Mogadisho in 1993–4.

soul of Islam   Misleading abstraction, something for which the West and 'moderate' leaders in the Muslim world were reportedly 'battling' or 'struggling'. Beyond its dubious epistemological status, and the fact that in Islam there is no equivalent of the Christian concept of the 'soul', this term also implied what all existent knowledge and common sense would contradict – that there existed, or could exist, one single, or dominant, opinion within the Muslim world. Distinct from 'Muslim Public'. See **Arab street**.

'Sultan of Chocolate'   Spanish *el sultan del chocolate*, where **chocolate** is Spanish slang for hashish. The media name for Andelwahid Mizzian Amir, a Moroccan drugs dealer active in the Barbate region of southern Spain, home to many British expatriates (*El País*, 9 May 2009).

superior   Italian premier Silvio Berlusconi's description in September 2001 of Western civilisation in relation to Islam (Elisabetta Povoledo, 'Berlusconi Is Target of Islamist Death Threat', *IHT*, 12–13 January 2008).

superpuissance religieuse   French for 'religious superpower', term used of Saudi Arabia (Samir Amchar, *Politique Etrangère*, No. 5138, March 2005, pp. 23–4).

T

Teddy-Bear *intifada* Protests in Sudan in 2006 following the use by an English school teacher in a local school of the name 'Muhammad' to refer to the teddy bear of one of the pupils. The teacher herself was then expelled from Sudan.

Terrorists Next Door Episode in the Fox TV (Emmy and Golden Globe award-winning) series *24*, starring Kiefer Sutherland as Jack Bauer, about the foiling of a plot by a Turkish Muslim family, in counterterrorism language *sleepers*, that had lived in America for five years while preparing to perpetrate a terrorist attack. In protest, the Los Angeles-based *Muslim Public Affairs Council* argued that the *Terrorists Next Door* strand of the script casts suspicion on 6 million American Muslims. As a result the programme began with a 'public service announcement' by Kiefer Sutherland, stating, 'I'm Kiefer Sutherland. I play counterterrorist Jack Bauer on Fox's *24*. While terrorism is obviously one of the most critical challenges facing our nation and the world, it's important to recognize that the American Muslim community stands firmly beside their fellow Americans in denouncing and resisting terrorism in every form'. See **Faux News**. ('24', *Dialogue*, February 2005). The initial episodes of the series *24* (see Chapter 1) predated 9/11, but the series itself, and in particular the interrogation tactics of Bauer, were later to inspire brutality by American prison guards against Islamist detainees. For a later, comparable, episode of *The Simpsons* see **Oliver**.

Third Temple Name and goal of extreme, minoritarian, Jewish movement, seeking to rebuild the Temple in Jerusalem on the site where the Second Temple, destroyed in 70 AD, once stood (now the site of the al-Aqsa Mosque and *Haram i Sharif*). In the 1940s this was a goal of Israel Eldad, the ideology of the terrorist group Lehi, also known as the Stern Gang. In 2004 an extreme group was reported as planning to crash a plane into the al-Aqsa mosque as part of a campaign to destroy it and rebuild the Temple. One under-recognised problem about rebuilding the Temple is that, were it to be reconstructed, it would be compulsory, under Jewish law and tradition, for the faithful to recommence mass animal sacrifices, as prescribed in the Bible. A religious-nationalist fantasy linked to other, Judaic and Christian, tendencies. See **Rapture Index** and **Zealot**, and, in some extreme Sunni Islamist programmes, with Muslim attempts to unite the (57) countries of the Muslim world into a single **Caliphate**.

towelhead   Term of abuse for South Asians, of any religion (including, of course, Sikhs, who wear turbans) now used more broadly of Muslims and Arabs. One of epithets used by British Prince Harry of his Arab fellow soldiers. Cf. **raghead**.

Tsar Lazar   Serbian national symbol, redefined and redeployed to justify anti-Muslim and anti-Turkish chauvinism in the 1980s and 1990s. In the anti-Islamic mythologies of Europe, equivalent to El Cid for the Spanish, Charles Martel (Victor at the battle of Tours in 750) for the French, Count Starhemberg (leader of the 1683 defence of Vienna) for the Austrians and **Chhatrapati Shivaji** for Hindus. **Lazar** died at the Battle of Kosovo in 1389, having vowed to shield the Christian heartland of Serbia from Muslim invaders. In the Serbian epic, he was visited by a grey falcon from Jerusalem that asked, 'Do you want an earthly kingdom?' The bird continued, 'If you want an earthly kingdom . . . , saddle your horses and drive out the Turks. // If you want a heavenly kingdom, build a church at Kosovo, // For all your soldiers shall be destroyed, // And you, prince . . . with them'. Lazar chose the latter. More than six centuries on, a Serbian militia group of the same name was formed in May 2007 and vowed to go into battle if Kosovo declared – or was given – independence (Humphrey Hawksley, 'Squaring off for the Wrong Fight', *IHT*, 9 November 2007).

V

veil   See Chapter 5.

Vlaams Belang   *Flemish Interest*, Belgian ultra-right party that advocates Flemish independence and strict limits on immigration, imposing the condition that immigrants must adopt Western culture. Although some of the founders of the party were Nazi collaborators, it is supported by a small, vocal Jewish group because of its anti-Arab xenophobia. The *Vlaams Belang* leader Filip Dewinter regularly meets Jewish leaders and is photographed with prominent rabbis. For Dewinter, Israel is 'the forward post of the free West fighting radical Islam'.

voluntary apartheid   Term applied in public discussion in Britain from 2006, e.g. by the then domestic affairs spokesman, 'Shadow Home Secretary', of the Conservative Party, David Davis, to practices and urban zoning that distinguished, and physically separated, Muslim from non-Muslim citizens. From the notorious Afrikaaner word for 'apartness', and the racist policy, i.e. *involuntary apartheid*, imposed by the white supremacist National Party in South Africa from 1948 to 1994 under the spurious slogan 'Separate But Equal'. Trevor Phillips, head of the Commission for Racial Equality, also warned that Britain was 'sleepwalking towards segregation'. Jack Straw, then Leader of the House of Commons (see also Chapter 1, **villains' charter**), tried some finesse, saying that 'some of my constituents who have been accepting of the *hijab* are greatly concerned about the **niqab**' (Tania Branigan and Vikram Dodd, 'Muslim Leaders "Risking Voluntary Apartheid" as Veil Row Escalates', the *Guardian*, 16 October 2006; Martin Wainwright et al., 'Dangerous Attack or Fair Point? Straw Veil Row Deepens', the *Guardian*, 7 October 2007). See Chapter 5, **hijab**.

vovchik   Russian term of abuse, short for *vahhabovchik*, 'Wahhabi', used indiscriminately of all opponents or critics of Moscow's policy in Chechenya and, more broadly, in the North Caucasus. Cf. **chernishopi**.

Images of Muslims

1. Ali Baba
2. Arab street
3. black arses
4. goat fuckers
5. Islamo-fascism
6. Jihadi Candidate
7. *Karcheriser*
8. Londonistan
9. Muslim headbangers
10. Muslim rage
11. permitted Arabic words
12. raghead
13. *Terrorists Next Door*
14. towelhead

CHAPTER 7

Palestine and Israel: 'Holy Land' and Other Inventions

A

abandoned properties Official Israeli term for private property of Arabs who live just outside the municipal boundaries of Jerusalem but whose adjoining properties are located within these borders, liable to confiscation without right of appeal or compensation (Henry Siegman, 'In the Mideast, Ask the Right Question', *IHT*, 5 May 2005).

Abu Ammar 'Father of Ammar', political name of Yasser Arafat, PLO leader 1968–2004.

Abu Ghanaim Arabic place name, literally 'the father of two goats', area on outskirts of Jerusalem, known to Israelis as *Har Homa*, where, from the late 1990s, Palestinians have protested at Israeli building projects.

Abu Qusai 'The father of Qusai', Qusai being one of the two sons of Saddam Hussein, hence a name adopted by someone who admired the Iraqi leader, such as the West Bank head of the Al-Aqsa Martyr's Brigade who was long imprisoned by the Israelis but released in July 2008 and immediately involved in repression and torture of Hamas rivals (*El País*, 18 August 2008).

administered territories Israeli term for lands occupied and retained after the June 1967 war. For critics, and in international law, *occupied territories*.

Against Normalisation Arabic *dhud al-tatbia*. Campaign in Arab countries in the 1990s and 2000s against diplomatic relations with Israel.

Al-Fatah Name of mainstream Palestinian group. See *fath*.

al-nakba   Arabic: 'the catastrophe'. A calque on the Hebrew term for
the Judaeocide, *Shoah*. Palestinian term for 1948–9 Arab–Israeli war and
expulsion of hundreds of thousands of Arabs. In Israeli terminology, the
'War of Independence'. Not to be confused with *al-naksa*, 'the setback', name
given to 1967 Arab–Israeli war.

`amaliat   istishadia   Suicide   bomb   attacks.   See   **martyrdom
operations**.

Amalek, Amalekite   Biblical term (Exodus 17: 8–16) for inferior tribe
whom, as a result of their attacking the Jews in the wilderness, the chosen of
God have the right to drive from their lands, exterminate, brutalise, in the
words of the Bible, 'blot out'. Term used by some extreme Jewish settlers of
Arabs on the West Bank, also by English troops sent by Oliver Cromwell to
Ireland in the 1640s.

anti-semitism   Prejudice, on religious or ethnic grounds against Jews,
widespread in Europe in late-nineteenth and early-twentieth centuries, providing ideological basis for Nazi genocide, later adopted by anti-Israeli
groups in the Middle East and more widely in the Muslim world. **Anti-
semitism** involves a packet of different prejudices, some drawing on Christian hostility to Jews, as a result of the execution of Jesus Christ, some
drawing on distorted hostility to Jews as embodiments of capitalist banking
(hence the remark by the German socialist August Bebel, describing anti-
semitism as 'the socialism of fools'). Many Jewish and pro-Israeli writers
regard **anti-semitism** as somehow inherent, across centuries, in Western –
when not all 'gentile', i.e. non-Jewish – culture: thus the Irish writer Conor
Cruise O'Brien said, 'Anti-semitism is a light sleeper'. While the Nazi genocide to a considerable, but not adequate, degree discredited anti-semitism
in Europe, the Arab–Israeli conflict has provided another, separate, context in Arab states and across the Muslim world for the resurgence of such
prejudice, in which stereotypes about Jews, and denunciations of Israel, go
well beyond any legitimate criticism: these include the campaign to define
Jewish nationalism, 'Zionism', as intrinsically a form of racism, and the propaganda identification of Israel with Nazi Germany. That Israeli society and
nationalist discourse embody some racist themes, towards Arabs and indeed all gentiles, such prejudice is hardly specific to Israel: the policies of,
for example, Iran and Syria towards Kurds are prime examples. Some of this
anti-Israeli propaganda draws on European themes and sources, including
the notorious forgery *The Protocols of the Elders of Zion*, while in more recent

years radical Islamist groups have forged a new religious hostility to Jews based on selective quotations from the Quran and prejudicial recycling of early Muslim history: see **Khaibar**. In the period since 9/11 some writers have identified a *new anti-semitism,* involving a more extreme, and racist, critique of Israel. While militant critics of Israel, in the Middle East and elsewhere, deny the charge of **anti-semitism**, some pro-Israeli writers use the charge to cover *all* criticism of Israeli policies towards the Palestinians.

Anti-Zionism   An elastic term, denoting hostility to 'Zionism' in different forms and on different definitions of the word itself, for which see **Zionism**. In general, pre-1948, opposition to the establishment of a Jewish state in Palestine within Jewish communities; since 1948, and especially since the rise of opposition to Israel internationally since the 1967 war, hostility to the exclusively Jewish character of Israel and/or hostility to the existence of the Israeli state as such. Anti-Zionists would favour, in earlier times, a solution to the persecution of Jews within the countries of the diaspora, in the more recent period, an end to discrimination against non-Jews inside Israel, and a repudiation of the claim that Israel is the state of all Jews in the world. The earlier forms of **Anti-Zionism** came partly from religious groups who argued that there could be no Jewish state on Earth prior to the return of the Messiah, and partly from left-wing socialist groups who saw the solution of the persecution of Jews within the context of a European anti-capitalist revolution. Both of these arguments rather lost relevance after the 1940s: the former because the state was established, the latter because the massacre of Jews under Nazism and the persistence of anti-Semitism in the USSR invalidated the aspiration to a socialist resolution of 'the Jewish question'. At the same time, arguments in favour of the abolition of Israel as a Jewish state persisted, sometimes in tacit or covert form. For example, the argument much trumpeted since an **Anti-Zionist** UN resolution to this effect was passed in the 1970s that Zionism is a form of 'racism' often contains such an, unstated, premise. That Zionist ideology and practice, like that of all forms of nationalism, exhibit elements of ethnic superiority and discrimination against non-nationals, is certainly true, but it is equally so of Arab nationalism, e.g. in its Ba'thist form and of Turkish and Iranian nationalism, etc., and does not entail that these nations have no right to their own state, this latter being the underlying claim of the 'Zionism = Racism' claim. On the same logic, neither Turkey nor Syria would have the right to exist as states because of their denial of the rights of their Kurdish citizens. Ditto Chinese, Russian, English and American nationalism. While proponents of **Anti-Zionism** seek to distinguish themselves from the racist ideology of **anti-semitism**, and may articulate valid criticisms of the Jewish state, based on considerations of international law and human rights norms, much of the rhetoric of the anti-Israeli movement, in the Middle East and in the West, contains **anti-semitic** themes. This has become increasingly the case with the rise of rabidly **anti-semitic** and racist rhetoric of Islamist groups such as Hezbollah and Hamas.

Armageddon   Site of battle between Jews and Philistines in ancient Israel, now taken as a term for the ultimate battle before the return of the **Messiah**. In the Cold War, it was associated with possible, all-destructive, nuclear war, in this case to be avoided.

ascent   To heavens, theme in Christian and Muslim religions, but with distinct, if often confused, meanings. Christianity has both the *Ascension* of Christ – physically, to heaven on the Feast of the Ascension, the fifth Thursday after his resurrection on Easter Sunday – and the *Assumption*, of the Virgin Mary – upon her natural death, 15 August, this latter a major public holiday in many Catholic countries (in Ireland, for example, the last holiday before the harvest). Islam has the *Night Journey*, Arabic *miraj*, of the Prophet Mohammad, when, guided by an angel, he visited the heavens for a few hours before returning to Earth. This latter event is said to have taken place at the 'furthest' place, *al-aqsa*, deemed by custom, but without any historical or other evidence, to have been the hill of Jerusalem, hence the location there of a major mosque of that name – not, however, to be confused with the much larger golden domed *Haram al-Sharif.*

B

Bantustan   Term frequently applied to Palestinian-controlled areas after the 1993 Oslo Accords. See Chapter 9.

barrier   Israeli term, also **fence, separation barrier**, used to denote wall constructed between Israel and the West Bank, denounced by opponents as the **wall**. Built by the Sharon government in 2003–4. Known to critics as the 'separation wall' and the 'Apartheid Wall', the eight-metre-high concrete wall replete with razor wire, sniper towers and electric fences enclosed thousands Palestinians by means of an elaborate separation barrier system that consists of a 'smart' fence in the centre. The average width of the barrier ranged from 50 to 100 metres. The implication of the term is that the construction is designed to keep out something unwanted, dangerous, toxic. Cf. use by East German authorities after construction of the Berlin Wall in 1961, of the term *die Sperrmauer* – the blocking wall. For West Germans it was often known as *die Schandemauer* – the wall of shame. Cf. term for wall built in 1970s between Catholic and Protestant areas of Belfast, *Peace Line.*

bizarre ratification of Osama bin Laden's view Criticism by magazine *The New Republic* of former Secretary of State Colin Powell for his views on Palestine. 'There is bin Laden attempting to persuade the Muslim world that what he wants is justice for the Palestinians, and here is Colin Powell attempting to persuade the Muslim world that what he wants is justice for the Palestinians' (Eric Alterman, 'Idiocy Watch: *The New Republic*', *The Nation*, 7–14 January 2002).

brigades Arabic: *kita'ib*. Term frequently used by Arab or Palestinian guerrilla groups to denote their organisation, with suggestion of at least paramilitary dimension, as in *al-Aqsa Martyrs*, or **Abu Hafs al-Masri**, etc. The term seems to have come into Arabic political terminology in the 1930s when the Lebanese Christian leader Pierre Jemayyil, influenced by Italian fascism and the use of the term Phalange (from Latin *phalanx*) in both Italy and Spain, founded his own organisation of that name.

C

Christian Zionism The belief, particularly strong among Evangelicals in the USA, that the restoration of the Jews to Palestine is a divine mandate and a necessary precursor to the return of the **Messiah**. Although supportive in political and military terms of Israel as a state, this attitude is also quite compatible with anti-semitism, and with a desire to force Jews out of gentile societies, such as the USA, where they currently reside. See **Armageddon, dispensationalism, End Times, Left Behind, Rapture Index**.

creeping right of return Israeli term denoting intermarriage between Arabs with Israeli citizenship and inhabitants of West Bank, Gaza or Arab countries. Used as basis for denying rights of family reunification when Israeli Arabs seek to bring their families home. See **right of return**.

D

dismantling of terrorist infrastructure Wide term used by US Congress to authorise coercive and punitive Israeli actions in the Occupied Territories. A resolution submitted to the 107th Congress, Second Session H (Res. 392) by Tom DeLay, *inter alia*, stated that The House of Representatives 'stands in solidarity with Israel as it takes necessary steps to provide security to its people by dismantling the terrorist infrastructure in the Palestinian areas;' 'Necessary steps' include military and nonmilitary action and the use of **New Israeli Population Centres** in the West Bank to destroy any contiguity that might make a Palestinian state viable. The resolution was passed at a time when Amnesty International had published a detailed report (2002) on the situation in the Israeli-occupied West Bank noting that 'the IDF [Israeli Defense Forces] acted as though the main aim was to punish all Palestinians. Actions were taken by the IDF which had no clear or obvious military necessity.' The report documents unlawful killings, destruction of civilian property, arbitrary detention, torture, assaults on medical personnel and journalists, and random shooting at people in the streets and houses (Henry Siegman, 'Is Bush Getting Serious about the Peace Process?', *IHT*, 21 June 2007).

dispensationalism   Aberrant US Christian belief that advocates return of Jews to Israel – hence strong support for the Israeli state – and envisages future nuclear war as desirable, leading to the return of the **Messiah**, Jesus Christ. A theological system based on literal interpretation of the Book of Revelation, and first popularised by John Nelson Darby, a nineteenth-century British evangelist. **Dispensationalism** divides history into seven dispensations, or epochs, beginning with the age of innocence (Adam). We are now preparing to enter the seventh time period, or the Millennial Kingdom, a 1,000 year reign of Christ on Earth. In Jerry Falwell's *Nuclear War and the Second Coming of Jesus Christ* (1983), nuclear war is welcome because it is inseparable from the Second Coming: 'the one brings thoughts of fear, destruction, and death, while the other brings thoughts of joy, hope, and life. They . . . are indelibly intertwined.' In order for a dispensational interpretation of prophecy to be fulfilled, the world's Jews must return to Israel (although dispensationalists also believe two-thirds of Jews will perish after the Rapture). To facilitate that process, dispensationalists have been among leading lobbyists seeking financial and political support for settlement programmes in Israel. One recent US poll showed that 36 per cent of respondents argued that the Book of Revelations should be read literally as prophecy, while the '**Left Behind**' series co-authored by the Christian right leader Tim LaHaye, which promotes a dispensationalist interpretation of the 'end of times', has sold 62 million copies. See **Christian Zionist, End Times, Left Behind, Rapture Index** (Colin Kidd, 'My God Was Bigger Than His', *London Review of Books*, 4 November 2004).

disputed   Frequently evasive, and purportedly even-handed term, much used by BBC radio news, to refer to places or areas in which territorial claims of different ethnic groups clash, implying that the two parties to the 'dispute' have equal moral and historical claim. Thus **disputed site** is a BBC term for the areas of Jerusalem or the West Bank where Israeli and Palestinian claims conflict. See **militants**. Also used in reports on Kashmit, *disputed territory*.

disputed site   Common Israeli and Western term for Dome of the Rock/Temple Mount in Jerusalem.

disputed territories   Israeli euphemism, and designed to displace 'Occupied Territories', for lands illegally retained after the 1967 Arab-Israeli war.

Dughmush   Armed clan operating in Gaza, separate from main political groups, Al-Fatah and Hamas. The 2007 kidnapping of British journalist Alan Johnson by the Dughmush clan drew attention to some of the complexities of political alliances in Gaza. Johnson's release after 16 weeks was negotiated with Hamas after dozens of Hamas militiamen surrounded Gaza City's Sabra neighbourhood where the Dughmush clan lives. The clan is constituted of a large family that controls part of Gaza and is notorious for the scale of its legal and illegal business activities. It has worked at different times with Al-Fatah and Hamas, mainly for commercial reasons. The 'ideological' side is represented by Mumtaz Dughmush and his 'Army of Islam' group, described by some Hamas sources as 'murderers and thugs who want money and jobs', while Palestinian Authority spokespersons say that the radical Islamic rhetoric is a cover for common criminal demands for money. However, the clan is protected by influential elements within the well-armed, resourceful and Fatah-dominated Preventive Security Force (Khaled Abu Toemeh, 'Gaza Clan Chief Holds on to Johnson', *The Jerusalem Post*, 22 July 2007; Benjamin Barthe, 'A Gaza, les rivalités entre le Hamas et le Fatah ont fait naître un 'nouveau courant extrémiste', *Le Monde*, 3 May 2007).

dynamic rapper   Usually shortened to DR, vocalist of a Palestinian hip-hop group – **The Palestinian Rapperz** – from Gaza, very popular among young people. Some Islamic youth object to its body language, yet, says DR, 'We don't sing about sex or drugs. We sing in Arabic and our songs are about Palestinian customs.' However, while traditional Palestinian songs are about love, DR lyrics, with a beat sounding like the rumble of tanks, speak of death and suffering. One song laments, 'Just because we're Palestinians // America and everyone suspects us of being terrorists // But all we're asking for is freedom' (Gwen Ackerman, 'Hip-hop musulmán en Gaza', *La Vanguardia*, 12 May 2007; *Time*, 22 February 2007).

E

End Times Biblical notion of the end of time, the coming of the Messiah, the deliverance of humanity. Much propagated by **dispensationalists**, believers in **Rapture, Second Coming**. The Quran, *Surat al Zilzal*, 'The Chapter of the Earthquake', has a similar historical vision, of terrible upheaval, followed by deliverance.

F

Farfour Figure in a Palestinian children's TV show. This Mickey Mouse look-alike, on a Hamas-affiliated television station, whose name means 'Butterfly', was the host of a children's programme called *Tomorrow's Pioneers*. In one episode he told child viewers, 'You and I are laying the foundation for a world led by Islamists'. He was finally killed off with a 'glorious martyr's' death in July 2007 while 'defending his land'. While propagandising for national values and pride are a legitimate part of such programmes, the injection of military incitement and romanticisation of death and killing into children's TV, like the common Palestinian practice of parading young boys in military uniform and with toy, or real, rifles, is above all a brazen violation of the rights of children ('Hamas TV Kills off Controversial Children's Character', *IHT*, 2 July 2007).

fath Arabic for 'conquest', or 'opening', a term with Quranic resonances. Great Islamic military leaders have often been called *al-fatih*, 'the conqueror', their conquests *futuhat*. Adopted as **Al-Fatah**, the name in English for a nationalist Palestinian group in the 1950s. The letters in Arabic '*f-t-h*' read as a reverse acronym for '*h-t-f* – *harakat al-tahrir al-watani al-falastini*, the Palestinian National Liberation Movement, long led by Yasser Arafat, until his death in 2004. Contrast acronym of its later, Islamic, rival **Hamas**. Strictly, in regard to the name of the Palestinian group, the definite article 'al' should not be affixed to the word *fath*. The same root can be used to form the word *mufattih*, an aperitif, or appetiser, and also *infitah*, the 'open door' policy introduced into the Egyptian economy by President Sadat in the 1970s. **Al-Fatah** is separate from the broader umbrella of the Palestinian Liberation Organisation (PLO), of which it is a dominant member.

fence   Israeli term, also **barrier**, for wall constructed in 2002–4.

fitful campaign   Palestinian leader Mahmoud Abbas's attempt to impose control in Palestinian-administered areas. So described in 2005, after he 'scored one small victory and suffered one awkward setback'. See also **iron fist** (Greg Myre, 'Abbas's Fitful Progress in Palestine', *IHT*, 5 May 2005).

Force 17   Elite presidential bodyguard created by Yasser Arafat and inherited by Mahmoud Abbas, used to protect the Palestinian leader and to silence critics within Palestinian society.

formaldehyde   Dov Weissglas, adviser to then Israeli prime minister Ariel Sharon, boasted that the 'road map' for settlement of the Palestine question and indeed the whole peace process had been 'safely' stashed away in this embalming fluid (Henry Siegman, 'In the Mideast, Ask the Right Question', *IHT*, 5 May 2005).

G

government with an address   In 2007 Israeli leaders were hopeful of negotiating peace with Syria and hence a halt to Syria's support for 'Palestinian extremists' and Hezbollah. One reason given was that Syrian President Bashar al-Assad, unlike Israel's other adversaries including Hezbollah, **Hamas, Al-Qa'ida** and **Islamic Jihad**, 'actually runs a government with an address' (Steven Erlanger, 'Israelis Make a Case for Talks with Syria', *IHT*, 28 May 2007). This, apparently optimistic, expectation did not stop the Israelis from bombing a suspected military target in Syria later in the year. In fact, the first of these groups, Hezbollah, did have an address, above all by dint of having elected members in the Lebanese parliament.

Grapes of Wrath   Name of 1996 Israeli military operation into Lebanon, recycled use of the title of John Steinbeck's 1930s novel, itself derived from a passage in the Bible (*Revelations* 14: 19–20) about the depression and dust bowl in America. See also **Katyusha**.

Green Revolution   Once a favoured World Bank agricultural policy for underdeveloped countries, the rise of **Hamas** in Gaza has also come to be known as the 'Green Revolution' because of the colour of the Hamas flag. Green is also considered to be the colour of Islam as the tribe of the Prophet Muhammad had a green banner, while the Quran describes Paradise (from the Persian word *pairi-daeza*, also a 'garden') as being filled with green, a place where people will wear 'green garments of fine silk'. In the run-up to **Hamas's** overwhelming victory in the 2005 elections, thousands of people were wearing green headbands saying *al islam huwa al-hal* ('Islam is the Solution'), a common Islamist slogan across the Middle East. Precisely and concretely what this 'solution' is supposed to be, other than imposing rigid social controls on women, banning alcohol and destroying modern educational and legal systems, is never made clear. Modern history has also seen a 'White Revolution', the Shah of Iran's early 1960s reform programme, and an 'Orange Revolution', the mobilisation for change in Ukraine and Georgia in 2003–5. Historically, radical revolutions have, of course, been 'Red', also, since the eighteenth century, the colour of the standard of the Sultan of Muscat.

H

Hamas   Acronym for *harakat al-muqawama al-islamiyya*, the Islamic Resistance Movement, a Palestinian branch of the Muslim Brotherhood, founded on 15 December 1987. Also the name of a more moderate, and quite distinct, Algerian political party. The Palestinian group's name is an implicit – *Islami*c – critique of the full title of its main rival, **Fath**, the Palestinian *National* Liberation Movement.

Hamas-lite   The new Palestinian government of 2006, in which Hamas would hold the majority in the Palestinian assembly and would therefore be able to exert a veto on any decisions, was so described by a 'senior [Israeli] military official, speaking anonymously because he was not authorized to speak publicly' (Ian Fisher, 'Hint of Progress in Palestinian Talks', *IHT, IHT*, 14 November 2006). The subsequent, June 2007, military seizure of Gaza by Hamas may have qualified this judgement.

Hannibal directive   In Hebrew *Nohal Hannibal*. This, according to *Schott's Almanac 2007*, was 'the unofficial Israeli order for soldiers to open fire on those kidnapping a comrade, even at the cost of his life, on the basis that a dead soldier is better than one whose life can be bartered for political gain'.

hasbara   Hebrew term for pro-Israeli propaganda and news management, literally the noun form of 'explaining', first used before the establishment of Israel in 1948 by representatives of the Zionist movement for 'explaining', i.e. 'making', the case for the Jewish state. Today it is generally used for explaining – in the sense of justifying – the Israeli case abroad. In

2004, Israel's Channel 2 launched a prime-time television programme called 'The Ambassador', in which 14 Israelis aged between 25 and 30 competed in different key locations (Cambridge University, Paris, Washington, New York, etc.) to make the best case (*hasbara*) for Israel in a largely hostile world, with a prize of one year in New York as a 'communications expert' for Israel. In an episode set in Paris, for example, contestants had to try to convince French citizens to buy air tickets to travel to Israel. The programme's blurb described *hasbara* as 'perhaps the biggest challenge facing Israel'. A Foreign Ministry report leaked just previously had warned that Israel's international image could soon deteriorate to that of South Africa in the late apartheid era and that support in America may slip. The explanation to be offered largely consisted in presenting Israelis as 5 million underdogs facing 100 million hostile Arabs, in an uncaring world where oil interests, Arab pressures and anti-Semitism hold sway. However, some hardliners argue that there is no longer any need for Israel to 'explain' its case and prefer the term much used in the USA in the 1990s and 2000s, **public diplomacy**. Alon Pinkas, the former Israeli consul general in New York, opposed *hasbara* on the grounds that Israel could not be both militarily strong and seen as the underdog: his government, he said, should be willing to pay the price of not having world empathy (Gary Rosenblatt, 'Israel Goes Prime Time', *United Jewish Communities*, 12 March 2004, www.ujc.org/page.html?ArticleID=89887).

Holocaust   Greek Biblical term for 'complete incineration'. Originally a large sacrifice, involving the burning of animals, as in temples of ancient Israel. In modern political usage, since used in this way by anti-Nazi investigator Simon Wiesenthal in the 1960s, the term has been applied to the genocide of 6 million Jews by Nazi Germany. Some historians objected to the term on the grounds that it separated the massacre of Jews from that of other murdered groups, such as communists, homosexuals, the handicapped and Gypsies and that it gave a spurious religious and providential, not to say fatalistic, character to what was an act of modern state mass brutality. This terminological querying, of the term but not of the genocide itself, is distinct from 'Holocaust Denial', the claim that no such genocide had taken place or that the figures for the numbers killed were deliberately exaggerated. See also **genocide, Judaeocide, *Shoah***.

Holy Land   Term used in recent centuries by Christians to note areas where the Bible and Gospel locate ancient people of Israel, the rise of Christianity, etc. The term itself is without any authority in the Bible, and was invented three centuries later by Eusebius of Cesearea (263–339 AD), one of the 'Early Fathers of the Church', in the time of the Emperor Constantine.

Merged in Western Christian imagination during the nineteenth century with Roman provincial denomination, **Palestine**. In recent decades, the term is also copied and adopted by Islamist fundamentalists, like **Hamas**, to denote lands occupied and dominated by Israel. For comparable contemporary sacralisation of territory, see Chapter 10, **Peninsula of the Prophet Mohammad**.

hostile entity   President George W. Bush declared the Gaza Strip a **hostile entity** in September 2007, three months after **Hamas** had taken power there. Ironically an echo of the Arab anti-Israeli term **the entity**, in both cases a way of referring to a territory and its political administration without giving it the status of being a 'state'.

hudna   Arabic for truce, term taken from the **Quran**, used by **Hamas** for possible ceasefire with Israel, while avoiding direct negotiations or commitment to longer-term recognition or final peace. Less tentative than *tahdia*, 'calming' or 'pacification', which implies a suspension of hostilities for a more limited period.

I

institutionally annoyed   Term used by the European Union (EU) to denote disapproval by officials in Brussels of Israeli settlement expansion plans, without this implying that any individual government member of the EU had also expressed such disapproval (Conal Urquat, 'US Deal "Wrecks Middle East Peace"', the *Guardian*, 24 August 2004).

Islamic *Jihad*   Extreme religious-nationalist group based in Gaza, not controlled by, and a rival of, **Hamas**. Source of some of the most irresponsible, and murderous, actions against Israelis. Strictly speaking, the term itself is nonsense, since **jihad** is by definition carried out by, and on behalf of, Muslims.

Israel   In Bible, name given by God to Jacob, and then to a whole people, *the people of Israel*, by extension to a geographical area. The gift of territory to the Jewish people by God, Genesis 1:18–21, does not specify a name. Name chosen, at last minute, by Jewish leader David Ben-Gurion for the Jewish state he proclaimed on 14 May 1948. Hitherto the area of Zionist settlement and aspiration had been referred to, by its British colonial name, as 'Palestine', while Jewish writers had suggested such names as *Eretz* (the land of) *Israel*, *Medinet* (the state of) *Israel*, *Judah*, *Zion*. The intention of choosing the name **Israel** was to make a claim not only over the land, in the name of the historic, if short-lived, United Kingdom of Israel of Kings Solomon and David, but, more importantly, and controversially, to make a claim over all the *people of Israel*, the original Biblical usage of the term, i.e., all Jews in the world. The establishment of Israel involved, therefore, not just a claim to land, but also a claim *over* all Jews in the world, who had an obligation to 'return' to their homeland.

Israel's Ayatollahs   Title of book by Israeli author Raphael Merguis (London: Saqi Books, 1987) on Israeli far right extremists such as Rabbi Meir Kahane.

Israeli-dominated *Bantustan*   Sceptical term used of statehood offered to Palestinians by Israel. The American journalist Thomas Friedman stated that the Palestine Liberation Organisation seemed willing to fight against its Islamist rival **Hamas** if it was offered a real state to rule over rather than 'some Israeli-dominated Bantustan' (Anatol Lieven, 'America Holds the Key to Mideast Peace', *FT*, 22 November 2007). See also **Ramallah model**.

Israeli controls   Western European diplomatic euphemism for Israeli occupation policies. Tony Blair's 'great summit' on the Middle East, held in London on 1 March 2005 in order to please Washington, was, despite being boycotted by Israel, potentially a useful get-together of 23 foreign ministers and six international organisations. The idea was to 'help' (pressure) the reluctantly attending Palestinian President Abu Mazen to control **Hamas** and the Palestinian Islamic *Jihad* movement, without this being linked with any concession from the Sharon government. While Javier Solana, the EU's *High Representative for Common Foreign and Security Policy*, lectured Abu Mazen on electoral structures and anti-corruption measures, the only balancing factor with regard to the absent Israel was a reference at the end of the final communiqué to **Israeli controls** (a euphemism for occupation) being 'economically counterproductive' (Rafael Ramos, 'Israel boicotea la reunión de Londres y no hará concesiones', *La Vanguardia*, 1 March 2007).

J

Jenin Martyrs Brigades   Radical Palestinian group based in the Al Bureij refugee camp in Gaza and taking its name from a camp on the West Bank which was site of particularly brutal Israeli-Palestinian confrontation in 2001. They took part in the July 2004 uprising against local police and other Palestinian Authority officials in July 2004 which challenged the authority of Yasser Arafat.

Jerusalem   City claimed in modern times as capital by both Israelis and Palestinians, site of Christian holy places, object of Crusader attacks in the eleventh and twelfth centuries, today symbol of intolerance, prejudice and manipulation of history and religion by partisan elements and fanatics. From the Hebrew *ir ha-shalom* (city of peace). The Arabic name for the city, *al-Quds* (the blessed, with same root as capital of Somalia, *Mogadishu*, 'The Blessed One'), corresponds to the ancient Hebrew *ir ha-kodesh* (the holy city). This place name is another political term that can mean a number of different things, the geographical area it denotes has expanded greatly in modern times, from the small historical centre, roughly one square kilometre – site of Christian, Jewish and Muslim shrines – to the expanded city and suburbs of today, in themselves of no religious, or historic, significance but vested with such by modern politics. The religious significance of this city for all three religions has ebbed and flowed over past centuries: it is, above all, a function of contemporary political concerns. For all the talk of Jerusalem as a city of the sacred, three religions, etc., it is in reality a symbol of intolerance, *between* religions, and, in the case of intermittent clashes between Christian communities, such as that in 1854 over the keys to the Church of the Holy Sepulchre which sparked the Crimean War, or the fight between Armenian and Greek worshippers in the same church in 2008, *within* religions. The only time in modern history when the patriarchal authorities of all three religions united was in opposition to a Gay Rights march to be held in the city in 2005.

Jesus Christ   Founder of Christian religion, self-proclaimed Son of God, central figure in the Christian New Testament. For all the influence of this personality, there is no firm historical evidence as to his existence, and the supposedly fundamental sources, the four Gospels, were written, on the basis of hearsay, decades after his death. An alleged reference in the *Histories* of the second-century AD Jewish historian Josephus is, at best, unclear and, in the view of many textual experts, a later interpellation by Christian copyists. Cf. **Holy Land, Three Kings**.

Judaeocide   Literally 'the killing of Jews', a term now used in parallel with, and sometimes as alternative to, the **Holocaust**. See also *Shoah*. Killing Jews did not, of course, begin with the genocide of the 1940s, but runs back through European and, to a considerably lesser extent, Middle Eastern history. For other uses of the suffix '-cide', see **Arabicide, genocide, politicide.**

K

Katyusha   Informal name for Russian-made truck-mounted rocket barrages, used by the Red Army in World War II, later applied incorrectly to hand-held missiles, more properly termed 'bazookas' used by guerrillas in Vietnam (to 1975), the Dhofar region of Oman (1968–75) and Afghanistan (1980s and onwards) and by Palestinians and Hezbollah in Lebanon (1970s onwards) firing at Israel, as well as in Iraq after 2003. A self-propelled but unguided and hence inaccurate and indiscriminate weapon: the advantage of these missiles was that, being highly mobile, they could be used, and their launchers then moved, before the enemy had time to counterattack. In origin the name **Katyusha** (Катюша) is derived from the Russian name for Catherine, Ekaterina, a double diminutive via Katya, and pertains to a song where a woman longs for her beloved, who is away on military service. The German army referred to these missiles as 'Stalin organs', both because the tubes mounted on trucks resembled the pipes of an organ, and also because of the sound they made passing through the air. **Katyusha** rockets were widely used by Hezbollah against Israeli territory during the 'summer war' of 2006.

Khaibar   Battle between the Muslims led by the Prophet Mohammad and Jewish tribes in the seventh century, cited today in Arabic slogans directed against Israel as symbol of Jewish defeat, e.g. *khaibar, khaibar, lil yihud*, in effect, 'Defeat, Defeat to the Jews'.

L

Lepanto   Naval battle (7 October 1571) off the west coast of Greece in which the navies of Venice and Spain, under the command of Don Juan of Austria, defeated those of the Ottoman Empire. Taken in European historiography as a strategic Christian victory over the Turks: in fact, the naval defeat at **Lepanto** did not stop the Ottoman advance overland through the Balkans and to the gates of Vienna, where they were only turned back in 1683, while the Spanish victory in 1571 was more than erased in their defeat by the English 17 years later, in 1588. What **Lepanto** in the end signified was a rough division of the Mediterranean into a western part, dominated by France and Spain, and the eastern part, dominated by the Ottoman Empire.

M

martyrdom operations   Approving Arabic term for suicide bombing attacks.

Mene, mene, tekel, upharsin   Words used by right-wing settlers on the West Bank to oppose territorial concessions. Originally an Aramaic curse visited upon the King of Babylon. According to the *Book of Daniel 5:1–31*, in what has subsequently become known in literature and opera as 'Belshazzar's Feast', the King of Babylon took hold of sacred golden and silver vessels, removed from the Jewish Temple in Jerusalem by his predecessor Nebuchadnezzar, and he and his court then used them to praise the (pagan) gods of gold and silver, bronze, iron, wood and stone. Immediately a disembodied hand wrote the mysterious Aramaic words *Mene, mene, tekel, upharsin* on the palace wall. Only the Prophet Daniel was able to interpret them: *mene* ('monetary toll') meant the days of Belshazzar's kingdom were numbered; *tekel* (a tokenary weight) meant that, weighed on the scales, he had been found wanting; and *parsin* ('division', but also 'Persian') meant that the kingdom would be divided. That night Belshazzar was murdered in his bed and Darius, King of Persia, became king. Though the historical details of the Bible story are disputed, the metaphorical meaning of the Aramaic words has endured as a portent of doom: today the more fanatical of the Jewish settlers in Gaza and the West Bank read the words literally and, in their righteousness, are not going to let the kingdom (in this case the 'historic' land of Israel as they claim it) be divided (Steven Erlanger, 'Era of Risks Weizman Might Have Relished', *IHT*, 30 April–1 May 2005).

Messiah   Hebrew, 'the anointed one', the saviour appointed by God who will come to deliver the world. In Christian theology, applied to Jesus Christ, who claimed to be not only the **Messiah** but also, sacrilegiously, the 'Son of God', a claim for which he was tried and executed by a Jewish court. Hence the Arabic term for Christianity, *al-masihia*, 'The Religion of the Messiah', *al-nasaria*, 'Nazarethism', confusingly the same word as for the Arab nationalist doctrine of the 1950s and 1960s, 'Nasserism', *al-salibia*, 'Cross-ism', but never 'Christianity', as this implies attributing origin of religion to an individual (hence the Western mistake in using terms **Mohammadanism, Wahhabism**, as in regard to other faiths, *Buddhism, Confucianism* and, indeed, *Marxism*, a term Karl Marx himself never used).

Messianic   Of or belonging to a **Messiah**, hence generally used of the Prophet, apocalyptic and other ideas and programmes.

militants   Somewhat pejorative term, less negative than **fanatics**, but still implying irrational and potentially dangerous opinions, applied to resisters and oppressed peoples. In a letter to the BBC Director of News, dated 11 April 2005, the League of Arab States' representative in London, Ambassador Ali Muhsen Hamid, pointed out that Palestinians – *all* the Palestinian people – are habitually described by the BBC as **militants**. Israelis, however, were called **right-wing groups** or **extremists**. Settlers and colonisers who had, in a highly provocative manner, moved into East Jerusalem and who opposed a just peace were just called **nationalists** by the BBC. While the Temple Mount is referred to as a holy site for both Jews and Muslims, the Aqsa Mosque is not referred to *per se*. If mentioned in connection with the Temple Mount, the two are melded into the euphemism of **disputed site** (*Arabfile News and Comments Bulletin*, London Office of the League of Arab States, Vol. 6, No. 14, 12 April, 2005). See also the slippage in much coverage of the West Bank and Gaza from **occupied territories** to **disputed territories**.

moser   Hebrew term of abuse: 'informer'. Halakhic, i.e. Judaic legal term used to condemn to death Jews who are accused of laying other Jews open to attack or danger. Used to discredit Premier Rabin in the early 1990s.

must and should   American writer Geoffrey Aronson pointed out the suggestive way in which President George W. Bush uses these modal verbs when speaking of an Israeli–Palestinian peace settlement. For example, in a release from the White House Office of the Press Secretary, dated 15 July 2007, the President said that the Palestinians *must* 'decide they want a future of decency and hope . . . match their words denouncing terror with action to combat terror . . . arrest terrorists, dismantle their infrastructure, and confiscate illegal weapons . . . work to stop attacks on Israel . . . enforce the law'. By contrast, Israel *should* remove 'unauthorized outposts' and end 'settlement expansion' and 'find practical ways to reduce their footprint' (Geoffrey Aronson, '"Follow Us Not Them". The Ramallah Model: Washington's Palestinian Failure', *A Conflicts Forum Monograph*, November 2007, conflictsforum.org/briefings/Follow-Us-Not-Them-Aronson.pdf).

N

natural growth   Euphemism used by US administration in 2004 to condone illegal expansion of Israeli settlements on the West Bank. Part of general, if underdeclared, accommodation to Ariel Sharon's plans (Steven Weisman, 'US Now Said to Support Growth for Some West Bank Settlements' *The New York Times*, 21 August 2004).

non-conventional deterrence   Israeli euphemism for its nuclear weapons, generally believed to encompass 300–400 nuclear warheads.

O

Orange   Colour which, like some others (e.g. blue, green, red), has had a variety of political uses and associations. In recent Middle Eastern terms, it is a symbolic colour used by opponents of Ariel Sharon's plan to evacuate the Jewish communities from Gaza and parts of the West Bank. Anti-withdrawal supporters adopted this colour, signifying the orange groves of Jewish settlers in Gaza, to protest. Orange ribbons rapidly appeared on cars, taxis and public transport, t-shirts and other items of clothing, backpacks, strollers and hats, in pedestrian malls, shopping centres, bus stations. Supporters of a democratic, liberal and secular Israel chose the colour **blue** (from the Israeli flag) but the colour was not so publicly exhibited as orange because it represented the 'silent majority' that opposed the fanatical minority. Orange was also used as the symbol of the 'Orange Revolution' in Ukraine in 2003, as the name of a lethal pesticide used by US forces in the Vietnam War – 'Agent Orange' – and as emblematic colour of the Protestant Loyalists in Northern Ireland (loyal, among other things, to the memory of King William of Orange, a Dutch ruler who led their forces against Catholics at the Battle of the Boyne in 1690).

outmoded armistice lines   Term used by Israeli and Western pro-Israeli writers to denote pre-1967 boundaries of Israel. The word 'outmoded', supposedly realistic and objective, usually betrays the wish of the user to over-ride existing agreements and laws, cf. *outmoded labour practices* to denote limits on the hours of the working week, protection against industrial accidents and health insurance. Perhaps could be extended to other cases, e.g. the 1840s US-Mexican frontier line, now clearly overtaken by Latin migration to the USA. The use of **outmoded** is similar to the manoeuvre involved in

Chapter 3, **new thinking on the laws of war**, involving the projection by the speaker of their own conception onto the object itself.

outpost Israeli alternative euphemism for **settlement**. As of 2009 there were reported to be 121 sanctioned Israeli settlements on the West Bank, and around 100 other, unsanctioned but largely tolerated, settler positions.

P

Politicide Literally 'killing of a *polis* or political entity/community', term used by Israeli sociologist Baruch Kimmerling to denote plans by the Sharon government to destroy Palestinians as a viable political entity (*Politicide. Ariel Sharon's War Against the Palestinians* [London: Verso, 2003]). **Politicide** 'involves a politico-military, diplomatic and psychological strategy which aims to liquidate the Palestinians people as a legitimate and independent economic, social and political entity' (*Le Monde Diplomatique*, Spanish edition, June 2004). Cf. **Arabicide, Genocide, Judaeocide.**

population centres Israeli euphemism, evading use of words like *settlement, town*, increasingly used after 2000 to denote larger Jewish settlements on the West Bank, e.g. Ariel, Gush Etzion and Ma'ale Adumim. Designed to reduce sense of these entities as being temporary or intrusive, and to 'normalise', i.e. make permanent, their status.

Post-Zionism Critique of conventional ideology of Jewish, and Israeli, political and social identity developed by Israeli writers in the 1990s, in particular rejecting the self-justifying history of Israel in the 1940s and 1950s and of the Jewish character of Israeli politics and society. Probably first used in a book edited by Israeli sociologist Uri Ram, *Israeli Society: Critical Perspectives* (in Hebrew) (Breirot Publishers, 1993). In popular usage, it became an umbrella term for left-wing criticism of Israel after the demise of communism and socialism (Jakob Feldt, *The Israeli Memory Struggle: History and Identity in the Age of Globalization* [Odense, University of Southern Denmark Press, 2007]). Initially included 'new historians' Ilan Pappé, Benny Morris and Avi Shlaim. Distinct from **Anti-Zionism**, in that it did not deny legitimacy of an Israeli state, and society, such that, unlike a significant section of the traditional **Anti-Zionist** Jewish movement, it did not base its critique on an alternative, ultra-Orthodox, interpretation of Judiasm. See Ephraim Nimni, ed., *The Challenge of Post-Zionism* (London: Zed Press, 2003).

Q

Qassam, Izzedin   Religious and social leader in Palestine, of Egyptian origin, associated with Muslim Brotherhood, killed in 1935, prior to a mass uprising against Jewish and British presence. See **Qassam rockets**.

Qassam Rockets   Homemade missiles, manufactured by the Palestinian group **Hamas**, in small workshops in Gaza. Made of long steel pipes, with payloads of nine kilograms and a range of up to seven miles. Used against Israelis living in and near the Gaza strip.

R

Ramallah model   Cornerstone of George Bush's policy for resolving the Israeli–Palestinian conflict. Ramallah is the West Bank town where the PLO and **Al-Fatah** were based, the 'Ramallah model' being the desired alternative to the 'Gaza model'. Based on the idea that international support for Abu Mazen and Fateh could undermine the support for Hamas is evident in its Palestinian election victory of February 2006. In one sense implemented, but with negative consequences, by the June 2007 **Hamas** coup in Gaza.

Rapture Index   Supposedly precise measure of state of (self-generated) religious excitement among US Evangelical Christians anticipating the Second Coming of Christ, reportedly a factor in shaping the policy of the Bush administration. In 2007 leaked government minutes revealed that Bush's White House has been holding frequent meetings with fundamentalists who believed that the Second Coming of Christ could happen only after Israel's re-emergence as a nation: hence support for Israel was at the top of their political agenda. They believed, too, that the great Jewish Temple in Jerusalem must be rebuilt for a third time before the Messiah could return. That meant destroying the al-Aqsa Mosque, said by some to be Islam's holiest shrine after Mecca and Medina. Conflict with Muslims was thus both necessary and desirable. There were reportedly some 8 million Christian fundamentalists in America waiting for such a final outcome, an **Armageddon** (Paul Vallelly, 'Whether God Speaks to Him or Not, Bush's Religious Fanaticism Has Shaped Our World', *The Independent*, 8 November 2007; Jon Carroll, 'Fasten Your Seatbelts: The Rapture Index', *San Francisco Chronicle*, 10 February 2005). See **Armageddon, National Terror Alert, promptings,** *Por el imperio hacia Dios.* In the Glossary of the *Rapture Index* (http://www.raptureready.com/rap2.html), the entry for the yearned-for 'Rapture' says, 'At an unknown hour and day the Lord Jesus will descend from heaven, while remaining in the air, he will snatch his Bride, the Church, out from among this sinful world. Christ then takes the Church to heaven for the 7-year wedding feast. The earthly reason for the removal of the Church is to make way for the rise of Antichrist and to fulfill [*sic*] Daniel's final 70th week.' The home page says, 'The Rapture Index has two functions: one is to factor together a number of related end time components into a cohesive indicator, and the other is to standardize those components to eliminate the wide variance that currently exists with prophecy reporting. The Rapture Index is by no means meant to predict the Rapture; however, the index is designed to measure the type of activity that could act as a precursor to the Rapture.' Rapture theology was mostly cobbled together in the nineteenth century on the basis of very selective readings from parts of the Old Testament: though it may look like gobbledygook, powerful people today take it seriously. The Index is based on 45 prophetic categories, for example drought, plagues, floods, liberalism and 'beast government' (the EU). Since the rapture is a good thing, human catastrophes are welcome as they bring the coming of the end of time closer. Even liberalism is good because a lot of Christ deniers are needed for this to come about. The political implications are spelt out, for example, in a *San Francisco Chronicle* article of 5 February 2005. One of George W. Bush's large core constituencies is actively praying for environmental degradation and the end of the world, because this 'is the beginning of the fun part of salvation' (for believers). The article considers the environmental budget: 'Money for clean water: down. Money for the cleanup of old nuclear sites, including the massive job at the Hanford (Wash.) Nuclear Reservation: way down. Number of Forest Service and Bureau of Land Management acres open for logging: up. Amount of territory in Alaska declared OK for oil drilling: way up.' As for deficit financing, 'Who cares how much debt we accrue? Christ will come and forgive it all. Why not borrow against the future to pay for the present? The future is gonna be a whole different deal. We're just placeholders for God's own totalitarian state.' If we find all this incredible, they assure us it is a 'reality-based' paradigm: 'We are still in the reality-based paradigm; we have not yet crossed over into the faith-based paradigm. In the faith-based world, the apparent inconsistencies within the Bush administration fade into nothingness.' See **Armageddon, End Times**.

refusenik   Israeli term for potential military recruits who refuse to serve in the West Bank and Gaza, and are, after hearings before tribunals, sentenced to periods in prison, also Hebrew *sarvaim*. Distinct from 'avoiders', Hebrew *mishtamim*, Israeli recruits who fail to report for service on grounds, real or fabricated, of ill-health. This usage of **refusenik** involves a misinterpretation of the original usage, from the USSR of the 1970s, *otkazniki* (from *otkaz*, 'refusal', 'denial' of something) to denote Russian Jews who wished to emigrate to Israel and who, after being *refused* exit visas by the Soviet state, were then denied employment and subject to other forms of persecution. Direct flights between the USSR and Israel, carrying Jews who wished to emigrate, began in October 1991, after the failed August coup in Moscow.

right of return   Right written into Israeli law in 1951 allowing all Jews to acquire Israeli citizenship, Hebrew *zklut ha-shiva*. Later taken by Palestinians to assert *their* right to return, in Arabic *haq al-'auda*, to the areas of Israel from which they or their families had originally come.

rodef   Hebrew: literally 'pursuer'. Word of religious derogation, used to denounce Jews who stray outside the faith and are, thereby, liable to be killed. Used, like *moser*, in the early 1990s of Prime Minister Rabin to incite his assassination. Similar in function to Islamic terms such as *kafir, munafiq*.

S

Second Masada   Slogan raised by far right activists in Israel, to convey resistance to government policies, evoking symbol of Jewish resistance to Roman forces at this site in south-eastern Israel in the first-century AD. In the account of the Roman historian Josephus Flavius, the fortress of Masada was captured by the Jewish sect, the Zealots, in their revolt against Rome in 66 AD. In 73 AD, after a harsh siege, the fortress was finally taken by the Romans who found that the 1,000 Zealots had committed suicide rather than be captured. Recent scholars, for example Machman Ben-Yehuda of the Hebrew University of Jerusalem, holds that the Masada myth was largely created by secular Zionism in the early twentieth century when the new movement desperately needed heroic Jewish myths. The term **Second Masada** was raised when, in mid-2005, some 200 ultra-rightists planned to resist the evacuation of the settlement from the Hotel Maoz Yam (Sea Fort) in the Israeli settlement Neve Dekalim in the Gaza Strip. They called their resistance the **Second Masada** (Sal Emergui, 'La policía israelí cerca un hotel de Gaza ocupado por colonos radicales', *El País*, 25 June 2005). In modern Israel young people, civilian and military, are taken to Masada for emotive rituals and ceremonies designed to promote patriotism and a sense of self-sacrifice.

self-hating Jew   Term of abuse and disqualification, with spurious psychoanalytic undertones, often applied to Jewish writers who criticise either elements in the Jewish religious and social traditions or the activities of the

Israeli state, for example, in the 1960s, to the writers Isaac Deutscher (author of *The Non-Jewish Jew* [Oxford: OUP, 1968]) and Maxine Rodinson (author of works on Israel and Arab nationalism) and Marxists who defended the case for an Israeli state, side by side with a Palestinian one, but who denounced the religious and military fervour that gripped Israeli in the 1967 war and condemned the denial of Palestinian rights. Similar derogatory terms, designed to deny legitimacy to critics of religious or national communities from which they come, can be found in other cultures and contexts: in the Irish case the use of terms such as 'Castle Catholic', and 'West Brit' to describe critics of Irish nationalism, or the many terms used in Arab politics to discredit critics, for example *munafiq* (hypocrite, fake believer) or 'Fuad Ajami', after the Lebanese-American academic who has been a policy adviser and public commentator in Washington, and was a strong supporter of the Iraq war.

separation barrier   See **barrier**.

shattered economic space   *World Bank* term, in a report published in May 2007, for the condition of Palestinian towns and villages on the West Bank. This denoted the fact that 'ever-smaller and disconnected cantons' were being strangled by physical obstacles (some 600 checkpoints), the bureaucratic pass system imposed by the Israeli army, and the breaking up of the West Bank into three distinct sections and ten enclaves. Half of the West Bank was altogether off-limits to most Palestinians. Even when permits were issued they were often summarily revoked in their entirety. In 2006 the whole Palestinian population had to stay at home for 78 days. As a result, two-thirds of the Palestinian population had been reduced to absolute poverty (less than $2 a day), while hundreds of thousands survived on food handouts provided by international relief organizations. Such economic, social and political fragmentation cast in doubt the attainment of what President George W. Bush continued to term 'the establishment of a Palestinian state that is viable, contiguous, sovereign and independent' (Roger Cohen, 'Israel and The Price of Blindness', *IHT*, 28 May 2007).

she'ket   Hebrew for 'quiet'. Used in two senses by Israelis, reflecting their desire for it: first, the wish for physical peace; second, security of identity in a context of what is known and familiar. Disturbances, noises, whether military or not, threaten this *ske'ket* (Amir Lupovici, outline of research project ' "Quiet, Please!" The Israeli Search for Physical and Ontological Security from 2000 to 2006'). This desire for political and social tranquillity contrasts, of course, with the vociferous character of much Israeli public debate and, in general, conduct in public places.

Shoah Hebrew word for 'catastrophe', synonym for **Holocaust** or **Judaeocide**. In contrast to **Holocaust** the word is a neutral, secular, term without religious, mystical or providential overtones. Also title of a famous documentary film made in the 1970s by Claude Lanzmann. See **Arabicide, genocide, Holocaust, Judaeocide, Politicide**. In the case of the Armenian genocide, an alternative term is that of 'the Great Catastrophe' (*medz yeghern*).

Swastika From Sanskrit *svastika* (lucky charm), a derivate of the common word, also an Indian women's name, *svasti* good luck. In the traditional form, with hook projections facing left, a common adornment of houses, dresses and charms for both Hindus and Muslims in South Asia. Adopted in altered form, with hooks projecting to the right, as part of cult of supposed *Aryan*, i.e. Indian, origins by the German National Socialist (Nazi) Party. Daubed on Jewish-owned buildings and tombstones in post-war Europe, especially after 2000, but, despite adoption of many other elements of European anti-semitism, not used to any significant extent by those in the Arab or Muslim worlds opposed to Israel, except as part of propaganda seeking to make out that the Israelis themselves behave like Nazis.

T

this individual Dismissive categorisation by State Department spokesman Tom Casey of former British Prime Minister Tony Blair in regard to the latter's announcement, on leaving office as British Prime Minister in 2007, that he would make it his 'absolute priority' to work as Middle East envoy on behalf of the Quartet of USA, Russia, the UN and the EU to reach a negotiated settlement between Israel and Palestine. In answer to a question at a press conference, Casey replied: '. . . there's certainly no envisioning that **this individual** would be a negotiator between the Israelis and Palestinians' (Geoffrey Wheatcroft, 'Mission Impossible for Bush's Best Friend', *IHT*, 4 July 2007).

Three Kings Another example of invention, and later sacralisation, of myth associated with Christianity. Centre of celebration on 6 January, associated in Spain especially with gifts for children, of Feast of the Epiphany (literally 'The Appearance') or, in Spanish countries, *Reyes*. The Gospel According to St. Matthew speaks of 'Wise Men from the East' who come to Herod, after the birth of Christ, attracted, as they say, by the appearance of a star. Herod, for his part, encourages them to find a 'Child' who has been born, and they offer the latter 'gold, incense and myrrh'. Aware of Herod's plan to kill Jesus, they go home by another route. There is nothing in Matthew about the fact that they are kings, or as to their number, or names, or that the star was 'of Bethlehem'. Other details, that they were three, were kings, had the names Balthasar, Lemchior and Gaspar, and came from Persia, are later accretions. Other sources claim there were 11 princes, and one king. Cf. **Holy Land, Jesus Christ.**

Titus 'Enemy of the Jewish people', Roman Emperor who destroyed the Second Temple in 70 AD, on par with Assyrian King Nebuchnadnazzar, who destroyed the First Temple in 586 BC. Both names were used against Prime Minister Ariel Sharon when he forcibly dismantled Israeli settlements in Gaza in February 2005 (*New York Times*, 20 March 2005).

Torah*, plural: *Torot Hebrew 'The Teaching', in various different meanings, denotes sacred texts used by Israeli religious and nationalist forces to legitimate their territorial and social policies, as in the slogan: 'There is no Israel without the Torah'. Can mean a particular teaching or practice, also the first five books of the Bible, 'The *Torah* of Moses', or the whole of the Bible, or, in much modern usage, the whole of Judaic written tradition, revealed and later commented upon. In the end, a political as well as social slogan. As with Muslim legal and political debates on *Shari'ah*, this orthodox and nationalist claim left entirely open the possibility of different interpretations of supposedly sacred text and tradition and, indeed, of who is more, or less, entitled to interpret this text.

transfer/transfer out Coded Israeli term, phrased in English, for possible expulsion, of Palestinians from the West Bank and Gaza. The most appropriate term for such an action, *Final Solution*, was precluded by its use in Nazi terminology to refer to the genocide of the Jews.

transplantation costs Financial compensation demanded by what are, under international law, illegal Israeli settlers in Gaza and the West Bank in return for an agreement to relocate within pre-1967 Israel.

U

usurper regime Term used to denounce Israel, and deny the Israeli state any legitimacy, used by the Supreme Leader of the Islamic Revolution, Ayatollah Seyed Ali Khamenei, in an address in April 2006 to the Third International Qods Conference supporting the rights of the Palestinian people (www.globalsecurity.org/wmd/library/news/iran/2006/iran-060414-irna08.htm).

V

viable   As in the significant and important diplomatic phrase, 'viable Palestinian state'. This phrase was itself a concession, avoiding the issue of the *legitimate* Palestinian boundaries after the expansion of the Israeli state in 1967, but it too was open to multiple and, in the end, ineffective, redefinition. Historically, the search for 'viable' state criteria was an issue associated with the earlier part of the twentieth century, since when states with almost no apparent objective basis for survival have, by dint of wit or accident, succeeded (Singapore, Monaco, Cayman Islands) while others, apparently endowed with natural criteria, have fared less well (Congo, Burma).

vision speech   Delivered on 24 June 2004 when President George W. Bush spoke in the White House Rose Garden of his dream of the day 'when liberty can blossom in the rocky soil of the West Bank and Gaza'. He also made a 'call for [a] new Palestinian leadership', one that is 'not compromised by terror'. He later claimed to be the first American President to call for the creation of a Palestinian 'state', although the White House had emphasised the 'regime change' aspects of the speech (Geoffrey Aronson, "'Follow Us Not Them" The Ramallah Model: Washington's Palestinian Failure', A Conflicts Forum Monograph, November 2007, conflictsforum.org/briefings/Follow-Us-Not-Them-Aronson.pdf).

W

world's largest prison   Term used by the 1.5 million inhabitants of the Gaza strip about the area in which they are confined.

Y

Yiddishland   See Chapter 10.

yorda   Hebrew: 'descent, going down from', i.e. departure from Israel. In contrast to *aliya* (ascent). *Yordim* are those Israelis who have left the country. In a land where statistics on everything else, except nuclear warheads, are plentiful, there is no official figure on the number of *yordim*. Estimates for 2004 suggested that up to 20 per cent of the population had left the country, as a result of continued violence, political infighting and, by Western standards, relatively low income, averaging around $1,200 per month. Among the most famous Israelis to leave the country, and to say they had done so, was the writer Amos Elon (d. May 2009), who emigrated in 2004 to Italy.

Z

zealots   Hebrew: *kana'im*. Religious or nationalist **fanatics**. Originally used of Jewish insurgents who rose against Roman rule in 70 AD, their defeat leading to the destruction of the Second Temple and the dispersal of the Jewish people. Associated in much Jewish tradition with needless violence and disputation. Now applied to extreme representatives of all religions, including Islam.

Zion   Hill just south of the gates of Jerusalem, then applied to the city as a whole and later to the physical, but in some cases spiritual, land claimed by Jewish nationalists. A metonym, i.e. a part used to represent the whole.

Zionism   Main form of modern Jewish nationalism, established at the 1897 World Zionist Conference in Basle, Switzerland, pioneered by Theodor Herzl in his 1896 book *Der Judenstaat* (correct translation 'The State of the Jews'). It is a movement to establish a Jewish state in Palestine. In subsequent usage, the term has acquired multiple meanings that are best kept distinct:
  (i) the actual historical ideology and movement that, from 1897 to 1948, aimed to set up a Jewish state in Palestine;
  (ii) since 1948, as general support and broad sympathy in both Israel itself and in the gentile world for that state and its continued existence;
  (iii) in a pejorative sense, used by both European fascism and anti-semitism and in much Middle Eastern rhetoric, of a global, secretive, conspiratorial force. This fantastical racism purports to identify a worldwide ('Zionist') conspiracy as in the anti-Semitic forgery *The Protocols of the Elders of Zion*. See **Anti-Zionist, Post-Zionist**.

CHAPTER 8

From 'Collateral Damage' to 'Mowing the Lawn': The Euphemisms of War

B

battlespace   Pentagon term for a military and strategic context in which their war planning will enable them to dominate.

Big Blu   A 30,000 pound bunker-busting bomb that, it was claimed, could be used for a US attack on Iran's nuclear installations (Harvey Morris, 'Israeli Appointment may up Tehran Stakes', *FT* 28 February 2005).

C

collateral damage   US military euphemism, developed in regard to nuclear targeting policies in the 1970s, for civilian casualties. From the Latin *collateralis* (*col-*, 'together with' and *lateralis*, from *latus*, 'side'), the word is now perhaps best used as a synonym for 'unintended'. The US Department of Defense defines collateral damage as, '[u]nintentional or incidental injury or damage to persons or objects that would not be lawful military targets in the circumstances ruling at the time'. Consequently 'collateral' is 'not unlawful': 'Such damage is not unlawful so long as it is not excessive in light of the overall military advantage anticipated from the attack' (US Department of Defense, Joint Publication, 3–60, 3 April 2007).

concentration camp   Term originating in the British policy of grouping the Boer population during the 1899–1902 South African War, 'the Second Boer War'. Later taken over by Nazi Germany to denote *extermination camps*, such as Auschwitz-Birkenau. Subsequently terms indistinguishable.

concertina wire   Euphemistic pseudo-musical and benign renaming of what was earlier known as *barbed wire*, major instrument for detention, mass roundup and isolation of civilians in conflict situations.

CONOPS   US military abbreviation for 'Concepts of Operations', a supposedly precise term designed to help military personnel to focus on the goals of what they are doing. According to the Air Operations Center (AOC) *Course Guide:* 'The US defence industry is being completely transformed. A strong *focus* on *Warfighters* and *First Responders* is putting renewed emphasis on *Operations Concepts (Ops Cons)* and *Concepts of Operations (CONOPS)*. This course provides a solid background in the differences between Ops Cons and CONOPS. Attendees will learn the five levels of CONOPS, how to write workable CONOPS and when to use them, what the threats to CONOPS are and how to mitigate them. The instructor describes in detail each *key* CONOPS component that operational users and *senior government* and *industry executives* now expect to see. Attendees will evaluate real-world examples of good and bad CONOPS from the USAF, US Navy and US Army and will *decompose* several representative CONOPS into their *key components*. Attendees will learn how Operational Concepts and JOpsCs are related to CONOPS and how CONOPS can support DOD instruction 5000.2, the DODAF and ACTDs. Several class exercises each day drive home *key* lessons and techniques.' (Writing solid CONOPS for US Government programs and projects course delivered by AOC [Air Operations Center], cited by Weasel Words, http://www.weaselwords.com.au/language.htm [last accessed 6 May 2008]).

D

daisy cutter bombs   Mass casualty bombs used in Afghanistan war in 2001.

decapitation strategy   Phrase used in the Cold War to denote US plan, using accurate nuclear targeting, to eliminate the leadership and command structure of, and hence hopefully immobilise, the Soviet Union and/or other adversaries. Later applied to anti-terrorist strategy and at the heart of President Bush's National Security Presidential Directive of October 2001, describing a narrow focus on capturing and killing Al-Qa'ida leaders. In Iraq, the emphasis on decapitation meant that Coalition cluster-bomb attacks and air strikes aimed at the Iraqi leadership occurred in densely populated areas. However, 50 decapitation attacks failed to hit a single target, yet caused dozens of civilian deaths and injuries. Meanwhile US Defense Department analysts were reportedly studying a scenario according to which China would opt for the **decapitation strategy** in a future attack on Taiwan. This would aim to short-circuit Taiwanese command and control systems and eliminate command nerve centres in accordance with the old saying, 'Kill the head and the body dies' (Susan B. Glasser, 'Review May Shift Terror Policies', *Washington Post*, 29 May 2005; Jim Lobe, 'Cluster Bombs, Decapitation Bombing Killed Hundreds Says Human Rights Watch', www.commondreams.org/headlines03/1212-01.htm; Wendell Minnick, 'The Year to Fear for Taiwan', *Asia Times Online*, 10 April 2004).

degrade   Sinister, and vague, US military term used after aerial attacks on enemy installations, e.g. those of Iraq in the 1990s, without claiming that anything has actually been destroyed or put permanently out of action.

drone   Originally a male bee, unable to sting, then a pilotless aircraft used for identifying targets to attack.

E

ethnic cleansing   Brutal and at the same time euphemistic Yugoslav term popularised in the 1990s, referring to forcible displacement of ethnic groups during conflict, initially in Croatia, Serbia and Bosnia. In this phrase the word 'cleansing' has a sinister polysemic character, appearing to stop short of killing or genocide, with mere displacement of populations, but also echoing the twentieth-century word 'purge', a euphemism, as used in Soviet Russia, for mass murder. In all of these cases a significant proportion of those 'cleansed' were actually killed, not least to encourage the others to leave. Seen as a synonym for forced population movements, 'ethnic cleansing' refers to the practice seen much more widely, and despite sustained vociferous denials by the perpetrators and their descendants, of driving out enemy populations by force under conditions of war: in the modern Middle East, of Palestinians by Israelis in 1948–9, of Kurds by the Ba'thist regime in Iraq in the 1980s, of non-Arab minorities in the wars of the Sudan and, earlier, of Greeks and Armenians from Turkey in the first decades of the twentieth century, and of Turks and other Muslim peoples from the Balkans and around the Black Sea over the nineteenth and twentieth centuries.

F

friendly fire   A military euphemism for careless and misdirected firing, or similar military activity, such as bombing or firing missiles. Another case of **deliberate and careful misrepresentations**. Originally adopted by the US military, the term refers to fire from allied or friendly forces, as opposed to fire coming from enemy forces. Friendly fire is one kind of **collateral damage**. Also known as *fratricide*, literally 'killing a brother' ... 'Friendly fire' can be accidental (described by another euphemism, 'fog of war') or murder, when premeditated. In Britain, the term has a widespread ironic use in referring to American military incompetence: this goes back a long way, as a World War I saying indicates: 'When the Germans fire, the British duck. When the British fire, the Germans duck. When the Americans fire EVERYONE ducks!' The reputation still seems merited. In the Kuwait War Operation Desert Storm (January 1991) 17 per cent of all US and allied service-member deaths were caused by 'friendly fire' (www.cbsnews.com/stories/2006/03/11/national/main1391626.shtml). After 2003, 'friendly fire' casualties – and US cover-ups thereof – created tensions at all levels between US and British forces in Iraq. One wounded British soldier said: 'I can command my vehicle. I can keep it from being attacked. What I have not been trained to do is look over my shoulder to see whether an American is shooting at me' (http://www.guardian.co.uk/world/2003/mar/31/iraq5 – [last accessed 10 April 2008]; 'Army Lied, US Athlete's Brother Says', *IHT*, 25 April 2007).

H

horde warfare   See **swarm warfare**.

K

kinetic   Euphemism for confrontational, when not simply violent and coercive, approach in conflict situations, where the word **kinetic**, literally 'moving' from the Greek word *kinesis* (also the source of the word *cinema*, i.e. moving pictures, hence 'movies'), serves as a substitute for 'aggressive'. In some US war-fighting manuals, the **kinetic** phase is that of actual combat (James Fallows, 'Why Iraq Has No Army', *Atlantic Monthly*, December 2005). So, too, was the term used to describe possible US actions against Iran in

2008–9. While British military officials in Afghanistan in 2007 favoured negotiation, the clashing attitude of their American colleagues, termed 'the **kinetic approach**', had brought relations to an 'all-time low'. One senior British soldier described the American approach, in contrast to that of British forces, as 'a lot less carrot, a lot more stick and considerably more projectiles' (Jason Burke, 'Taliban Town Seizure Throws Afghan Policy into Disarray', *The Observer*, 4 February 2007).

M

mowing the lawn   British military term, used of air warfare against Taliban fighters in Afghanistan and for mass killing of enemy forces using air power.

N

non-hostile weapons discharge   US military euphemism for shooting, wounding and killing by own forces, or also used to refer to suicide by serving military. Thus, official records said that the US Army specialist Alyssa Peterson died on 15 September 2003 from a 'non-hostile weapons discharge'. Military documents revealed that Peterson shot herself with her service rifle. Her suicide came just two weeks after she refused to take part in further interrogations of Iraqi prisoners and had asked to be reassigned (Weasel Words, www.weaselwords.com.au/language.htm).

non-lethal transfers   Military supplies that are not directly used for killing, such as military-applicable information technology and precision targeting technology. The distinction between 'lethal' and 'non-lethal' is, of course, spurious since even the most apparently innocent item can be the link in a killing chain. As observed by the folksy Soviet leader Nikita Khrushchev in the early days of strategic arms negotiations with the USA, even the buttons on his trousers are strategic weapons since, if they were not holding his trousers up, a soldier would not be able to fight.

P

payload   Euphemism for explosives carried by a plane.

Predator   Intimidatory term for unmanned attack aircraft, used in Afghanistan and elsewhere to carry out targeted assassinations.

R

rabbits in a sack, turkey shoot   Dehumanising language used by
US forces in the 1991 Kuwait war. Cf. **get some**.

run-up to war   As if it is a game of athletics. Cf. **next round**.

S

servicing the target   One of several US Army terms to denote killing
the enemy. Other terms include **decommissioning the aggressor, ex-
ceeding the threshold of physiological damage, neutralising, substantive
negative outcome, wasting**. See http://www.sourcewatch.org/index.php?
title=Doublespeak   and   http://www.stim.com/Stim-x/8.2/doublespeak/
doublespeak.html (last accessed 10 May 2008).

Shock and Awe   Supposedly resolute and intimidatory phrase espoused
by the US administration prior to the 2003 Iraq invasion, to denote use of
overwhelming force to break opposition forces and will power, and impose
control on that country. Six years later, as George W. Bush prepared to leave
office, with over 100,000 US troops still tied down in Iraq, and over 4,000
US soldiers dead, the words had changed to **morass, nightmare, quagmire**
and other self-exculpatory terms (see Chapter 11). The term **Shock and
Awe** was originally coined in a book published by the US National Defence
University in 1996, *Shock and Awe: Achieving Strategic Dominance* by Harlan
Ullan and James Wade. Designed as a post-Cold War strategy for the US
military, that would use its superiority in firepower, precision and information control, it resumed concepts long present in military thinking, such as
Blitzkrieg, full spectrum dominance and *rapid dominance*. The word **awe**, its
resonance strengthened in the 1990s in the slang word *awesome,* served to
attribute superhuman, possibly invincible, qualities to the US armed forces.
Like many supposedly scientific military doctrines, it made assumptions
that in reality never applied, such as complete knowledge of the enemy and,
not least, of one's own side. Later adopted as a term of commercial promotion by, among others, sellers of golf clubs, condoms and financial services.
It is also the name of a Scottish pop group. In phonetic terms, an example of
the English language trope of supposed greater emphasis given by pairing of
two, sometimes rhyming, monosyllables such as *cut and run, huff and puff,
kiss and tell,* **pump and dump***, rock and roll, spit and polish.*

swarm warfare   Otherwise known as **horde warfare**, based on the offensive strategy of Genghis Khan. Another pseudo-scientific, ultimately banal, military concept, fostering the illusion of battlefield control and rationality: the idea is to make all the components of war – land, naval, air, missile, space, virtual and information – operative at multiple levels and settings. See http://peacepalestine.blogspot.com/2007/10/fabio-mini-italian-general-operation.html [last accessed 9 October 2007].

T

transfer tubes   US Army euphemism for coffins bringing home the bodies of the dead from wars in Iraq and Afghanistan. Cf. in Vietnam War *body bag;* in the 1991 Gulf War, Pentagon staff called them *human remains pouches* (Tim Harper, 'Pentagon Keeps Dead out of Sight', *Toronto Star*, 2 November 2003). By contrast, British soldiers in World War I referred to cigarettes as *coffin-nails.*

transformation from 30,000 feet   Description of the arrogance and ignorance of much Washington discussion of international issues. Reviewing a book co-authored by David From (author of the phrase **axis of evil**) and Richard Perle and entitled *An End to Evil: How to Win the War on Terror*, Fareed Zakaria wrote, 'Frum and Perle want transformation from 30,000 feet, without the moral taint of compromise. They scorn the diplomats who must deal with foreigners, not to mention the foreigners themselves' (Fareed Zakaria, 'Showing Them Who's Boss', *The New York Times*, 8 February 2004).

U

umbrella effect   Euphemism for the impact of a landmine blast.

CHAPTER 9

'Bad Guys', 'Circular Firing Squad', 'Slum Dunk': The Vitality of US Colloquial

8,000-mile screwdriver   Term used by Viceroy Paul Bremer and senior military staff to describe micromanagement (by Rumsfeld) in the running of Iraq from Washington (Paul D. Eaton, 'For His Failures, Rumsfeld Must Go', *IHT*, 20 March 2006).

A

adversary   US Secretary of Defense Donald Rumsfeld, when addressing Pentagon workers on the then fashionable subject of reforming the armed forces, began: 'The topic today is an adversary that poses a threat, a serious threat, to the security of the United States of America'. It 'crushes new ideas', is a foe 'more subtle and implacable' than the former Soviet Union and is 'closer to home' than 'the last decrepit dictators of the world'. The enemy: the 'Pentagon bureaucracy'. The date: 10 September 2001 (Frank Rich, 'Donald Rumsfeld's Dance with the Nazis', *IHT*, 4 September 2006).

anti-soldier   Term applied by US right to critics of US military activity, usually linked to other liberal causes such as support for gay marriage.

ants   As in Admiral William Fallon, in an interview on Iran in *Esquire* (March 2006): 'These guys are ants. When the time comes, you crush them'.

Arabian Candidate   Variant on the Cold War story of the *Manchurian Candidate*, involving a US presidential aspirant who uses anti-communist rhetoric as a cover for a communist takeover. In the words of Paul Krugman,

This time the enemies would be Islamic fanatics, who install as their puppet president a demagogue who poses as the nation's defender against terrorist evildoers. The Arabian candidate wouldn't openly help terrorists. Instead, he would serve their cause while pretending to be their enemy. After an attack, he would strike back at the terrorist base, a necessary action to preserve his image of toughness, but botch the follow-up, allowing the terrorist leaders to escape ... Meanwhile, he would lead America into a war against a country that posed no immediate threat ... The Arabian candidate might even be able to deprive America of the moral high ground by creating a climate in which US guards torture, humiliate and starve prisoners, most of them innocent or guilty of only petty crimes.

(Paul Krugman, 'The Arabian Candidate',
International Herald Tribune, 21 July 2004)

Contrast with **Jihadi Candidate**.

attention whore   Abusive term applied to Cindy Sheehan, whose son Casey, a US Army reservist, was killed in Iraq in April 2004, and who became the 'face' of the anti-war movement. In May 2007 she gave up her campaign, citing her frustration with the apathy of the public, the failure of the Democratic Party to try to bring the troops home, and routine abuse from both liberals and conservatives, which included accusing her of being an 'attention whore.' In 2008, she unsuccessfully ran for Congress as an independent (Andrew Buncombe, 'Cindy Sheehan Quits as 'Face' of Anti-war Campaign', *The Independent*, 30 May 2007). See **swiftboating**.

B

bad guys   Term, loosely derived from *Westerns*, frequently used by George W. Bush and the US military for terrorist and other opponents. Implies an additional element of moral superiority and mission not present in conventional terms such as *enemy, foe, opponents*. An informal variant of **evil-doers**.

Baghdad is for wimps, Tehran is for real men   Only half-ironic Washington saying in the period between the President's January 2002 'Axis of Evil' speech and the March 2003 invasion of Iraq.

bill of goods   Euphemism for false information. Thus a 'retired American four-star general with close ties to the British military' noted that it was widely believed in London that the Blair Government was 'sold a bill of goods by the White House in the build-up to the war against Iraq'. This had created a high 'burden of proof' (Seymour M. Hersch, 'Shifting Targets: The Administration's Plan for Iraq', *The New Yorker*, 8 October 2007).

birth pangs of a new Middle East   Categorisation by US Secretary of State Condoleezza Rice of the summer 2006 Israel–Hizbullah war. The image of 'birth pangs' usually suggests the birth, albeit with pain, of something welcome, an occasion for joy: on this occasion, the war presaged, in the eyes of many experts, the start of a new phase of internationalisation of the Palestine question, involving a region-wide Iranian–Israeli rivalry, more extensive and less manageable than that between Israel and the Arabs of the decades after 1948.

Bolton baubles   Along with everything else Bush's UN envoy John Bolton bequeathed to a troubled world were a few samples of his singular turn of phrase applied to things and people he did not like. Among them were: The High Minded, The True Believers, Candle Lighters, Crusaders of Compromise, The Weak-kneed, The Chattering Class, Euroids, Mattress Mice and EAPeasers (for members of the Bureau of East Asian and Pacific Affairs in the State Department) (Brian Urquhart, 'One Angry Man', *New York Review of Books*, 6 March 2008). See also **close their eyes and press the lever, immediate family, critical that we get him in place, Old man, Old Yeller, poster child, quintessential kiss-up, kick-down sort of guy, unleash**.

Bomb Iran   During a public appearance, the year before he ran for US President, a jocular Senator John McCain responded to a question from the audience about military action against Iran by singing the chorus of the Beach Boys song, '*Barbara Ann*'. 'Bomb, bomb, bomb . . . ' The audience was amused (AP, *IHT*, 20 April 2007).

box   Derogatory term used by US and UK politicians with regard to the policy towards Saddam Hussein between 1991 and 2003. Cf. **cage, come to heel**. An earlier term, similar in denotation and tone, was **reservation**, as in 'X has escaped from the reservation'. This latter word originally referred to a confinement area for native Americans. Cf. also the term 'Indian country', the opposite of **reservation**.

bring them on   Stated by George W. Bush on July 2004, in answer to the question on US ability to deal with the security situation in Iraq. The full quote runs: 'My answer is, bring them on. We've got the force necessary to deal with the security situation' (quoted in Lawrence Freedman, *A Choice of Enemies, America Confronts the Middle East* [London: Weidenfeld and Nicolson, 2008], p. 439).

Bushisms   Infelicitous, clumsy and other sayings of George W. Bush. The following of many possible examples are self-explanatory:

– 'They misunderestimated me' (Bentonville, Ark., 6 November 2000).

– 'If this were a dictatorship, it'd be a heck of a lot easier, just so long as I'm the dictator' (Washington, DC, 19 December 2000).

– 'I know what I believe. I will continue to articulate what I believe and what I believe – I believe what I believe is right' (Rome, Italy, 22 July 2001).

– 'Do you have blacks, too?' (to Brazilian President Fernando Cardoso, Washington, DC, 8 November 2001).

– 'The most important thing is for us to find Osama bin Laden. It is our number one priority and we will not rest until we find him' (Washington, DC, 13 September 2001). 'I don't know where bin Laden is. I have no idea and really don't care. It's not that important. It's not our priority' (Washington, DC, 13 March 2002).

– 'I am here to make an announcement that this Thursday, ticket counters and airplanes will fly out of Ronald Reagan Airport' (Washington, DC, 3 October 2001).

– 'I wish you'd have given me this written question ahead of time so I could plan for it . . . I'm sure something will pop into my head here in the midst of this press conference, with all the pressure of trying to come up with answer, but it hadn't yet . . . I don't want to sound like I have made no mistakes. I'm confident I have. I just haven't – you just put me under the spot here, and maybe I'm not as quick on my feet as I should be in coming up with one' (after being asked to name the biggest mistake he had made, Washington, DC, 3 April 2004).

– 'Our enemies are innovative and resourceful, and so are we. They never stop thinking about new ways to harm our country and our people, and neither do we' (Washington, DC, 5 August 2004).

– 'Too many good docs are getting out of the business. Too many OB-GYNs aren't able to practice their love with women all across this country' (Poplar Bluff, MO, 6 September 2004).

- 'Because the – all which is on the table begins to address the big cost drivers. For example, how benefits are calculate, for example, is on the table; whether or not benefits rise based upon wage increases or price increases. There's a series of parts of the formula that are being considered. And when you couple that, those different cost drivers, affecting those – changing those with personal accounts, the idea is to get what has been promised more likely to be – or closer delivered to what has been promised. Does that make any sense to you? It's kind of muddled' (explaining his plan to save Social Security, Tampa, FL, 4 February 2005).

- 'See, in my line of work you got to keep repeating things over and over and over again for the truth to sink in, to kind of catapult the propaganda' (Greece, NY, 24 May 2005).

- 'The same folks that are bombing innocent people in Iraq were the ones who attacked us in America on September the 11th' (Washington, DC, 12 July 2007).

(For more, visit http://politicalhumor.about.com/od/bushquotes/a/ dumbbushquotes.htm [last accessed 6 January 2008] and other sites.)

C

cage   Demeaning and insulting term used by US and British politicians of the policy towards Saddam prior to the 2003 invasion, with implication that he was a wild animal, as in 'Keeping him in his . . .' or 'Putting him back in his. . . .' Similar terms include *back in his box*, *come to heel*, *off the reservation* and also the all-purpose UN-speak **comply**.

cakewalk   Afro-American slang, originally derived from a kind of funfair competition, much used in Washington prior to the 2003 invasion of Iraq to imply that the operation would be easy. Analogous to the UK phrase 'a piece of cake'. Kenneth Adelman, a former Reagan security official, writing in *The Washington Post*, believed that 'demolishing Hussein's military power and liberating Iraq would be a **cakewalk**'. To some extent this anticipation was correct: the Iraqi regular army did not put up major resistance, but, within weeks, substantial popular, irregular, resistance to the American presence began. Later Adelman would write in the same newspaper that President Bush was 'ultimately responsible' for the 'debacle' in Iraq. The military planners had ignored Napoleon, it seems: the 280-page US military counterinsurgency field manual released in December 2006, *FM 3-24*, has some sobering reflections on Napoleon's intervention in Spain in 1808, which he believed would be little more than a **military promenade** but which eventually depleted the resources of the French Empire. The manual notes, 'Napoleon's campaign included a rapid conventional military victory but ignored the immediate requirement to provide a stable environment for the populace ... It was the beginning of the end for Napoleon' (Ken Adelman, 'Cakewalk in Iraq', *The Washington Post*, 13 February 2002; Kristen Williams, 'Counterinsurgency 101', *In These Times*, March 2007).

chicken hawks   Disparaging US term, originally gay slang for someone who preys on younger men, later applied to men who did same to younger girls. Applied in the 1990s to right-wing advocates of military force who have themselves never experienced war or military service, e.g. Richard Perle, Paul Wolfowitz, George W. Bush. The American usage of *chicken* implies cowardice, as in the derogation of CNN as **Chicken News Network**, and the game of '*Chicken Run*', immortalized in the James Dean film *Rebel without a Cause*, in which two drivers accelerate towards a cliff to test which of them will brake first.

Chicken News Network   Neo-conservative abuse of *CNN, Cable News Network*, accused of liberal reporting in regard to US wars.

Chinese water torture   Self-pitying George W. Bush term for difficulties his administration faced in securing support for the invasion of Iraq and having to wait for reports of UN weapons inspectors, used in conversation with Spanish Prime Minister José María Aznar, 22 February 2003, at a meeting in Crawford, Texas (*El País*, 26 September 2007). At a time before the chief UN inspector, Hans Blix, whose teams had been searching for the non-existent weapons, had delivered his report, Bush was chafing for war. Referring to the inspections, he said to Aznar, 'This is like Chinese water torture. We have to put an end to it.' While Aznar, worried about opposition to the invasion in Spain, was concerned about getting **international legitimacy** by means of a second UN resolution, Bush informed him that the decision to go to war was a *fait accompli*. 'If anyone vetoes, **we'll go** ... There are two weeks left. In two weeks we'll be militarily ready. We'll be in Baghdad by the end of March'. As Aznar argued for the diplomatic route, Bush issued veiled threats. 'Countries like Mexico, Chile, Angola and Cameroon have to know that what's at stake is the United States' security and acting with a **sense of friendship** toward us.' He continued to threaten that Chile's **negative attitude** could jeopardise Senate confirmation of the Free Trade Agreement while, if Angola did not show a **positive attitude**, its funding from the Millennium Account could be 'compromised'. Bush then spoke of being guided by a **historic sense of responsibility**, describing himself as an **optimist** and saying, 'I am **at peace with myself**'. He was confident of getting international support in the second UN resolution because, in his words, 'we're developing a **very strong humanitarian aid package**' (Mark Danner, ' "The Moment Has Come to Get Rid of Saddam"', *NYRB*, 8 November 2007).

circular firing squad   Journalist Frank Rich's description of the in-group Washington blame game for things falling apart in Iraq. The full phrase is 'circular firing squad of the war's enablers' (Frank Rich, 'Is Condi Hiding the Smoking Gun?' *IHT*, 7 May 2007). Cf. British journalist Rupert Cornwell, writing of the US Presidential campaign as it neared its polling date in October 2008: 'This year traditional roles are reversed. Normally fractious Democrats are united, but Republicans resemble a **circular firing squad**' (*The Independent*, 26 October 2008).

close their eyes and press the lever   The strategy of lawyers who, having been presented with reams of documentary evidence as to John Bolton's unsuitability to be the Bush administration's nominee for the post of US Ambassador to the UN, apparently continued to believe that he deserved the post. See also **poster child** (*IHT*, 30 May 2005).

cojones   Spanish for 'balls', 'testicles'. US political slang, applied by, among others, George W. Bush to friendly leaders from other countries deemed to have courage. Cf. the Persian expression towards a person without will power, *tokhm nadarad* ('he hasn't got any balls'), and the Arab use of the term for unflinching nationalist leaders, as in a frequently heard statement up to 2003 that Saddam Hussein, Osama bin Laden and Yasser Arafat were the only Middle Eastern leaders with this attribute. In no case does it imply that the person so characterised also has any brains.

Colinectomy   Removal of Colin Powell as US Secretary of State by neo-conservative critics (Calvin Trillin, 'Farewell Colin Powell', *The Nation*, 13 December 2004).

come to heel   Symptomatic racist language of some columnists and strategists, treating another state and people as if they were a tame dog. Cf. **Box, Cage**. As in an article by US strategist Edward Luttwak, 'America Should Threaten to Pull Out of Iraq' (*International Herald Tribune*, 19 August 2004), where he writes that if the US threatens to allow an independent Kurdish state in Iraq, 'Turkey would soon come to heel'.

corkscrew journalism   Instant comment, bereft of research or orig-inality, leading to a cycle of equally vacuous, staged polemics between columnists who have been saying the same thing for the past decade, or more. The term originated in the film *The Philadelphia Story* (George Cukor, 1940).

culture wars   Conflict within the USA that grew in the 1990s between those promoting secular, rational values and defenders of traditional, Christian thinking, across a range of issues including abortion, Creationism, gun control, homosexuality and censorship. Not related to the concept of the **clash of civilisations** as much as to domestic US debate. So known after the influential book *Culture Wars: The Struggle to Define America* by the University of Virginia sociologist James Davison Hunter, who saw that the conflict was one between *orthodoxy* and *progressivism*. Further promoted by the speech of Republican candidate Pat Buchanan at the 1992 Republican Convention, the '**culture wars** speech'. Believed to be a translation of the German term, of rather different political import, referring to the conflict between Chancellor Bismarck and the Catholic Church in the 1870s, *Kulturkampf*. In contrast to a raft of other such American terms that also found echo in Europe, e.g. *political correctness, anti-sexism* – this term was largely confined to debates in the USA and Australia.

curveball   Baseball term, rough equivalent of English cricketing word *googly*, a breaking pitch in which the ball is thrown with topspin, code name of mendacious Iraqi 'defector' used to justify 2003 invasion. See Chapter 4, **Curveball**.

cut and run   White House demonisation of any plan for eventual withdrawal of US troops from Iraq, hinting at cowardice, and quickly slipping thence into the call for 'substantially more' troops (Frank Rich, 'The Longer the War, the Larger the Lies', *IHT*, 18 September 2006).

D

damaged goods   Term used in the UK and US to discard and disown former allies, e.g. Pakistani President Musharraf in 2007. Like the business and government phrase *on the way out*, or the employers' euphemisms for firing workers, such as *let go, lose, shed*, a supposedly neutral term that projects responsibility onto the person so departing.

darn good liar   Characterisation of President George W. Bush in August 2004 anti-war New York demonstrations, play on his use of the term 'darn good' to praise allies and friends.

defeatocrats   White House coinage for Democratic congressmen trying to force President George W. Bush into withdrawal from Iraq (Frank Rich, 'Donald Rumsfeld's Dance with the Nazis', *IHT*, 4 September 2006).

devil   Embodiment of evil in Christian and Islamic traditions, said to be the fallen archangel Beelzebub. In the US presidential campaign of 2008, the two candidates were asked, at a meeting in an Evangelical church in California on August 16, if they believed in the devil. Barack Obama said he saw the devil in the streets of America as much as in the conflict in the Sudanese province of Darfur. John McCain declined to find the devil anywhere in America, and said he found him in the figure of Osama bin Laden (*El País*, 18 August 2008).

do   As in 'Do Iraq', 'Do Iran', but also 'Do Drugs', 'We do not do nation-building'. All-purpose seemingly casual verb, usually betraying some barely suppressed impropriety or vagueness in the mind of the user. See **nation-building**.

dumb luck   See Chapter 4.

E

elephant in the room   Picturesque term for an issue, problem or person that is repressed in conversation or public discourse. Thus, Salma Yaqoob, a Labour candidate in the May 2006 local elections in Britain, pointed out that, while the war in Iraq was not treated as an electoral issue, as in Spain and the USA, it was still 'the elephant in the room' (Alan Cowell, 'Making an Issue of the War', *IHT*, 22 November 2005). Also used in regard to US press coverage of the Alaskan Vice-Presidential Republican candidate, *the moose in the bedroom*.

empire lite   Termed used by Canadian philosopher, writer and politician Michael Ignatieff to describe US power and actions in the early twenty-first century. See also **grace notes** (Michael Ignatieff, 'The Burden', *The New York Times Magazine*, 5 January 2003).

endgame   Derived from chess, where it has the precise meaning of the phase when checkmate occurs. Now used imprecisely, to denote the final phase, and final outcome, of any conflict or problem. Thus, in regard to the fate of the dozens of **Al-Qa'ida** captives held by the US after they were no longer useful as informants, the US Secretary of State Condoleezza Rice reported in May 2005 that the government had to decide how long to keep suspects in a **legal limbo** without bringing them to trial: however, when one unnamed official asked what the '**endgame**' was, the answer was not forthcoming (Michael Isikoff and Mark Hosenball, 'Got Him. Now What?', *Newsweek*, 16 May 2005).

evil   Term often resorted to by President George W. Bush, as in his 12 September 2001 speech where he spoke of a 'monumental struggle between good and **evil**', and then in his January 2002 State of the Union address, **axis of evil**, and in frequent references to terrorists as in Chapter 1, **evil-doers, bad guys**. In modern US political usage, it was first revived in the 1980s by President Ronald Reagan, as in *empire of evil*, then used by President George W. Bush in his memoirs: '. . . it was a matter of good versus evil. Saddam had begun the epitome of evil in taking hostages and in his treatment of the Kuwaiti people' (George W. Bush and Brent Scowcroft, *A World Transformed*, New York: Vintage, 1998, p. 375).

F

Fahrenheit 9/11   Film, released in 2004 directed by Michael Moore, and 'quoting' the title of the earlier Ray Bradbury novel *Fahrenheit* 451, about US policy on terrorism and Iraq. Enthusiastically critical of George W. Bush, breaking with all American conventions of deference to the President, and the US policy on terrorism and Iraq. While in his writings Moore showed himself to be a characteristic US anti-imperialist naïf (indulging, as many had done before him, the IRA), the main charges of his film (e.g. the connections between President Bush and the Saudi elite) were substantiated. (Philip Shenon, 'Fact-checking a Cinematic Broadside', *International Herald Tribune*, 19–20 June 2004). Moore was also accurate about the 43rd US President's attitude to his job: according to the film, the President spent 42 per cent of his first eight months in office on vacation, instead of concentrating on a possible Al-Qa'ida terrorist attack for which there was already precedent and anticipatory evidence. Corroborative evidence for claims in the film can be found at www.michaelmoore.com.

Faux News   From French *faux* meaning 'false', and, in English, with overtones of clumsiness, as in the expression *faux pas*. A disparaging term for the right-wing US TV channel **Fox News**.

financial weapons of mass destruction   Description in 2003 by financer Warren Buffett of banking arrangements, particularly derivatives, that were to lead to the global economic crisis of 2008. For his part, Barack Obama, in warning of the need to take urgent measures to stabilise the world financial system, evoked in a speech on 19 September 2008 the danger of a '*financial 9/11*'. In fact, the Wall Street financial crash of 8 September 2008 had, in many ways, a far greater impact on the US economy, and the life of most Americans and of most people in the world, than the 9/11 attacks. (I am grateful to my LSE colleague Michael Cox for this latter observation.)

folks   Bushspeak for a terrorist enemy, as in 'those folks who did this'. Other examples of unhegemonic, supposedly 'folksy', West Texas judicial terminology used by the US President in response to 9/11: 'dead or alive', 'posse', 'outlaw', 'smoke out', 'turn him in'. In his last few weeks in office, Bush, in an interview with CNN Television (12 November 2008), said that he regretted using the 'dead or alive' call in regard to bin Laden.

Fox News Channel   Right-wing American TV channel, which gained ground in the early 2000s, with no pretence of journalistic objectivity. Osama bin Laden was termed a 'dirtbag', a 'monster', running a 'web of hate'. His followers were 'terror goons', and the Taliban 'diabolical' and 'henchmen'. Owned by Rupert Murdoch. See **Faux News**.

Freedom Fries   Used in 2003 to replace 'French Fries' on the menu of the US Congress after France opposed a US attack on Iraq. Analogous to the decision of the Turkish government, after Turkey joined NATO in 1952, to rename *Russian salad* as *American salad*.

full court press   Wrestling term, denoting absolute control of the opponent, who is pinned to the ground, much used by US politicians and strategists to describe war goals.

full-scale invasion   Graphic example of psychological mechanism known as **displacement**, term used by US conservative politicians not of the 2003 invasion of Iraq, which neoconservatives called a 'liberation', but of the alleged consequences of Latin American immigration into the USA. In his formulation, the founder of the House Immigration Reform Caucus, Tom Tancredo, himself a grandson of Italian immigrants, was protecting America from a '**full-scale invasion** of Latin immigrants'. That this immigration was first and foremost a result of the needs of US employers, industrial, agricultural and domestic, for cheap and casual labour did not seem to occur to him. Another member of the Caucus (Steve King of Iowa) called this immigration 'a terrorist attack on the United States'. The measures they proposed included deporting every undocumented worker in America – at a cost of about $200 billion – and stopping all, including legal, immigration. Tancredo wanted America to reject 'the siren song of multiculturalism' and declared that Islam was 'a civilization bent on destroying ours.' See also **citizen patrols** ('The 10 Worst Congressmen', *Rolling Stone*, http://www.rollingstone.com/politics/story/12054520/the_ 10_worst_congressmen/6 [last accessed 18 March 2008]).

G

get some   By analogy with Friday-night-on-the-town wish to 'get some sex', or drugs, the desire voiced by edgy American troops in Iraq to kill. See **rabbits in a sack, turkey shoot**, Chapter 4, **Whopper**.

gin up   Expression used in latter part of the George W. Bush administration to denote stirring up of a possible confrontation with Iran. 'I would not be surprised later this fall to see an **uptick in Iran-bashing** from elements of the administration and associated constituencies trying to **gin up** confrontation' (Ken Silverstein, 'Six Questions for Laura Rozen on Iran', *Harper's Magazine*, 4 May 2007). Also used, in the sense of talking up, of putting most emphasis on and of the pro-Iraq war faction in the earlier Bush Presidency. Thus, Condoleezza Rice, at that time National Security Adviser, did this, after ignoring reports debunking the Iraqi nuclear tubes and shrugging off the presidential brief dated 6 August 2001 which tried to prioritize another threat, that of Al-Qa'ida. The August memo was entitled: 'Bin Laden Determined to Attack Inside the United States'. See also **sexing up Iraq** (Maureen Dowd, 'Unleash John Bolton', *IHT*, 28 April 2005).

God Bless America   Title of nationalistic US song, hence all-purpose slogan. Functionally equivalent to Islamic *Allahu Akbar*, 'God is Great'. The original song was composed by Irving Berlin in 1918, on the basis of an earlier popular Jewish melody, and was made famous in 1938 in a version sung by Kate Smith. To avoid the appearance of partisanship, the 1938 version altered the original words 'Guide her to the right' by 'Guide her through the night'. Of simple melody and words, it has often served as a more accessible song than the musically more complicated official US anthem, *The Star Spangled Banner*.

God-drenched   Phrase used, in a play on 'sun-drenched', by Ronald Reagan's speechwriter Peggy Noonan of right-wing Evangelicals in the USA (*The Economist*, 29 January 2008).

grace notes   Musical term for additional, optional notes in a musical score. Used by Canadian writer and politician Michael Ignatieff to denote the relationship of such things as free markets, human rights and democracy to US military policies. See also **empire lite**.

H

Hail Mary   Tactic in American football, where a quarterback who is desperate for a touchdown at the end of the game, steps back, rallies his fellow team members and then rushes down and lobs the ball. Applied by US commander Norman Schwarzkopf to rapid deployment of the US Eighteenth Corps to block Iraqi retreat at end of the Kuwait war (Lawrence Freedman, *A Choice of Enemies, America Confronts the Middle East* [London: Weidenfeld and Nicolson, 2008], p. 249)

harbour   All-encompassing word for tolerance and support of opposition groups by states. As used by George W. Bush on 9/11: 'We will make no distinction between the terrorist who committed those acts and those who harbour them'. Such a policy would, *inter alia*, have justified Cuba, Nicaragua, the UK and India going to war with the USA at any time in the 1980s or 1990s.

haves and have mores   Uncharacteristically accurate and pungent term used by George W. Bush of his core voting constituency.

Holy Warriors   English rendering of *mujahidin*, Washington liberal term for some neoconservatives.

homelanders   US term for core conservative voters.

I

immediate family   Term used by John Bolton, then nominee US Ambassador to the UN, in the context of his barring aides from outside his own office from meetings so as to confine the sessions to 'immediate family' (Douglas Jehl and Steven R. Weisman, 'Senators to Hear Critic of Bush's UN Nominee', *IHT*, 8 April 2005). The term is normally applied to those entitled to attend a funeral or to visit someone with a serious illness.

ironing the wrinkle around the shirt   Metaphor for ineffective and belated measures, similar to *reordering the deckchairs on the Titanic, spitting* *in the wind, exercise in futility.* As troops were taken from the southern approaches to Baghdad where they had been ordered to secure the towns of Mahmudiya, Latifiya and Iskandariya and sent to the north, a commentator described this policy thus ('Special Report: Iraq' *The Economist,* 18 June 2005).

J

Jihadi Candidate   A term used by opponents of Barack Obama in the 2008 US presidential campaign to suggest he harboured pro-fundamentalist sentiments, was still really a covert Muslim, etc. See also **Arabian Candidate** and **Manchurian Candidate**.

K

kicking the can down the street   Troublemaking, fishing in troubled waters, used by a US military official of Iran's role in Iraq in 2004 (Christopher de Bellaigue, 'Bush Iran and the bomb', *NYRB*, 24 February 2005).

M

muscular   Like 'robust', swaggering, when not thuggish, and self-aggrandizing euphemism, much used in the 1990s and later, for brutal, violent and at times illegal action against detainees, as well as belligerent and unilateral moves in foreign policy.

My Pet Goat   Name often erroneously given to the children's story ('The Pet Goat' in the book *Reading Mastery II: Storybook I* by Siegfried Engelmann and Elaine C. Bruner) that George W. Bush continued to read, for nine minutes at a school in Sarasota on 9/11, after being informed of the Twin Tower explosions. Famously recorded in Michael Moore's film *Fahrenheit 9/11*. In his statements after 9/11, Osama bin Laden was to mock at the US President for this incident.

One subsequent commentary found a suitable political moral in the tale: 'In the end, "The Pet Goat" is the story of an authority figure – the dad – who learns to exercise his powers with restraints. When the security of his home is threatened by the goat's appetite for mass destruction, the dad's initial impulse is small-minded and simplistic. He focuses on one evildoer – the goat itself – to the exclusion of anything else. He thinks he knows goats, and they're trouble. Other voices – specifically, the girl's – raise less drastic possibilities: Possibly the goat can be reasoned with, or coerced, into altering his behaviour. Possibly the goat is not the threat the dad thinks it is. Possibly the family is even complicit, for having trained the goat poorly. Possibly the goat is really … a scapegoat. The dad proves a wise enough leader to heed his advice. In so doing, he avoids a costly overreaction, since, in the end, taking any action against the goat would have let the car robber get away scot-free. The car robber is the real enemy, and because the dad was so smart, the car robber was captured. It should come as no surprise that the president chose to stick around for the end to this riveting story. Only the petty or small-minded could fault him for it. After all, there is much to learn from literature' (Gene Weingarten, *Washington Post*, 18 July 2004).

N

nomadic year   George W. Bush's term for his period of military service in 1972. That is, time spent doing nothing, consuming too much alcohol. Close synonyms for **nomadic** here would be '**vagrant**', '**of no fixed address**', '**living like a vagabond**'. Opposite of traditional German term **Wanderjähre**, 'wander years', which implies education and exploration, and modern English **gap year**, time between leaving secondary school and going to university, sometimes spent on charitable work in other countries, travel, etc.

nuclear *souq*   Nuclear (Arab or Muslim) market. A term used by American writers for the Pakistani policy of selling nuclear technology to a range of other countries. Also *nuclear bazaar*. In both cases, the use of the Middle Eastern-related terms **souq** and *bazaar* carry the implication that this kind of nuclear proliferation is the consequence of non-Western, corrupt and informal practices: in fact nuclear proliferation – first to Britain, then to Israel, South Africa, Iran in the 1970s, later Pakistan, Libya and India – was all the result of covert Western policies, some state-supported, some carried out by the business sector.

O

objectively pro-terrorist   Thus did Michael Kelly of *The New Republic* describe those Americans whom he deemed to lack enthusiasm for the then imminent war in Iraq (Eric Alterman, 'Idiocy Watch: *The New Republic*', *The*

Nation, 7–14 January 2002). Reminiscent of earlier usage, in the Cold War, of *objectively pro-communist.*

Old Yeller   One of the names by which the Bush administration's envoy to the UN, John Bolton, was known. See **close their eyes and press the lever, immediate family, critical that we get him in place, poster child, quintessential kiss-up, kick-down sort of guy, unleash John Bolton** (Maureen Dowd, 'Unleash John Bolton', *IHT*, 28 April 2005).

on/in the hunt together   Pseudo-reassuring, also Texan phrase for military collaboration (cf. **bad guys, folks**). Hence whatever the differences between the USA and Pakistan (see **Stone Age**), they were united in pursuing terrorists, especially Osama bin Laden. In the words of President George W. Bush: 'We are on the hunt together'. He was echoed by the Pakistani President, General Pervez Musharraf: 'We are **in the hunt together** against these people' ('Bush Was "Taken aback" by US Threat to Pakistan', *IHT*, 23–24 September 2006).

our way or the highway   Arrogant attitude characteristic of American occupation forces and associated politicians and diplomats post-2003. Cf. **come to heel, Shock and Awe.**

out of our lane   US military version of 'above my pay grade', or 'don't-know-won't-speak', as justification for pretending not to know about sensitive issues. Thus used in 2007 by an aide of Major General William Caldwell, top spokesman for the US military in Iraq, when asked about **contractor** casualties. It would seem that no Pentagon office has records of these casualties. 'Contractors are out of our lane and we don't comment on them', said the officer concerned. According to one estimate, the total number of **contractors** killed by the end of May 2007 was at least 917, with more than 12,000 wounded in battle or on the job (John M. Broder and James Risen, 'War Takes Toll on Iraq Contractors', *IHT*, 21 May 2007).

P

perceived liberal bias   Right-wing American term used of the media when the least hint of criticism is divined, the term 'perceived' being used to suggest some validated or objective assessment. Usually a cover for, undeclared, right-wing bias.

Petri dish   Benazir Bhutto, just before her ill-fated return to Pakistan in 2007, used Petri's invention as a metaphor for her country. Under Musharraf, she said, radical schools and mosques had mushroomed with a consequent extremist influence. The country was 'the **Petri dish** of the international extremist movement'. Originally, a shallow glass or plastic cylindrical dish that biologists use for obtaining cell cultures, named after the German bacteriologist Julius Richard Petri (1852–1921) (Salman Masood, 'Musharraf Will Remain General If Not Elected', *IHT*, 25 September 2007).

poster child   Description of two prominent, and controversial, representatives of the Bush administration, popular with the neoconservative wing of the Republican Party: Lewis 'Scooter' Libby, assistant to Vice-President Dick Cheney, forced to resign in 2007 for lying to investigators about his role in the **Plame Affair** (see **distinguished public servant**); term also used of John Bolton on his nomination to be US Ambassador to the UN by Republican Senator George Voinovich of Ohio, who called him a 'poster child of what someone in the diplomatic corps should not be' ('The Warnings about Bolton', *IHT*, 30 May 2005). The term **poster child** came into vogue in the 1990s, as a result of the, often cynical and manipulative, use of children in advertising, hence an infantile version of older but latterly deemed to be somewhat jaded terms such as *bright-eyed boy, darling, pin-up boy/girl*. The spurious implication of the term is, of course, that the person so portrayed in the 'poster' is innocent and pure.

Pottery Barn principle   Term used by former US Secretary of Defense Colin Powell when warning President Bush and his Cabinet about their responsibility for the results of the invasion of Iraq. Rough US equivalent of the British 'You have made your bed and now you must lie in it'. From the principle applied by the US *Pottery Barn* retail chain where customers who damage goods before having paid for them are then expected to purchase the item, on the principle 'You broke it, you bought it' (Paul Krugman, 'Staying What Course', *IHT*, 17 May 2005).

Q

quintessential kiss-up, kick-down sort of guy   Opinion of Carl Ford, former head of the US State Department's bureau of intelligence and research (INR), of John Bolton, former US Ambassador to the UN. He also described him as a 'serial abuser'. See also **close their eyes and press the lever, immediate family, critical that we get him in place, Old Yeller, poster child, unleash.**

R

rearrange the sand   Description of ineffective 1998 rocket attacks on supposed Al-Qa'ida bases in Khost, Afghanistan, using 66 cruise missiles, along with attacks on factory in Sudan, as retaliation for East African embassy bombings. Cf. **ironing the wrinkle around the shirt**.

rearrange wiring diagrams   Term used to denote unwelcome and elaborate plans to restructure Washington's intelligence community, and in particular to break up or demote the CIA, in wake of the 9/11 Commission report and other official investigations.

renegade   As in 'renegade cleric'; alternatively 'wanted' and 'radical' cleric. Terms variously applied to the Iraqi Shi'i extremist Muqtada al-Sadr. '**Renegade**', in origin a Portuguese word, from *renegar*, to renounce or abjure, is a term of colonial derogation, referring to an escaped slave, later much used in the USA in the nineteenth century to denote Native Americans who refused to accept settler control.

S

security moms   US women voters, usually with sons, who backed Bush in the 2004 elections.

silver bullet   American expression for a one-off, complete or 'magical' solution, synonym for *magic wand*. From the *Lone Ranger* stories, as the hero's trademark (a reminder that a life was as precious as silver), and the legend of the werewolf, according to which only a 'silver bullet' can slay the beast. Rather misused, to suggest invincibility of the enemy, as in the testimony by then-National Security Adviser Condoleezza Rice before the 9/11 Commission when she said that there was no 'silver bullet' that could have prevented the attacks of 9/11.

slam dunk case   Image from basketball, a forceful, definitive shot in which a player jumps up and pushes the ball down through the net. Phrase used by then CIA Director George Tenet in December 2002 when asked by President Bush about the quality of intelligence on Iraqi weapons of mass destruction.

smoke 'em out   Part of George W. Bush's West Texas phrasebook. See **bad guys, bring them on, stand-up kind of guy**.

smoking gun   Term referring to some incontrovertible evidence for a matter under dispute or investigation. Misused as a metaphor by Condoleezza Rice in calling for military action against Iraq before the threat became nuclear, 'We don't want the smoking gun to be a mushroom cloud'.

stand-up kind of guy   Characterisation by George W. Bush of British prime minister Tony Blair at a press conference during the latter's visit to Bush's ranch in Crawford, Texas, in April 2004.

stop button   After President Mahmoud Ahmadinejad of Iran defiantly said that the Iranian nuclear programme had no *reverse gear*, the US Secretary of State Condoleezza Rice responded, 'They don't need a *reverse gear*. They need a **stop button**' (Brian Knowlton, 'Iran Takes Bold Tone of Eve of Meetings', *IHT*, 26 February 2007).

sucker-punch   Media strategy developed by the Bush White House in 2007 aimed at covering up its failing policy in Iraq, spinning new and old stories 'to keep the war going until Bush can dump it on its successor', according to journalist Frank Rich. The **sucker-punch** propaganda strategy involved a sharp **uptick** in references to **Al-Qa'ida**, a decline in references to Sunni-Shi'i violence, and a change from the original definition of the mission as being to establish 'an Iraq that can govern itself, sustain itself, defend itself'. The replacement policy emphasised 'Victory is defeating **Al-Qa'ida**', on the inaccurate grounds that **Al-Qa'ida** was the chief organizer of mayhem within Iraq. See **public diplomacy** (Frank Rich, 'Don't Laugh at Michael Chertoff', *IHT*, 16 July, 2007).

swiftboating   Word coined by 2004 Democratic Presidential candidate John Kerry, referring to Vietnam War veterans who had cast doubt on his war record, when he worked in units using rapid naval craft. The term later came in US political parlance to mean an attack, often insidious, on a candidate's strengths rather than weaknesses. Thus, during the 2008 Presidential campaign, references to Barack Obama's African-Indonesian racial and religious background and reputation for integrity carried the smear that he was a secret Muslim ('Did you know his middle name is Hussein?') and/or at least not *a real American* ('Well, his name isn't Smith, is it?'). One trick in this campaign was for opponents, including for a time his Republican rival, John McCain, to make a point of including, and placing emphasis on, his second name, thus 'Barack *Hussein* Obama'. The fact of his belonging to the Trinity United Church of Christ was also used against him, references being made to its website where it states that the Church is 'unashamedly black'.

Before she was knocked out of the Presidential race by Barack Obama, Hilary Clinton, referring to the controversial 'black values' of the pastor of his church, hinted that her opponent had not been properly 'vetted' (Sarah, 'Dirt Begins to Fly at Obama', *The Sunday Times*, 13 January 2008, http://www.timesonline.co.uk/tol/news/world/us_and_americas/ us_elections/article3177684.ece [last accessed 13 January 2008]). In the end, when the election was held in November 2008, Obama's name, childhood abroad and Muslim names (Barack is a Kenyan rendering of the Islamic term for divine blessing, *baraka*) seem to have made little difference to voter's choices, an indication of the remarkable good sense, and practical priorities, of most Americans.

T

terror talk   Used by US teenagers of post-9/11 slang, as in 'Ground Zero' to denote a messy bedroom; 'Total Jihad' for school punishment; 'so September 11' for a minor concern; the insult 'Your Mama, Osama'; and 'Taliban', 'Terrorist' and 'Fundamentalist' as terms of abuse ('In Times of Terror; Teens Talk the Talk', *IHT*, 20 March 2002).

terrorism humour   Lynne Cheney so admired the sense of humour of her Vice-President husband, Dick, that at a Gridiron dinner in Washington on 11 March 2006, she gave an example. 'Just the other day I asked him, "Do you know how many terrorists it takes to paint a wall?" And he answered right back, "It depends on how hard you throw them."' Her audience laughed (Maureen Dowd, 'Running on Empty', *IHT*, 16 March 2006).

thugocracy   Term of abuse coined by Tom DeLay, leader of the House Republican majority, to refer to Fidel Castro's regime. A staunch supporter of the US trade embargo against Cuba, he was nevertheless photographed smoking a Cuban cigar on a visit to Israel in July 2003, even though the purchase and consumption of cigars was illegal in the USA. Under the Helms-Burton Act of 1996 'trading with the enemy' was made illegal. The *thugees* were originally an Indian sect.

tough-guy shtick   That is, 'tough guy act/pretence', from Yiddish *shtick*, German *Stück*, literally 'piece', by extension, as in English, a party act, the regular comedian's turn. Here pretence of toughness used to cover timidity, **fundamental cowardice'** and underhand practices, in particular Bush's resort to *signing statements*, a practice allowing him surreptitiously to subvert more than 750 laws enacted since he took office, rather than vetoing them in public view. In this way he bypassed the ban on torture, *inter alia*. 'It allowed him to make a coward's escape from the moral (and legal) responsibility of arguing from so radical a break with American practice' (Frank Rich, 'A Profile in Cowardice', *IHT*, 9 July 2007).

turkey shoot   See Chapter 8.

U

uptick   The word 'uptick' was once limited to a stock market transaction at a price higher than the preceding one for the same security. In recent years, it has increasingly been used in the context of US policy towards Iraq and Iran, as more or less equivalent to *increase*: in some senses, the stock market connection is probably not fortuitous, given the role of speculation, misinformation and alarm in shaping perceptions about these states. Another word taken from stock market usage and given another, military, usage was **surge**. Thus, in 2005 there was 'an **uptick** lately in technology to Iran' (*The New York Times*, 14 April 2005), in 2006 there was '**uptick** in interest in Iran' (*Washington Post*, 7 April 2006) and in 2007 there was an '**uptick** in Iraq violence' (*Reuters*, 11 March 2008).

V

vertical stovepipe   Term used of process of US planning for the 2003 Iraq War, implying lack of inter-agency coordination, blinkered vision, **group-think**. Thus, according to the US Chief of Operations in Iraq, General Jay Garner, speaking to the British government's *Future of Iraq Commission*: 'the problem with that planning is that it had been done in the **vertical stovepipe** of that agency and the horizontal connection of those plans did not occur' (Patrick Wintour, 'Iraq on Verge of Genocidal War, Warns US General', the *Guardian*, 18 June 2007).

Vietnam on speed   Journalist Frank Rich's definition for occupied Iraq (Frank Rich, 'A Quagmire for the MTV Attention Span', *IHT*, 29–30 January 2005).

W

Whopper   See Chapter 4.

American Colloquial

1. 8,000-mile screwdriver
2. attention whore
3. bad guys
4. bring them on
5. cakewalk
6. chicken hawks
7. circular firing squad
8. cut and run
9. darn good liar
10. elephant in the room
11. folks
12. full court press
13. get some
14. gin up
15. ironing the wrinkle around the shirt
16. Pottery Barn principle
17. quintessential kick-up, kiss-down kind of guy
18. rearrange the sand
19. rearrange wiring diagrams
20. security moms
21. silver bullet
22. slam dunk case
23. tough-guy shtick
24. vertical stovepipe
25. Vietnam on speed
26. Whopper

CHAPTER 10

Spaces, Real and Imagined

Bali to Beslan to Baghdad.

—Panoramic alliterative phrased used by President George W. Bush in speeches on terrorism, 2006

The situation on the Iraqi-Pakistan border.

—Area of supposed concern to Republican Presidential candidate John McCain, in TV comment, 15 October 2008, on Barack Obama's failure to address this (non-existent) shared border during his 2008 election campaign visit to the region

A

Absurdistan   Addition, in the form of a title (of a book by Gary Shteyngart, Random House, 2007) to the growing number of '**-istans**' invented since 9/11 (*FT* Magazine, 8–9 March 2008). See also **Hamastan, Richistan, Talibanistan**.

Af/Pak   See Chapter 4.

Afghanistan   Term invented in 1747 to denote new buffer zone between British, Chinese, Russian and Persian empires. Literally 'land of the Afghans' denoting at once all inhabitants of that country and, more specifically, the Pushtuns/Pathans, the largest ethnic group who often refer to themselves as 'Afghans'. Ruled until 1973 by the Muhammadzai monarchy, a family of Pashtuns of tribal origin, but using Persian, here termed 'Dari', the language of the court, as medium of government and artistic expression. Controlled from 1978 to 1992 by the communist **People's Democratic Party of Afghanistan (PDPA)** as the Democratic Republic of Afghanistan, from 1992 to 1996 by the *mujahidin* alliance, as the Islamic Republic of Afghanistan, and from 1996 to 2001 by the Taliban as the Islamic Emirate of Afghanistan.

Andalucia/Andalus   Historically, all of Spain ruled by the Muslims, from the eighth to the fifteenth century, source of inspiration for much music and culture in the contemporary Arab World. In North Africa many bookshops and chemists are called **Andalus**. In the words of the Moroccan political scientist Mohammad Tozy: 'Andalus is a myth, of the unity of all Muslims, of a great civilisation, an alternative to the west, and dominated by Muslims' (*El País*, 14 May 2007). Intermittently claimed by a few Islamist militants, but not by groups active in Morocco and Algeria, who limit their claims to the two remaining Spanish enclaves in North Africa, Ceuta and Melilla. Sometimes referred to as *Bilad Tariq*, 'the Land of Tariq', after Tariq ibn Zaid, the military commander who conquered Spain in 711 AD, and who gave his name to the peninsula of Gibraltar, *jabal tariq*, 'the Mountain of Tariq'. The modern Spanish region of Andalucia, comprising nine autonomous regions, among them Seville, Cordoba, Granada and Cádiz, is a creation of administrative reform in the nineteenth century.

Arabia   Romantic but often imprecise geographical term, English for the Arabian Peninsula, in Arabic *al-jazira al-'arabia*. See *Jazeera/Jazira*. The English term 'Saudi Arabia' is in Arabic *al-mamlaka al-'arabiyya al-sa'udiyya*, 'The Arab Kingdom of Saudi Arabia'. The older English term '*Araby*' and comparable terms in other European languages can be used to cover the Arab world, as well as Iran, real or imagined, as a whole. As an example of how the word has come to be a synonym for the generically exotic, Hans-Werner Henze's song cycle, *Sechs Lieder aus dem Arabischen*, translated as 'Six Songs from the Arabian', derives its title from just one of the six items, in the event a *Persian* poem by Hafez. See **Peninsula of the Prophet Mohammad**.

Arabistan   Literally 'Land of the Arabs', *not* a term used to denote any Arab state, or the Arab world as a whole, but applied to the south-west province of Iran, Khuzistan, home to a significant Arab minority and, intermittently, claimed by Iraq as part of its national territory.

Arc of Crisis   Term used in the late 1970s to denote a range of countries running from Afghanistan, through Iran and the Arabian Peninsula, to Ethiopia, where established pro-Western regimes had been overthrown or challenged. Invented in 1978 by Presidential adviser Zbigniew Brzezinski, popularised as the *Crescent of Crisis* in a *Time* magazine cover story dated 15 January 1979. For some analogous terms see **axis of evil, Shi'i crescent**, and satirical late 1970s variants.

Arc of Extremism   Tony Blair in his speech of 1 August 2006 in Los Angeles, 'There is an arc of extremism now stretching across the Middle East and touching countries far away from the region'. See following item.

Arc of Instability   US diplomatic and military term, c. 2005, for large intercontinental area, much larger than the earlier **Arc of Crisis**, comprising much of the Middle East, Africa, Central and South Asia, estimated to remain unstable for another 50 years.

Arc of Islam   Alarmist, when not paranoid, category used by Hindu nationalist politicians in India to claim encirclement of their country.

Arc of Reforms   Optimistic term used by US officials in the period 2003–4 to describe US-promoted process of democratisation, good governance, reform in the wider Middle East, from Morocco to Afghanistan. Complete failure, soon abandoned.

axis of evil   President George W. Bush used this term in his State of the Union address of 29 January 2002 of governments he accused of sponsoring terrorism and developing weapons of mass destruction. Here, he alleged, 'states like these, and their terrorist allies, constitute an **axis of evil**, arming to threaten the peace of the world'. The term 'axis', earlier in modern history applied to the fascist allies Germany, Italy and Japan before and during World War II, is incorrect as there is no coordination between the countries in question. The countries he mentioned were Iraq, Iran and North Korea. Invented by Michael Gerson, chief presidential speech writer, and his assistant David Frum, tasked with writing the January 2002 State of the Union address. Frum, who did the first draft of the speech, sought inspiration from Roosevelt's 'day of infamy' speech after Pearl Harbour, and proffered the term *axis of hatred*, justifying the word 'axis' on the grounds that while Iran, Iraq and, by extension, **Al-Qa'ida** were suspicious and rivalrous of each other, this had also applied to the states forming the 1941 Axis Powers, Germany, Italy and Japan. Frum's original phrase was reworked by Gerson to give it a more 'folksy' image, as suited the President's general style.

   In a speech on 6 May 2002, John Bolton, then US Under-Secretary of State, added Libya, Syria and Cuba to the list. Alternative uses include that of Hugo Chávez, President of Venezuela, who described 'Washington and its allies' as an 'axis of evil'. In a satirical mode, *The Economist* ran a cover headline, 'Axis of Feeble', about the end of the Bush–Blair partnership (11 May 2006). For other pseudo-geometric and geo-strategic terms, see **Arc of Crisis, Shi'i Crescent.**

B

Balkans   Originally a medium-sized mountain range in Bulgaria, the Haemus or Balkan (from a Turkish word for thickly wooded hills) mountains, extended in early nineteenth century by German geographer August Zeune to cover all of what had previously been termed 'Turkey in Europe'. Used throughout the nineteenth and twentieth centuries to cover western Turkey, Greece, Albania, Bulgaria, Romania and the components of former Yugoslavia – Serbia, Bosnia, Croatia, Slovenia, Kosovo, Montenegro – as well as the Moldovan former republic of the USSR. Croatia and Slovenia sought, after independence in the 1990s, to deny their membership of this region. The division of the once unified Ottoman region, beginning in the late nineteenth century and concluding with the independence of Kosovo in 2008, yielded the term *Balkanisation*: a dozen or so states where hitherto there was one.

Bantustan   Derogatory term used in South Africa in the 1960s and 1970s to denote supposedly autonomous 'tribal' homelands, such as Transkei and Kwazulu, set up, with spurious autonomous rights and institutions, as part of the *separate but equal* policy of *apartheid* ('Apartness') under the white supremacist National Party government. Later applied by extension to the Palestinian-controlled areas delimited under the 1993 Oslo Accords. The word *Bantu* itself is racist, being a generic, and pseudo-ethnic, term for black South Africans.

Bharat   Hindu chauvinist term for India, from the Hindu God and alleged ancestor of all Hindus. Inserted in the name of main right-wing party, the Bharatiya Janata Party.

C

cradle   As in 'cradle of civilisation': atavistic term used to suggest that all civilisation, religion, agriculture or whatever originate from the country in question, e.g. Syria which claims, in a bid to outstrip rivals such as Turkey, Egypt, Iraq and Israel, to have 10,000 years of civilisation.

crescent   Literally something that is 'growing', hence half-moon, the symbol of Islam, and, by extension, applied to geographical areas, and imagined political spaces, associated with it. Earlier example *The Fertile Crescent*, agriculturally productive lands stretching from Palestine, Lebanon, Syria over to Iraq in the inter-World War period, scene of rivalry between Egypt, Syria and Iraq.

Crescent of Crisis   US-European Strategy for the Greater Middle East.

crucible of terrorism   Description by UK Prime Minister Gordon Brown of border areas of Pakistan and Afghanistan on a one-day visit to Afghanistan, 27 April 2009.

D

dar al harb, dar al islam   Literally 'House of War', 'House of Islam', historic Islamic categories for distinguishing the non-Muslim from the Muslim worlds. These terms are not, however, present to any significant extent in modern Islamist or general Arabic discourse, and it is mistaken to project them onto contemporary Islamist discourse, as does, e.g., Samuel Huntington in his *The Clash of Civilisations*. No Muslim states conducts its diplomacy on the basis of this distinction. No newspaper in any Muslim country divides its pages along the lines of these categories.

E

East and West   Two frequently used words, purporting to denote at once *a geographical and a cultural identity*, that are the source of many misunderstandings, clichés, prejudices and meaningless generalisations. If east and west are two cultural poles, then 'west' is more easily recognisable than 'east', which refers to a variety of countries sometimes the whole of Asia, sometimes the Middle East or Near East alone, sometimes, as in earlier British colonial usage, India. In Arabic, *Maghreb*, 'the land of the west', refers to North Africa, while *gharb* refers to the 'west' in general (from the word *gharaba* 'to set', i.e. of the sun) and *mashriq/sharq*, from *sharaqa* to 'rise' refers to Arab East (i.e. Syria, Lebanon, Palestine, Jordan, Iraq), what in Western European languages is often termed 'the Middle East'. The Quran, Surat al Nur, has the words *la sharqia wa la gharbia*, literally 'neither eastern nor western', thus providing modern nationalist politicians with a supposedly canonical legitimation for their policies, be it President Arif of Iraq in the 1960s or the slogan of Ayatollah Khomeini in Iran, *nah gharb nah sharq*, 'Neither East nor West'. As in all such reuses of classical religious texts, the modern usage nears little or no relation to the Quranic meaning, which is part of a passage on mysticism, denying the relevance of particular places.

Eurabia   That is, an Arab/Islamic takeover of Europe, multi-purpose alarmist term denoting either possible future takeover of Western European cities and countries by fundamentalist and culturally unassimilable Islamic communities or subordination of European politics and foreign policy to the Muslim and Arab world. In the Dutch European elections of June 2008 the anti-Muslim Geert Wilders, leader of the PVV, the 'Party of Freedom, and which came second in the polls repeated the slogan 'No to **Eurabia**'; openly Islamofobic, the PVV also called for the expulsion of Bulgaria and Romania from the European Union. In support of the **Eurabia** thesis, Giselle Littman argued in *Eurabia: The Euro-Arab Axis* that Europe's alliance with the Arab world has been at the expense of the Jews and the trans-Atlantic alliance. It is distinguished from *Euro-Arab Dialogue*, the long-running and almost wholly ineffectual series of meetings between European and Arab, especially Gulf, countries on matters of international and economic importance. This paranoid fantasy of a European-Middle East fusion contrasts with the alternative fantasy, widely held on the French right, of an Islamic-US conspiracy against Europe, this mediated via shared Puritanism and, of course, anti-Europeanism of the two sides.

F

Fatahland   Area of southern Lebanon controlled by the Palestinian guerrillas from the mid-1970s until the Israeli invasion of 1982.

Federally Administered Tribal Areas (FATA)   Seven districts in north-west Pakistan, between the **North-West Frontier Province**, with its capital at Peshawar, and Afghanistan, scene of tribal and Taliban activity. Comprised North and South Waziristan, Bajaur, Tank, Khyber and Dera Ismail Khan.

G

Gulf   In reference to the Middle East/West Asia usually 'The Gulf' is a waterway bordered by Iran, Iraq, Saudi Arabia and smaller Arab states. Cf. in the Western Hemisphere 'the Gulf' is usually 'The Gulf of Mexico'. Site of over half of the world's known oil and a quarter of its known gas reserves. Known for much of the twentieth century as the 'Persian Gulf', the region began to be called 'the Arab Gulf' by Arab states in the 1970s, thus initiating a dispute that continued after the Iranian Revolution. Various alternatives have been tried, notably using the former Ottoman title 'the Gulf of Basra' or, briefly after the Iranian Revolution, 'the Islamic Gulf'. In the 1970s the Iranian Kurdish writer, Hazhir Teimurian, suggested that since his people did so much of the work in these countries, it should be called 'the Kurdish Gulf'. The dispute over this nomenclature, like that over the three small Arab islands (total population less than 200) taken by Iran in November 1971, was a fine example of what Freud has termed 'the narcissism of small differences'. It also calls to mind the observation by the Argentinian writer Jose Luis Borges about the Anglo-Argentine War in 1982 over the Falkland Islands (population 2,000): 'Two bald men quarrelling over a comb'.

H

Hamasistan/Hamastan   Literally 'the land of **Hamas**'. Name for Gaza and the West Bank that gained currency in Israeli political circles and among hard-line supporters of Israeli government policy. Contrast with equivalent **Fatahland**, applied by same people to the PLO-controlled areas of Southern Lebanon in the 1970s. The term **Hamasistan** also found its way into a note published by the British National Union of Journalists, warning young and unwary freelancers about going off on dangerous missions alone, of '... the temptation for some, in particular the young and gung-ho and inexperienced, to hare off to the latest place in the Pentagon's bomb-sights as soon as they can find **Hamasistan** on a map. The simplest and most obvious advice we could offer to such people would be: Don't ... ' (Mike Holderness, 'Safety at Work', 2002, www.londonfreelance.org/safety.html]).

Hindu Kush   Literally 'Kill Hindus' or 'Kill Indians', mountain range along Pakistan–Afghanistan frontier.

Holy Land Factitious Christian term for Palestine, more recently adopted by Islamic fundamentalists as well. See Chapter 7.

I

Iran Traditional name, in the Persian language, for the country referred to for many centuries as *Persia*. In 1935 Reza Shah decreed that the country should officially be known henceforth as **Iran**. The name is believed to derive from the same root as *Aryan*, in the past a neutral term for linguistic, geographical or ethnic identification, but since the rise of Nazism in Europe it was associated with German and other racist, white supremacist doctrine. The word *Persia* derives from the southern province of *Fars*, site of the ancient imperial capital known in Persian as *takht-i jamshid*, 'the Throne of Jamshid' (Jamshid being a mythical ancient monarch) but to the ancient Greeks, who burnt it down in 334 BC, and to the rest of the world as *Persepolis*, the 'City of the Persians'. See **Gulf**.

Iraq Name given by British colonialists to area created after World War I from three former Arab provinces of the Ottoman Empire, those of Mosul, Baghdad and Basra. Site of ancient civilisations of Mesopotamia (including Sumerian, Akkadian, Assyrian and Babylonian) and of the medieval Muslim Abbasid Empire (750–1258 AD). The word *'iraq* was in the past a geographical, not a political or administrative, term, possibly derived from the word for dark earth, applied to what is now the northern part of Arab-inhabited Iraq and the adjacent, western, part of Iran, hence a traditional geographer's distinction between *'iraq 'arabi* and *'iraq 'ajami*. This denotation was, however, without political import, and it was only in the twentieth century that the term **Iraq** came to denote a fixed, territorial and political, entity. As a way of rebuffing suggestions of Arab claims or connections to the relevant part of Iran itself, the government of Reza Shah decreed that the town of *'Araq*, known until the early twentieth century as *'araq i 'ajami*, south-west of Tehran, hitherto spelt with the same root as *'iraq*, be retitled *Arak*, thus losing both the initial *'ain*, this to be replaced by the latter *alef*, 'A', *'ain* being a letter not pronounced in Persian in any case, and converting the final *'q'* into a *'k'*.

Islamistan Despite apparent temptations, and parallel concepts such as *Christendom*, there is no evidence of this term ever being used, in part because **Islam** as a religion is universal, and hence cannot be associated with a particular geographical area. But see *dar al harb, dar al islam*.

'-stans'/'the stans' The suffix 'stan/istan', meaning 'land of', is of Persian origin, but now used generally of regions and areas, real or imagined, with some Muslim association. See **Islamistan, Londonistan, Pakistan, the stans.** Significantly, no state or region in the Arab world, however, adopted this suffix, the word *Arabistan* being applied to the Arab-populated region of south-west Iran, otherwise known as Khuzistan.

L

Land of the Two Rivers Arabic *bilad al nahrain*, common name for Iraq, whose most fertile areas lie between the two rivers, the Tigris and Euphrates. The Arabic is probably a translation of the classical Greek name, with the same meaning, *Mesopotamia.*

Londonistan Used in much the same tone as **Eurabia**, first by French alarmist writers, then taken up in British press usage, e.g., Melanie Phillips, *Londonistan. How Britain Is Creating a Terror State Within* (London: Gibson Square, 2006). Chapter headings included 'The Human Rights Jihad', 'Multicultural Paralysis', 'Scapegoating the Jews', 'The Red-Black Alliance', 'On Their Knees before Terror', 'The Appeasement of Clerical Fascism'. According to Phillips, the 'dirty secret' in the war against terrorism was that 'Britain's capital had turned into "Londonistan" – a mocking lay on the names of such state sponsors of terrorism as Afghanistan – and become the major European centre for the promotion, recruitment and financing of Islamic terror and extremism' (pp. 11–12). One of several books in different European countries denouncing apparent appeasement of Muslim extremism. Cf. Chapter 6, **Fallaci, Oriana; Hirsi Ali, Ayaan.** Comparable terms in regard to rich Russians in London, *Londongrad, Moscow-on-Thames.* While registering a number of legitimate criticisms of the indulgence of Islamist militants and of their 'hate speech', the elementary weakness of all such arguments about London and Islamist terror is that they operate with a wholly outdated model of how terrorism works: in the modern world, there *is no centre of promotion, recruitment and financing* since much is done by informal networks across the world, via the Internet and remote control and that it is images of war and oppression, and the outrage they provoke that, as much as anything, lead young men to commit terrorist crimes.

M

Middle East   Geographical and geopolitical term first coined by US Admiral Alfred Thayer Mahan in 1902 ('The Persian Gulf in International Affairs', *National Review*, September 1902, pp. 27–35). An attempt to delineate the area between the Mediterranean and India, also in contrast to Far East. Somewhat, but never completely, displaced terms 'Near East' (delineating Turkey and Arab areas along the Eastern Mediterranean), 'Levant' or, more recently, 'West Asia'. Generally includes the Arab countries of the eastern Arab world, Turkey, Iran and Israel but, conventionally, excludes Afghanistan and Pakistan. Despite its casual and imperial origins, it became generally accepted in modern Middle Eastern languages: hence Arabic *al-sharq al-awsat*, Persian *khavar miane*, Hebrew *ha-mizrach ha-tikhon*, Turkish *orta doğu*. Contrasted to 'Greater Middle East', a term coined with regard to US policy in 2003, which includes Afghanistan but not Pakistan, and my 'Greater West Asia', which includes both of the latter (see *Two Hours that Shook the World* [London: Saqi, 2001]). Significantly, at a time when other geographical terms are being questioned, e.g. 'Far East', 'Central Europe', 'British Isles', remarkably little nationalist objection to this term has, as yet, been noted in the region. A wider term than the former *Near East* which covered states bordering the Mediterranean, but, in most usage, narrower than *West Asia*.

N

Not Part of Europe   Dismissive term, on a par with the rejection of an individual as 'not one of us'. Used to denote countries, notably Turkey but also Ukraine, Russia and the South Caucasian states, which some in the EU want permanently to exclude from membership in the Union. The term demonstrates an arbitrary and ignorant view of European history and borders. Often accompanied by the suggestion that more distant lands such as Australia, the USA, etc. *are* part of the Continent. Among other things, the term ignores the fact that the Iberian Peninsula and the **Balkans** were for centuries under Islamic rule and that many of the core cultural components of Europe, not least religion, food and vocabulary, are derived from interaction with the Middle East, not to mention the effects of past decades of migration of millions of Muslims to cities of European states.

Nusantara   Aspirational Islamic geographical term, used in Indonesia, first by medieval leaders, later by nationalists, and, more recently, by Islamists. The concept is a composite of the Javanese words *Nusa* (island) and *Antero* (whole) and refers to all regions of Indonesia from Sabang (Sumatra) to Merauke (West Papua). The term originates with an oath made by the fourteenth-century Javanese Emperor Gajah Mada: he swore he would not eat any spiced food until he had conquered all of *Nusantara*. Indonesia's first President, the nationalist Sukarno, made 'From Sabang to Merauke' his main slogan, thus indicating that the whole of the Dutch colony of the East Indies would be included in newly independent Indonesia, whether minority peoples such as the West Papuans, Achenese and Ambonese, for example, wished this or not. Nowadays, Islamist groups such as *Jemaah Islamiyah, Abu Sayyaf* and *Kumpulan Militan Malaysia* are calling for a new utopian *Nusantara*, an Islamic state – *darulah Islamayah nusantara* – that is even larger than the medieval or post-independence entity. This Islamic aspirant state stretches from southern Thailand, home to many, oppressed, Thai Muslims, through Malaysia, Singapore, the Philippine Muslim island of Mindanao and the Indonesian archipelago. Ironically, the international organisation the *Association of East Asian States* (ASEAN) was formed in 1967 in large part as a response to Sukarno's *Indonesia Raya* (Greater Indonesia) nationalism and today, at least in the minds of the new pan-Islamic nationalists, it has spawned its own destruction (Loretta Napoleoni and Rico Carish, 'Quién paga a los asesinos', *El País*, 10 July 2005).

P

Pakhtunistan/Pashtunistan/Pushtunistan   Territory claimed by successive Afghan governments in Pakistan since the latter's independence in 1947. Afghanistan has contested the border defined in 1893, the Durand Line.

Pakistan   State of South Asian Muslims formed in 1947 after the partition of British India into Muslim and, predominantly, Hindu states, viz. Pakistan (at that time comprising West and East Pakistan, the latter is today's Bangladesh) and India. The word itself, is said, variously, to be based on the Urdu/Persian for *pak*, pure, i.e. 'Land of the Pure', or on the initial letters of some of the major provinces comprising it, Punjab, Afghanistan, Kashmir and Sindh (where 'Afghanistan' denotes the Pashtun, North-West Frontier, region). According to some accounts, it was invented by the Indian Muslim politician Chaudhary Rahmat Ali, in his manifesto *Now or Never,* published in Cambridge, in 1933. Apart from recurrent anti-Hindu prejudices, an important goal of the founders of Pakistan was to free South-Asian Muslims from what they termed 'Arab imperialism'.

Peninsula of the Prophet Mohammad   Arabic *jazirat Muhammad,* term used by Osama bin Laden for Saudi Arabia, a state whose name he rejects, on the grounds that it gives ownership of the state and land to a particular family, the Saudi rulers. An example, as in Chapter 7, **Holy Land**, of the sacralisation of territory, without any historical or scriptural authority, by modern politics. The use of this inclusive term by the **Al-Qa'ida** leader would seem to imply, first, that *all* of the Arabian Peninsula is one territory, with no distinction between Saudi Arabia – which is four-fifths of the territory – and the other six states, Yemen, Kuwait, Oman, Bahrain, Qatar and the Emirates, and, second, that the whole of this territory, not just the holy cities of Mecca and Medina and their environs, is sacred territory (see **Mecca**). The former assumption is seen by non-Saudis as an expression of expansionism; the latter has no legal or Islamic scriptural foundation.

pretzel of preposterousness   Spoof term of late 1970s, along with **rhomboid of rhetoric**, of pseudo-geometric terms much used by purveyors of alarm in regard to the Middle East and Islam. See **Arc of Crisis, Shi'i Crescent**. Also **Eurabia, Olive Belt**.

R

Richistan   Mythical land inhabited by the very wealthy, another variant on the extended use of **-istan**, given a somewhat shady connotation by association with the Islamic-sounding toponymic suffix. Cf. **Hamasistan, Londonistan**. The classic source is Robert Frank's *Richistan: A Journey through the American Wealth Boom and the Lives of the New Rich* (Crown Publishers, 2007). According to Frank, 'true wealth' starts at $10 million. **Richistan** has a vocabulary of its own. Household managers have superseded the old-fashioned butler and are something akin to 'chief operating officer for My Life Inc.', while the 100-plus household staff includes arborists. **Richistanis** have stationery wardrobes of envelopes and letterheads that reflect their wealth and standing as true masters of the banal, having made their fortunes from selling ceramic villages, inventing a new kind of mozzarella and coming up with the Dogloo (igloo-shaped doghouse).

Most become 'citizens' through a liquidity event, when someone buys out their company, rather than through an inheritance. Philanthropy has a new slant now that the **Richistanis** have disdain for donating to charities with large overhead costs and have set up their own philanthropic ventures run on business principles, some of them as for-profit organisations analysing what is the best investment per dollar with regard to progress made with their donations. They have their own health-care staffed by 'concierge doctors' but they still suffer status anxiety. When asked how much money would make them feel secure, they invariably quote a figure that is twice their own net worth, and since they want to live forever, they are very 'germ-oriented' people (Alex Beam, 'Richistan', *IHT*, 8 June 2007; Robert Frank, 'Welcome to Richistan', *The Sunday Times*, 17 June 2007).

S

Scottish Guantánamo   Term used for the poorer East End regions of Glasgow, such as Easterhouse, Parkhead and Barlinnie. It is used by inhabitants to underline the impossibility of moving elsewhere.

Shi'i Crescent   Purportedly accurate term propounded by King Abdullah of Jordan in an interview with the *Washington Post* in December 2004 (cf. **Arc of Crisis, Eurabia**). In the face of rising Shi'i, and Iranian, influence in Iraq to his east and in Syria and Lebanon to the north and north-west, the King, descendant of a noble Sunni family long established in Mecca and Medina, the Hashemites, charged that a 'Shi'i Crescent' was threatening to split the Arab and Islamic world. According to the King, Iran's 'vested interest' was 'to have an Islamic republic of Iraq; if that happened, we've opened ourselves to a whole set of new problems that won't be limited to the borders of Iraq'. Moshe Ma'oz, Professor Emeritus of Islamic and Middle Eastern Studies at the Hebrew University of Jerusalem, differed, arguing that far from being about to be torn apart along Muslim sectarian lines, 'the pattern in the Middle East has been for mixed Sunni-Shi'i states to remain intact' because 'important differences remain among Shi'i communities. In many cases, the Shi'ah are more concerned with changing their lot within their existing countries than in binding themselves to Iran, the largest Shi'i community in the region, or in creating any other form of pan-Shi'i alliance' (Moshe Ma'oz, 'The "Shi'i Crescent": Myth and Reality', *Brookings*, 1 May 2008).

Shi'istan   American term for possible Shi'i state in partitioned Iraq, post-2003.

Sunni triangle   Term first coined by the Iraqi political scientist Dr. Abbas Kelidar in 1975 to denote the wider area of Mosul, Ratba and Baghdad. More recently used to denote the area bounded by Baghdad, Fallujah and Tikrit, where, in contrast to the rest of the country in which either Kurds or Shi'i predominate, Sunni Arab are in the majority.

Sunnistan   American term for possible separate Sunni state in partitioned Iraq, post-2003.

Swat   Pashtu-speaking region in the **North-West Frontier Province** of Pakistan, ruled by autonomous princes till its incorporation into the Pakistani state in 1969 (population 1.3 million). It was previously the location of historic Hindu and Buddhist sites, and of ski facilities, and was taken over by Islamist militants, foreign fighters and the Taliban in 2006–7. The scene of fierce fighting with the Pakistani army in 2009. Historic residence of the ruler known as *The Akond of Swat.* See Chapter 5, **akhund.**

T

Talibanistan   Informal denomination of the zone comprised by Pakistan's North-West Frontier Province (NWFP) and the **Federally Administered Tribal Area** (FATA) agencies. In 2006–7, as concern about violent Islamists in the area rose, the term came to be used more frequently in the US press as, for example, in 'The Truth about Talibanistan' by Aryn Baker in *Time* (22 March 2007). According to Baker, 'Remote, tribal and deeply conservative, the border region is less a part of either country than a world unto itself, a lawless frontier so beyond the control of the West and its allies that it has earned a name of its own: **Talibanistan**'.

Temara   Detention centre ten miles south of Rabat, Morocco, used for detention in secret and brutal interrogation of suspects in the **war against terrorism**. Developed by the Rabat government to replace other, notorious, political prisons closed and destroyed in propagandistic claims about a new respect for human rights. Run by the country's Directorate for Territorial Surveillance, an organisation without legal authority to detain. Denounced in an Amnesty International Report of July 2004. Following bomb attacks in Casablanca in May 2003, an estimated 7,000 people were arrested.

Toulouse   Southern French city, site of major explosion of 300 tons of ammonium nitrate in an AZF factory, owned by TotalFinaElf, a few days after 9/11. Thirty people were killed, and damage valued at 2 billion euros was caused. Three years after the event it was still not clear if this was an accident or the work of an Algerian Islamist identified by the police as working in the factory. When I conducted a seminar on 'globalisation' at the Total headquarters outside Paris in March 2007 with senior executives of the company, and casually asked about the cause of the blast, I was told that none of those present, senior managers and engineers, were prepared to comment.

V

Vietnamalia syndrome   US aversion to using force abroad in early 1990s, fusion of 'Vietnam' and 'Somalia'. Coined by the diplomat Richard Holbrooke.

W

Wadi Silicon   Term for computer industry in Israel, a reworking of *Silicon Valley*.

Y

Yiddishland   'A borderless realm of east European Jewish life and letters in the inter-war period' ('Contested City', *The Economist*, 2 May 2009). The state of Israel made considerable effort to suppress the use of the Yiddish language (German, written in Hebrew letters and with a large Hebrew vocabulary) in favour of the newly revived Hebrew. Yiddish was regarded by Zionism as a language of the diaspora, of weakness and of cultural dilution.

A World of 'stans': Lands Real and Invented

Absurdistan

Afghanistan

Arabistan

Bantustan

Hamastan/Hamasistan

Islamistan

Londonistan

Pakhtunistan/Pashtunistan

Richistan

Shi'istan

Sunnistan

Talibanistan

CHAPTER 11

Obscuring Responsibility: Euphemisms, Circumlocutions and the Vagaries of the 'Exculpatory Passive'

'Exculpatory Passive'   Practice frequently resorted to by those in power and those engaged in news management, propaganda, censorship, etc. of using in English in the passive form of verb to distance themselves, and the organisation they work for, from responsibility for policies and actions – in Latin languages, such as French and Spanish, the reflexive serves the same function. From everyday life 'my bag has not showed up', i.e. *I lost it.* Thus, in business, 'This is not a procedure that we have', i.e. *we refuse to do this;* from a radio report about Nigeria, 'Money simply has not filtered down to the people', i.e. *the rich and powerful have kept the money for themselves;* 'there were flaws in the way the scheme was planned and implemented', i.e. *we made a mess of things.* Examples abound from the contemporary Middle East. Thus President Bush, on the eve of his departure from office in January 2009, regretting 'that the intelligence was not what it was', i.e. *that he and his administration faked intelligence reports to justify their invasion of Iraq;* on future negotiations over Palestine, 'Israel will resist any such timetable', i.e. *Israel refuses to change its policy;* 'confidence in the security plan is not high', i.e. *no-one trusts the plan* (this from a 2008 report out of Iraq); 'we have to recognize that we have a long-run problem here', i.e. *the west has done nothing about this for the past 60 years* (Tony Blair on the Palestine question, January 2009). The term is mine.

Stuff happens.

> —Donald Rumsfeld, US Defense Secretary, on the looting,
> of Baghdad 2003, while the troops under his command stood by

I regret that the intelligence was not what it was.

> —President George W. Bush

That's how our training goes.

> —US military excuse for the killing of civilians

The boom in loans has been supported over the past ten years by a relative lack of regulation.

> —BBC radio report, 16 November 2008, on the boom in British
> loans and bank financing over the previous decade

There was an error in my accounting system.

> —British MP during the 2009 parliamentary accounts scandal

While the programme is not classified, there is a lack of transparency surrounding it, though US military officials said the lack of publicity was not an attempt to keep the programme secret.

> —US military trained Georgian commandos', *FT* 5 September 2008

A

automatic pilot   As applied to politicians, such as George W. Bush, who answered questions in a detached, rote-like manner, i.e. while not thinking or listening.

B

blowback   Evasive term, said to be CIA slang, for activities carried out by former Western clients, such as the Afghan guerrillas, who later turn against the West. Example of **exculpatory passive**. Cf. **morass, nightmare, quagmire**. Title of book on US involvement in Afghanistan by John Cooley, linking later Islamist terrorism to CIA policy in the 1980s.

bruising   Like **searing**. Adjective used by states which encounter opposition when they invade or occupy other countries.

C

complicit enablers   Description of US media relationship with the Bush White House, in which they collaborated with the 'carefully orchestrated campaign to shape and manipulate sources of public approval'. This comes from the memoirs of the former White House press secretary Scott McClellan, *What Happened: Inside the Bush White House and Washington's Culture of Deception* (*IHT*, 29 May 2008).

conflict-affected   One of a set of compound adjectives and technical terms, propagated in the 1990s, that allow the user to avoid mentioning causes of the conflict, or responsibility thereof. It frequently qualifies 'populations', 'countries' and 'states', much used in humanitarian and World Bank circles.

confusing   Self-exonerating word for politics and society of a country invaded without prior study or consideration of local realities. Cf. **bruising, messy, quagmire, searing**.

D

declassify   In the George W. Bush White House, an evasive term for 'leak'. Word normally applied to making available to the public of 'classified', i.e. secret or restricted circulation, documents relating to recent policy making, but also used in off-the-record, *i.e. not public*, briefing by Vice-Presidential assistant Lewis 'Scooter' Libby in briefings to reporters about pre-invasion intelligence on Iraq.

denial   One of several commonly used terms taken, but then misused, from psychoanalysis. First appearance in English in 1914 as the translation of the psychoanalytic term *Verneinung*, to denote various forms of refusal, by individuals, government institutions or whole nations and people, to recognise, or admit suffering. Distinct from *negation*, a philosophical term, and *annihilation*, physical destruction. For Freud, denial is a protection against pain, a defence against ego-menacing external reality or unbearable news. It is also a highly evolved psychological trick to enable us to live with our every-day misdoings. It can go from benign inattention to outright rejection in the form of lying, rage, blustering and other forms of violence. It is frequently expressed in the form of euphemisms (Benedict Carey, 'Denial: A Defensive Skill That May Help Everyone to Stay on Speaking Terms', *IHT*, 22 November 2007). A fine example of the accurate, but broad use of the term is the work by South African criminologist Stan Cohen, *States of Denial* (Cambridge: Polity Press, 2001), which covers a range of 'modes of avoidance' by those in-volved, as victims or perpetrators, in human suffering. Part of the problem in the slippage associated with **denial** is the lack, in English, of a suffi-ciently diverse vocabulary that distinguishes different meanings of the term: (i) refusing, often mendaciously, to accept something is the case; (ii) refus-ing to admit to oneself that something painful has occurred; (iii) negating, eliminating, seeking to render null, a fact, feeling or situation. As a result, more widely and, in terms of psychoanalytic origins, inaccurately used from the 1980s, especially the term **in denial**, to cover failure of a person, or a collective group, to accept responsibility for criminal action: hence of a political leader 'he is in denial', meaning he cannot face or admit what has happened. Thus **denial** has come to encompass not so much the denial of pain and suffering experienced by the 'denier' as failure to accept legal and moral responsibility for past acts: a good example of this latter usage is the 2006 book by Bob Woodward on the Bush administration, *State of Denial*. See also **Global War on Terror**.

distinguished public servant   Description of Lewis ('Scooter') Libby, in the file compiled by his lawyers on the basis of accolades by such luminaries as Henry Kissinger, before Libby was sentenced to 30 months' imprisonment on federal obstruction and perjury charges following the grand jury inves-tigation into the CIA identity leak, the **'Plame Affair'**. His lawyers claimed that he was the **poster child** for everything that had gone wrong with the occupation of Iraq (David Stout and Brian Knowlton, 'Libby Is Sentenced to 30 Months in Prison', *IHT*, 5 June 2007).

E

ease   As in regard to daily posted prices of oil, a euphemism for 'fall', as if the high prices were a form of tension or that needed to be relaxed. When the prices are of something being sold for which there is general support for price rises, such as houses, or works of art, the terms used are negative. Thus in reports on these prices the terms used are *weaken, slide, slip.*

elusive   All-purpose word designed to justify and suggest continued support for policy that is plainly failing, thus 'elusive search for peace', 'elusive pursuit of victory'.

embattled   Self-pitying term, like **blowback, nightmare, quagmire**, used by the US government and corporate representatives, and craven journalists, to describe entities which have run into difficulties as a result of their own folly, greed and aggression.

expectation management   Official euphemism for propaganda designed to backtrack on earlier commitments and deflect criticism of Western policies, e.g. 'after all the promises made by the coalition before and after the invasion of Iraq that the country would be rebuilt once the fighting was over, the chaos and violence after liberation fell far short of expectations – and these expectations had to be "managed"' (Steve Tatham, *Losing Arab Hearts and Minds: The Coalition, Al Jazeera and Muslim Public Opinion* [London: Routledge, 2007]). Also, when the final announcement of a British troop withdrawal from Iraq was made, in December 2008, the BBC reported that 'it was met with relief'. This apparently positive message serving to deflect any discussion of what the more than five years of involvement in Iraq had actually achieved.

I

incurious   That is, stupid, dogmatic word often used of President George W. Bush.

investigative shortfalls   That is, cover-up, see **missteps**.

J

joint tragedy   Mawkish American term for conflict that it had helped exacerbate but where it subsequently claimed right to self-pity. Cf. of Vietnam **quagmire**. Thus, US Secretary of State Condoleezza Rice on Afghanistan said: 'After the Soviet Union left I think it is well understood that we did not remain committed, and I said to the president earlier that in many ways

September 11 was a **joint tragedy** of the Afghan and American people out of that period' (Zahid Hussein, 'US Wants Free Pakistan Elections', *The Wall Street Journal Europe*, 18–20 March 2005).

M

messy   Description of country or situation which the speaker themselves so turned into a mess.

missteps   Evasive, euphemistic term for official manipulation and obfuscation of evidence in cases of brutality or corruption. Like the cognate world, much used in corporate and political circles, to *misspeak*, meaning 'to lie', an attempt to disguise deliberate action as accident, or slip-up. Thus in a two-year-long investigation into the deaths of two detainees in the US military detention centre at Bagram, Afghanistan, crucial witnesses were not interviewed, documents disappeared and evidence was mishandled, and mandatory reports of possible misconduct were not filed – all this was then termed '**missteps**'. The '**missteps**' were also described as **investigative shortfalls** by the Criminal Investigation Command, which had said it could not see any 'clear responsibility' for the deaths. See **blunt force trauma** (Tim Golden, 'US Army Inquiry Slow to Act on Abuse', *IHT*, 23 May 2005).

morass   Country in which the invader finds themselves in difficulty. Cf. **quagmire**.

P

pain   In political contexts, as in the phrase 'feeling **pain**' (this itself a pleonasm or linguistic redundancy, since pain, if not 'felt', does not exist), sentimental and often mendacious term used by perpetrators of political action, e.g. in the invasion of other countries, in the settlement of occupied lands after, to fend off critics of their actions, to demand state compensation and generally to refuse to take responsibility for their illegal actions. Those loudest in trumpeting their own '**pain**' are the most silent on the pain they cause to others, e.g. organizers of terrorist actions against civilians in Lebanon, Israel, Iraq, Kashmir, etc., Israeli settlers in Gaza and the West Bank. One of a set of terms used to displace responsibility from the perpetrators by implying their victimhood or, at the least, innocence and passivity. Cf. **bogged down, nightmare, quagmire**. Similar displacement evident in oft-used American expression, nearly always asserting equivalence between quite different situations, *we're hurting too.*

poor tradecraft, poor management   Exculpatory term applied to US intelligence error in alleging that, prior to 2003, Iraq had a significant programme to produce **weapons of mass destruction**. According to a report by a bipartisan US investigative commission, co-chaired by Republican appeals-court judge Laurence Silberman and a Democratic former governor and senator from Virginia, Charles Robb, issued in March 2005, the intelligence 'errors' about the weapons of mass destruction in Iraq, which were used to justify the invasion, 'stem from **poor tradecraft and poor management** ... We conclude that it was the paucity of intelligence and poor analytical tradecraft, rather than political pressure, that produced the inaccurate pre-war intelligence assessments.' The *Silberman-Robb Commission* chose not to consider how Bush and his top aides used the intelligence they received or whether they misled the public. The main targets of the commission were top CIA officials, in particular George J. Tenet, who resigned as director of central intelligence shortly thereafter. President Bush later awarded him the Presidential Medal of Freedom. The report notes that the frightening claim of the White House that Saddam was building a secret network of mobile labs in Iraq capable of producing a 'witch's brew' of biological weapons rested 'almost exclusively' on the dubious claims of the well-known 'fabricator' **Curveball**, noting that 'a culture of forced consensus' inside the CIA acted to suppress and resist any doubts raised (David Barstow, 'Doubts on Iraq Intelligence Were Rebuffed, Report Says', *International Herald Tribune*, 2 April 2005).

Q

quagmire   Marsh into which people can sink, without being able to extricate themselves, hence metaphor, and usually self-exculpating euphemism, for disastrous situations which US policy has helped to create. Much used of Vietnam War of early 1970s. Cf. **bogged down, messy, morass**. Donald Rumsfeld did not '**do**' them. In the transcript of a US Department of Defense news briefing he gave on 24 July 2003 with Paul Brenner, presidential envoy to Iraq, somebody asked, '**Quagmire?**' Rumsfeld replied, 'No. That's someone else's business. Quagmire is – I don't **do** quagmires (laughter)' (US Department of Defense News Transcript, www.defenselink.mil/transcripts/transcript.aspx?transcriptid=2894).

S

searing   Another variant of the self-pitying terminology used by imperial powers after their occupation of other countries goes wrong.

self-imposed climax   An old hand at the **exculpatory passive** turn of phrase, Henry Kissinger used this (auto-erotic?) phrase in 2007 when he argued that the war in Iraq was approaching this stage – all by itself, so it would have appeared (Henry A. Kissinger, 'A Political Programme to Exit Iraq', *IHT*, 3 July 2007). Cf. **bogged down, nightmare, quagmire.**

selling the threat   Closely linked to the concept of 'threat inflation', this is a process by which governments seek to mobilise public support for military action by promoting alarmist analyses, thus projecting outwards their own fantasies and exaggerations, and then pretending it was to these facts that they were responding. In this case, the actions taken by the US and UK governments to mobilise support for the 2003 Iraq War.

slow to act   As in 'the government/army was slow to act' on complaints of mistreatment. A euphemism for official obstruction of enquiries and complaints. See **blunt force trauma, non-judicial punishment.**

stuff happens   The ultimate instance of the *exculpatory passive*, phrase attributed to US Secretary of Defense Donald Rumsfeld after the looting in Baghdad in April 2003. See **freedom is untidy.**

T

That's how our training goes   Exculpatory philosophy of military accused of killing innocent people. The response of Sergeant Frank Wuterich who was accused of being involved in the killing of two dozen Iraqis in Haditha on 19 November 2005. In an interview in the CBS '60 Minutes' programme, he admitted that his squad tossed a grenade into a residence without knowing who was inside. The interviewer Scott Pelley remarked, 'But when you roll a grenade in a room through the crack in the door, that's not positive identification, that's taking a chance on anything that could be behind that door'. Wuterich's response: 'Well, that's what we do. **That's how our training goes**' (Robert Parry, 'Bush's Global "Dirty War"', *Consortium*

News, 1 October 2007). Those accused of war crimes in other wars have been known to say, '*We were only following orders*'.

tilt   A favourite exculpatory Washington weasel-word, used of change in foreign policy, or internal political preference, to favouring one side more than the other, e.g. between Israel and Arabs, or Arabs and Iranians, or Sunnis and Shiʻias in Iraq. Contrast with **evenhanded**. The word allows for a change of policy without implication that the previous one, which had, by definition, not worked, was a mistake.

V

veracity   A curious locution of then Secretary of State Condoleezza Rice, who stated that the USA lacked this with regard to Iran. Perhaps confusion with *visibility, accurate reading*, or perhaps the subliminal recognition of distortions inherent in US policy towards Tehran. Dr. Rice admitted that Iran has a 'political system I don't understand very well' and that her whole department was in the dark. 'We don't really have people who know Iran inside our own system . . . We don't have Farsi speakers any more in the service. I mean, we really are not well positioned . . . We are also operating from something of a disadvantage in that we don't really have a very good **veracity** or a feel for the place' (Edmund O'Sullivan, 'Tragedy of Errors Drives US Policy in the Middle East', *MEED*, 22–28 June 2007, quoting interview published in a *Wall Street Journal* website on 11 June 2007). In 1979, some months after the victory of the Iranian Revolution, I met with the recently retired CIA desk officer for Iran, Jesse Leaf. He revealed that he had never been to Iran, and had never met an Iranian: however, as he told it to me, on the basis of a reading of history, including the historian of the French Revolution Alexis de Tocqueville, he had intuited earlier than most of his colleagues that the regime of the Shah was in serious trouble.

CHAPTER 12

Some Other Distortions: History, Politics and International Relations

The starving, the wretched, the dispossessed, the ignorant, those living in want and squalor, from the deserts of northern Africa to the slums of Gaza, to the mountain ranges of Afghanistan: they too are our cause . . . The kaleidoscope has been shaken. The pieces are in flux. Soon they will settle again. Before they do, let us reorder this world around us.

—Prime Minister Tony Blair, 2001

Why are we fighting and opposing you? The answer is very simple. Because you attacked us and continue to attack us. You attacked us in Palestine . . . You attacked us in Somalia; you supported the Russian atrocities against us in Chechenya, the Indian oppression against us in Kashmir, and the Jewish aggression against us in Lebanon. Under your supervision, consent, and orders, the governments of our countries which act as your collaborators, attack us on a daily basis.

—Osama bin Laden, 'Message to the Americans', in *Messages to the World*, 2 October 2004, pp. 162–3

Only those who are ignorant of the world can believe that any nation, even so great a nation as the United States, can stand alone and play a single role in the history of mankind.

—President Woodrow Wilson (quoted in *The Nation*, 4 May 2009)

'6+2' UN negotiating process, initiated in 1993, under which the six states bordering Afghanistan (China, Pakistan, Iran, Turkmenistan, Uzbekistan, Tajikistan) plus the USA and Russia joined discussions to end the conflict in and around Afghanistan. Basis for international negotiation regarding the post-Taliban regime in late 2001, and one noted case of reasonably successful diplomatic coordination between Washington and Tehran. More or less finished off by a January 2002 speech by President George W. Bush branding Iran as part of an **axis of evil**. In 2008–9, faced with a dramatic escalation of violence in Afghanistan and then Pakistan, Washington, without using the term, began again to try to work within such a regional framework.

'41 and 43'   Mawkish pseudo-familial terms used by George Bush (US President 1989–93) and his son George W. Bush (US President 2001–9), following the twin presidencies of the Adams family, John and John Quincey ('2' and '6' in Bush-speak), some 200 years ago (Rupert Cornwell, 'How the War Came to the White House', *The Independent on Sunday*, 22 October 2006).

A

appeasement   Originally applied to the policy of seeking to avoid war with Nazi Germany in the 1930s by making concessions (e.g. agreeing to impose territorial concessions on Czechoslovakia in the Munich Agreement of 1938), then widely and loosely used by neoconservatives in Washington to discredit opponents in regard to war with Iraq, also Iran and Syria. Defined by the British wartime Prime Minister Winston Churchill as 'feeding the crocodile in the hope that it eats you last'. See **Second World War language**.

assertive multilateralism   Neoconservative term for **unilateralism**.

assumption train   Apologetic term used in decision-making theory for unquestioned premises. See Chapter 1, **groupthink** and other entries.

Anti-Americanism   General and often carelessly used term for hostility to, or criticism of, US foreign policy, culture, way of life, aspiration to world domination. Long confined to journalism or polemics, the term acquired specious academic and public policy recognition after 9/11, leading to conferences, books and other supposedly objective discussions of the topic. Described by Philippe Roger in his book *The American Enemy* (a 'masterpiece' according to *Le Monde* after its publication in France in 2002) as 'the only "**French passion**" that calms the other passions, wipes out antagonism and reconciles the harshest adversaries ... It is impossible to understand French anti-Americanism or its timelessness if you don't see the social-national benefits it represents in manufacturing a **tissue of consensus**' (John Vinocur, 'Sarkozy's New Grip on Anti-Americanism', *IHT*, 22 May 2007). For one academic treatment, see Ivan Krastev and Alan McPherson, eds., *The Anti-American Century* (Budapest: Central European University Press, 2007).

astroturfing   As a political term said to have been coined by Senator Lloyd Bensen, to yield a satirical redefinition of 'grassroots democracy', in regard to faking by politicians or companies of opinion or behaviour that is supposedly supported by the public. Originally, the term refers to corporate practice, in particular the *Big Pharma* companies that fabricate illness out of symptoms that are supposedly chemically reparable. For example, shyness becomes a 'depressive disorder' but the solution is at hand in the form of SSRIs, 'selective serotonin reuptake inhibitors', marketed as Prozac, Zoloft, Paxil, Luvox, Exefor and Celexa, *inter alia*. Ditto the vast *wellbeing* and *anti-aging* industry designed to pathologise, and make money from, normal biological change. In politics and international affairs, the same practice is applied in threat inflation, e.g. fabricating a threat of WMDs and then creating a national security crisis that requires urgent and costly action.

asymmetric conflict   In contrast to *symmetric conflict,* that between two or more sovereign states. Multi-purpose term developed by social scientists and US strategists in the 1970s, above all in regard to the war in Vietnam, to denote a war between fundamentally dissimilar powers, the orthodox state having an advantage in firepower and economic resources, the guerrilla opposition having greater endurance and tactical agility. The aim of the latter is to undermine the dominant state through political pressure on its regional allies and on its domestic, political and financial system. For a classic analysis, see Andrew Mack, 'Why Big Nations Lose Small Wars: the Politics of Asymmetric Conflict', in *World Politics*, Vol. 27, No. 2, 1975. More recently, used of possible cyber warfare as part of attacks on economies and communications of developed states.

B

behaviour change   A less extreme alternative to 'regime change'. US policy on Syria in 2005 involved military strikes on the Syrian border with Iraq, but, according to an unnamed US official in Washington, this was not aimed at regime change, in the sense of forcibly replacing one government with another, as had happened in Iraq, only 'behaviour change' (Guy Dinmore, 'US "Seeks New Syrian Leader" as Pressure Mounts', *FT*, 10 October, 2005). Cf. **compliance, regime change**.

black hole state   Term used to denote countries without effective government, sources of transnational criminal activity. The original astronomical term *black hole* first used in the 1960s, apparently by reference to the **Black Hole of Calcutta**, to denote an area of space with gravity so strong that no radiation or matter can escape. In what is, in literal terms, a misunderstanding of the scientific meaning, since quite a lot of things (drugs, kidnapped women, stolen cars, laundered money, illegal guns) do escape from them, as they are forcibly sucked into them, in the 1990s **black hole state** was widely applied to countries, or areas of countries, with no apparent state control, from which threats emerge, and with widespread transnational criminal activity, e.g. Trans-dniester, Kosovo and the Waziristan district of Pakistan. In another, more accurate, usage, the UNDP *Arab Human Development Report* for 2004 found several *black holes* in the Arab world. For example, throughout the region, the concentration of power in the hands of the executive (monarchy, military dictatorship or civilian president elected without competition) has created a *black hole* at the centre of Arab political life. Again, the modern Arab state resembles the astronomical model because the executive apparatus is like a *black hole* that converts the social environment into a setting in which nothing moves and from which nothing escapes. The authors also say that the executive authority at the centre of these *black hole states* prevents the judiciary from safeguarding the rights of the citizenry as the regime swiftly sweeps aside the independence of the judiciary without any hesitation' (I. Cembrero, *El País*, 6 April 2006).

by all necessary means   Term used in UN Security Council Resolutions, such as those related to the Iraqi occupation of Kuwait in 1990–1, to authorise the use of force by Council members, in the event of other forms of sanction and pressure failing to achieve the desired result, in this case, the removal of Iraqi forces from Kuwait.

C

Christianist culture   Term used by author Christopher Collins, by analogy with 'Islamist', to describe the USA as a country that 'is no less . . . nostalgic for an idealized past than its Islamist foes'. Collins describes how biblical narratives have justified policies and institutions ranging from Indian genocide, the slave trade, and exploitation of immigrant workers and, in more recent times, the militaristic foreign policy of the Bush administration (*Homeland Mythology: Biblical Narratives in American Culture* [Penn State Press, 2007]). See **Manifest Destiny**.

coalition of the willing   UN members who chose to take part in specific military operations without being so formally instructed to do so by the Security Council. Polite form of nineteenth-century irregular punitive force composed of armed citizens, 'posse'.

Compassionate Conservativism   Bushite euphemism for greed. See **haves and have mores**.

containment   Originally used to describe the policy alternative to all-out war, the concept was formulated by diplomat George Kennan in his classic 1947 *Foreign Policy* article, 'The Sources of Soviet Conduct', where he advocated limiting expansion of the USSR and so provoking an internal crisis. Used, in the term 'dual containment', for US Gulf policy towards Iraq and Iran in the 1990s. As the Clinton policy that had, allegedly, failed against Iraq, this became a justification for the 2003 military offensive.

context   Frank Rich points out that this word, used by senior US officials, as in 'the context in which I made that statement last year', usually means 'I'm going to tell a lie'. For example Vice-President Dick Cheney invoked the word on 'Meet the Press' to explain away his false 'predictions' that Americans would be greeted as liberators in Iraq or that the insurgency was in its last throes (Frank Rich, 'The Longer the War, the Larger the Lies', *IHT*, 18 September 2006). Analogous to Soviet/Russian *videteli*, 'Well, you see . . .' and Arabic *bi-siraha*, 'To be frank . . .'

cosmopolitanism   Political ideal, much abused in recent times by conservative politicians in the West and by nationalist and Islamist demagogues in the Middle East. Equated in the former with treason, disloyalty to the state and the community, in the latter with 'cultural imperialism'. Literally the idea that the world, or humanity, as a whole, the *cosmos*, rather than a particular nation, or city-state, is the appropriate point of reference for loyalty and identity. Episodically espoused by utopian, liberal and revolutionary thinkers since classical times, and also represented in some of the classical texts of Islam, Judaism and Christianity, it has been the object of repeated attack, and mockery, by thinkers, from Plato and Rousseau, whose frame of reference is limited to a particular state, or community/nation. In modern times, attacks on cosmopolitanism have come from, among others, orthodox communists, Islamic fundamentalists and proponents of 'English', 'American' and other national-specific values. Also used to attack people, such as Jews or intellectuals, who do not conform to national conventions of practice and thought. Thus, in his *The Captive Mind*, Czeslaw Milosz (referring to East European Communist intellectuals) describes how the official order is to 'evince the greatest horror of the West', to scoff at any Western artistic or intellectual products, 'for to fight against "cosmopolitanism" is one of the basic duties of a citizen'. In his book *The Word and the Bomb*, Hanif Kureishi finds echoes of anti-cosmopolitanism in young Islamists but also notes another often-ignored aspect of cosmopolitanism in Western societies who deny to others rights they espouse for themselves: 'The freedom to speak is not only our privilege but it is essential to the oppressed, unheard and marginalised of the Third World, as they struggle to keep their humanity alive in conditions far worse than here. To retreat into a citadel of "Englishness", to refuse to link up or identify with them, is to deliver them over to superstition and poverty of the imagination.' In the end, 'The roll-call of the censored is an account of our civilisation' (Hanif Kureishi, *The Word and the Bomb* [London: Faber and Faber, 2005]). The authorities in the Islamic Republic of Iran, borrowing themes from Stalinism and extreme nationalism, have made much of the 'cultural aggression', *tahajom i farhangi*, to which Iran is supposedly being subjected by foreign ideas, satellite TV, the Internet, etc.

cowardice   According to journalist Frank Rich, cowardice was 'as important to understanding Bush's cratered presidency as incompetence, cronyism and hubris'. See **tough-guy shtick** (Frank Rich, 'A Profile in Cowardice', *IHT*, 9 July 2007).

critical that we get him in place   That is, the policy designed to legitimate and implement unconstitutional appointments in the US government system, where all ambassadorial nominations, including that of Ambassador to the UN, have to be approved by the Senate (the principle of 'Advice and Consent'). The policy used by the Bush White House, in words of spokesman Scott McClellan, when sidestepping Senate resistance to the appointment of conservative obsessive John Bolton as UN Ambassador by sliding him in with a **recess appointment** (Reuters, 'Bush Team Urges Vote on Bolton', *IHT*, 21 June 2005).

D

democratic cheerleading   President Bush's second-term inaugural address in January 2005 was thus described, with the implication that his administration would issue calls, as if cheering from the sidelines, in favour of democracy but not actually do anything. He soon had to smooth ruffled feathers and explain that his call to 'end tyranny' did not represent a plan to put an end to strategic relations with countries like China and Saudi Arabia. The 'policy' seemed to boil down to the President's response to allegations of human rights violations in Jordan: 'I urge my friend His Majesty to make sure that democracy continues to advance in Jordan' (James Harding, 'Bush Tries to Ease Foreign Policy Fears', *FT*, 27 January 2005).

democratisation industry   A strand of applied or policy-oriented political science that has evolved into a significant, career-based practice where the task is undertaken by NGOs, bilateral and multilateral donors and philanthropic foundations to foster and promote the growth of Western-style democracy. The phrase is attributed to Robert Springborg, at that time Professor at the School of Oriental and African Studies, London, in a 2005 lecture (Dean Nicholas, 'Professor Robert Springborg: The Democratization Industry and the Middle East', 6 June 2005, www.culturewars.org.uk/2005-01/springborg.htm). One of the main functions of this 'industry' was to serve Western strategic interests by (i) funding and aiding in kind, e.g. with air tickets, computers, groups opposed to rival authoritarian states, particularly Russia, and (ii) to 'certify' or authenticate as 'democratic' or as 'in transition to' democracy states such as Yemen, Morocco, Kuwait and Jordan that remained, in fact, undemocratic, but with an appearance of political pluralism and freedom of expression. A leading exponent of (both) these practices was the right-wing Washington-based National Endowment for Democracy.

dialogue   Much-used term to suggest open and respectful debate between different religious and/or political interests in the region and representatives of the West. Often a pretext for officially managed theatrical events in which nothing of originality or independent character is said, serving to reinforce authority of state and/or religious officials. On the most substantive East-West issue of all, where calls for such a process have been made for 30 years, that of oil prices and output levels, no substantive discussion of an organised kind, between producers and consumers, has taken place: all has been left to speculation, and the market.

E

embed   Euphemism for *muzzle, control,* official news management term for journalists attached to, and hence formally controlled and briefed by, US and British armed forces during military operations, basically a means of offering greater access and security in return for favourable coverage. Opposite of **unilateral**, a reporter not so controlled.

empire   Historically, term applied to major imperial systems of history: Persian, Chinese, Roman, British, French, Dutch, Spanish, etc. Rejected as unsuitable by major powers in the Cold War, each of which proclaimed itself a champion of anti-colonialism and the freedom of people. Used by each side as a way to denounce the other – thus *US imperialism, empire of evil*. After the end of the Cold War, however, US commentators and politicians increasingly came to adopt the term, modelling themselves, with some self-satisfaction, on the previous cases. While the historical substantive *imperialism* was not used in this self-enhancing sense, **empire/imperial** came into acceptable usage. Thus on one occasion, when a White House official tried to tell President Bush that a particular policy would not work, he was told that he was part of the **reality-based community**. *We're an empire now and when we act we create our own reality'.*

energy war   Wide-ranging, often alarmist and sometimes imprecise term for conflicts that are caused, sustained or in other ways occasioned by competition between states, either producer and/or consumer, as a re-sult of the desire to control oil resources. 'War' in this context can refer to the corruption and conflict associated with extractive industries in countries where oil and natural gas are used as a weapon by politically corrupt regimes. Again, in a context where the implications of Western energy use are rarely pondered, the evermore frequent use of this term could be preparing the ground for an all-out resource war. Between, e.g., the USA and radical third world producers. The film *Energy War* by Shuchen Tan, Ijsbrand van Veelen and Rudi Boon takes up some of the issues, showing how the Russian govern-ment used the giant GAZPROM, Russia's biggest company and the world's biggest natural gas extractor, to force Georgia back into Russia's orbit and away from NATO. The film predicts that the primary struggle of the twenty-first century will be the result of a pitiless drive to secure America's position as the energy superpower. It also depicts the alliance between Venezuela and Iran as explicit in its plans to destabilise the USA via its Achilles heel – its de-pendence on oil (Frank G. Zarb, 'How to Win the Energy War', *IHT*, 24 May

2007). Whatever the future brings, however, the record of the Middle East in modern times, a region that has seen numerous wars, is that, as yet, in none of these has energy been the sole or, plausibly, prime cause, even as it has certainly allowed some states, e.g. Iraq and Iran, to sustain military activity they might otherwise have found impossible to continue. For an informed, and profoundly disturbing, analysis of future possibilities and trends, see Michael Klare *Resource Wars.*

Euroids   Derogatory Washington term for Europeans, particularly European critics of US foreign policy, in regard to Iraq before and after the 2003 invasion.

evil-doers   Biblical term much favoured by President George W. Bush, a more formal version of the term 'bad guys', to refer to terrorists and military opponents of all kinds, e.g. in Afghanistan and Iraq. The Old Testament has at least 17 references, e.g. Job 8:20, 'Neither will we help the evil-doers'; Isaiah 1:4, 'Ah sinful nation, a seed of evil-doers' (Alexander Cruden, *Cruden's Complete Concordance to the Old and New Testaments* [Grand Rapids, MI: Zondervan Publishing Co., 1999]).

executive orders   George W. Bush's presidency will be remembered, *inter alia*, for his frequent use – much more than any other US President – of 'executive orders', a form of arbitrary policy making that circumvents normal checks and balances of US legislative and judicial systems. In 1952, the Supreme Court disallowed an executive order of President Truman (in an attempt to avert a national steelworkers' strike), ruling that an executive order must have either direct statutory or constitutional authority. Bush tended to base his executive orders on his Commander-in-Chief authority established in Article II of the Constitution. One example of Bush's many executive orders is that issued on 17 July 2007 entitled 'Blocking Property of Certain Persons Who Threaten Stabilization Efforts in Iraq'. This permitted the President to confiscate the assets of anyone who opposed the US-led 'war against terror' and effectively criminalised the US anti-war movement. Again, hours after the UN endorsed US control of the 'Development Fund' for Iraq, Bush signed Executive Order 13303 that decreed that 'any attachment, judgment, decree, lien, execution, garnishment, or other judicial process is prohibited, and shall be deemed null and void', with respect to the Development Fund for Iraq and 'all Iraqi petroleum and petroleum products, and interests therein'. In May 2007, Bush issued a presidential National Security Directive (National Security and Homeland Security Presidential

Directive NSPD 51/HSPD 20), which would have suspended constitutional government and established broad dictatorial powers under martial law in the case of a 'Catastrophic Emergency' (for example a terrorist attack). NSPD 51 can effectively annul Constitutional government by enabling the President to declare a 'national emergency' without Congressional approval. In other words, the implementation of NSPD 51 could lead to a closing-down of the Legislature and the militarization of justice and law enforcement. Some scholars have contended that without a formal congressional declaration of war, the President cannot exercise this authority and hence his executive orders are unconstitutional (Michael Chossudovsky, 'Bush Executive Order: Criminalizing the Antiwar Movement', *Global Research*, 20 July 2007; also www.globalresearch.ca/index.php?context=va&aid=6377). See also, in regard to doctrine of executive supremacy in US government, **unitary**.

F

faith   Literally adherence to a view for which there is no evidence; word used increasingly in the 2000s in Britain and elsewhere to describe religious institutions and communities, usually with indulgent, when not irrational, suggestion of 'respect', i.e. refusal to engage in any critical moral, legal or historical way with the claims of such communities' self-appointed, and often 'ethnically entrepreneur', leaderships.

faith communities   Mawkish term, frequently used by political leaders indulgent to religion, such as Tony Blair. Usually applied, like the word 'ethnic', to some 'other' groups such as Muslims. Also a means of avoiding the word 'minority'.

faith-related crimes   Banal, evasive, alternative to more forthright 'hate crimes' or 'racist attack', expression used to describe attacks on Asians and religious minorities in London after the suicide bombing attacks in London on 7 July 2005. In the three weeks following 7/7, the London police recorded more than 230 'faith-related crimes' as opposed to 36 for the same period in 2004 (Robert F. Worth, News Reports, 'US Jails Yemeni Cleric for Financing Terrorists', *IHT*, 29 July 2005). By contrast, in the weeks following the 11 March 2004 bombings in Spain, there were no reports of such incidents.

freedom   Whereas in earlier decades words like 'liberation' and 'emancipation' were generally associated with left-wing and liberal causes, the term 'freedom' has since the 1980s been associated with the right, and in particular with US foreign policies. Thus, the invasion of Afghanistan in 2001 was termed **Operation Enduring Freedom**, while *Freedom House* became the name of a conservative think-tank in New York. The name of the monument at the World Trade Center site, which was to have been originally called the International Freedom Center, was criticised as being **anti-American** and disrespectful to the dead: as a result the offending 'International' was removed and the monument was retitled 'Freedom Museum'. The term was also used when the US Congress, angry with the French government's opposition to the 2003 invasion of Iraq, deemed that its menus should refer to fried potatoes as '**Freedom Fries**' rather than 'French fries' (see **French passion** and **Anti-Americanism**).

Freedom Speech   Term given by supporters to George W. Bush's second inaugural speech in January 2005, where he proclaimed a worldwide **war against tyranny**. In this speech he also committed himself to reforming the tax system, the legal system and pensions.

French passion   See **Anti-Americanism**.

G

genocide   Recently coined legal term, later used in looser and often polemical political and historical sense. The 1948 *Convention on the Prevention and Punishment of the Crime of Genocide*, Article II, defines it broadly as 'acts committed with intent to destroy, in whole or in part, a national, ethnical, racial or religious group'. Such acts may include killing, causing serious bodily or mental harm, inflicting conditions of life that could bring about the group's physical destruction in whole or in part. By contrast, the US-based 2008 Genocide Prevention Task Force talks of 'a deliberate attempt to destroy a racial, religious or political group in its entirety'. Policy of killing all, or part, of a people, from Greek: *génos* ($\gamma \acute{\epsilon} \nu o \varsigma$) *family*, *tribe* or *race* and Latin *– cide*, from *occido –* to *massacre, kill*, as in older words such as *regicide*, killing a king, *infanticide* killing a child, *fratricide* killing brothers. The word 'genocide' was invented in 1943 by Raphael Lemkin, a Polish-Jewish lawyer who had found refuge in the USA: Lemkin single-handedly drafted the prototype Genocide Convention that was then approved by the UN General Assembly in 1948. Although commonly used thereafter to imply the attempt to kill a *whole* people, as was the case with the persecution of the

Jews under Nazism, 'genocide' in the legal sense also covers any systematic
attempt through murder to destroy the culture or will of a people, including,
as occurred in the Balkan Wars of the 1990s, the selective killing of members of a particular class or professional group, including the intelligentsia.
See **Arabicide, Holocaust, Judaeocide, Politicide,** *Shoah* (*The Economist,*
'Preventing Genocide', 13 December 2008).

globalisation   Term in economics and sociology, popularised in the
1990s, often vague in definition and careless in application. Arabic renders
the term as *al-'awlama* (world-becoming). Persian has oscillated between the
pejorative *jahangiri* (world-grabbing) and the more positive *jahanshodan*
(world-becoming); the latter has, for the moment, prevailed. Both the
Arabic and second Persian terms are renderings of the slightly different
French word *mondialisation.* Used to denote a range of concurrent international trends in three main spheres: liberalisation and increase of trade
and investment in economics, democratisation and the increased linking of
societies in politics, and the breaking down and intermingling of societies
and cultures. Experts dispute the extent and distribution of each of these,
their interaction and the degree to which the trends involved are a continuation of earlier forms of global interaction, based on North–South inequality,
going back decades or even centuries. In the Muslim world the majority of
politicians and writers, re-using the themes of Western and Latin American
critiques, denounce 'globalisation', while a minority argue in favour, often
on the grounds that Islam was the first, and for sure the greatest, globalising
force in world history.

God gulf   Difference of opinion and outlook that divides Bible-believer
Republicans from the more secular Democrats in the USA: as one index of
the hold of literalist Biblical thinking, only 28 per cent of the US population
in 204 said they believed in evolution (Nicholas D. Kristof, 'The God Gulf',
The New York Times, 7 January 2004). Cf. **grief gap**.

grand strategy   Pompous term much used in Washington to describe
and give bogus coherence to random bits of aggressive and bellicose fantasy.

Great Game   International rivalry in Central Asia between Britain and
Russia during the nineteenth century, which ended with the 1907 convention
defining relations in Persia, Afghanistan and Tibet. Loosely and rather inaccurately applied to the situation in the Trans-Caucasian and Central Asian
regions after the collapse of the USSR in 1991. In the end, and with the
exception of the Afghan War of the 1980s, the conflicts of twentieth-century

history turned out to have almost nothing to do with this supposedly vital strategic region.

grief gap   Term used to denote the distance between the strong US and other more muted Western reactions to the 9/11 attacks, and the response in many other parts of the world.

Gulf War   Term applied to both the 1980–8 Iran–Iraq war, sometimes called 'the first Gulf war', and the 1990–1 Iraq–Kuwait war. Should also be applied to the precursor of both, the 1969–75 Iran–Iraq conflict, which ended with the Algiers Agreement between the Shah and Saddam Hussein in 1975. It was the renunciation after the 1979 Iranian Revolution by Iranian leader Ayatollah Khomeini of that agreement, in particular the commitment not to interfere in the internal affairs of each country, that laid the ground, if not the legitimation, for the two later wars. If the war that began with the US invasion of Iraq in 2003 is also included, there have, since the late 1960s, been no less than *four* cases of 'Gulf War'.

H

Hague invasion clause   Section of US law, passed in August 2002, justifying US action, including invasion of another country, to counter the authority of the International Criminal Court based in The Hague, Netherlands. Members of the US administration teamed up with Republican lawmakers to pass a law to this effect. It contains a blanket authorisation for American troops to use 'all means necessary and appropriate' to liberate any American servicemen if they are ever imprisoned and in danger of being forced to appear before an 'unaccountable tribunal' such as the International Criminal Court (Samantha Power, 'Darfur and the International Criminal Court: The Court of First Resort', *IHT*, 12–13 February 2005).

hyperpower   French *hyperpuissance*, term coined by Hubert Védrine, a French socialist with the portfolio of Foreign Minister in the Chirac government, to describe Bill Clinton's USA while calling on the **international community** to join together in restraining the Americans (John Vinocur, 'Sarkozy's New Handle on Anti-Americanism', *IHT*, 22 May 2007).

I

imperial presidency   Critical term applied to the US President, in a country which prides itself on its republic traditions, and to the administration of George W. Bush. Yale Law School law professor Eugene Fidell described the 81-page legal brief written by John Yoo (then the second-ranking official at the Office of Legal Council at the Justice Department) to support broad White House powers to capture, detain and interrogate suspects (using 'extreme methods') around the globe as 'a monument to executive supremacy and the **imperial presidency**' (Mark Mazzetti, 'Few Limits for Military Interrogators', *IHT*, 3 April 2008).

influence   Euphemism for diffusion of pro-US propaganda and promotion of favourable, and often false, news stories in regard to conflicts, such as Iraq after 2003. An example was the private contractor *Lincoln Group*. According to Pentagon documents, the company had 12 US Government contracts, totalling more than $130 million: for this it had planted more than 1,000 articles in the Iraqi and Arab press and had placed pro-US editorials on an Iraqi website. A *Washington Post* article (26 March 2006) described their work as follows: 'They've planted those fake news articles trumpeting pro-US stories. They've conceived and distributed anti-terror comic strips and leaflets. They ran a campaign that distributed water bottles bearing a phone number that Iraqis could call to report terror activity to US authorities. They do research, media analysis, polling and focus groups. They seek to completely understand a culture, so they can better influence it.' Another company trafficking in influence was the **Rendon Group**: it too had received multimillion-dollar Pentagon contracts. According to *Sourcewatch*, 'The **Rendon Group** is a secretive public relations firm that has assisted a number of US military interventions in nations including Argentina, Colombia, Haiti, Iraq, Kosovo, Panama and Zimbabwe'. The company founder, John Rendon, once described himself as 'an information warrior, and a perception manager'. Some manipulation of perception may have been involved even in this case, as the USA did not, in modern times, play any direct military role in Argentina (www.sourcewatch.org/index.php?title=Rendon_Group). See also **truthful messages** (Jeff Gerth, 'US on the Attack in Information War', *IHT*, 12 December 2005).

Insecurity Council   Mocking Iranian term for UN Security Council. Warning the West in early 2006 about the dangers of confrontation with Iran, the Iranian Ayatollah Ahmad Jannati declared in one of his sermons, 'If they behave like madmen, they can be sure they'll lose more than we do ... They say, "We'll take you to the Security Council. But I call it the Insecurity Council"' (*La Vanguardia*, 18 February 2006). Similar sardonic references to supposedly supreme international institutions include the disparagement of the UN as 'the Disunited Nations', and the term applied by Bolshevik leader Vladimir Lenin to the precursor of the UN, the interwar *League of Nations* (German *Völkerbund*) – Lenin used to refer to the body as *der Räuberbund*, 'the League of Robbers'. Ayatollah Khomeini used to refer to the opposition Islamist group *mujahidin-i khalq* (the Holy Warriors of the People) as *munafiqin-i khalq*, 'the Hypocrites of the People', where *munafiqin* is a Quranic term for those who profess belief, in this case support for the Islamic Republic, but in fact oppose it. His counterparts in Afghanistan, the leaders of the communist regime that came to power in 1978, referred to the opposition Muslim Brothers, *ikhwan-i muslimin* as *ikhwan-i shayatin*, 'the Satanic Brothers', literally 'the Brothers of Satans', *shayatin* being the plural of *sheitun*, 'Satan'. In a less exalted vein, British Conservatives used to refer in the 1950s to the recently introduced 'Welfare State' as the 'Farewell State'.

intelligence–industrial complex   Term used by US intelligence expert James Bamford to refer to the CIA, itself under staff pressures but with increased budget allocations, contracting out intelligence work to private companies and contractors, themselves largely staffed by ex-CIA personnel. Bamford speculated about thousands of such people working outside formal CIA organisational structures and disciplines, at a cost of hundreds of millions of dollars. He raised serious doubts about the competence, financial oversight and general efficacy of such contractors ('Rent a Spy', *International Herald Tribune*, 21 June 2004).

international community   All-purpose euphemism for whatever international policy the speaker, usually an official of the US or British government, approves of. First used in the 1920s as part of the rhetoric of liberal internationalists like Gilbert Murray to denote collective will, and determinations, of the League of Nations, a synonym for 'collective security'. Later became a tool of hegemonic abuse, especially when reflecting US–UK policies that are opposed even by a majority of the permanent members of the Security Council, as in regard to Iraq before March 2003. In the 1990s it was used commonly to mean decisions of the UN Security Council supported by the USA and Britain, more broadly any form of concerted international pressure by the USA and its allies. See Hidemi Suganami's *The Domestic Analogy* for means by which the word *community*, originally given legitimacy in regard to a single society, or domestic setting, was then transposed to the international arena.

iron fist   Boastful, and usually ineffectual, term used by Middle Eastern rulers in the face of unmanageable security threats. Thus, in 2005 under

pressure from Hamas, the Palestinian leader Mahmoud Abbas released a
Hamas militant hours after his arrest even though he had been found with
a rocket-launcher in his car. Not long before, Abbas had pledged to apply an
'iron fist' to truce-breakers. See **fitful campaign** (Greg Myre, 'Abbas's Fitful
Progress in Palestine', *IHT*, 5 May 2005).

K

Kemalism   Ideology of Mustafa Kemal Pasha, 'Atatürk' or 'Father of the
Turks', after the establishment of the Turkish Republic in 1923 as a secular and unitary state. The six pillars of Kemalism are republicanism, populism, nationalism, secularism (Turkish *laiklik*), statism and revolutionism.
Kemalism remains the ideology of the Turkish state and military to this day,
contested by Islamist parties and Kurdish opponents alike.

L

legitimate reprocessing state   Term used to justify US acceptance
for Indian nuclear proliferation, in contrast to, implicitly, 'illegitimate' states
such as Iran and North Korea. Almost 30 years after a ban that was imposed
in 1978 following India's first 1974 nuclear test, India achieved this status in
July 2007 after negotiations in which the USA agreed in principle to allow
India to reprocess American reactor fuel and to transfer sensitive nuclear
technology to India for enrichment and reprocessing purposes. In return
for its new-found legitimacy, India agreed to build a new processing facility
in accordance with the UN atomic energy agency's safeguards. India had
never signed the Nuclear Non-Proliferation Treaty, which the USA has tried
to enforce as a global rule (Sharon Squassoni, 'The Top Rule-maker Bends
the Rules', *IHT*, 17 August 2007).

M

malign stability   Acquiescence to dictators in the interests of stable re-
pression is how the political historian Paul Berman characterised American
Middle East policy in the six decades before the invasion of Iraq (Roger
Cohen, 'Of Sarajevo and Baghdad', *IHT*, 25 June 2007).

mango crate   Phrase used to put pressure on General Pervez Musharraf in his last months as President. During the mango season of 2007,

Musharraf's critics were quoted as saying: 'He either goes the mango crate way or he goes gracefully' (Carlotta Gall, 'Grumbling in the Army Bodes Ill for Musharraf', *IHT*, 28 June 2007). According to one of the theories about the death of Pakistan's General Mohammed Zia ul-Haq in a plane crash in 1988, the plane was sabotaged by explosive gas secreted inside crates of mangoes that were loaded on to the plane as a last-minute gift. In the end, Musharraf left office peacefully. Some Pakistani military sources give a different account of the plane crash, attributing it to prior interference with the plane's navigation system.

Manifest Destiny   Highly influential phrase in US foreign policy, used by John O'Sullivan, editor of the influential publication *Democratic Review*, to express the belief that the country was destined to expand from the Atlantic seaboard through the Pacific Ocean. First coined, it seems, by Jacksonian Democrats, it was used after 1845 to promote the annexation of much of what is now the Western USA, including Texas, the Mexican Cession and the territory of Oregon to which Great Britain also laid claim. While the term *per se* is rarely uttered today, its presence, given global scope and implementation, was evident in the post-Cold War belief, espoused by Democrats and Republicans alike, in an American 'mission' to promote and defend 'democracy' throughout the world, and, more generally, in the entitlement to and necessity for 'American leadership' across the globe. Some academic commentators, journalists and critics regarded George W. Bush's brand of American nationalism as an updated version of Manifest Destiny. He spoke often of 'destiny' but the adjective 'manifest', in its time an attempt to prioritise American interests above those of other colonial powers, became redundant in a supposedly 'unipolar'post-1991 world. See **Christianist culture**.

mercenary–evangelical complex   Variant on earlier US-critical term 'military–industrial complex', first used in his farewell address by President Eisenhower, to denote close, and improper, relations between the Pentagon and arms manufacturers, with consequent distortion of US policy, here denoting the same linkage between **private security contractors** and right-wing Christians. See Chapter 4, **Blackwater**.

militarism   Seemingly well-defined social science term denoting role of military concerns, personnel and interests in a society and in the determination of its foreign policy. In discussions of European society before World War I, and in some analyses of the role of nuclear weapons in the Cold War, it was common to use the term to imply that the priority given to military matters, and preparation for war, had come to determine social and political life as a whole. In the first case, the word was also often a synonym for **imperialism**, this word being used in its, original, sense of a European political entity run by a, presumably **militaristic**, imperial leader. On closer examination the word is much less clear than it seems: it has several distinct meanings – influence of the armed forces at government, a high percentage of the state budget spent on military matters, general public support for war, general public enthusiasm for a belligerent and warlike culture, high social standing of armed forces in society and high propensity of that society to go to war.

moral clarity   Self-righteous term much used in post-9/11 Washington to pump up support for simplistic historical and foreign policy judgements. Often laced with quotes from suitably paraded authorities such as Winston Churchill and Woodrow Wilson.

N

neoconservatism   Confident, belligerent and blinkered variant of US Republicanism, arising out of the Reagan Presidency of the 1980s, the guiding philosophy of the Bush administration 2001 and onwards and, more broadly, of much Washington debate and opinion in those years. In foreign policy, domestic policy and economic policy, one of the most disastrous, and rapidly and comprehensively discredited, doctrines of modern times. For proponents, such as columnist Charles Krauthammer (see **raw power and victory**), neoconservatism marked 'the maturation of a governing ideology whose time has come'. New leaders, 'realists, newly mugged by reality', for example Condoleezza Rice, Richard Cheney and George W. Bush, 'have given weight to neoconservatism, making it more diverse and … more mature'. Naturally, 'Bush Doctrine', for Krauthammer (who coined the term 'Reagan Doctrine' for the American foreign policy of supporting anti-communist insurgencies around the globe), was essentially 'a synonym for neoconservative foreign policy'. See http://en.wikipedia.org/wiki/Charles_Krauthammer. For a good background analysis see James Mann, *The Rise of the Vulcans* [London: Penguin, 2004].

P

petrolism   Distorting reliance on oil production, in both producer and consumer countries. Cf. phrases such as *addiction to oil, curse of black gold,* *rentier state.* Thomas L. Friedman sees **petrolism** as the 'biggest threat to America and its values today'. In his definition, '**Petrolism** is ... the corrupting antidemocratic governing practices – in oil states from Russia to Nigeria and Iran – that result from a long run of $60-a-barrel oil. **Petrolism** is the politics of using oil income to buy off one's citizens with subsidies and government jobs, and using oil profits to build up one's internal security forces and army to keep one ensconced in power – without any transparency or checks or balances.' However, for Friedman, 'oil states', the producers, are only part of the problem: responsibility also lies with avid consumer states that are maintaining this 'petrolism' (Thomas L. Friedman, 'Green *Is* White and Blue', *IHT*, 7–8 January 2006). Friedman is on to something here, but, as always with over-opinionated, and intellectually underperforming, columnists, he fails to record the discussion of this topic which exists in more measured, academic literature, e.g. Terry Lynn Karl, *The Paradox of Plenty Oil Booms and Petro-States* (London: University of California Press, 1997). It is not 'oil' itself that produces this expenditure pattern, but the character of the state, and society, into which the revenue is paid: a country like Norway has made very different use of its revenue than Russia, Saudi Arabia or, for that matter, the US state of Louisiana. Much of the air of corruption and scandal surrounding the oil industry originates not from the new producer dictatorships, but from the history of backhanders, reckless spending and tax 'incentives' associated with oil production in what has for many decades been the largest oil producer in the world, the USA. See the classic study by Harvey O'Connor, *World Crisis in Oil* (London: Monthly Review Press, 1962) and Michael Tanzer, *The Political Economy of Oil and Underdeveloped Countries* (London: 1969). Friedman is, however, right to emphasise that with oil, as with drugs, responsibility lies not only with the often excoriated producers, but also with the consuming countries and their almost unfettered demand for these products. The prefix **petro-** has yielded its own list of new coinages: thus *petrocaudillo*, name applied to Venezuelan leader Hugo Chávez; *petrodollar* since 1970s, oil revenues paid to producer states; and *Petro-Islam*, term coined by French Middle East expert Gilles Kepel, denoting use of oil revenues, e.g. by Saudi Arabia, to promote conservative Islamic values.

petty mosquitoes   Reference to the big powers according to Iranian President Mahmoud Ahmadinejad, who also liked to warn that if these 'petty mosquitoes' continued to 'bully' other nations they would be sent to the 'dustbin of history'. Another pleonasm, since all mosquitos are small insects (Najmeh Bozorgmehr, 'On the Road with a Populist President', *FT*, 23 April 2007).

pragmatist   Term of disdain, if not of abuse, in usage of Bush administration officials, implicitly contrasted with ideologues, believers, etc., of neoconservative vision to reshape the Middle East, possibly the world. After 2003 this word replaced 'dove' in some military circles: for example, when in 2007 the White House was exploring the appointment of a central overseer of the wars in Afghanistan and Iraq – by elevating the post of deputy national security adviser – one of three retired four-star generals who refused the job said it would be 'unworkable' because 'hawks' like Vice-President Dick Cheney were more influential than 'pragmatists' who were seeking 'ways to wind down the conflict' (Brian Knowlton, 'White House Seeks War Leader, Finds No Taker', *IHT*, 12 November 2007).

projects of a missionary style   Term applied by human rights expert David Kennedy to Western humanitarian action; these **projects** included moral betterment, religious conversion, economic development and democracy ('International Humanitarianism: The Dark Sides', *The International Journal of Not-for-Profit Law*, Vol. 6, No. 3, June 2004, http://www.icnl.org/ knowledge/ijnl/vol6iss3/special_2.htm [last accessed 2 October 2007]).

protect schoolchildren   Dismissive neoconservative term for international and US peace-keeping operations. In the words of Condoleezza Rice, advising George W. Bush when he was still a candidate in the 2000 presidential campaign that US forces should not be used, as they were in the Balkans, to **protect schoolchildren** (Francis Fukuyama, 'America's Parties and Their Foreign Policy Masquerade', *FT*, 8 March 2005). Rather more to the point is that the forces in the Balkans were not used to protect the thousands of inhabitants of Sarajevo and Srebrenica killed by Serbian forces, and the members of all three warring communities – Serbs, Croatians, Bosnians – killed by their enemies in the period 1992–5. It goes without saying that the protection of children in the West Bank and Gaza was also not on the US agenda. The curious, and morally repulsive, implication of this remark is, of course, that the lives of children have even less value than those of adults.

protection crisis   That is, inability of international institutions and concerned governments to protect lives. Term used in August 2004 by UN officials to refer to mass rape and other forms of violence against the population in the Darfur region of Sudan.

public diplomacy   One of the great Washington illusions of recent times. This term for 'public relations', and often attempted manipulation of media and public opinion, by governments, came into use in the 1970s with the creation of an *Office of Public Diplomacy for Latin America and the Caribbean*, the White House organ for demonising the Sandinistas in Nicaragua and used as a cover for the secret war against them. More recently used to refer to US efforts, as in public appearances by Secretary of State Condoleezza Rice, designed to present US policy in a more favourable light in the Arab world. The argument for **public diplomacy** was backed up by claims, often made by military officials, that the *battle for ideas, the battle for hearts and minds* was, in any way, as important as the military battle itself. In terms of deciding, and evaluating, the political outcome of combat this was, for sure, often the case. What it did *not* entail was that information, news, access and tailored video clips could, and should, be used during any conflict as a form of weapon, irrespective of truth, to promote the war aims of the government in question. Equally, the belief, present in much US policy in regard to Palestine, Iraq and elsewhere, that major political and military blunders on the ground could by compensated for, or overridden, by a press or diplomatic campaign, was an illusion. The problem in regard to US policy in, for example, Iraq was not presentation, or the lack of **public diplomacy,** but the policy itself: it was the product, not the packaging, that was decisive. Cf. definition of diplomacy offered by the comedian Will Rogers (1879–1935), 'The only real diplomacy ever performed by a diplomat is in deceiving their own people after their dumbness has got them into a war' ('Coddling Condi', Editorial, *IHT*, 20 January 2005; Sourcewatch, /www.sourcewatch.org/index.php?title=Public_diplomacy).

pundit   From the Sanskrit *pandita*, a learned man, specifically an adviser on Hindu law to the British courts in India. Also 'pandit' as in Pandit Nehru. Now, a media expert, usually both ponderous and superficial.

put on notice   Condescending and imperious term – cf. **come to heel** – applied to third world countries that dissent from Western policy. Thus executives and bankers in the Arab world were informed on 7 March 2007 by Stuart Levey, the US Undersecretary for Terrorism and Financial Intelligence, that even innocuous trade with Iran could help to bankroll the 'disputed Iranian nuclear program'. He warned them: 'Those who are tempted to deal with **targeted high-risk actors** are **put on notice**: If they continue this relationship they may be next to be targeted for action' (AP, 'Arabs Get Warning on Dealing with Iran', *IHT*, 8 March, 2007).

R

Ranger   Pre-1776 term for a US irregular soldier, now used for special intervention US forces. Not the exact equivalent of the UK's SAS, as they are more numerous, less elite.

reality-based community   In contrast to 'faith-based community', term of disparagement in the Bush administration for those who did not share their international goals and aspirations. Quoted in an article by Ron Suskind in *New York Times Magazine*, 17 October 2004, 'Faith, Certainty and the Presidency of George W. Bush'. In response to a criticism of administration policy, an unnamed White House aide charged his critic with being a member of the **reality-based community**, who based their judgements on research and facts. The aide then declared: 'We're an empire now, and, when we act, we make our own reality'. In response to the publication of this article, opponents of the President wore t-shirts with the words 'Proud to be a Member of the Reality-Based Community'.

redact   Less commonly used word for *edit, prepare for publication*, also carries overtones of *correction*. In the post-9/11 context, the US euphemism for censor. A back formation from the noun *redaction*. Cf. **censoring impulses, public diplomacy**. Hence title of Brian De Palma film *Redacted*, on censorship and self-censorship in the US media. De Palma qualified the policy of the US media as 'a mission to misinform' (Nigel Andrews, 'Hollywood's Explosive Talent', *IHT*, 8–9 March 2008). Other critics have referred to the *stenographic* character of much US news reporting, i.e. giving an abbreviated summary of what some official said, without assessing or providing independent background material on such claims.

regime   In terminology of international relations and diplomacy, term borrowed from French, popularised in the Cold War to denote the political system of a hostile country, a pejorative alternative to 'government', 'administration' or 'state', applied to enemies of the USA in the post-Cold War period.

regime change   Term used in US politics since 1920, revived by General MacArthur during the Korean War in regard to the communist regime in North Korea, also used by the Clinton administration in the 1990s: denotes radical change in policy, and political character, of target state, the latter implicitly authoritarian and illegitimate, as well as hostile to the USA, but short of invasion, intervention or counter-revolution. Applied, retrospectively, to collapse of communism in Eastern Europe and the USSR in the late 1980s, then, prospectively, to hostile regimes, such as North Korea, Iraq and Cuba. In the earlier, Cold War, context it would more probably have been termed *counter-revolution* by supporters of such regimes, or *liberation* by those advocating change. Cf. the milder policy of **behaviour change**.

Rice, Condoleezza US Presidential National Security Adviser, later Secretary of State in the Bush administration. Among other utterances of monumental, but generally uncontested, banality, 'The **hearts and minds issue** is back', this in July 2004 was a belated recognition of failure of reliance on coercion and killing alone after a year of rising insurrection in Iraq. In her university and graduate days, Condoleezza Rice adhered to a group of hard-line international realists named 'The Vulcans', later to form, with Paul Wolfowitz and Douglas Feith, part of the neoconservative foreign policy clique around George W. Bush. The unusual first name of the US Secretary of State was coined by her mother from the Italian musical notation *con dolcezza* (with sweetness) – rendered as 'Kinda-Lies-a-Lot' by the 'Jersey Girls', a group of widows of 9/11 victims (*IHT*, 6 February 2008; review of Philip Shenon, *The Commission. The Uncensored History of the 9/11 Investigation* [New York: Twelve, 2008]). Sweetness was probably not what Chevron Oil had in mind when it appointed her a board member and later, in 1993, named a 129,000-ton super-tanker the *SS Condoleezza Rice*, in gratitude for her invaluable services in Kazakhstan, where Chevron had a $10 billion project and whose President (Nursultan Nazarbayev) Rice happened to know. Following revelations of Bush family ties to the oil industry and charges against Chevron of human rights abuses in Nigeria, the tanker was given a new name *Altair Voyager*, this time referring to a bright star and perhaps indirectly to Condi, as she likes to be called ('What's in a name?' Russell Baker, 'Condi and the Boys', *New York Review of Books*, 3 April 2008; James Mann, *The Rise of the Vulcans* [New York: Viking, 2004]).

right-thinking Americans The Bush administration's term for officials appointed for their political loyalty, not for competence or fitness for the job. Cf. **loyal Bushies**.

rogue state Term popularised in Washington in the 1990s, in a post-Cold War context allegedly shorn of ideological conflict, for those countries, such as Iraq, Iran and North Korea, who did not comply with US wishes. Later it was argued that perhaps the most dangerous state was one no-one included at that time on the list, because it was a US ally, Pakistan. It was probably not possible to say *outlaw state* as even those so castigated remained part of the international diplomatic, commercial and legal system. Ironically, one of the countries which evinced most resistance to international law, refusing to ratify a range of UN and other conventions, including the *Covenant for the Elimination of Discrimination Against Women* (CEDAW) of 1979 and the *International Criminal Court* was the USA. Needless to say, the USA often abided by international norms even when not formally signing up to them, while many of those who signed paid, in practice, little or no need to them.

Rumsfeld's rules   Sayings, maxims and adages adopted by US Secretary of Defense Donald Rumsfeld, the man who oversaw the invasion of Iraq and the altering of rules on the interrogation of US prisoners. Rumsfeld first published these 'rules, reflections and quotations' in 1974, saying they had been gathered 'over forty years'. He began with the quote (author not cited) 'If it's not true, it's still well-founded', perhaps an English rendering of the Italian phrase, *si non e vero, e ben trovato.* Other gems included: 'As former Missouri Congressman Tom Curtis said, "Public money drives out private money"'; 'In politics, every day is filled with numerous opportunities for serious error. Enjoy it'; 'The oil can is mightier than the sword' (Senator Everett Dirksen, R-IL); 'No plan survives contact with the enemy' (Old military axiom); 'The advantage of a free market is that it allows millions of decision-makers to respond individually to freely determined prices, allocating resources – labor, capital and human ingenuity – in a manor [*sic*] that can't be mimicked by a central plan, however brilliant the central planner' (Freidrich von Hayek); and 'If a problem cannot be solved, enlarge it' (Dwight D. Eisenhower), a rule that Rumsfeld seems to have observed to the letter in Iraq. Fuller coverage at http://library.villanova.edu/vbl/bweb/rumsfeldsrules.pdf (last accessed 30 September 2007). See **stuff happens** and **snowflakes**. (See also James Goodby, 'Enlarge the North Korean Problem', *IHT*, 21 June 2005.)

S

smart sanctions   Measures that target the leadership of a state and their families rather than the whole population. Tried against Iraq and Zimbabwe in the1990s. Never known to be effective. The 1990s vogue for international sanctions, preferred to outright invasion or other forms of military pressure, failed in most of its objectives, *sanctions fatigue* leading, at least in the case of Iraq, to *sanctions exhaustion*.

T

tax terrorism   Figurative extension of the concept of **terrorism** by Russian President Vladimir Putin and his advisers in late 2004, in an attempt to reassure private investors in the Russian oil industry that the harassment of private oil companies, such as *Yukos Oil*, would cease. The problem was, of course, that the issue was not one of *taxation* as such, the level of tax levied, but of overall *control and ownership*, an issue on which the Russian state, of which Putin remained in charge as President and later Prime Minister, showed itself unwilling to alter in its trend towards greater intervention. Days after the President's speech, tax authorities presented TNK-BP, a Russian-British joint venture and Russia's second-leading oil producer, with a bill for nearly US$1 billion and the threat of more to come (Erin E. Arvedlund, 'Investors of the World, Here's the Word on Putin Inc.', *The New York Times*, 2 March 2005; Pilar Bonet, 'Los juices aplazan la lectura de la sentencia de Jodorkovski', *El País*, 28 April 2005).

Theocons   Play on **neoconservative** and *theocrat*, title of book by Damon Linker (New York: Doubleday, 2006), *The Theocons: Secular America under Siege* – a study of a group of American Catholic thinkers who deemed themselves to be at the heart of a religious revival, in which religion was supposed to be playing an increasingly significant role in public life. However, these Catholic strategists were still a long way behind the evangelical movement in terms of influence (Adrian Wooldridge, 'Church as State', *The New York Times*, 24 September 2006).

traditional values coalition   Christian Right US organization, headed by Reverend Louis P. Sheldon, which claimed to represent over 43,000 conservative Christian churches throughout the USA. It proclaimed on its website its belief in Bible-based traditional values as '[a] moral code and behavior based upon the Old and New Testaments'. To give a taste of Sheldon's grasp of politics: 'A dangerous *Marxist/Leftist/Homosexual/Islamic coalition* has formed – and we'd better be willing to fight it with everything in our power. These people are playing for keeps. Their hero, Mao Tse Tung is estimated to have murdered upwards of 60 million people during his reign of terror in China. Do we think we can escape such persecution if we refuse to fight for what is right?' See 'The War on Christianity' (13 December 2005; www.traditionalvalues.org/modules.php?sid=2533).

transformational diplomacy   Use of diplomacy to bring about political change in third world countries, name given in 2006 to major shake-up in the US State Department, involving the 'redeployment' of hundreds of diplomats from Europe to the Middle East and Asia in order to confront the rise of 'global anti-Americanism'. In an address given at Georgetown University, Secretary of State Condoleezza Rice noted that in the future it was going to be tougher to be an American diplomat. Though she insisted that this did not mean *forcing* American values onto people, she said that she wanted a commitment to **transformational diplomacy** in order to *influence events* and *promote democracy* (Julian Borger, 'Rice Reveals Shake-up in US Diplomacy', the *Guardian*, 20 January 2006).

truthful messages   Official term for material put out by the US Army's 1,200-strong psychological operations unit at Fort Bragg. The state-of-the-art centre formed part of a military operation and the writers and producers were soldiers putting out **truthful messages** 'to support US objectives'. Colonel Jack Summe, Commander of the 4th Psychological Operations Group, said, 'We call our stuff information and the enemy's propaganda' (Jeff Gerth, 'US on the Attack in Information War', *IHT*, 12 December 2005).

U

unilateralism   Literally 'one-sidedness', hence a state acting on its own, an example of a nomadic political term used in the 1950s and 1960s European movement against nuclear weapons, calling for *unilateral* disarmament, i.e. with this being part of a negotiated agreement with the Soviet Union. The 1990s and 2000s denoted US rejection of *multilateral* diplomacy, a one-sided resort to military action, disdain for views of other peoples. Sometimes cynically rendered as *assertive multilateralism*. Paul Wolfowitz, Deputy Secretary of Defense during the preparation and launch of the Iraq War, claimed that '**unilateralism** is the high road to multilateralism'.

unilaterals   Disapproving official term for journalists who, in conflict situations, refuse to accept news management controls, and to be controlled by military information officials, i.e. **embedded**. See **channel with a reputation, embed** (*Democracy Now*, 29 May 2006, [www.democracynow.org/2006/5/29/ex_british_navy_spokesperson_steve_tatham]).

unitary   Word with multiple contemporary political and/or religious applications. In US political parlance, applies to the belief in a strong, and unchallenged, Presidential/executive power, overriding checks of Congress, the law and media, as espoused by Vice-President Dick Cheney and associates in the George W. Bush administration. In broad terms, an attempt to push back the increase in Congressional oversight achieved in the 1970s and 1980s. In Arabic political vocabulary a *wahdawi* is someone who espouses Arab unity, or *wahda*. In recent times it usually refers to a person associated with the legacy of Egyptian President Nasser (d. 1970). In Northern Ireland, by contrast, a *Unionist* is someone who supports the Protestant domination and the continued link between the province and Great Britain, opposite of a *nationalist* (more or less synonym for 'Catholic'). In a religious context, the word has other connotations: thus in Christianity a *Unitariarian* is someone who denies the Trinity doctrine of God, while orthodox and fundamentalist Muslims, notably so-called **Wahhabis**, often call themselves *muwahhidun*, 'people who assert the oneness of God', in this case against polytheism, **shirk**.

V

victims of terror   People who have suffered from the physical and mental effects of torture, often including members of their family, often manipulated for political campaigns. In the USA, President George W. Bush declared that Syria and Iran 'deserve no patience from **victims of terror**'. In Spain victims of the Basque terrorist group ETA and of the March 2004 Madrid bombings were used by the right-wing *Partido Popular*, thus creating serious division among the victims and their families (Guy Dinmore, 'US "Seeks New Syrian Leader" as Pressure Mounts', *FT*, 10 October 2005).

W

Weapons of Mass Destruction   Category of weapons covering nuclear, biological and chemical weapons, i.e. broader than nuclear weapons but beyond what were previously called 'conventional' weapons. The term was first used by *The Times* (28 December 1937) to report the German bombing of the Basque town of Guernica in the Spanish civil war and revived in US arms control and official vocabulary of the 1970s. Despite the canonical usage of the abbreviation *WMD*, this term is far less precise than is often claimed: many biological and chemical weapons are, while capable of wreaking terrible suffering on their specific targets at any one time, not capable of 'mass destruction'. Thus Professor Lawrence Freeman, writing of the lumping together of chemical, biological and chemical weapons through use of this term: 'Their routine elision, which is now so ingrained as to be beyond remedy, encourages carelessness in public debate in failing to distinguish between systems that cause containable tragedies to those that would lead to the most unimaginable catastrophe' (See *Survival. The IISS Quarterly*, Vol. 46, No. 2, Summer 2004, p. 40n2).

'We're an empire now'   See **reality-based community**.

Wilsonianism   From US President Woodrow Wilson (1917–20), a proponent of active American role on the international scene: while Wilson was a liberal, the term **Wilsonianism** was much used by neoconservative supporters of a unilateral US role in the years of the second Bush administration, these advocates of war sometimes terming themselves *hard Wilsonians*.

World War III   *Not* the **war on terror**, but the prospect of a major interstate war involving new and old nuclear states, usually in or around the Middle East. Intermittently used during the Cold War, then revived in the mid-2000s as Russian and American policies began to conflict: thus when President Vladimir Putin of Russia warned President George W. Bush in 2007 that he should abstain from any military strikes against Iran, the latter responded that to permit Iran to possess a nuclear weapon was to risk '**World War III**'. In his inimitable style he elaborated, 'So I told people that if you're interested in avoiding World War III, it seems like you ought to be interested in not letting Iran acquire the capacity for developing nuclear weapons' (Brian Knowlton, 'Iran Risks "World War III," Bush Says', *IHT*, 18 October 2007).

World War IV   Title of 2008 book by veteran alarmist and self-publicising 'security expert' Norman Podhoretz, on Western relations with the Islamic world.

Claims of American Power

1. assertive multilateralism
2. cakewalk
3. grand strategy
4. hyperpower
5. *Mission Accomplished*
6. moral clarity
7. neoconservatism
8. our way or the highway
9. Plan for Victory
10. Project for the New American Century
11. regime change
12. Shock and Awe
13. war of choice
14. 'We're an empire now'

Acknowledgements

For having, in many ways and over many years, inspired in me an interest in, and unpredictable curiosity about, language and words, there are many people I should thank. First, a special debt is owed to those friends and relatives who, in the course of decades, have nourished and pushed my fascination with words and meanings and who stimulated and, not least, validated a curiosity that has remained with me all my life: my brothers David and Jon, both accomplished and enthusiastic linguists; my teachers at secondary school, in particular Philip O'Riordan Smiley and Fr. Barnabas Sandeman; my Arabic teacher at SOAS, Owen Wright; at Bernard Johnson, Tanya Chambers and Paul Marsh, my much tried teachers of Russian; and my feisty domestic interlocutors of many years, Maxine and Alex, who more than kept me on my linguistic and semantic toes. Also friends and colleagues with whom I have shared conversations, at times meandering and recondite, and later unexpected and quirky emails about language and words: in Britain, Yasser Suleiman, Mark Cohen, the late Dominique Jacquin-Berdal, Baqer Moin, Denis McCauley, Peter Wilson, *Claire Beaugrand*; in Tehran, Karim and Goli Emami; and in Barcelona, Simone Venturi, Gregory Qushair and Carmen Claudin.

A most particular thanks is due to Julie Wark, a fellow resident of Barcelona and distinguished translator of Catalan and Spanish literature, for sharing with me her general enthusiasm for language and obscure words, for encouraging me to go ahead with writing this book and, most particularly, for her help in organising, drafting and pursuing many of the entries in this volume. Without her encouragement, support and collaboration, it could not have been written.

In preparing the manuscript and, with patience and precision, helping me to keep track of multiple versions, bits and pieces, many thanks to Andrew Sherwood in London and Silvia Forno in Barcelona. Finally, to those most crucial and indispensable mentors, my publishers, Abigail Fielding-Smith and Iradj Bagherzade of I.B.Tauris who had the vision, perhaps rashness, to commit themselves to publishing this book, undoubtedly the most unusual I have ever written, but one which, in a tone different from my others, conveys a fascination, sometimes obsession, with the oldest and most important of all forms of human interaction and social life as with the issues of power, truth and democratic control which underlie it. It is for this reason, the linkage of speech to control, that those in power or seeking to appropriate it, and who seek thereby to dominate, or destroy us, pay such particular attention to controlling the words we use. As a consequence, we should indeed not be shocked, or awed, but, in linguistic as in other matters, should remain informed, fastidious and vigilant.

This book, and an earlier work of attempted demystification, *100 Myths About the Middle East* (London: Saqi Books, 2005), are beyond their specific relevance to the contemporary Middle East and to international relations, part of an ongoing if somewhat diversified interest of mine in the critique of language, identity and tradition. As such, they form part of my work on contemporary forms of internationalism, a topic for which I was awarded a Senior Research Fellowship by the Leverhulme Trust in 2003–5. These two books, and a set of essays, *For Internationalism*, to be published in 2010 and more directly concerned with issues in political theory and international relations, are the, perhaps unanticipated, outcomes of SRF: in this regard, the support of the Trust is here most gratefully acknowledged.

Note on Transliteration, Standardisation and Abbreviation

As generations of scholars, translators and writers on the Middle East have recognised, there is no single, fully consistent, way of transliterating into any one European language words from Arabic and Persian, let alone of establishing a system that encompasses different European phonetic and linguistic systems (thus English *Khomeini* and *jihad* become in Spanish *Jomeini* and *yihad*). In this volume I have taken the conventional path of applying consistently to all but the most common words one of the standard transcription systems, in this case that of the *International Journal of Middle Eastern Studies,* minus the diacritical marks. Again following convention, I have left in the usual if inaccurate form words, personal names such as Nasser or place names such as Jordan or Syria, which have come to be most widely known in this rendering. I have, however, sought to avoid renderings that are, on any informed transcription system, inaccurate – thus only one *s* in *madrasa* and one *d* in *mujahidin.*

A distinct, but also intractable, problem is that of how to deal with the many differences of American and English spelling, especially evident in this book where so much of the material comes from the USA. I have followed British usage, except where the US rendering is official: thus *neo-conservative,* but *Secretary of Defense.*

In giving website sources, I have followed OUP practice: omitting 'http://' except where there is no 'www' prefix, and dispensing with 'last accessed' details. Most of the sources are given in full, but a few abbreviations have been used for publications: thus *FT (Financial Times), IHT (International Herald Tribune), MEED (Middle East Economic Digest), NYRB (New York Review of Books).*

Works Consulted

Arendt, Hannah, *Eichmann in Jerusalem. A Report on the Banality of Evil*, London: Penguin Twentieth-Century Classics, 2000.

Artigas, Mónica, '200 palabras para una década', *La Vanguardia Magazine*, 14 December 2008.

Attali, Jacques, *Dictionnaire du XXIe siècle*, Paris: Fayard, 1998.

Ayalon, Ami, *Language and Change in the Middle East. The Evolution of Modern Arabic Political Discourse*, Oxford: OUP, 1987.

Ayton, John, *A Century of New Words*, Oxford: OUP, 2007.

Bromwich, David, 'Euphemism and American Violence', *New York Review of Books*, 3 April 2008.

Brophy, John and Eric Partridge, *The Daily Telegraph Dictionary of Tommies' Songs and Slangs, 1914–18*, Barnsley, S. Yorkshire: Frontline Books, 2008.

Corominas, Joan, *Breve Diccionario Etimólogico de la Lengua Castellana*, Madrid: Editorial Gredos, 2006.

Esposito, John, ed., *The Oxford Encyclopaedia of the Modern Islamic World*, 4 vols., Oxford: OUP, 1995.

Evening Standard, 23 October 2001.

Freedman, Lawrence, *A Choice of Enemies. America Confronts the Middle East*, London: Weidenfeld and Nicolson, 2008.

Gerges, Fawaz, *The Far Enemy. How Jihad Went Global*, Cambridge: CUP, 2005.

Giustozzi, Antonio, *Koran, Kalashnikov and Laptop. The Neo-Taliban Insurgency in Afghanistan*, London: Hurst, 2007.

Glassé, Cyril, *The Concise Encyclopaedia of Islam*, London: Stacey International, 1989.

Gresch Alain and Dominique Vidal, *The New A-Z of the Middle East*, London: I.B.Tauris, 2004.

Hoggart, Richard, *The Uses of Literacy*, London: Penguin, 1957.

Jackson, Richard, *Writing the War on Terrorism. Language, Politics and Counter-terrorism*, Manchester: Manchester University Press, 2005.

Jacobs, Louis, *A Concise Companion to the Jewish Religion*, Oxford: OUP, 1999.

Jezernik, Božidar, *Wild Europe. The Balkans in the Gaze of Western Travellers*, London: Saqi, 2004.

Johnson, Samuel, *A Dictionary of the English Language*, first published 1755, reprinted *Samuel Johnson's Dictionary*, ed. Jack Lynch, London: Atlantic Books, 2004.

Kovacsics, Adan, *Guerra y lenguaje*, Acantilado: Barcelona, 2007.

Lambton, A. K. S., *Persian Vocabulary*, Cambridge: CUP, 1961.

Lawrence, Bruce, ed. *Messages to the World. The Statements of Osama bin Laden*, London: Verso, 2005.

Levy, Reuben, *The Sociology of Islam*, Cambridge: CUP, 1965.

Lewis, Bernard, *The Political Language of Islam*, London: University of Chicago Press, 1988.

Lewis, Jeff, *Language Wars. The Role of Media and Culture in Global Terror and Political Violence*, London: Pluto, 2005.

Mozaffari, Mehdi, 'Bin Laden's Foreign Policy. Paths of Amity and Enmity', in *Islamist Policy*, Centre for Studies in Islamism and Radicalisation, University of Aarhus, Denmark, April 2009.

Orwell, George, *Nineteen Eighty-Four*, London: Penguin Classics, 2000, first published 1949, pp. 312–26, '*Appendix*. The Principles of Newspeak'.

Rottman, Gordon L., *FUBAR. Soldier Slang of World War II*, Botley, Oxford: 2007.

Sanmartín Sáez, Julia, *diccionario de argot*, Madrid: Editorial Espasa Calpe.

Shorter Oxford English Dictionary, 2 vols., sixth edition, 2007.

Stedman Jones, Gareth, *Languages of Class. Studies in English Working Class History 1832–1982*, Cambridge: CUP, 1983.

Tatham, Steve, *Losing Arab Hearts and Minds: The Coalition, Al Jazeera and Muslim Public Opinion*, London: Routledge, 2007.

Thorne, Tony, *Dictionary of Contemporary Slang*, London: A&C Black, third edition, 2007.

Truss, Lynne, *Eats, Shoots and Leaves. The Zero Tolerance Approach to Punctuation*, London: Profile Books, 2003.

Vercellin, Giorgio, *Istituzioni del Mondo Musulmano*, Turín: Einaudi, 2006.

Webster The New International Dictionary of the English Language, third edition, 1961, reprinted Cologne: Köneman, 1993.

Wehr, Hans, *Arabic-English Dictionary*, ed. J.M. Cowan, fourth edition, Wiesbaden: Harrassowitz, 1979.

Wikipedia, The Free Encyclopedia, online reference, accessed 2007–9.

Williams, Raymond, *Keywords. A Vocabulary of Culture and Society*, London: Fontana, 1976.

Wilson, Andrew and Nina Bachkatov, *Russia Revised. An Alphabetical Guide to the Former Soviet Union and the New Republics*, London: André Deutsch, 1992.

Yule, Henry and A. C. Burnell, *Hobson-Jobson. A Glossary of Colloquial Anglo-Indian Words and Phrases, and of Kindred Terms Etymological, Historical, Geographical and Discursive*, first published in 1886.

Index

Fox News Channel, 247
franchise, 10
freedom, 294–295
Freedom Fries, 247
freedom is untidy, 106
Freedom Speech, 295
freelance counterterrorist, 69–70
French passion, 295
frequent flyer program, 70
FREs, 106
friendly fire, 232
full court press, 247
full-scale invasion, 247–248
fusilocracy, 106
fuzzy-wuzzies, 183

G

Gadahn, Adam, 43
Gang of Eight, 10–11
gated communities, 107
general level of arrogant
    incompetence, 11
Geneva Conventions, 70
genocide, 295–296
George Washington of Iraq, 107
get some, 248
ghost detainee, 70
Ghost Plane, 70–71
ghost ship, 107
gin up, 248
Gitmo, 71
Gitmo-ize, 71–72
Glennville, 11–12
glide path, 107–108
global counterinsurgency, 12
global intelligence failure, 12
Global Threat Reduction Initiative, 12
Global War against Terror/Terrorism
    (GWAT), 12
globalisation, 296
glocal phenomenon, 12
glorifying, exalting or celebrating
    terrorism, 13
gloves off, 72

go massive, 108
goat fuckers, 184
God Bless America, 248
God-drenched, 248
God gulf, 296
golden shield, 72
government with an address, 209
grace notes, 249
grand strategy, 296
granularity, 108
Grapes of Wrath, 209
gratitude level, 108
Great Game, 296–297
Green Revolution, 209–210
grief gap, 297
Ground Zero, 13
groupthink, 13–14
GSPC. *See Salafist Group for Preaching
    and Combat* (GSPC)
Guantánamo Bay, 72–73
Gucci muj, 44
guilt and innocence, 73
Gulf, 265
Gulf War, 297

H

habeas corpus, 73
habeas lawyers, 73
Hague invasion clause, 297
Hail Mary, 249
halal, 153
halal hippy, 184
Halliburton, 108–109
Hamas, 210
Hamas-lite, 210
Hamasistan/Hamastan, 265
hammour, 153
handful of foreign terrorists, 44
hanging gestures, 73
Hannibal directive, 210
Happy Mohammed mask, 73
harbour, 249
hard facts, 74
harsh interrogation techniques, 74